MW00805453

FIERCE AND FEARLESS

Fierce and Fearless

Patsy Takemoto Mink, First Woman of Color in Congress

Judy Tzu-Chun Wu *and* Gwendolyn Mink

NEW YORK UNIVERSITY PRESS

New York

NEW YORK UNIVERSITY PRESS
New York
www.nyupress.org

References to Internet websites (URLs) were accurate at the time of writing. Neither the author nor New York University Press is responsible for URLs that may have expired or changed since the manuscript was prepared.

Library of Congress Cataloging-in-Publication Data
Names: Wu, Judy Tzu-Chun, author. | Mink, Gwendolyn, 1952–   author.
Title: Fierce and fearless : Patsy Takemoto Mink, first woman of color in Congress / Judy Tzu-Chun Wu, and Gwendolyn Mink.
Other titles: Patsy Takemoto Mink, first woman of color in Congress
Description: New York : NYU Press, [2022] | Includes bibliographical references and index.
Identifiers: LCCN 2021031269 | ISBN 9781479831920 (hardback) | ISBN 9781479868247 (ebook) | ISBN 9781479826292 (ebook other)
Subjects: LCSH: Mink, Patsy T., 1927–2002. | Legislators—United States—Biography. | Women legislators—United States—Biography. | Legislators—Hawaii—Biography. | Women legislators—Hawaii—Biography. | United States. Congress—Biography. | United States—Politics and government—20th century. | Japanese American lawyers—Hawaii—Biography. | Japanese Americans—Biography. | Japanese American women—Biography.
Classification: LCC E840.8.M544 W8 2022 | DDC 328.73/092 [B]—dc23
LC record available at https://lccn.loc.gov/2021031269

New York University Press books are printed on acid-free paper, and their binding materials are chosen for strength and durability. We strive to use environmentally responsible suppliers and materials to the greatest extent possible in publishing our books.

Manufactured in the United States of America

10 9 8 7 6 5 4 3 2 1

Also available as an ebook

CONTENTS

FIGURES

A NOTE ON THE TEXT

As is fitting for a work that explores Patsy Mink's achievements and collaborations, this book emerged from an intellectual partnership. A feminist historian of Asian American identity and politics, Judy Tzu-Chun Wu began research into the life of Patsy Mink in 2012. Early on, Judy was advised to consult with Wendy (Gwendolyn) Mink, Patsy's daughter and a political scientist. Wendy grew up in a tightly knit family; she was Patsy and John Mink's only child. Both she and her father served as political interlocutors and strategists for Patsy. During Wendy's childhood and adolescence, they discussed issues and ideas over breakfast, during commutes, and at the daily dinner table. Later, they continued to work through policy and political questions together over daily phone, fax, and email exchanges, as well as during frequent visits.

We decided to join our work on Patsy Mink, and thus to bring together the personal and the political, the specificity of a story with the perspective of history. We met regularly during Judy's trips to Washington, DC. Judy conducted research elsewhere, but the bulk of sources were at the Library of Congress, specifically the over two thousand manuscript boxes that constitute the Patsy T. Mink Papers. When in town, Judy usually met with Wendy twice a week for dinner. Reflecting our ethnic backgrounds and culinary comfort zones, we ate Japanese and Chinese food. Wendy shared stories and knowledge of American politics during these meals.

Each chapter begins with a vignette by Wendy, reflecting on her family's life, her mother's political activities, and her analysis of their mutual political collaborations. Judy drives the narrative chapters with historical analysis and at times revisits topics and events from a different vantage point. We hope the duet of vignettes and chapters together tell a layered and textured story of the remarkable woman Patsy Mink.

Introduction

Speaking Truth to Power

In 2002, at the age of seventy-four, Patsy Takemoto Mink rose before Congress to celebrate the thirtieth anniversary of Title IX. The first congresswoman of color, Mink served as a US representative from Hawaiʻi from 1965 to 1977 and again from 1990 to 2002. She had a special relationship to this landmark piece of legislation, which "prohibits sex discrimination in any educational program that receives federal funds."[1] Reflecting on her long political career, Mink stated, "I consider Title IX to be one of my most significant accomplishments as a Member of Congress."[2]

Mink recounted the sea change in women's involvement in sports from the 1970s to the early twenty-first century. In the 1970s, "Women athletes were so few and unknown that the only well-known athlete we could bring in to testify was Billie Jean King."[3] The record-breaking tennis player became even more famous for her 1973 match against Bobby Riggs, a notorious sexist. King challenged Riggs to a "battle of the sexes" and won. Thirty years later, Mink celebrated the widespread elation over the US soccer team victory in the 1999 Women's World Cup: "Hundreds of thousands of spectators attended the games, and millions more watched on television."[4] In fact, Mia Hamm, "one of the team's brightest stars, was born in 1972—the same year that Title IX was signed into law. Without Title IX, she and many of her teammates may have never had the opportunity to develop their talents and their love of the sport."[5]

Title IX meant more than transforming the ability of girls and women to participate in athletics. Mink reminded her audience, "Since its enactment, Title IX has opened the doors of educational opportunity to literally millions of girls and women across the country. Title IX has helped to tear down inequitable admissions policies, increase opportunities for women in nontraditional fields of study such as math and science, improve vocational educational opportunities for women, reduce discrimination against pregnant students and teen mothers, protect female students from sexual harassment in our schools, and increase athletic opportunities for girls and women."[6] Various critics have questioned Title IX, and the recent administration of Donald J. Trump directly undermined it.[7] Nevertheless, Title IX still provides the legal foundation for gender equity in schools. When Mink passed away in 2002, just a few months after the thirtieth anniversary celebration, Title IX was renamed the Patsy T. Mink Equal Opportunity in Education Act.

Who is Patsy Mink? Why is she not widely recognized among the feminist pantheon in US history? How did a third-generation Japanese American from Hawai'i become such an influential political voice in Washington, DC? After all, Mink made her mark advocating for racial equality, antiwar politics, environmental protection, and women's rights.

Born on December 6, 1927, and passing away September 28, 2002, Mink lived nearly three-quarters of a century. She was born on the rural outposts of a US territory. In 1893, haole, or white, business and missionary interests illegally deposed Native Hawaiian sovereign Queen Lili'uokalani and called for annexation. The white settlers installed a plantation economy, and Mink's grandparents arrived from Japan as contract farm workers. They were subject to racialized naturalization laws that designated them forever foreigners, "aliens ineligible for citizenship."[8] Only in 1952, as the United States allied with Japan during the Cold War, did Japanese immigrants gain naturalization rights to become US citizens. It took another seven years before Hawai'i became the fiftieth state. The delay stemmed from mainland concerns about the sizable nonwhite population on the islands and fears of Communist-inspired labor organizing.

Mink was a first in so many ways. She was the first Japanese American woman in Hawai'i to practice law, the first to run for and win a seat in the Hawai'i legislature, the first woman of color to serve in the US House of Representatives, and the first Asian American to run for the US presidency in 1972. Beyond these achievements, Mink also advocated for progressive initiatives, such as government-funded childcare, an end to nuclear testing in the Pacific, peace in Viet Nam, welfare programs to alleviate poverty, and educational access for all.

Despite Mink's impressive accomplishments, no book-length study has analyzed her extensive political career. Research on the 1960s and 1970s tends to focus on women and people of color as grassroots activists, as "outsiders" demanding change. Scholars interested in "traditional" political history incline towards white male protagonists. Analyses of US race relations foreground white-Black interactions, with much less attention given to Asian Americans. Mink's Japanese American ancestry, her origins in Hawai'i, and her engagement with legislative activism challenge what we know about race, feminism, and politics.

Mink's career reveals how outsiders strove to become full citizens, how a woman of color shaped the policies and values of the United States. Her political involvements in Hawai'i and in Congress over the course of the twentieth century raised questions of who can be recognized as a US citizen and who has the right to fully participate in the national polity. These debates concerning legal and cultural citizenship held global implications, given the importance of the Pacific to US international ambitions.

In Hawai'i, Mink, along with a generation of Japanese Americans, transformed themselves from suspected fifth columnists during World War II to integral party insiders of the Democratic Party during the early Cold War. The claiming of citizenship rights by Japanese immigrants as well as their Hawai'i-born children emerged alongside the islands' efforts to achieve a new political status. As a member of the territorial legislature in the mid-to-late 1950s, Mink advocated for statehood. Her electoral efforts in Hawai'i, however, frequently met with obstacles from the Democratic Party, including its Japanese American members, because she was one of the few women involved in the male-dominated realm of politics.

At the national level, Mink emerged in the midst of a pioneering cohort of female leaders. They arrived on the electoral scene just as mass activist movements across the United States demanded social justice for people of color and women. Mink's colleagues included the first African American woman in Congress, Shirley Chisholm, and Jewish American congresswoman Bella Abzug.[9] Together, they collaborated on progressive legislation, including the authorization of the 1977 National Women's Conference.

Mink's political career began during the ascendancy of Cold War liberalism. She defined key features of this political agenda by demanding civil rights, promoting gender equity, and protecting the environment. She also countered Cold War liberalism by attempting to limit US military interventions in Southeast Asia and across the Pacific. Mink's initiatives emerged from the margins and became contested positions within the Democratic Party and among the US public.

Mink left the House of Representatives in 1977 but returned in 1990 to a politics dominated by conservative retrenchment and the rise of neoliberalism, an approach to governance that promoted reductions in public oversight of corporate practices, cuts in funding for social welfare, US intervention abroad, and the maintenance of a security state at home. Cumulatively, these political trends challenged the policies and values that Mink advocated for in the 1960s and 1970s. Furthermore, neoliberalism went hand in hand with conservative racial and gendered ideologies that envisioned the white, middle-class, heteronuclear family as the fundamental basis of US society. By the 1990s, Mink, along with members of other marginalized groups, had gained increased formal political access to the US state. Yet, she faced intense resistance towards her efforts to position women, people of color, immigrants, and the poor as deserving of government support and social acceptance.

It is important to note three aspects of Mink's political identity and strategy. First, she served as a political "bridge." She worked in tandem with grassroots advocates to effect legislative change. Rachel Pierce coined the phrase "capitol hill feminism" to capture how "women on the Hill adopted and adapted the rhetoric, ideological precepts, and policy goals of the women's movement."[10] Also, Anastasia Curwood uses the term "bridge feminism" to describe how Shirley Chisholm connected the African American civil rights movement and the women's movement as well as the grassroots and the legislative arena.[11] Similarly, Mink partnered with allies in and outside of Congress, amplifying the voices of those not traditionally welcome at the political table. She was an exceptional woman, but her achievements and political battles were not hers alone. Instead, Mink considered herself a representative of the people. She was not afraid to take controversial positions. She did so to advocate *for and with* those whose voices were often ignored.

Second, Mink's political leadership and achievements challenge how feminism is traditionally understood. Her terms in Congress coincided with the so-called second and third waves of feminisms. The first wave commonly refers to the diverse movements that culminated in the passage of the Nineteenth Amendment and women achieving the vote. The second wave serves as a shorthand for women's activism during the 1960s and 1970s. And the third wave refers to the gender activism of the 1990s that foregrounded intersectional understandings of oppression and resistance. That is, these latter movements understood gender hierarchy as intertwined with other forms of structural inequality based on race, class, and so on. Various scholars have critiqued the wave metaphor as a way of characterizing US feminist history. The tendency is to privilege white, middle-class women, particularly on the East Coast, as the main protagonists. Even the history of the second wave tends to tell a sequential story of feminism as a white, middle-class women's movement that then gave rise to other forms of feminisms.[12]

Mink's political career reveals that so-called liberal feminists, those who prioritize legislative change and equal opportunity, were not all white women who cared only about the middle class. "Liberal" approaches could lead to transformative policies and practices that address the needs of diverse women. Also, feminist activists came from various backgrounds and drew political inspiration from assorted movements. They espoused many and evolving perspectives that spilled beyond categories such as liberal, radical, and Third World.[13] As feminist scholar Chela Sandoval argues, the feminist methodology of women of color operates through a "differential consciousness" that refuses any singular approach to resisting multiple intersecting oppressions.[14] Mink's political approach reveals this productive blurring of and experimentation with diverse political approaches.

In essence, Mink was an *intersectional legislative feminist*. In her 1989 groundbreaking essay, Kimberlé Crenshaw introduced the term "intersectionality" to critique the limitations of the law as well as feminist theory and antiracist politics. By centering Black women's experiences and theorization, Crenshaw pointed out the inadequacies of treating "race and gender as mutually exclusive categories of experience and analysis."[15] Crenshaw drew from the insights of previous scholars, who emphasized how race, gender, and other systems of inequality were interlinked. At the electoral level, Mink, in conversation with community activists, feminist thinkers, and progressive elected officials, was creating and promoting intersectional feminist legislation. Through political innovations, she sought to go beyond single-axis frameworks to address the needs of those traditionally marginalized in US society.

Finally, Mink's political vision reveals a Pacific World understanding of feminism. Her identity as a racialized woman from Hawai'i shaped her ideas regarding nuclear testing, the environment, labor, gender, race, and sovereignty. Mink's experiences growing up in a plantation society and becoming a lawyer during Hawai'i's Democratic Revolution of the 1950s shaped her understanding of and desire to address injustice. She demanded full inclusion into the US polity, seeking equal opportunity and equal protection. Native Hawaiians advocating sovereignty have challenged the rubric of civil rights and the goal of inclusion. In fact, Native Hawaiian scholar Haunani-Kay Trask and others characterize Asian Americans as settler colonialists.[16] Even with unequal political and economic power compared to haoles (whites), Asians in Hawai'i nevertheless contributed to the impoverishment and disfranchisement of Native Hawaiians.

The Pacific origins of Mink's worldview led her to identify particular wrongs of the US national state and nurtured a range of strategies that she deployed. In contrast to Trask's important critiques of US and Asian settler colonialism, Mink navigated the tricky waters of political liberalism, seeking full citizenship rights in order to challenge US militarism in the Pacific. Mink demanded government intervention to address racism, sexism, and Indigenous dispossession. Playing on the famous Audre Lorde quotation, we might say that Mink sought to utilize the master's tools (political liberalism) in order to renovate the master's house (create a seat at the table for those traditionally left out).[17] Mink charted radical possibilities within political liberal constraints.

This book tells Mink's life in four parts. Part 1, "The Party of the People," offers an origin story, exploring the confluence of personal and political events in Hawai'i and on the US mainland that led to Mink's election to Congress in 1964. Part 2, "A Great Society at War," focuses on Mink's first set of terms in the House of Representatives (1965–1977) with chapters on her antiwar, feminist, and environmental politics. Part 3, "Oceans and Islands," analyzes Mink's life away from Congress at the national and local levels. During this interlude (1977–1990) she served as President Jimmy Carter's assistant secretary of state for Oceans and International Environmental and Scientific Affairs. Mink also became the first woman to serve as national chair of Americans for Democratic Action, a progressive organization cofounded by Eleanor Roosevelt. During the 1980s, Mink decided to return to her island roots and chaired the Honolulu City Council. Part 4, "A National Reckoning," zeroes in on Mink's intersectional legislative feminist activism during the last twelve years of her life in Congress (1990–2002).

There is much more to say about Patsy Mink. This telling will hopefully invite others to remember, share their own stories, and reconsider the histories of feminisms and modern US politics. Reenvisioning the past offers the opportunity to rethink possible futures. As Mink modeled in her thirtieth anniversary Title IX speech, she did not just celebrate previous achievements; she emphasized the persistent need to perfect an imperfect democracy: "While it is wonderful that many young girls and women today take it for granted that they will be offered equitable educational opportunities, we must not forget our struggle for the passage of Title IX. Further, despite our many successes, women and women leaders are still underrepresented in many important areas of society including government, business, and academia. To remedy these and other inequities that continue to persist, we must all remain vigilant."[18] Mink was a lifelong fighter who demanded social justice. A remembrance of her determination to speak truth to power will hopefully inspire us to do the same.

PART I

The Party of the People

I personally regard the choice of a political party of equal importance and significance to that of selecting one's religious faith. While the latter has to do with your ultimate purpose in life, your political faith has to do with how you believe your daily affairs should be handled by your own government. Choosing your political party is not a casual matter, but is one which should be preceded by careful consideration of one's own political philosophy and attitude.
—Patsy Takemoto Mink, 1963

Patsy Mink came to the platform to face a huge crowd that for more than an hour had been restive and often so noisy the speakers on the platform could not be clearly heard.
Dressed in white, and so small she hardly measured up to the microphones before her, she quieted the crowd with her first sentences.
Thereafter the only interruption was frequent cheers. When she finished there was a roar of applause and a rush of people to congratulate her.
—*Honolulu Star-Bulletin*, ca. 1960

In July 1960, five months after African American students in Greensboro, North Carolina, launched a sit-in movement to challenge Jim Crow segregation, the Democratic National Convention erupted over a proposed civil rights plank for the party's platform.[1] All the southern states opposed it, but it passed. Unlike the Dixiecrats in 1948, the southern Democrats did not walk out. Patsy Takemoto Mink, a thirty-two-year-old Japanese American lawyer from Hawai'i and a first-time delegate, addressed the crowd of more than ten thousand people to support the call for civil rights. Coming from the newest state of the union and a

member of the platform committee, Mink did not hold back: "I cannot sit silent at this historic moment without defending . . . one of the
truly great planks of this platform. . . . So long as there remains groups
[sic] of our fellow Americans who are denied equal opportunity, and
equal protection under the law; so long as they are deprived of their
basic right to vote—we must remain steadfast—till all shades of man
may stand side by side in dignity and self respect."[2] Only a portion of
Mink's speech was televised. Her eloquence, political commitment, and
physical attractiveness (one commentator described Mink as "the lovely
Oriental doll of a delegate") launched her into the national limelight.[3]
Four years later, Mink became the first woman of color to be elected to
the US Congress, eventually serving twenty-four years as a member of
the House of Representatives.

Mink's involvement with the Democratic Party in Hawai'i, before and
after the 1960 national convention, laid the basis of her extensive career
in politics. She developed a lifelong commitment to the party, despite
deep differences she sometimes had with members and leaders at the
national and local levels. Mink's dedication speaks to a broader phenomenon of Americans of Japanese ancestry (AJAs) coming of age in Hawai'i
after World War II. Collectively, they sought to overturn their caste status by seeking economic and political rights for racialized and working
people. For AJAs, the ultimate symbol of equality was the achievement
of Hawai'i statehood in 1959.

As much as Mink supported the Democrats, she also consistently advocated that the party shift towards even more liberal politics. Mink
demanded peace, an end to nuclear proliferation, protection of labor,
equal rights for women, a greater investment in education, and transparency in the legislative process. Mink's political commitments led her to
advocate within and without the Democratic Party. Her outspoken politics attracted loyal supporters and aroused fierce opposition, particularly
from those unused to the leadership of a Japanese American woman.

Mink owed her personal and political trajectory to the feats and sacrifices of her forebears, beginning with the journey of her grandparents
from Japan to Hawai'i. Their travels across the Pacific laid the foundation for Patsy's claims of belonging and social justice. Their story was
not an immigrant tale of assimilation into a democratic nation. Two
of her grandparents arrived just before the United States overthrew

the Native Hawaiian kingdom, and her other grandparents arrived in the midst of forced annexation. At the dawn of the twentieth century, Hawai'i became a US territory, a designation that relegated the islands to secondary political status and froze the hierarchy that conferred vast social and political privilege upon white settlers, or haoles. As Japanese immigrants, Mink's grandparents were desired for their labor but denied the ability to become citizens. The 1790 Nationality Act restricted naturalization to free white people. While the Fourteenth Amendment (ratified in 1868) recognized citizenship of persons naturalized or born in the United States, including formerly enslaved persons, it did not undo the exclusion of Asian immigrants from naturalization. And, for Asian Americans who were citizens by birth, holding citizenship was not a guarantee of acceptance. Both Japanese immigrants and their children were suspected of being enemy spies during World War II. Witness to interlocking policies and practices of exclusion, subordination, and marginalization, Mink entered public life to demand that the United States fulfill its promise of democracy and equality for all.

Travel to a neighbor island in the 1950s was magical but fraught: we soared through glorious skies in barely pressurized cabins on propeller aircraft. The first interisland trip I remember was a forty-minute flight from Honolulu to Kahului, Maui, in June 1955 to attend my great-grandfather Gojiro Tateyama's funeral. Despite the weight of the moment, Mom dressed me in my prettiest dress, a pale pink dotted swiss thing with lots of crinoline underneath. I flew to Maui in the early morning with my grandparents Mitama and Suematsu Takemoto; my parents would come later that same day for what was going to be a long weekend of grieving, remembering, and feasting.

Gojiro's funeral was my introduction to the extended Tateyama family. For the first time, I saw all nine of my grandmother's living brothers and sisters in one place (one brother died in World War II), hung out with my great-grandmother Tsuru, and discovered that although I had only one first cousin at the time, my mother had oodles of them, all of whom were family to me.

At age three, I was one of the youngest children in the extended family, and the second oldest of four great-grandchildren who had been born by the time Gojiro passed away. Although in Japanese culture the arc of life entails great sacrifice for children, family gatherings were not child-centered events. We romped in the brush and entertained ourselves playing jacks or catch, ordinarily leaving adults to their merry gossip and hanafuda card games. But on the passing of the family patriarch, children were kept close to adults, integrated into bereavement activities.

Tateyama boys and girls, men and women, usually split off into gender groups, with the guys talking sports or sneaking off to swim and fish, while the women tended to cooking, dishwashing, and very giggly chatter. I tagged along with the womenfolk, part fly on the wall, listening to conversations that later would help me piece together the family's history, and part shadow, following and emulating my elders as I internalized our cultural practices and traditions as my own.

The family gathered at Gojiro and Tsuru's home in Kailua, Maui, a blip on the map far from population centers. Kailua was east of the towns of Pā`ia, Kahului, and Wailuku, reachable only by driving a narrow, winding road, now known as the Hana Highway, for what could seem like hours.

The trip was not for the faint of stomach, as the route included a relentless succession of hairpin curves. The road was so ruthless that sometimes car-sick passengers would have to walk the most twisty parts to abate violent discomfort.

Although they raised eleven children there, Tsuru and Gojiro's Kailua home was a small house with very few amenities. To bathe, one went out to a shed that housed a furo (wooden tub filled with water), which was heated by a fire. There was one toilet in the house, another in an outhouse. The kitchen had running water supplied by a well, with pipes leading to a sink spigot that was covered by a Drum tobacco bag to filter out debris. With only sketchy electricity, Tsuru baked her iconic bread using a kerosene stove.

Tsuru and Gojiro moved to their Kailua home in 1915, a year and a half after the birth of their youngest daughter but before the births of their youngest sons. Prior to 1915, the growing Tateyama family lived in a tent and a shack along Waikamoi stream, a place even more remote than Kailua. On a northeastern slope of Haleakalā, Waikamoi stream flowed through a rain forest far from any town or village and about three miles from the nearest road. In its isolation, Waikamoi was the perfect place for two fugi-tives. Gojiro had fled his labor contract, so was an unauthorized immigrant; Tsuru had fled her drunken and abusive first husband, with whom she had emigrated from Japan. In Waikamoi and for a decade after, they concealed their status by living under an assumed last name, Tokunaga.

Life in Waikamoi was primitive and difficult. Gojiro midwifed all of Tsuru's births, as doctors and clinics were inaccessible. The older girls tended to the younger siblings as Gojiro and Tsuru cultivated, prepared, and preserved their very local food. Once a month, Gojiro would hike to the nearest village for supplies, sometimes delighting his daughters with surprises of candy and oranges upon his return.

Bamboo forests surrounded the Waikamoi home, yielding an ample sup-ply of takenoko (bamboo shoots) and warabi (fern sprouts) to eat. Trees bore luscious fruit like guava and mountain apples. The ground offered wild watercress and taro, which the family pounded into poi. Gojiro, who had a lifelong green thumb, grew vegetables, most famously sweet pota-toes. In 1979, during a Tateyama family reunion, the Tateyama sisters—my mother's aunties, Taneyo, Asayo, Sakae, Shige, and Chiyo, along with her mother, Mitama—took some of the younger generation up to Waikamoi to show us where they had spent their childhoods. It was lush with foliage, wet, and muddy—a mosquito's paradise. Amazingly, we found remnants of bowls and plates poking up out of the mud near where the family had been encamped seventy years earlier.

In Kailua, Gojiro and Tsuru raised their family in somewhat improved circumstances, developing good relations with a haole manager at East Maui Irrigation, where Gojiro worked as a ditchman, and with the few other residents of the area, some of whom were Native Hawaiian. Less remote than Waikamoi, Kailua was nevertheless isolated, both from agglomerations of people in towns and from Japanese immigrant communities on the plantation. But the Tateyama parents transmitted a strong sense of Japanese cultural identity to their children, especially through Buddhist religious observance and holiday traditions surrounding Oshogatsu, or Japanese New Year.

Japanese New Year, celebrated according to the Western calendar, was the most important family event each year. Tsuru and Gojiro's children and their families converged on Kailua to help prepare for and then enjoy New Year's rituals. Most of the Tateyama siblings still lived on Maui while Gojiro and Tsuru were alive, although several had relocated to Honolulu during the 1940s. Many of the Honolulu Tateyamas traveled to Kailua for New Year's, some annually without fail. Together, the family pounded mochigome (glutinous rice) into mochi, for use in the ozoni (New Year's soup) eaten for breakfast to greet the New Year. To bid farewell to the old year and welcome the new, my grandfather Suematsu orchestrated fireworks, and the Tateyama brothers, my mother's uncles, played ukulele and led everyone in song.

Tsuru was monolingual, in Japanese. I don't know whether Gojiro spoke any English. Their eleven children all learned English at the missionary schools Gojiro's boss sent them to; most seemed to use English as their first language. Most of the Tateyama siblings also were Christianized to some degree by their schools, though all honored Buddhist practices as well, especially in relation to their parents. By the time my mother's generation could speak, English was the primary language at family gatherings, though communication with Tsuru and possibly also with Gojiro required Japanese translation.

When I met Tsuru at Gojiro's funeral, I could not converse with her or ask questions as I didn't speak Japanese. So I observed. After the viewing of Gojiro lying in repose in the living room, several female family members retired to a small room to sit with Tsuru. Invited to join them, I eagerly did. Seated on a zabuton (cushion) on the floor, Tsuru, called "Obaban" by her granddaughters, including my mother, was small but sturdy, welcoming but somber. Dressed in drab funeral clothing, she rolled a cigarette while sipping a brown liquid that she poured from a bottle into a teacup. I somehow knew that the brown liquid was whiskey, my suspicions confirmed when the aunties wouldn't let me have a taste.

Obaban's demeanor set fireworks off in my brain. The female family members I had observed up to that point were very gender traditional, proper, and sober. No Tateyama woman I knew imbibed alcohol, let alone smoked or rolled cigarettes. (In fact, the women who were in the room with Obaban and me that day later insisted she had been drinking tea.) I didn't have a vocabulary to describe my impressions at the time, but in retrospect I can say Tsuru struck me as her own kind of woman, independent and indomitable. Much later, I learned that my whiskey-sipping, cigarette-rolling great-grandmother had stood up to her impossible first husband, Sootsuchi Yamada, leaving him though laws were not available to her to divorce him; raised a family with Gojiro though she could not legally marry him until 1926, after Yamada passed away; and, with Gojiro, arranged for Yamada's burial and regularly tended his grave as one does for family. Tsuru and Gojiro even taught their children and grandchildren to include Yamada in the family's honoring of ancestral spirits during the annual obon festival. I did not come to know all these details until I was well into adulthood, but my first impressions of Obaban foretold a back story of strength and resilience.

Gojiro's funeral took place at Mantokuji Buddhist Temple, near Pā`ia, and he was buried in Mantokuji cemetery, which gazes upon the ocean in the distance. Tsuru joined him there a few years later. Both graves are not far from Yamada's.

The funeral itself involved rituals that were unfamiliar to me. I was unaware of our family's Buddhist roots until Gojiro's funeral. The strategic role of missionaries in the Christianizing and assimilating education of so many second-generation Tateyamas (as well as of my grandfather Suematsu Takemoto) meant that religion-wise, most of the family leaned toward churches, not temples. But Buddhist ritual was part of the whole family's vernacular, and the service resonated with everyone.

From Mantokuji we returned to Kailua, to memorialize Gojiro over a traditional Tateyama meal. From my mother's childhood through my own, Tateyama meals comingled cuisines, reflecting the family's own integration of Native Hawaiian culinary preparations with their Japanese cultural heritage. Sometimes the meals would be accompanied by peripheral table accents such as tatted doilies and crocheted placemats crafted by one of my grandmother's sisters. The Tateyama daughters had been introduced to crafting at Mauna'olu Seminary in Makawao, where they received a heavy dose of Anglo-American domestic arts as part of their education through eighth grade.

I don't remember our mourning meal for Gojiro, but it was likely a typical family meal. His grandchildren remember that traditional Tateyama feasts included Hawaiian dishes like lomi lomi salmon, lau lau, poi, and chicken long rice, as well as Japanese staples like nishime, namasu, and hekka made with fresh bamboo. If the menfolk had time to hike down to the sea, fresh fish and opae (tiny red shrimp) could be added to the menu. Back in the day, Gojiro's special contribution to family celebrations was his kalua pig, roasted deep in the earth in an imu (underground, rock-lined pit). Minus the imu, many of these dishes remained part of our reunion menus until the turn of the twenty-first century, served in homage to the family's traditionally multicultural feasts.

Gojiro held many jobs—ditchman, mailman, owner of a small country store—but his vocation was farming and gardening. He and Tsuru raised chickens and a few pigs for eggs and meat, while cultivating the land around them with patches of pineapple and sweet potato, groves of gardenia and ginger, and thickets of ti leaves. Much of this bounty fed the family, but Gojiro also sold some of it. The family's dependence on the land fostered great respect for nature, the environment, and sustainability. This love of the soil, water, and forests of Maui was quite possibly Gojiro and Tsuru's greatest legacy to my mother.

Mom's parents nurtured this love of the land and respect for its bounty in their own home life. As young children, Mom and her brother, Eugene, helped raise chickens and grow fruits and vegetables. Their Hamakuapoko home was much closer to towns and communities than was their grandparents' Kailua home, but it was still country living. Because my grandfather Suematsu was a technical worker rather than a farm worker, he was provided a house apart from the plantation camps. Separated geographically from Japanese American neighborhoods, the home was also isolated from neighborhoods of haole, professional or managerial plantation employees. The nearest neighbor was a couple of football fields away, and there were no playmates nearby.

Though playmates were scarce, Mom had plenty to do—feeding the animals, watering plants, pulling weeds, harvesting the day's gifts from nature. My grandmother Mitama transmitted to her daughter all of the domestic skills she had learned at Mauna'olu, preparing Mom for her expected future role as homemaker. Mom assimilated those skills, doing her fair share of sewing, knitting, and cooking. But even as a child, Mom favored chores that involved the land. As a mom, she continued to prefer yardwork to housework.

Mom's Tateyama childhood permeated my own childhood home life, though I didn't know that before visiting Kailua. Going to Kailua showed me that many practices in the Takemoto Mink household were not unique, but rather interpretations of folkways learned from Tsuru and Gojiro. Now I understood that Mom's love of *koge* rice (the burnt crust at the bottom of a metal pot used for rice cooking) was not about salvaging a culinary mistake; it was about savoring family memories evoked by that crispy crunch. Now I saw why my mother glowed with joy when she puttered in the garden watching bananas grow.

I don't know what my parents discussed on their first date. But I suspect that their mutual awe of the earth—of its land, water, and life—entered the conversation. Matters of war and peace, progressivism and McCarthyism, not to mention bridge strategy, certainly bound them together, as well. Yet the presence of the environment at the center of our family's ontology almost certainly sealed their bond.

The Tateyama family revered two things—the patriarch Gojiro and the land. Gojiro's funeral was my father's baptism into the extended family. In Hawai'i for less than three years when Gojiro died, my father was new to our extended family rituals and culture. To some in the family, my father no doubt was a strange white man—an interloping mainland haole who was clumsy with chopsticks and who had no parental family of his own nearby. My father was the first haole to marry into the extended family; he was the only haole in the family for decades. But over time, the family embraced him as one of their own. The family's relationship with the land lubricated his passage into its midst, as the land provided common ground for conversation, mutual learning, and respect. My father, a geologist and groundwater specialist, frequented Hawai'i's mountain forests as part of his work. Waikamoi stream, the Tateyama family's point of origin, became familiar terrain to him, as were the challenges of water delivery and coexistence with wildlife. In this my father shared interests with family menfolk who had worked as ditchmen or who had mapped plantation irrigation routes, or who knew the forests inside out and could teach Pa how to behave in the presence of wild boar.

With Gojiro's funeral, my father and I began the process of becoming Tateyamas. Of course, we were part of the Tateyama family already, my father by marriage and me by birth. But with that June weekend in 1955, we began to feel like Tateyamas in our souls.

1

Plantation Society

Born on the island of Maui, Patsy Matsu Takemoto grew up in a caste-based plantation society. At the top were haoles, particularly those who controlled the sugar industry through five big conglomerates, known as the Big Five.[1] At the bottom were Native Hawaiians, dispossessed of sovereignty and land. Hawai'i officially became a US territory in 1900 after haole economic leaders and the US military overthrew the Kingdom of Hawai'i in 1893 and annexed the islands in 1898. Near Native Hawaiians on the social hierarchy were other nonwhites, mostly Asians and Puerto Ricans. They were recruited to provide manual labor on plantations and eventually moved into low-level service industries.

Plantations were company towns. Workers owed their wages, housing, access to credit, health care, and schools to their bosses, who were allied with the Republican Party. Those towards the bottom tended not to challenge these power relationships, but they did find ways to resist. Significant labor strikes racked the sugar, pineapple, and transportation industries in the first half of the twentieth century. Politically, however, Asian immigrants were disfranchised as they could not become US citizens due to racially exclusive naturalization laws. Their island-born children, though, received birthright US citizenship. Even so, all political activities, either in the electoral arena or through labor organizing, were carefully monitored by the plantation hierarchy.

World War II both reinforced these power dynamics and sparked transformational changes. Following the attack on Pearl Harbor, the imposition of martial law on the islands reinforced racial anxieties and social control, particularly regarding Japanese immigrants and their American-born children. By then, there were 157,000 people of Japanese ancestry living in Hawai'i, constituting one-third of the overall population and the largest ethnic group on the islands.

Despite hostility against them, many sons of Japanese immigrants signed up to fight for the United States. The wartime experiences and sacrifices of these racialized soldiers increased expectations of full citizenship, a phenomenon that scholars have characterized as martial citizenship.[2]

Neither a veteran nor a man, Mink was nevertheless part of this generation of Americans of Japanese ancestry (AJAs). She came of age under the national leadership of Franklin Delano Roosevelt, who both created the New Deal and authorized the mass incarceration of Japanese Americans during World War II. Despite this mixed political record, Mink and other AJAs would eventually turn collectively to the Democratic Party to challenge the caste system in Hawai'i.

Plantation Families

Patsy's family history followed a familiar pattern of Japanese migration to Hawai'i. She never met her paternal grandparents, Yakichi Takemoto (1864–1909) and Shiyumu Nakamura Takemoto (1867–1900). They both died relatively young, when Patsy's father was still a child. They sailed for Honolulu in March 1892, both in their mid- to late twenties.[3] The Takemotos left behind one, or possibly two, of their sons in Japan. Such family separation was not uncommon among immigrants of all backgrounds. Some expected to return to their home country better able to support families, and others hoped to reunite their families in their adopted country at a later date. Patsy's maternal grandparents also arrived in Hawai'i by the late nineteenth century. Her grandmother Tsuru Wakasugi Yamada (1877–1958) landed in 1898 at the age of twenty.[4] Patsy's grandfather Gojiro Tateyama (1879–1955) arrived one year later at the same age.[5] All four grandparents were among the approximately two hundred thousand Japanese who migrated to Hawai'i over the course of the late nineteenth and early twentieth centuries.

These labor recruits left an industrializing and militarizing economy that burdened workers and farmers. The spread of tenancy, along with stagnating prices and a new tax system, impoverished many agrarian families. Younger sons, and sometimes daughters, looked beyond Japan's borders to help their families survive. Both Tsuru, who came from Yamaguchi, and Gojiro, who came from Kumamoto prefecture on Kyushu Island (the most southern of the main Japanese islands), came from farming families.[6]

As Japanese migrants sought wages abroad, the plantations of Hawai'i recruited laborers to cultivate and harvest commercial crops. Plantation workers performed long hours of back-breaking labor under the supervision of overseers who could mete out physical punishment as well as verbal abuse.[7] Due to shortages, plantation owners in Hawai'i imported workers. Native Hawaiians tended to resist performing such labor. Their population drastically declined due to epidemics introduced by settlers and economic dislocation.[8] Given the islands' location in the middle of the Pacific Ocean, obtaining laborers from Asia was cost effective. Some Japanese traveled to Hawai'i as early as 1868, but the poor working conditions there led the Meiji government to institute a ban on emigration that lasted until 1885. After that, the governments in Japan and Hawai'i worked together to arrange plantation labor migration.

Japanese migrants like Gojiro arrived in Hawai'i having signed a multiyear contract. They agreed to perform labor for an extended period in exchange for wages, lodging, and food. Japanese women also were sought after as plantation laborers. Like the men, they worked in the fields but for less pay. Also, women were considered civilizing influences that dampened activism. Plantation owners and managers regarded family men as more reliable and less likely to protest poor working conditions. However, some workers did protest, eventually forming unions and organizing strikes. Others, like Gojiro, simply left. He arrived in Honolulu on the island of O'ahu as contract worker #6536 for the Hackfield Company. He soon escaped to a remote area of the island of Maui and assumed an alias, Tokunaga.[9] He formed a family with Tsuru, who had sailed from Yokohama as the wife of another Japanese immigrant laborer.

Nearly twenty thousand women, mostly from Japan but also from Okinawa and Korea, arrived in Hawai'i in the early decades of the twentieth century as "pictures brides." Their families and their go-betweens arranged marriages with Asian men abroad and "married" the couples through an exchange of photographs. These marriages were essential to the social reproduction of Japanese American communities in Hawai'i and on the mainland. After the 1907 Gentlemen's Agreement between the

United States and Japan, Japanese laborers could no longer enter the United States or its territories. This agreement was patterned after the 1882 Chinese Exclusion Act, which prohibited Chinese labor migration and barred all Chinese, regardless of class, from naturalized citizenship. However, because Japan had been victorious in the Russo-Japanese War of 1904–1905, the country was regarded as a rising world power. Consequently, certain concessions were made to the exclusion policy. Japanese children in San Francisco could attend integrated schools; their segregation had ignited international tensions that resulted in the Gentlemen's Agreement. Also, Japanese immigrants could bring their family members to the United States; "picture bride" marriages allowed Japanese men to marry without having to leave the United States and potentially be barred from reentry.

Arranged marriages might be regarded as a form of female subordination, and many women certainly experienced these marriages in that way. Some men, who labored many years in order to earn enough to marry and transport their wives across the Pacific, sent younger photos of themselves. Other men sent pictures of more handsome friends. Regardless of such misrepresentations, women who arrived as picture brides were bound for life to men whom they did not know and sometimes could not even recognize from their photos. However, women who became picture brides also had aspirations of their own. Some utilized arranged marriages to escape economic and familial circumstances in Japan and explore new opportunities abroad.

Tsuru was not a picture bride. She traveled to Hawai'i with her first husband, Sootsuchi Yamada, on the *S.S. Mogul*.[10] It is possible that the marriage was arranged, since that was the common practice. However, participants in arranged marriages can nevertheless become acquainted with one another and even choose or veto potential partners. Sootsuchi and Tsuru were of similar ages, both in their early twenties, and had similar economic and work backgrounds; both were farm laborers from Yamaguchi and were most likely bound for plantation labor on Maui. Once in Hawai'i, Tsuru discovered that her husband was physically abusive and a heavy drinker. Sootsuchi may have always been prone to both before his departure from Japan. Being near the bottom rung of a racial and labor caste system no doubt exacerbated his sense of frustration and helped to fuel impulses to escape through alcohol consumption as well as to physically control and harm his wife. Just as Gojiro escaped

Figure 1.1. Gojiro and Tsuru, with their first four of eleven children, living under the surname Tokunaga at the time of this photo, circa 1908. Patsy's mother, Mitama, stands at Gojiro's knees. Courtesy of Gwendolyn Mink.

plantation work, Tsuru escaped her first marriage. She was not the only immigrant woman to do so. Japanese-language newspapers featured advertisements demanding the return of runaway wives and sometimes their lovers.[11]

Tsuru and Gojiro chose each other as life partners, eventually bearing and raising eleven children together. They could not legally marry until 1926, after Sootsuchi passed away. Gojiro and Tsuru were grandparents by then, and lived under the assumed name of Tokunaga instead of Gojiro's family name of Tateyama. Patsy's mother was their third child, Mitama (1905–1987).

Patsy grew up with a large extended family on her mother's side, but her father, Suematsu Takemoto (1898–1972), was an orphan. His parents had four children in the United States. Suematsu was the youngest, born in 1898, before his mother passed away two years later giving birth to a stillborn child. Suematsu's father followed in 1909 due to illness. Reflecting the precarious conditions of a plantation society with limited health care, only one of Suematsu's siblings in Hawai'i survived beyond childhood and early adulthood.[12] And, Suematsu had no contact with his family in Japan.

Patronage and Paternalism

Despite these difficult beginnings, both Suematsu and the Tateyama/ Tokunaga family ironically benefited from haole patronage. Early white settlers in Hawai'i were motivated not only by financial gain but also by faith. Christian missionaries established religious and educational institutions to convert Native Hawaiians and immigrants. These expressions of paternalism sometimes softened the hardships wrought by the plantation society. Indigenous and Pacific Islander studies scholars have critiqued these missionary initiatives for the cultural, physical, and sexual violence they inflicted on Native people.[13] Both sides of Patsy's family, though, advanced through educational opportunities provided by haole benefactors and missionary institutions.

After becoming an orphan, Suematsu found his way to Mills School, a private, missionary-run boarding school on the island of O'ahu that was

Figure 1.2. Gojiro and Tsuru, living under Gojiro's given surname, Tateyama, by the time of this photo, circa 1940s. They were grandparents before they could legally marry in 1926. Courtesy of Gwendolyn Mink.

in the process of becoming the Mid-Pacific Institute. The school offered English-language as well as Christian religious instruction to Native Hawaiians and Asians. In essence, the school offered cultural capital for outsiders in the haole-dominated plantation society. Despite the low tuition at Mills, Suematsu likely worked in order to attend and board at the school. He graduated in 1918 and four years later received a college degree from the University of Hawaiʻi (UH).

Suematsu was not the only person of Asian ancestry in his college graduating class. Wealthy haoles sent their children to the mainland for college. So, three out of the four senior class officers had Chinese last names, and the fourth had a Hawaiian one.[14] Reputedly, Suematsu was the first AJA to receive a civil engineering degree from UH.[15] Following graduation, Suematsu obtained a job as a skilled professional, a surveyor for the East Maui Irrigation Company (EMI). With his college education, Suematsu entered the plantation hierarchy several rungs above most plantation workers.

Mitama also received a white missionary education, though only through eighth grade. An unauthorized resident after he escaped contract labor, Gojiro settled his family far away from the plantation. After living in the Waikamoi forest for many years, Gojiro moved the family to the isolated village of Kailua. There, they were befriended by a haole employer and his wife. As the Tokunagas/Tateyamas settled in Kailua, located on the northeast coast of Maui, Gojiro dug ditches for EMI. The wife of an EMI manager took an interest in the growing Tateyama family and arranged for all six of the Tateyama daughters to attend the Maunaʻolu Seminary, a Christian boarding school in Makawao, Maui. William Pogue, a supervisor for EMI, even paid for their education. Similar to the Mills Institute, Maunaʻolu taught Western religion, language, and culture to nonhaoles. The Tateyama girls traveled by foot and horseback to reach the school, which was about fifteen miles from Kailua, up the midslopes of Haleakalā. Mitama found Maunaʻolu, which ended at eighth grade, to be "very austere and the discipline strict."[16] Nevertheless, she enjoyed the experience and learned to cook Western foods. Her classmates were Hawaiian and Chinese, and they shared their cultural practices and foods with one another. In part due to the Maunaʻolu experience, Mitama, like the rest of her family, combined elements of Asian and Western as well as Native Hawaiian traditions in their daily lives.

Figure 1.3. Patsy's father, Suematsu Takemoto, at the edge of an east Maui bamboo forest, ca. 1930s. Suematsu was a land surveyor for the East Maui Irrigation Company. Courtesy of Gwendolyn Mink.

As a result of their exposure to haole language, culture, and education, Patsy's parents led a more privileged life than the average Japanese American plantation family. Suematsu and Mitama met in Kailua, and they married in the summer of 1925. Since he was a skilled employee, they were allocated a modern house. Patsy's cousin, Ruth Okazaki Mukai, recalled that Patsy's family "had what we called a supervisor's house which is a big living room, a big kitchen, and a big yard."[17] In contrast, Ruth "lived in a little plantation house. The back steps were gone, rotted away, but they didn't feel it was important enough to fix. And, the front side door was rotted away too and they thought it wasn't important to fix and we lived in a house that had an outhouse. . . . We had no bathtub in the house."[18] In addition to having a bigger and more modernized house, the Takemotos were physically removed from the other plantation laborers, who tended to live in ethnically and racially segregated camps. The Takemotos were situated closer to, but still distant from, the haole managers. Patsy's older brother, Eugene, recalled that their home was "right smack surrounded in . . . [a] pasture, flanked with two railroads on . . . either side so we were isolated . . . really isolated from the community. In fact, I think it's about a hundred yards or more to Mr. Force and other plantation official[s]."[19]

Patsy and Eugene enjoyed their country home life, despite their geographic isolation from playmates and family. They relished the outdoors, climbing trees, riding bikes, and attending family get-togethers at their grandparents' house. They were surrounded by animals and vegetation—a dog, cats, chickens, rabbits, a vegetable garden, and a watermelon patch, as well as mango and papaya trees and their mother's lily garden.[20] Despite life in the remote Maui countryside, they were connected to an increasingly tumultuous world by a Silvertone Sears radio that they used to listen to music, news, sporting events, and President Franklin Delano Roosevelt's fireside chats.[21]

A Maui Girl

On Maui, Patsy became a leader as she sought and gained educational and social opportunities. She also developed a painful awareness of racial, linguistic, and class hierarchies, instituted into the fabric of the school system. These dynamics intensified during World War II. After all, the attack on Pearl Harbor led to the formal entry of the United States into the global war, and Japanese Americans in the islands and on the mainland became suspect for their presumed connections to an enemy nation. Coming of age in a plantation society in the crucible of war shaped Patsy's political outlook for decades to come.

Patsy was a motivated and intelligent child. She and Eugene, one year older, grew up as close friends. Their cousin, Calvin Tamura, described

Figure 1.4. Toddler Patsy with big brother, Eugene Takemoto, circa 1930.
Courtesy of Gwendolyn Mink.

them as "the best of pals."[22] When Eugene started attending school,
Patsy demanded to go as well. At age four, she began school and enjoyed
excelling in her studies. Patsy and Eugene also participated in a variety
of activities outside of school. She was a Girl Scout and took piano as
well as hula lessons; Eugene played the ukulele.[23]

The Takemoto parents encouraged their children, not holding Patsy back because of her age or gender. Eugene recalled that his father "was very quiet" and only spoke when he had something very important to say. Both Suematsu and Mitama had "very strict rules"; Eugene and Patsy learned that they "gotta study," and their parents "wanted us to be very good at" things.[24] Their mother took care of the housework and children. She "really cared for us because she did all the cooking . . . washing the clothes, all that kind of task plus driving us to school."[25] According to Mitama's nephew Calvin, "She was very specific about [how] she thought the world should function. . . . She was in control of the space that she lived in, she oversaw it, she was the mistress of the house."[26] Mitama and Suematsu channeled Patsy towards particular skills because she was a girl, but they also allowed her freedom to pursue interests though they did not encourage them. Patsy learned to cook and sew, but she also played outdoors with her cousins, who initially were all boys. She attended school with her brother and developed an abiding interest in the natural sciences.

Patsy and Eugene eventually enrolled at Kaunoa School, an English Standard school. These institutions enforced racial and class separation by allowing access only to students who spoke Standard English and could pass a language test. This restriction resulted in a predominantly haole student body with a smattering of Asian and Hawaiian students. At Kaunoa, "in the mid-1930s 95 percent of the students . . . were white"; in addition, "All of its teachers were white."[27] Most working-class, nonhaole children in Hawai'i spoke pidgin, a language that emerged in the plantations through the mixing of Hawaiian, Asian, Spanish, Portuguese, and English languages. Patsy spoke both pidgin and Standard English, the latter acquired initially from her father and then perfected by listening to Franklin Roosevelt on the radio. Harriet Holt, one of Patsy's classmates when they both attended Maui High School, was a more typical English Standard student. Harriet grew up in Wailuku, the main town of Maui, where "there were no plantation camp kids"; the residents were "mostly people, whose families were business people in the community or worked for the state or the county or the territory at that time."[28] For her, the English Standard school was the norm. She did not remember "ever taking an English Standard test" in order to enroll.[29] In contrast, Patsy's cousin Ruth recalled that students of her background who

Figure 1.5. Three generations of Tateyama women—Obaban (grandmother) Tsuru (*right*), mother Mitama (*left*), Patsy (*center*). Courtesy of Gwendolyn Mink.

wanted to enter Kaunoa had to take a test, and "we spoke pidgin so strong that we didn't know pidgin from good English."[30]

These racial and cultural hierarchies at Kaunoa made the school an uncomfortable learning environment for Patsy. She found the place "intimidating and unfriendly."[31] Even though Patsy earned good grades, "she felt unrecognized for her accomplishments."[32] Furthermore, attending Kaunoa required a long commute, and few of Patsy's friends nearby attended the school. The structures of exclusion, which only allowed select Asian and Hawaiian students into English Standard schools, created the educational experience of social and cultural isolation.

Despite stringent differentiation in the elementary grades, the students who attended English Standard schools matriculated at Maui High School alongside those who did not. When Patsy and Harriet were seniors, Ruth Mukai entered Maui High as a ninth grader. And, Elmer Cravalho, a future Democratic politician, also attended the school without the benefit of an English Standard elementary education. Elmer was a descendent of Portuguese immigrants to Hawai'i. They occupied an in-between racial position between haoles and Asians.[33] Elmer caustically criticized the English Standard schools as educational segregation and worked to dismantle them when he became an elected official.[34]

Patsy excelled academically at Maui High and also became a school leader. Reflecting her own in-between status, Patsy had the ability to move between social cliques at the school. As Harriet recalled, "Patsy mixed with various groups. . . . She was well known in the . . . entire class. . . . I can remember she was always moving from place to place, very energetic, very determined. She . . . always knew what she wanted to be and what . . . she wanted to do."[35] In her senior year, Patsy entered her first electoral race. She ran for and won the class presidency. Her competitors included Harriet Holt (whose father was a politician) and Elmer Cravalho (who claimed to have never lost another vote after high school).[36] Patsy graduated in 1944 as class valedictorian.

Though Patsy eventually thrived in the more mixed environment of Maui High, she came of age during an anxiety-filled period of history. Japan's attack on Pearl Harbor on December 7, 1941, one day after Patsy's fourteenth birthday, ignited fears about Japanese in the United States and its territories. In a 1970 newspaper article, Patsy recalled that her family "had been up late the night before, celebrating my birthday, and we slept

Figure 1.6. Patsy readies for the first day of high school, 1940. Courtesy of Gwendolyn Mink.

very late that day. We didn't know what was happening—we were 100 miles from the Naval Base, on the island of Maui—until the Boy Scouts came and told us to turn out our lights. . . . We might be considered 'Jap Spies.'"[37]

Japanese Americans on the West Coast, approximately 120,000 people (two-thirds of whom were US citizens), were forced to leave their homes for concentration camps. They constituted a tiny minority of the mainland population. However, a long history of racial antagonism, recurrent white economic resentment, and bigoted military leadership created the conditions that resulted in Japanese American incarceration. General DeWitt, commander of the Western Defense Command, actively lobbied for forced relocation, and West Coast newspapers published editorials like the one in the *Los Angeles Times* stating that "a viper is nonetheless a viper wherever the egg is hatched. . . . So, a Japanese American born of Japanese parents, nurtured upon Japanese traditions, living in a transplanted Japanese atmosphere and thoroughly inoculated with Japanese . . . ideals, notwithstanding his nominal brand of accidental citizenship almost inevitably and with the rarest exceptions grows up to be a Japanese, and not an American."[38]

Japanese in Hawai'i were too numerous to relocate en masse, but they nevertheless faced racial suspicions, harassment, and discrimination. Patsy's father, Suematsu, became president of the Hamakuapoko Japanese Community Association at the outbreak of war. As a Nisei, or a member of the second generation, Suematsu was a US citizen. Despite editorials like those in the *Los Angeles Times*, Japanese immigrants and their Hawai'i-born children hoped that citizenship would provide some protection. However, after the Hamakuapoko cane fields were shelled by a Japanese submarine, Suematsu was among those who were interrogated. In fact, he "was immediately suspected of having sent a signal" to assist the attack.[39] The suspicion against Suematsu and his interrogation generated anxiety and fear in the Takemoto and Tateyama families. Ruth Mukai remembered, "After Pearl Harbor, we were afraid that we would be taken into the concentration camps so I took all the Buddhist symbols, images, whatever I could find in the house and climbed into the attic and put it in there."[40] Eventually Suematsu was cleared of suspicion. Nevertheless, the Takemoto family "for two years . . . lived in an interior closet lit by one light" after sunset.[41] And, Patsy remembered "how it was to be called 'Dirty Jap' in school."[42]

Despite anti-Japanese suspicion and surveillance, the Takemoto children contributed to the US war effort. Patsy volunteered at the Red Cross, knitting scarves and rolling bandages. Eugene enlisted in the US military. Suematsu initially discouraged Eugene from military service. Perhaps Suematsu wanted to protect Eugene and continue the Takemoto lineage. Also, the US military did not want AJAs initially, assigning them the status of 4C, enemy aliens. Eventually, the military changed its policy, although suspicions remained, and called for volunteers; ten thousand AJAs came forth in Hawaiʻi, while a much smaller number, understandably, volunteered from mainland concentration camps. AJAs in Hawaiʻi helped to form the 100th Infantry Battalion and combined with the 442nd Combat Team. Together, they became the most highly decorated units in US military history. Eight members of the Tateyama extended family served in the US armed forces during World War II, and one, Mitamaʻs second-youngest brother, Haruyoshi, died in Italy, as a member of the legendary 100th Battalion.

As young Japanese American men proved their loyalty on the battle-fields of Europe, Suematsu discovered that racial prejudice persisted on the plantation. Despite his seniority and technical knowledge, he never broke the glass ceiling to enter the managerial ranks. Instead, appointments were given to less experienced, haole individuals. With Eugene away in the army, and Patsy a student at the University of Hawaiʻi, Suematsu and Mitama decided to relocate to Oʻahu. They initially struggled financially. Mitama, who had not worked outside the home while on Maui, "went to work at a lunch counter, a hat store and a tropical fish store to help pay the bills and keep Patsy in college."[43] Eventually, Suematsu opened his own surveying business, and Mitama worked with him as the office manager. Within a decade of their move, Suematsu and Mitama had built a home on the outskirts of Honolulu, on Kāhala Heights.

A Foreigner in Her Own Country

The next eight years after high school were filled with transitions for Patsy. When she was four, she decided to become a medical doctor. A kindly family physician on Maui, Dr. Frank St. Sure, encouraged his young patients to study.[44] Patsy wanted to help people as Dr. St. Sure did and so set her sights on becoming a physician. It was an unusual career choice for women in the mid-1940s. Cousin Ruth recalled that the standard professional options for educated women were nursing, teaching, or being a secretary.[45] In college, Patsy double majored in zoology and chemistry while pursuing a variety of extracurricular activities, including debate, oratory, theater, and student government. Her studies as an undergraduate and eventually in law school took Patsy to the mainland. She encountered new opportunities to develop intellectually and personally. She also experienced pervasive gender and racial discrimination in her educational and professional pursuits. These life journeys laid the basis for her future political involvements with the Democratic Party.

Patsy found success in her early years at UH, but the more promising students were encouraged to study on the mainland. She was part of a generation of Japanese Americans who pursued higher education in the islands and on the continent. Following World War II, the GI Bill provided financial support for veterans to receive further education. Those in Hawai'i took advantage of this opportunity, enrolling at UH and various mainland institutions. The GI Bill in essence created a professional class among the male children of plantation workers.

Patsy spent her junior year on the mainland. One of her UH professors encouraged her to enroll at Wilson College for Women, a small Christian college in Pennsylvania. Upon arrival, Patsy, despite her US citizenship, was automatically classified as a foreign student. The local branch of the American Association of University Women even invited Patsy to give a talk on a topic related to "internationalism." The other speaker was a student from Luxembourg.

Perhaps responding to the assumption that she was not American, Patsy chose to speak about Hawai'i's campaign for statehood. She pointed out the drawbacks of being a territory versus a state. As a territory, Hawai'i was taxed by the US federal government, but residents did not have the "political right of voting for their own governor, the President of the United States and other high officials."[46] Patsy challenged presumptions of island primitiveness by emphasizing that "Hawaii is very up to date, very Americanized."[47] She argued that denial of statehood should not be based upon assumptions of cultural difference. Instead, Patsy revealed that opposition to statehood had to do with the political process as well the sugar industry. Statehood held the possibility of democracy, while territorial status granted the Big Five greater latitude to influence appointed officials.

Dissatisfied with her educational experience at Wilson, Patsy transferred to the University of Nebraska. There, she encountered a more blatant form of racism, which led her to protest, perhaps for the first time, for racial equality. In a letter to the student newspaper, Patsy criticized the segregation and prejudice that she experienced on campus: "When I arrived here on January 31st, 1947, I hoped and prayed that here I could find some link with what I was told America was like. I am a premedical student and naturally inquired immediately about the College of Medicine. I found that institution likewise polluted with germs, germs of a discriminating nature."[48] Patsy also encountered residential segregation. She "found that the dormitories were not open for people like myself."[49] Patsy could only lodge at the International House, where other Japanese Americans, African Americans, and "an Indian girl" lived.[50] Finally, Patsy discovered that she could not join college social organizations. She "found that affiliation with sororities and fraternities was impossible for anyone with skin any darker than the superciliously arrogant whites."[51] In response, Patsy vowed to fight these injustices. She started a "campaign to open the dormitories"; her efforts met with resistance from parents, but the residence halls were desegregated the next year.[52] Patsy was even elected "president of the unaffiliated students of the University of Nebraska which has a membership of more than 6,000, two-thirds of the student body."[53]

Becoming ill at the end of the term, perhaps a response to what she had experienced, Patsy decided to return to UH to complete her senior year. Her activities there reveal her growing involvement with political issues. In addition to being a finalist for campus queen, performing in theater productions, and being inducted into the women's honorary society, Patsy also participated in debate, oratory, and student government.

In a debate against the University of Colorado, Patsy and her varsity teammate argued for an activist and expansive government. They maintained that "The Federal Government Should Provide for the Economic Security of All American Citizens." Patsy emphasized the need for government intervention in free enterprise. She opened with the cyclical nature of economic recession and depressions and highlighted various social problems that the nation was facing in terms of education, housing, health, social security, and unemployment. Perhaps thinking of the economy in Hawai'i, Patsy pointed out that "an economy such as ours based on profits leads to exploitation and speculation."[54] In response, Patsy advocated turning "to our government" to ensure "equality of opportunity, equality in the pursuit of happiness."[55] Referencing the Great Depression, Patsy asserted that "government alone has the tools which now lie rust covered in a tool chest locked by complacency."[56]

Patsy continued this theme of government responsibility for social welfare in the All-Hawai'i oratorical contest. She won first place by arguing for socialized medicine for "Our Nation's Health."[57] Citing Franklin Delano Roosevelt that "medical care [is] a basic human right," Patsy asserted that "adequate medical care for the sick and injured is a social function, a right and duty, not a private or public charity."[58] Here again, Patsy revealed her faith in the government to provide equitably for the welfare of its people.

Patsy also chaired the Associated Students of the University of Hawai'i (ASUH) statehood committee, which staged a constitutional convention to draft a model state constitution.[59] The convention generated publicity for statehood. Patsy and other organizers wrote to one hundred mainland universities to explain their initiative and ask for support for Hawai'i statehood. Also, island politicians opened the convention, and local media covered the proceedings extensively. The event showcased the leadership and intellect of UH students. As chair of the ASUH statehood committee, Patsy was the primary organizer for the constitutional convention. A radio interviewer asked her whether she was planning to pursue a career in politics after graduation. In response, Patsy affirmed, "I hope I can. I'd like to very much."[60]

Despite her political activities, Patsy was still committed to attending medical school. She applied to over a dozen schools. She had excellent grades and had demonstrated her initiative and leadership skills. However, all the schools turned her down, a devastating experience for Patsy.[61] Female students constituted at most 5 percent of the medical school body in the United States from the 1920s to the 1960s.[62] Applying to start in 1948, Patsy faced not only gender bias but also competition from returning veterans.

Encouraged by a mentor, Patsy decided to apply to law school. There were no other Japanese American women who practiced law

Figure 1.7. The Takemotos celebrate Patsy's graduation from the University of Hawai'i, 1948. *Left to right*: Patsy, Suematsu, Mitama, Eugene. Courtesy of Gwendolyn Mink.

in Hawai'i. It also was past the application deadline, but she decided to take a chance and send in an application anyway. Surprisingly, the University of Chicago law school admitted Patsy. The elite institution still had space for international students, and Patsy was once again mistaken for one.

At the University of Chicago, Patsy lived at I-House, a residence for international students as well as American students interested in global affairs and foreign cultures. A newspaper article described it as a graduate student residence with people from forty-nine countries:

On a stairway an American girl and a British youth are trying to decide whether to listen to the record concert or go folk dancing in the auditorium.

Kay Mya Yee of Burma comes skipping from the mail boxes carrying a letter from home. She mixes East and West in her dress. It consists of a longyi (brocaded shirt) and aingyi (cotton blouse) and a pink cardigan sweater.

A Filipino youth carrying a bag of laundry stops her to borrow a dime. He's going to use the automatic washing machine in the basement.[63]

Patsy thrived in this environment, playing bridge and engaging in fireside conversations with fellow residents.

Patsy also met her husband at I-House. John Mink, a World War II veteran, grew up in a coal mining town in Pennsylvania with a social configuration similar to Hawai'i's plantation society. His grandparents immigrated from Lithuania and Slovakia, laborers recruited by coal companies. When John and Patsy met, he was using the GI Bill to earn a master's degree in geology and geophysics. They became close to one another very quickly and married in 1951, within a few months of meeting. Interracial marriages were not common in 1950s America. A 1958 Gallup poll revealed that "approval" for these unions was 1 percent among white southerners and 5 percent outside of the region.[64] There is little evidence as to whether Patsy's and John's marriage aroused curiosity or antipathy in Chicago. In 1827, Illinois had passed an antimiscegenation law against Black and white marriages, which was repealed in 1874. Fourteen states banned Asian-white unions, but Illinois was not among the list.[65] However, racial prejudice went beyond legislated barriers. Perhaps the community at I-House offered support for their union. Or, perhaps Patsy and John decided to marry regardless of social attitudes. They both possessed scientifically inclined minds and shared political interests. John even had some electoral experience as a volunteer for the 1948 Progressive presidential candidate, Henry Wallace. When Patsy eventually ran for office, John almost always served as her campaign manager. They were true life partners.

Although the University of Chicago Law School was associated with conservative approaches to law, Patsy found the experience an exciting challenge and an opportunity to develop and articulate her political

Figure 1.8. Nineteen-year-old John Mink stands beside his B-17 Flying Fortress near Cambridge, England, during World War II. John was a highly decorated US Army Air Corps navigator. Courtesy of Gwendolyn Mink.

views. As in her speeches in college, she expressed strong political beliefs through law school assignments. She condemned disfranchisement of African Americans in the American South and discrimination against Asian immigrants through exclusion and alien land laws. She also credited labor unions, particularly the International Longshoreman and Warehouse Union (ILWU), for improving the lives of workers. In Hawai'i, the ILWU "organized the sugar, pineapple and the shipping industries. . . . Aside from the increased wages, shorter hours, and better working conditions, the unions fought against the paternalistic practices of the employers."[66] She acknowledged that those who were unfamiliar with plantation society might not understand "what is objectionable about living in a company house, burning company fuel, drinking company water, etc., since in effect these are all by way of compensation."[67] Familiar with plantation conditions, Patsy explained that "viewed from the aspect of freedom it is not difficult to visualize a worker under this system bound to the plantation through his dependency upon the perquisites and that even after a lifetime of work" such a worker would "be without property and very small savings. Gift[s] of perquisites allowed the companies to offer very low wages, which in most cases were only nominal figures."[68] To address these inequalities, Patsy argued, trade unionism provided workers the possibility of independence and dignity.

Patsy also expressed strong views regarding the role of education in resolving global conflict. She argued in an essay that "there must be cooperation and subordination to a sovereign international law. . . . Therefore, before peace and order can prevail, nations must be educated in the ways of peace and constructive aggression. . . . Peace can become a reality only by the extensive and thorough re-education of the peoples of the world."[69] Patsy's writings in her early twenties reveal her political beliefs and sense of idealism. These perspectives regarding race, labor, international conflicts, and education laid the foundation for her future political career.

When Patsy graduated from the University of Chicago Law School in 1951, she was one of two women and one of two Asian Americans in her class. Among her schoolmates were future politicians, legal advocates, and jurists with whom she would collaborate in the coming years. They included Abner Mikva, a Democrat who served in the US House

Figure 1.9. Patsy poses for a class photo on graduation day at the University of Chicago Law School, 1951. Source: Hanna Holbrook Gray Special Collections Research Center, University of Chicago Library/Stephen Lewellyn photographer.

of Representatives with Patsy before joining the bench of the US Court of Appeals, and Ramsey Clark, who served as US attorney general under Lyndon Johnson and who advanced civil rights and civil liberties. Mink and Mikva were on friendly terms in law school and became political allies in Congress. Clark eventually represented Mink in a legal challenge to executive-branch secrecy regarding nuclear testing.

Even with a JD from a prestigious university, Patsy found it impossible to work as a lawyer. Chicago law firms would not hire her, a Japanese American married woman. To make ends meet, she worked a variety of odd jobs, including as a clerk and model in a department store and a library worker at the University of Chicago. When newborn Wendy developed a health condition in reaction to the heat and humidity of Chicago, the Minks decided to relocate to Hawai'i.

Suematsu and Mitama were initially reluctant to accept Patsy's decision to marry a haole. Interracial marriages, particularly among Japanese Americans in Hawai'i, were not common in the 1950s. However, they welcomed their granddaughter, were happy to have their daughter near, and eventually developed a strong affection for John. John shared some commonalities with Suematsu. They both loved baseball and listened to

Figure 1.10. Baby Wendy rides her rocking horse under mother Patsy's supervision, 1953. Courtesy of Gwendolyn Mink.

games together on the radio. In addition, both had grown up without a father. John spent six years of his childhood in an orphanage. Widowed on the eve of the Great Depression, John's mother placed four of her six children there as a temporary measure, while she struggled to find steady work. The two men, who both grew up without parental supervision, invented how to be husbands and fathers who could support their strong wives and daughters.

"PINK MINK"

It was well past my bedtime, but I was napping, not sleeping. I knew that at some point late in the evening the phone would jangle, letting us know that a nuclear bomb would soon be detonated by the United States above Johnston Island in the Pacific. When the call came—around 10:00 p.m. on August 11, 1958—my parents carried me to the car and plunked me in the back seat next to a pillow, blanket, and mosquito repellent. It was the kind of muggy summer night only biting insects enjoy, but still they worried I might catch a chill at the edge of the cane field where we would park to await the nuclear blast.

We had recently moved to our new tract home in Waipahu, an old sugar plantation town a dozen miles west of Honolulu. Nestled between identical homes in a low- to middle-income residential development, our house became my parents' anchor for nearly three decades. First-time homeowners, my parents pampered every square foot of both house and garden. Outside, my mother coddled banana, mango, and papaya trees, while my father sculpted crotons and other hedge plants for privacy. Inside, my mother kept things neat while my father kept things clean. Both house and yard were quite small, but they were ours, and my parents took great pleasure in that.

Once we got the call about the impending nuclear blast, we drove from our Waipahu home up Kunia Road toward Wahiawā. After about fifteen minutes on the road, we spotted a handful of cars parked on a rise facing south and west toward Barber's Point and Waiʻanae. We pulled over and joined the group. My parents wanted me to stay in the car, so they took shifts visiting with the others and helping me feel safe as we awaited the explosion.

This was the second atmospheric nuclear test at Johnston Island in less than two weeks. The first had been conducted in extreme secrecy by the US government—until the atomic blast revealed itself in a giant red and yellow fireball that overwhelmed the Honolulu horizon shortly after midnight on August 1.[1] Only night owls and early birds saw that blast, as the government gave no notice to the public; and only the governor and military brass knew that Hawaiʻi was not under attack when concentric circles of fire encapsulating a cloud of radioactive devastation came into view.[2]

The outcry against the secrecy of the August 1 test was widespread. Some argued that given the trauma of the Pearl Harbor attack only seventeen years before, it was cruel of the US government to keep Hawai'i residents in the dark. Others, Mom included, argued that given the potential dangers and certain terror of the nuclear blast, people had the right to know when the blast would occur.[3] Johnston Island was just seven hundred nautical miles southwest of Honolulu. The danger zone for the nuclear test radiated 520 miles from Johnston Island in all directions, putting Hawai'i barely 180 miles beyond direct danger and within viewing range of an atmospheric explosion.

The Department of Defense decided that "because of public interest in Hawaii," the second blast would come with forewarning.[4] On August 11, the Navy announced that a nuclear test would be conducted late that night or in the predawn hours of August 12. As the clock struck 10:00 p.m., the local antinuclear phone tree warned people that the blast could come at any time. The call was our cue to head to higher elevation, where an unobstructed view beyond the sugar cane and pineapple fields would allow us to witness a moment in the nuclear arms race.

When the warhead detonated, the sky first flashed a brilliant white-blue. Then a smoky haze formed a kind of puffy cloud, surrounded by a purple-blue-green-red rainbow-like silhouette that slowly faded over the course of five minutes. What people saw depended on where they were when they viewed the blast. In downtown Honolulu, people saw a brilliant flash, which "dimmed to a rose glow and faded away" in about a second. Further to the east on Maui, from high on Haleakalā, the view was described as a "dark brownish red mushroom" that rose in the sky, then turned to white with a dark red rainbow as the spectacle died away. By all accounts, the August 11 blast was less visually coherent and astounding than what was seen on August 1.[5] But no one who watched the sky that night on Kunia Road would ever doubt the power and peril of nuclear bombs.

The Johnston Island tests culminated four months of Hawai'i-based antinuclear protest and controversy. The protests began in early April 1958, when four pacifists sailed a small ketch named the Golden Rule from California toward the Marshall Islands in the central Pacific Ocean. They intended to moor at Eniwetok Atoll, site of twenty-two nuclear tests by the United States between April and September 1958.[6] A Quaker-inspired protest, the Golden Rule was part of a small but vocal campaign to ban nuclear testing as well as the use of nuclear weapons in war. Halfway across the Pacific, the *Golden Rule* took port in Honolulu to refuel before crossing to Eniwetok. Anticipating the protest, the Atomic Energy Commission (AEC) issued a rule barring US citizens from entering the testing area. A federal judge in Honolulu enforced the AEC rule with an injunction specifically barring the pacifist crew from the environs of Eniwetok and Bikini Atolls and prohibited the *Golden Rule* from leaving its mooring in Honolulu without permission from the court. In an act of civil disobedience, the crew set sail for Eniwetok anyway, at which point they were arrested and thrown in jail.[7]

When she learned of the planned *Golden Rule* protest in March 1958, Mom allied with the local Quaker community to prepare political, legal, and material support for the crew.[8] On the eve of the ketch's arrival in Honolulu from California, she called upon the Hawai'i public to extend a rousing welcome.[9] When the crew was arrested on May 2, Mom visited them in jail (with me in tow), wrote to the judge for clarification of prison rules on the crew's behalf, and lent her voice to a public defense of the *Golden Rule*'s choices and actions. When they finally won release from jail, the crew came over to our house for an afternoon of chili, rice, and "talk story," as Hawai'i locals refer to relaxed conversational exchanges.

Mom's unequivocal solidarity with the *Golden Rule* crew received media attention—in the Hawai'i press, of course, but also on the national news-wire. Some of the attention accrued from her role as one of a handful of political leaders who stood up for the crew's conscientious action. Some was generated by the editors of the *Honolulu Star-Bulletin*, whose editorial "Still No Protest to Moscow?" questioned the allegiance of anyone who supported the *Golden Rule*.[10] For weeks, letters to the editor debated the "Americanism" of antinuclear protest, with many letters singling out Mom, both for condemnation and for praise.[11] One of the enduring effects of the red-baiting attack on Mom during the *Golden Rule* controversy was the epithet "Pink Mink," which was bandied about morning drive-time talk radio for years afterward.

The idea that Mom might be a communist sympathizer was not new to public discourse in 1958. That idea had been implanted one year earlier by talk radio and newspaper opinion pages. In the winter of 1957, a resolution opposing British nuclear tests at Christmas Island was Mom's first legislative venture as a newly elected member of the Territorial House of Representatives.[12] An editorial in the *Honolulu Star Bulletin* called local opposition to the British nuclear tests a Soviet ploy,[13] while Joe Rose, a precursor to Rush Limbaugh, hurled vicious red-baiting commentary on Hawai'i talk radio. Although Mom's resolution was cosponsored by all Democrats in the Territorial House and passed that body with a unanimous vote, reactionary forces singled Mom out for abuse. Some went on to fuse the antinuclear issue with the statehood question, linking her support of both causes to a communist plot.[14]

Seasoned by the 1957 controversy and by a year in the public spotlight as a legislator, Mom stood her ground about nuclear testing when the *Golden Rule* pressed the issue in 1958, even though it meant aiding civil disobedience. Although Mom never embraced true pacifism as her philosophy, she believed that our actions always should skew toward peace and that war should never be a strategy, only a last resort.

As important as peace was to her, the effects of weapons and warfare on innocents was an even higher priority. Even before becoming a legislator, Mom kept abreast of research news about the impact of nuclear weapons on human populations. Ever the science major, she kept notes and news clips on rising strontium 90 levels, variations in radioactive fallout affecting crops and dairy products, the long-term effects of radioactive material on human health, and efforts by scientific groups to ban all nuclear testing.[15] Her study of the many problems created by the use of nuclear weapons led her to publicly question the morality of the US bombing of Hiroshima and Nagasaki during World War II.[16] Her naysayers had a field day with that.[17]

Coming on the heels of her 1957 legislative resolution against British H-bomb tests in the Pacific, the *Golden Rule* protest crystallized Mom's politics, honed her principles, and summoned her resilience. Support for the *Golden Rule* protest required her to challenge the US government, as nuclear weapons testing by the United States was what the *Golden Rule* sought to stop. It required her to embrace civil disobedience as a method of political expression, for it was the crew's defiance of the law—injunctions— that landed them in jail. It also inspired her to resolute advocacy for causes she believed in, regardless of adversity and defeats along the way.

She explained to a supporter whose letter to the editor defended her,

My public career has only just been christened and yet there are those who work to see its abrupt end. . . . All I ever wanted to do is to help work for a better community and to fight for the preservation of life, liberty and happiness for ourselves and for our children. So long as these are my goals, obviously status quo is not enough. This is the key to why my foes are determined to ruin me and others like me. I pray for the courage I shall need as these attacks increase.[18]

Clearly, support for the *Golden Rule* required Mom to run into the headwind of Cold War politics in 1950s America; if it didn't knock her down, it would make her fierce and fearless.

I learned a lot during those months between the *Golden Rule* protest and the Johnston Island atmospheric explosions. The gravity of the nuclear arms race and the visibility of my mother's work against it forced my parents to educate me about Hiroshima and Nagasaki, about civil disobedience, about red baiting, and about solidarity. They took special care to discuss with me why the *Golden Rule* crew was detained in the city jail, how it was that my parents had friends who might be considered criminals, and why the crew chose jail rather than sign a court-ordered pledge to never again break the law. They engaged me repeatedly and at length about hate trafficking and name calling and the importance of standing up to both. They tried to assure me that our work to prevent nuclear war would keep us safe from nuclear devastation.

A few weeks after witnessing the blast on August 11, I entered first grade. I was both blessed and burdened by being the only six-year-old I knew who had visited jail to support pacifist conscientious objectors, whose mother had been publicly condemned as un-American, and who had seen an actual atomic bomb light up the sky.

My mother, too, was both burdened and blessed by her work against nuclear testing. Henceforth, she would have to suffer relentless hair-trigger red baiting whenever she expressed a politically unpopular opinion. But henceforth, she also would find strength in the rightness of the principles that guided her and in the alliances of conscience that powered the politics of peace. Four years after Johnston Island, Mom spoke at a Mother's Day Peace Rally in Honolulu. Her concluding words underscored the importance of the rally on that day in May 1962, when progress toward a nuclear test ban treaty between the United States and the Soviet Union seemed more urgent than ever—but also more impossible. But they could just as well have described what she learned from the *Golden Rule*: "Those of us who are asked to explain what good will come from a peace rally such as this realize that we will not solve the problems of nations today. But what we feel we can accomplish is that our community will have cause to ponder the consequences of nuclear preparation even for just a day by reading about your testimony for peace. That from this, others will pick up from here and work as hard for peace as there are those who work at the preparations for war."[19]

2

A Democratic Revolution

After her return to Hawaiʻi, Patsy Mink became a committed Democratic Party member. As an organizer and campaigner, she helped launch Hawaiʻi's "Democratic Revolution." In 1954, the Democratic Party in Hawaiʻi mobilized nonwhite voters and union members to become the elected majority of both the House and the Senate for the first time in the territory. Patsy stumped for candidates like John (Jack) Burns, the titular head of the Hawaiʻi Democratic Party. She also started a branch of the Young Democrats (YD) and became an elected vice president of the organization nationally. Through the YD, Patsy created a semi-independent political base and achieved political recognition beyond Hawaiʻi for the first time. She made important political connections and traveled to Europe as a political representative of the United States. Patsy also became the first Japanese American woman elected to office, initially in the Territorial House of Representatives and then in the Territorial Senate. She eventually served in the state Senate, a few years after Hawaiʻi was admitted as the fiftieth state in 1959.

As Patsy designed legislation and debated ideas, she faced criticism of her politics and her gender from the extreme right and from Hawaiʻi Democrats. She embraced how her identity as a woman shaped her politics. Yet, she also insisted on her right and ability to engage in politics regardless of gender. During this early phase of her political career, Patsy focused her energies on preventing nuclear testing, protecting labor rights, advocating for gender equity through the equal-pay-for-equal-work policy, insuring transparency in the political process, and improving public education. She achieved hard-fought victories but also suffered difficult defeats. Throughout these twelve years, Patsy remained loyal to the Democratic Party, in spite of the local party leadership's tendency to marginalize and undermine her.

Preparing for the Revolution

Patsy returned to Hawai'i in hopes of launching her legal career. Instead, she met with similar obstacles as in Chicago. When Patsy applied to take the bar exam to practice law, she was informed that she had lost her Hawai'i residency and hence her eligibility to take the test. Patsy had married someone from another state. Under the legal custom of coverture, a woman's political identity is covered by her husband's. Although the Nineteenth Amendment mandated that the right to vote cannot be prohibited on the basis of sex, a variety of other laws and practices still posited women's legal dependence on male heads of households. As a result of her marriage, Patsy's residency presumably changed to that of her mainland-bred husband.

Patsy disagreed with and challenged the principle of coverture. In fact, she initially adopted her maiden name, Takemoto, as opposed to her married name, Mink, for professional purposes.[1] Doing so asserted her independent identity and also highlighted her Japanese ancestry, an asset in Hawai'i. In what she described as her first win over sexism, Patsy challenged her exclusion from the bar. After securing the right to practice law, she wrote to the territorial attorney general, "You might recall that at the time of my interview with you, you questioned my status as a resident of the Territory of Hawai'i."[2] After a close review of the law, Patsy discovered that since she did not live in John's home state, Pennsylvania, she had not lost her residency. Patsy took and passed the bar exam in 1953, becoming the first Japanese American woman to practice law in Hawai'i.[3]

Being licensed, however, did not guarantee a job. Along with other Americans of Japanese ancestry (AJAs), Patsy could not get a position at a prestigious law office on O'ahu. These firms with strong financial ties to the Big Five tended to hire haole lawyers. Lesser firms did hire AJA men, but none would hire Patsy, because she was a woman and a mother. In 1956, three years after she passed the bar, a local paper published an article about female lawyers. By then, only thirteen women practiced law compared to "an estimated 325 male attorneys in general practice on the Island."[4] Being a distinct minority in the profession, female lawyers clustered in government service work. One of these lawyers claimed that "women like quiet work" and that she "enjoy[s] government work more than competitive practice because I have home responsibilities."[5] In other words, she perceived government work as more compatible with her caretaker role and her less aggressive feminine personality. Another female lawyer condemned those who pursued government work rather than "get[ting] out and scratch[ing] more."[6] She wanted women to compete more with men and explained gender clustering as a lack of effort on the part of women. Neither of these perspectives acknowledges systemic discrimination that channeled women into certain forms of legal labor by denying them employment and mentoring opportunities as well as condoning a hostile work environment for women.

In 1956, Patsy Mink was among five female lawyers not employed in government service. She lectured on business law at UH and opened her own practice. She shared office space with her father's surveyor business and initially gained some clients through his work. A Jill of all legal trades, she accepted cases related to family law, personal injury, criminal defense, immigration, and so on. Her practice never proving particularly lucrative, Patsy accepted barter for legal services early on. Wendy recalled that her mother's first client offered a fish for payment.

As Patsy established her legal practice and settled her family on O'ahu, she became involved with politics. The Democratic Party in Hawai'i formed in 1900 but had little political sway or power. The Big Five Republicans dominated the islands. After World War II, though, John A. Burns (1909–1975), who eventually became governor of Hawai'i, began building the Democratic Party. Born into an Irish Catholic and Democratic family in Montana, Burns moved to Hawai'i in 1913, when he was still a young child. He grew up in Kalihi, a working-class, multiethnic, multiracial community. His future wife, Beatrice, recalled that John "could relate to people of any ethnic background," because he grew up in that neighborhood.[7] A police officer, John became head of the Honolulu Police Department's (HPD) Espionage Bureau before the United States entered World War II. As the liaison between military intelligence, the FBI, and the HPD, Burns assembled a diverse team of officers (one Hawaiian, one Japanese, one haole, and another mixed-race) to investigate potential acts of disloyalty and sabotage.[8] Shortly before the Pearl Harbor attack, he encouraged a network of Japanese Americans to report to the HPD. After the war began, these AJA contacts apprised him of violations of martial law. Burns used his team to encourage "Americanism" among Japanese Americans, to promote "a definite break . . . from those things and institutions which are or represent Japan itself" and to "stop the spread of rumors."[9] He also urged both the community and the authorities to embrace military participation of Japanese American men. According to some, Burns's wartime efforts proved AJA loyalty, thereby preventing mass relocation and incarceration. He did so, though, through a culture of surveillance.

After World War II, Burns utilized his working-class background and wartime connections to build the Democratic Party. He reached out to plantation workers and organized labor, most notably the International Longshoreman and Warehouse Union (ILWU). He also created a multi-racial political party, recruiting nonhaoles, including Native Hawaiians and Asian Americans. He developed close ties to male AJAs, especially veterans. The 442nd veterans even gave Burns an honorary membership. They possessed strong networks and organizations that could be politically mobilized. Also, after 1952, the Issei, or immigrant generation, was no longer barred from naturalized citizenship. They could vote.

Daniel Inouye (1924–2012), who became the nation's first Japanese American congressman, exemplified this generation of Democrats. Son of an immigrant father who worked as a jewelry store clerk in Honolulu and a Nisei mother who was a homemaker, Inouye was the eldest of four children. The family was poor, all six living "in a one-bedroom cottage . . . just across the way from the fashionable Pacific Club, which barred all" Asians.[10] During World War II, Inouye became an officer in the highly decorated 442nd regiment, which tolled vast losses in battles. During an assault he led, Inouye was shot, his arm shattered by a grenade. It took two years for him to recover.

Fighting in World War II gave Inouye and other AJAs access to educational opportunities and raised their expectations regarding civil rights. Inouye utilized the GI Bill to complete his college education at UH and earn his law degree from George Washington University. In his opinion, "Without the G.I. Bill most of the so-called leaders of Hawai'i today would be clerks."[11] Despite these achievements, Inouye and others were acutely aware of persistent racial barriers. For example, AJA veterans could not join the American Legion "because Orientals were not always accepted."[12] When Inouye returned to Hawai'i, he and other AJAs transformed and revitalized the Democratic Party. According to Inouye, at that time "only drunks and bums joined the Democratic Party."[13] However, the membership quickly and dramatically changed.

Patsy Mink became involved with the Democratic Party in 1953. Invited by a fellow UH alum to attend a Democratic discussion group, she soon became an active participant and leader. One day after her twenty-sixth birthday in December 1953, Patsy issued a letter asking if other Democrats might want to form "a group to act as a sounding board for ideas and who presently either have no outlet for the expressions of their opinions, or do not wish to make committals or become associated with one of the groups already having an influence upon policies."[14] Patsy and others envisioned the group, eventually called the Everyman Committee (EC), as a political forum for those interested in Democratic politics but wanting to avoid party factionalism. By holding discussions and generating ideas, the group could serve as a sounding board for the Democratic Party. Patsy and others envisioned their group as a means towards democratization: "It is our purpose in organizing to promote representative government within our Party by giving more persons a voice in the management. . . . By achieving this, we will acquire a more responsible leadership, and develop a stronger internal structure for the Party."[15]

Shortly after this call, a group of ten Democrats met. Patsy was the only woman in the group. They developed several recommendations for how the party should function and promote its political views. They also decided to continue meeting in order to "sit down together and swap opinions—frankly and openly, in a permissive atmosphere."[16] In addition, the group recognized that it "could exert a stronger influence upon party activities than could the same people acting as individuals."[17] Inouye attended the first meeting but not the subsequent gatherings. As an elected member of the Territorial Central Committee of the Democratic Party, he was already in a leadership position. Mink and others continued, though. EC members criticized the existing party laws as too focused on the "punitive"; instead, they recommended the redrafting of "new rules . . . with a constructive purpose . . . toward aiding in the development of an effective Democratic organization."[18] Patsy consulted with friends in other states to redraft the party rules for Hawai'i. The EC presented their proposals to the Hawai'i Democratic Party, which adopted the recommended general laws in 1954.

The EC eventually renamed itself the Young Democrats (YD) of O'ahu in the summer of 1954. They became affiliated with the national YD three years later after other branches also formed on outlying islands. Patsy served as president of the O'ahu YD for two years and then as head of the Territorial YD in 1957. The nationwide organization, intended for younger Democrats (typically forty and under), provided opportunities for dialogue, leadership, and recruitment.

This independent Democratic base in Hawai'i aroused both admiration and suspicion from the regular Democratic Party. During the September 1954 meeting of the Democratic Party's Territorial Central Committee that Burns chaired, "An application from the O'ahu Young Democrats was read and a very lively discussion was brought up indicating the very healthy condition of the Democratic Party of Hawaii. It was agreed that there was a possibility that such an organization might hurt the County Committee set up in the various counties. It was also pointed out by members of the Oahu and Maui Central Committees that the young Democrats have been contributing a considerable amount of work and candidates in the present campaign and in the special election."[19] The O'ahu YD were praised for their contributions, as their existence exemplified "the very healthy condition" of the party. Yet, they were regarded as a potential disruption, a competitor for resources that might "hurt" the existing party structure. This tension between applauding grassroots activism and feeling fearful of its outcomes would persist and grow in the Democratic Party.

In 1954, energized by its new constituency, the Hawai'i Democratic Party decided to mount a full slate of candidates. Democrats had run in previous elections, but it was unprecedented to have a full slate on the ballot. Of the twenty-six candidates who ran in 1954, twelve were AJAs, and five were haole. The rest were Hawaiian, Korean, Chinese, Filipino, Portuguese, and multiracial. All were men, except for Anna Furtado Kahanamoku. She was of Portuguese, Hawaiian, and Chinese descent and a teacher by training. She also was the sister-in-law of Duke Kahanamoku, a five-time Olympic medalist who popularized surfing.

Native Hawaiians tended to hold the Democratic Party at arm's length. Soon after annexation, Native Hawaiians formed the Hawaiian Independent Party, a party that advocated home rule. The "party briefly captured both the houses of the territorial legislature and sent a delegate to Washington, D.C."[20] Until the mid-1920s, Native Hawaiians "comprised a majority of those elected to the territorial legislature" and "more than one-half of the registered voters."[21] Republican Party efforts to court Native Hawaiians led many Indigenous leaders to align with the elite, haole establishment. This political alliance formed despite the fact that Native Hawaiian socioeconomic status declined overall as haole economic and political interests ascended. Some Native Hawaiians, like Anna Kahanamoku and her sister, Dolores Furtado Martin, became active Democrats.

During the 1954 elections, eleven Democrats were elected, including Daniel Inouye, George Ariyoshi (the eventual first AJA governor), Anna Kahanamoku, and Elmer Cravalho (then the Democratic Party Maui County chairman). They joined eleven other Democrats already in the House and the Senate. They dominated both branches of the Territorial legislature, since only eight Republicans remained. It was this 1954 election that marked the Democratic Revolution in Hawai'i.

In 1954, Patsy was an active campaigner for the Democratic Party. In fact, she cochaired Burns's campaign for delegate to Congress. She had previously played a key role when Delbert E. Metzger, a judge and a Democrat, had run for the delegate position in a special election earlier in 1954. Republican Joseph R. Farrington died while serving as Hawai'i's delegate. Metzger ran and lost against Betty Farrington, the widow of Joseph. For the regular election, Burns entered the race, but again Farrington won. Patsy worked tirelessly for his campaign, though, coordinating the efforts of organizers, keeping track of fundraising and expenditures, and speaking for and writing about Burns. During this phase of her political career, Mink and Burns were close political colleagues, and she was regarded as a party asset.

"A Full-Blooded Politician"

Within one election cycle, Patsy moved from being a behind-the-scenes political organizer to being an elected official and political leader. In the 1955 legislative sessions, Patsy served as one of six attorneys for the Territorial House of Representatives. This appointment was likely an award for her loyal service to the party. She witnessed firsthand the Democrats' political efforts and was rather disappointed and disillusioned by what she observed. Patsy described her experiences in a letter to a friend:

> It has been [a] nerve-wracking, demoralizing, disheartening experience by and large. The results have fallen short of the numerous campaign promises—the bickering among legislators has been very apparent, and legislation has greatly suffered as a result—the old timers have not been willing to accede to the wishes of the freshmen legislators—the deals have continued. . . . The Party appears less unified now than it did before the convention last May. I guess you can live long in this game with naïve idealism, but you soon learn to tolerate compromises, and graciously accept small victories on behalf of the principles of the Democratic Party.[22]

Some of these dynamics resulted from the inexperience of the rookie legislators. Tom Gill, the Democratic Party Oʻahu County chairman in 1954 and an eventual leader within the party who challenged Burns's influence, was serving as an attorney for the Territorial Senate in 1955. He recalled that "most of the Democrats—not most but a large percentage of them—didn't know what they were doing. . . . Some of the bills were poorly drafted, and if they had been enacted we probably would have had trouble."[23] Ironically, Gill credits the Republican governor appointed by President Eisenhower, Samuel King, for "saving" the Democrats: "I think he vetoed seventy-two bills or some such thing."[24] Even taking into account this inexperience, the tensions between different generations of politicians and the common practice of political compromise troubled Patsy. Rather than scaring her away, though, her involvement motivated her to run for office.

In 1956, Patsy became a candidate for the Territorial House of Representatives from the Fifth District in Hawaiʻi. The district was large, stretching from Nuuanu Avenue (on the edge of downtown Honolulu) west along the leeward coast to Waiʻanae and across the mountains to Waialua on the North Shore. It was primarily agricultural, dominated by sugar and pineapple plantations. In the 1956 elections, just under forty-nine thousand people registered to vote and eventually just under forty-four thousand actually voted in the general election.[25] Patsy ran for one of the five seats for the district.

Recognizing that she was a relative unknown, Patsy designed a campaign to introduce herself. She chose the slogan "Think, Vote Mink" to encourage voters to critically consider what they wanted for their government and how her political vision and goals could align with theirs. One of her foldout brochures featured one page on her political beliefs and another on her political platform. Patsy's statements articulated her commitment to an activist government that ensured the welfare of its people. She explained, "I BELIEVE that the rights of the individual are the highest trust and responsibility of government and that government exists for the people; to provide for the well-being of all; to raise the level of life above that of mere existence; to assure and achieve the fullest possible employment; and to increase the opportunities for a better life for ourselves and for our children."[26]

Patsy's political platform applied her stated philosophy to policy questions affecting economics, government, and social welfare. Her economic goals included repealing a regressive 2 percent wage tax, supporting the fishing industry, expanding unemployment compensation to include agricultural laborers and government employees, and working towards full employment, particularly for young first-time workers. Notably, Mink highlighted the need to "make available more public lands for home sites, for public housing, for agricultural enterprises, and for parks and recreational facilities."[27] This last agenda item was the top priority of the Democratic Party. The Big Five controlled the islands' economy through land taken from Native Hawaiians. Creating economic opportunities for the have-nots involved a redistribution of land from the plantation elite.

To enact this agenda, the central government needed to play a significant role in the economy and reorient towards local concerns on behalf of marginalized peoples. At the same time, Patsy called for the territorial authority to "return greater control of the affairs of county government to the respective counties."[28] The demand for economic justice through democratization and local control resonated with the Democratic Party's critique of Hawai'i's territorial status.

Mink concluded her policy platform with a focus on children. She vowed "to fight for better laws so that our children can be better housed, better clothed, better fed, better educated, and so that they may look forward to a better life in the years to come."[29] Her call to prioritize the lives of children is striking. The other elements of her platform were gender neutral, but this particular item evoked maternalist politics. Maternalism refers to the justification of women's political contributions based on their status as mothers. Bringing attention to the needs of children highlighted Patsy's own status as a mother.

Patsy presented a political persona that harnessed her identities as assets rather than as obstacles. Her brochure shared four aspects of her life that showcased her gender and Japanese ancestry. First, she was a "local girl," a third-generation AJA with family ties in Hawai'i. Patsy emphasized her role as a daughter and utilized her extensive kinship network in her campaigns. Second, Patsy highlighted her legal profession; here, too, she stressed her unique achievements as the "first and only woman of Japanese ancestry to be admitted to practice before the courts of the Territory."[30] Third, Patsy highlighted her Democratic credentials. The political ascendency of AJA politicians in the Democratic Party was clear to her audience, as was how few women ran for political office. Finally, Patsy introduced herself as a "housewife and mother."[31]

Male politicians frequently highlighted their family status in political campaigns; however, doing so resonates differently for men compared to women. In the context of the early Cold War, in which nuclear families and traditional gender roles were culturally emphasized, Patsy very easily could have been dismissed. Instead, she embraced her roles as mother and wife as valuable for her political career. A 1956 campaign speech explained how gender added rather than detracted from Patsy's qualifications as a candidate. She shared, "As a woman, as a housewife, and as a mother I know and understand your problems and wishes, your hopes and dreams for a better and happier life, and therefore, if you will give me the opportunity I shall put all my education, my experience, and ability to try to make Hawai'i a better place for our children."[32]

Even though Patsy emphasized her gender identity in campaigning, she did not yet engage in organizing female Democrats. Others in Hawai'i were interested, however. One person wrote to Patsy, as head of the YD, for advice about forming a "League of Democratic Women."[33] Patsy supported the idea and offered encouragement but also noted the difficulty of creating such a group: "Women's organizations are sorely needed in the Democratic Party, but strangely, they have not been able to thrive. Personal ambitions, petty jealousies and deep cleavages within the ranks make the formation of fully representative organizations nigh impossible. At least this has been my observation in my limited experience in politics. My belief is that the goal is there to be conquered, however."[34] Patsy's comments about jealousies and cleavages could easily describe the party more broadly, but her assessment of Democratic women indicates that they, too, were prone to factionalism.

Patsy utilized newspapers, radio, and television for her campaign. She reached out via English- and Japanese-language media. She and her supporters also canvassed door to door and worked the polling stations.[35] Patsy was in her element at large outdoor rallies. These events were social occasions; all members of the family, including children, attended. Patsy was a compelling public speaker, having extensive experience through debate and oratory. In addition, the novelty of being the first AJA woman running for office worked in Patsy's favor. As her husband observed, "The curious are soon converted to her camp by her remarkable speaking ability. Few other candidates can approach her oratory."[36]

Patsy succeeded in her first electoral attempt, and the Democrats followed up the 1954 revolution with another series of victories in 1956. There were six open seats for the Fifth District in the House of Representatives, and Patsy placed a surprising second in the Democratic primary. She was just one vote behind incumbent George Ariyoshi. In the general election, Burns finally succeeded in his effort to become Hawai'i's delegate, and Patsy was elected to the Territorial House of Representatives. In a letter to a friend, Mink described her elation: "I am now a full-blooded politician of the first order."[37]

Cold War, Civil Rights

Patsy thrived in politics. She focused on a range of territorial matters that held national and global significance. Nuclear testing, statehood, and racial equality were hot-button issues in the midst of the "Cold War Civil Rights" movement and the era of decolonization.[38] Hawai'i, due to its territorial status, location in the Pacific, and sizable nonwhite population, played a central role in the United States' endeavor to win the "hearts and minds" of Third World people.

Of all of Patsy's initiatives, her efforts to prevent nuclear testing in the Pacific captured the public's attention and aroused fierce criticism.

Figure 2.1. John removes his shoes before entering the Mink's Waipahu home as Patsy and pup Tawny greet him. Source: Getty Images, The LIFE Picture Collection/Ralph Crane photographer.

On February 20, 1957, the first day that the Territorial House met, Patsy introduced a resolution to protest British nuclear tests on the Christmas Islands. The House passed it the next day, but the Territorial Senate held hearings before taking action. Mink wrote to Burns, Hawai'i's delegate in Washington, DC, to request that he represent the House resolution to the appropriate federal and international offices. Patsy's antinuclear resolution actually preceded national congressional investigations, which did not take place until May and June of that year.

Both the United States and its NATO allies conducted aboveground nuclear tests in the Pacific Proving Grounds, a region created in 1947. To demark this testing site, the United States requested and received permission from the United Nations to create a Trust Territory of the Pacific Islands (TTPI). Equivalent to the size of the continental United States, the TTPI encompassed one hundred Micronesian islands. Residents were at times forcibly evacuated in order to facilitate nuclear testing or else exposed to radioactive fallout without adequate protection or informed consent. Scholars Setsu Shigematsu and Keith Camacho characterize the relationship between the United States and the Pacific as a form of "nuclear colonialism."[39]

Patsy opposed British and US testing in the Pacific. She pointed out the potential impact for all of the people and lands in the Pacific. In her letter to Burns, Mink explained,

> I have done a good bit of research on this problem of the harmful effects of radiation, from a vast source of available bibliography on the subject. Granted being some 900 miles from the bomb site we will probably not experience local and immediately fatal doses of radioactivity. But with the same violence of the Southernly, Southwesterly, and Westerly winds, traveling 110 miles per hour, even at the 60,000 feet heights, which we experienced just this past weekend, we are not free of the possibility that the smaller winddriven particles will . . . be discharged over Hawaii.[40]

In addition to this Hawai'i-centered argument against nuclear testing, Patsy also warned of the impact on the Marshallese. She expressed skepticism towards the assurances by Washington and the "British government, that no harm will come to the populated islands of the Pacific. These same assurances were given to the poor people of the Marshall Islands, 300 of whom were exposed to large amounts of radioactive fallout in the 1954 tests."[41] The fallout, Patsy stressed, had long-term genetic consequences, so "it is equally bad and harmful to our future generations."[42] In Patsy's critiques of nuclear testing, she emphasized the ecological connectedness between the Marshall and the Hawaiian Islands. The former was under trusteeship, and the latter was a territory with the possibility of statehood. Even so, Patsy did not highlight the exceptional status of Hawai'i. Instead, she underscored the common nuclear dangers that threatened to cross oceanic distances and political borders.

Although the Senate eventually passed a similar resolution as the House, Patsy received the brunt of public criticism for initiating these protests. Joe Rose, a conservative radio commentator, began calling her "Patsy Pink" and "Pink Mink." He and anonymous letter writers to the local papers alleged that she was a Communist and condemned her as anti-American. One writer charged that Patsy supported the attack on Pearl Harbor, since she condemned the use of atomic bombs on Japan. Defending her antinuclear politics took a toll emotionally. In one letter to the *Honolulu Advertiser*, Patsy stated, "I introduced the resolution at no one's suggestion but from the dictates of my own conscience and from my own deep concern for the future welfare of the people of this Territory."[43] In another letter to an individual, Patsy expressed her feelings: "I fully realize that as an elected politician, I must accept the good with the bad. But I am discouraged at these scurrilous attacks upon my character and integrity. . . . I [was] warned that politics was dirty, but I never thought it would be like this. These people would stoop to anything to crush, annihilate and defeat. . . . And to think that I ever imagined that McCarthyism was dead!"[44] As Patsy discovered, the Cold War was very much alive, both globally and in Hawai'i.

Despite her efforts and increased national and global attention to the dangers of nuclear testing, the practice continued. In 1958 alone, thirty-five weapons were tested aboveground or underwater in the Marshall Islands as part of Operation Hardtack I. To protest these tests, a sailing ship operated by members of the American Friends Services Committee, the *Golden Rule*, attempted to sail into a nuclear testing zone. The four crew members stopped in Hawai'i en route from California and were imprisoned for attempting civil disobedience. Patsy publicly supported the protesters, visiting them regularly in jail and assisting their defense.

Patsy's strong political stances drew criticism from within the Democratic Party as well. Inouye, the majority leader of the Democrats in the Territorial House, complained to Burns about Mink: "Patsy Mink has been a personal problem of mine. She has great potentialities, great talents and I am certain great dedication as a legislator. But, because of her aggressiveness, because of her desire to carry out certain 'principles,' she has antagonized many of her colleagues. . . . I have tried to impress upon her that especially in legislative life we can carry out our principles and ideals by methods not requiring a head strong, aggressive, forward move."[45] Inouye's charge that Mink was too aggressive and too principled reflected her inclination to advocate for her political beliefs regardless of popularity. In addition, the charge of aggressiveness had gendered implications. Men who stand on principle are frequently admired for their integrity. Women who do so are commonly viewed as too strident, as stepping out of bounds. Inouye thought Patsy should be more accommodating and deferential, both stereotypically feminine traits. Instead, she stood her ground and led like a man.

As an elected official, Patsy possessed a platform upon which to speak about national and international politics. Through her involvement with the YD, Patsy received opportunities to gain political recognition beyond Hawai'i. In mid-February 1957, right before the Territorial House started its session, Patsy traveled to San Francisco to attend the Democratic National Conference (not to be confused with the Democratic National Convention [DNC]). Representing the Hawai'i YD, Patsy spoke in a session on "Alaska-Hawaii Statehood." The panel was cochaired by Edith Green, US congresswoman from Oregon and a future political colleague of Patsy's in DC. The other cochairs were the Hawai'i and Alaska delegates, John Burns and Del Bartlett. Hawai'i actually sent a Republican to this session to address one of the main arguments against the island's admission into the union. Lorrin P. Thurston, publisher of the *Honolulu Advertiser* and chair of the Hawai'i Statehood Commission, argued that the islands were not a hotbed of communism. His speech, entitled "Communism Does Not, and Never Will, Control Hawaii," explained how the people of Hawai'i rejected and sought to contain communism.[46] Patsy addressed the other main argument against Hawai'i's admission. She stated, "We all know that the real reason for the delay is because of Hawaii's large Oriental population. The day has come when you must face this issue squarely. Are all men born equal?"[47] The answer to this question held global implications.

Patsy framed the issue of racial equality in the context of post–World War II decolonization and the Cold War competition for Third World allies. Patsy argued that "Hawaii is your laboratory for the East. We are an example of a successful intermixing of many races. Parts of America do not accept this way of life. The world watches to see American democracy at work. . . . The world watches and closely scrutinizes your record. The principles of American democracy must be proven to the oppressed peoples of the East."[48] Patsy asserted that Hawaiʻi's campaign for statehood and the United States' failure to achieve racial equality held global significance. In the context of the Cold War, Third World peoples, particularly Asians, were scrutinizing the US racial record and awaiting Hawaiʻi's political fate.

Through the YD, Patsy gained additional opportunities in national political circles. In November 1957, she traveled with her parents to Reno, Nevada, for the national convention of the Young Democrats Clubs of America (YDCA). The Hawaiʻi YD, just admitted into the national organization, would be represented for the first time. It also was the first trip to the mainland for Suematsu and Mitama. Patsy purchased a car in San Francisco and drove to Reno with her parents, before shipping the vehicle home to Hawaiʻi.[49] At the convention, Suematsu and Mitama celebrated Patsy's election as a vice president of the national organization.

Patsy's candidacy had not been planned. In Reno, she became acquainted and formed alliances with progressive politicians, most of whom were from the western states. Mirroring national dynamics in the Democratic Party, southern representatives and even some eastern ones promoted more conservative politics at the YDCA conventions. Philip Burton, the youngest elected assemblyman in California and a future colleague of Patsy's in the US House of Representatives, ran for the presidency of the YDCA. However, Nelson Lancione of Ohio also wanted to run. Both current vice presidents, their candidacies would have split the progressive vote. To avoid this, Burton agreed to step aside while also endorsing Patsy as a VP candidate. Her position was designated for the representation of women in the YDCA, and she was elected as part of an unprecedented slate. All the other officers were men, and almost all were white. Richard L. Crawford from Chicago, an African American, also was elected as vice president. In a letter to Burton, Patsy expressed her gratitude as well admiration: "It has been my greatest thrill at the convention to meet a person of your stature and integrity. It isn't often that one is able to witness the great sacrifice which you made in order to assure the victory of the liberal movement."[50]

As vice president of the YDCA, Patsy gained more opportunities for political exposure. She traveled to meetings and conventions in Washington, DC, Miami Beach, Pittsburgh, and Toledo, Ohio. She met current and former YDs, including the youngest member of the US Senate, Frank Church of Idaho. She also met prominent politicians, such as future US president John F. Kennedy (then US senator from Massachusetts), future vice president Hubert Humphrey (then US senator from Minnesota), and Adlai Stevenson II (the Democratic candidate for president in 1952 and 1956). Patsy stayed with Burns and his wife while in DC and was also admitted to practice before the US Supreme Court.[51] She even appeared on national television, on a program called *See It Now*, to lobby for Hawai'i statehood.[52]

Patsy ironically benefited from the Democratic Party's limited efforts to recruit women for auxiliary political roles. The party recognized the need to increase women's participation and created various positions and organizational structures to facilitate this process. The predominantly male leaders, though, did not necessarily envision women as full and equal political leaders. Patsy served as an officer, because the YDCA designated a women's vice presidency. Under Lancione's leadership, a Women's Division also was created. He explained that the purpose of the division was "to emphasize the role of young women in the Y.D.C.A. and to coordinate the activities of Young Democratic women within the Women's Division of the Democratic National Committee."[53] Lancione, who had tremendous respect for Patsy, nevertheless understood women's roles in relation to other women, not in terms of the overall YDCA or the national Democratic Party. Patsy did not lead the women's division, but she assisted with its efforts. She also announced her intention to organize female Democrats in Hawai'i.[54]

Due to her YDCA position, Patsy became one of five Americans to attend a NATO Conference of Young Political Leaders, held in Paris in summer 1958. Approximately one hundred representatives attended the conference. They came from the fifteen nations that constituted NATO (the United Kingdom, France, Italy, Norway, Denmark, the Netherlands, Luxembourg, Portugal, Belgium, Iceland, Canada, West Germany, Turkey, Greece, and the United States). Patsy diversified the US delegation: she was a woman, an AJA, and a resident of a US territory. Just as people around the world observed the fate of Hawai'i, Patsy's presence at the NATO conference symbolized the inclusiveness of US democracy. After the opening of the conference, the attendees were divided into three commissions, each assigned a different topic. One focused on the "policies and principles of NATO."[55] Another focused on "the role of youth organizations in helping to achieve the spirit of cooperation and unity."[56] And, the final commission, the one that Patsy was assigned, focused on "the controversies and problems which seem to presently divide the Alliance."[57] The issues considered by Patsy's commission included Algeria's opposition to French colonialism, self-determination for Cyprus, reunification of Germany, disarmament, and territorial fishing limits by Iceland.[58] Even though the locales were far from Patsy's home, the topics resonated with political debates in Hawai'i as an archipelagic territory and one of the many epicenters of the Cold War.

It was an exhilarating experience for Patsy, and John was able to share it with her. It was his first trip back to Europe since flying missions there during World War II. Wendy accompanied them as far as Pennsylvania, where she spent the next ten days getting to know Grandma Helen, John's mother. In Paris, Patsy and John soaked up their international political adventure and then enjoyed what Patsy described as a second honeymoon.

Friends and Enemies

Motivated by her successes in the Territorial House, the YDs, and at the NATO conference, Patsy successfully ran for the Territorial Senate in 1958. The achievement of Hawai'i statehood in 1959 opened a new phase in her young political career. However, statehood also exacerbated power hierarchies within the Hawai'i Democratic Party, and these divisions led to Patsy's first, and particularly devastating, political loss.

Patsy was a front runner for the Territorial Senate in 1958. Due to redistricting, there were five senatorial spots allotted to the Fifth District. Patsy's first term in the Territorial House had aroused controversy, and according to John Mink, "The Republicans [we]re out to get her."[59] During this campaign, Patsy now had a track record to showcase, and she had been honored and recognized both nationally and internationally. Her supporters broadcast her achievements through a testimonial dinner that highlighted her involvement in the NATO conference in Paris. She won the primary easily, with over seventeen hundred votes over her nearest competitor. As her political career ascended, she became a target for conservatives and some liberals.

The ILWU, the target of anticommunist witch hunts, was not always a reliable partner for the Democratic Party. In the 1958 senatorial race, the Pacific Action Committee (PAC) of the ILWU endorsed Patsy along with three Republican candidates. Less than a week before the election, the ILWU PAC circulated a flier criticizing other Democratic candidates and placed Patsy's name at the bottom of the accusations. When Patsy confronted the PAC, "They gleefully chided her to do something about it."[60] In response, she took out a quarter-page ad in the newspapers, "disclaiming, discrediting, and disavowing the tactics of the ILWU campaign methods."[61] Patsy still placed first in the general elections, but she seemed to have lost some votes due to the flier. She came in only fifty-five votes ahead of Frank Fasi, who eventually became the longest-serving mayor of Honolulu. She was the only woman in the Territorial Senate. The Democrats dominated again, winning sixteen seats; the Republican won nine positions.

In the Senate, Patsy faced opposition from Republicans as well as Democrats. She advanced an equal-pay-for-equal-work bill, an initiative that she began while in the Territorial House. In the Senate, the bill was repeatedly deferred and underwent seven drafts. Inouye supported the legislation, calling it "one of the Democratic Party's priority measures."[62] However, Senate president and Democrat Herbert Lee faced accusations of blocking the bill.[63] It finally passed the Senate, but contained an amendment that allowed heads of households to receive more benefits. Since most heads of households were male, the amendment countered the purpose of the bill, which was to guarantee women equal pay for equal work.

Patsy and other members of the Territorial government celebrated when the US Congress finally voted Hawai'i in as the fiftieth state in March 1959. Burns played a crucial role in this campaign. He developed close relationships with key legislators and was particularly friendly with powerhouses from Texas, such as speaker of the House Sam Rayburn and Senate majority leader Lyndon Johnson. Burns also allowed Alaska to proceed with the statehood vote before Hawai'i. This lessened the chances of defeat, since the two territories did not have the same opponents. Also, once Alaska became a state in January of 1959, the argument against including noncontiguous territories became moot.

Achieving statehood elated Patsy. In a letter to the YDCA president, she enthused, "We finally made it! . . . Overnight we have become full-fledged Americans."[64] And, in a speech anticipating Hawai'i's statehood, Patsy elaborated on the significance of becoming the fiftieth state: "Having a full and equal voice as free men and women in the affairs of the government of our citizenship—this we will have won with statehood, not because of our racial composition or despite it, but because, though it has taken time, our country truly means and believes that all men are created equal and that they are endowed by certain inalienable rights of life, liberty, and the pursuit of happiness."[65] While Patsy emphasized how statehood validated the US principle of equal rights, other AJAs had pecuniary reasons to celebrate the change in Hawai'i's political status. As the plantation economy receded during and after World War II, some Asian Americans took advantage of new prospects to invest in land, tourism, and banking.[66] Statehood expanded these opportunities.

Statehood required a vote in Hawai'i as well as in Congress, and seventeen voters to one supported statehood. Despite the overwhelming result, there were opponents among large plantation owners and Native Hawaiians. Alice Kamokilaikawai Campbell testified against statehood at the first congressional hearings in 1946. Her haole father, James Campbell, was one of Hawai'i's largest landowners, and her mother, Abigail Ku'aihelani, petitioned in 1897 against US annexation. A Territorial senator, Kamokila distanced herself from the Democratic Party over statehood, seeking instead "an independent form of government."[67] She also filed a lawsuit in 1948 "that challenged the legality of the financing of the Hawaii Statehood Commission," whose mission was to advocate statehood.[68] The commission would spend hundreds of thousands of dollars, shaping the political discourse about statehood both in Hawai'i and on the mainland. As a result, the 1959 ballot only provided two choices: statehood or the continuation of territorial status. There was no option for political independence.

Following Hawai'i's admission, Patsy declared her candidacy to become the islands' sole representative to the US Congress. Inouye filed for one of the two US Senate seats. Neither Mink nor Inouye had the prior approval of Burns, who exerted control over candidate slates though he was far away in Washington, DC. Burns declared his candidacy for governor, then turned his attention to the congressional slate. He knew that the elder statesmen of the Democratic Party, Oren Long and William Heen, both aspired to run for the Senate. Long was haole and aged seventy. Heen was seventy-six and of Hawaiian-Chinese heritage. Burns wanted Dan Inouye, who was turning thirty-five that year, to become a candidate for the US House rather than the US Senate. That way, Long and Heen could campaign for the Senate seats without competition from Inouye. Also, the congressional slate would then be racially "balanced." Since concerns about race delayed Hawai'i's admission, Burns sought to avoid a delegation that consisted entirely of AJAs. Burns did not support Patsy's candidacy at all, preferring her out of the race altogether. She was too independent minded.

Mink resisted the pressure to abandon her candidacy, but Inouye, initially reluctant, eventually acceded to Burns's plan. As Patsy recounted to a senator in Oregon, "Efforts were made to get me out and to have Dan [Inouye] move down to the House seat. The reasons suggested and rumored were too horrible to believe or mention. I could not accept them. Neither could Dan—until the last moment, three days before the deadline for filing."[69] Inouye announced his decision to change races at a press conference attended by Oren Long. He stated that he had made his decision after "much soul searching."[70] He decided to switch his candidacy to the US House of Representatives because of his "great aloha for Mr. Heen and Mr. Long."[71] Inouye underscored "sincere desire for a unified and harmonious Democratic Party."[72] He supported the fiction of a unified and harmonious Democratic Party by bowing out of the Senate race. He was perfectly willing, though, to create political friction by challenging Mink for the House seat. Patsy did not back down. As she stated, "For the sake of principle, and to prove my independence from the machine, I decided to hold strong and run anyway."[73]

Inouye claimed years later that he ran a clean race against Mink, but male chauvinism played an important role. Since they had similar liberal records, they tended to draw from the same constituency. Inouye and his supporters proclaimed him the better candidate due to his gender. At an election rally, one of the speakers for Inouye "urged his listeners to be 'practical' and elect a Congressman 'of the male gender.' Mr. Izumi noted that Congressmen often hold meetings in the corridors, the cloak room, and 'even in the men's rest room.'"[74] The speaker went on to say that only one of the candidates could participate in these bathroom political deals: "Dan Inouye—the hero, lawyer, legislator—a man."[75] Inouye's status as a veteran of the 442nd, physically evident through the loss of his arm, was a key asset. Patsy responded at the same rally that "a campaign should be waged on the candidates' qualifications, and not on extraneous matters such as whether one is a Catholic or Protestant—or man or woman."[76]

Inouye's campaign did not just broadcast his superiority as a man. His supporters also spread gossip to question Patsy's ability to be a wife and a mother. John Mink observed,

> The opposition effectively circulated the following rumor . . . with excellent results:
>
> 1. She [Patsy] was pregnant.
> 2. We were to be divorced after the election.
> 3. She had a nervous breakdown due to the strain of campaigning.[77]

Inouye's supporters also suggested that Patsy's daughter, Wendy, was developmentally disabled.[78] This allegation fueled speculations that Mink should not be running for political office, when her energies were clearly needed at home. To counter the rumor, Wendy, then around age seven, taped a television spot, offering voters to observe that she was the number one fan of her mother's political work.

Patsy campaigned vigorously, but she lost in a landslide. Overall, Inouye had greater organizational support. The Democratic Party backed him, as did party-affiliated labor unions. These groups would not circulate or display Patsy's political materials. In addition, veterans' organizations stood solidly behind Inouye, an expression of martial citizenship as they channeled their military service into political capital.

The disproportionate support for Inouye flowed from cultural assumptions about male superiority. As Patsy learned from a colleague of her husband's, "My vote and only my vote will go to Dan Inouye, *the candidate*. For me, there would be no choice if the consideration were between Dan Inouye the person and Patsy Mink the person. Why? With everything else being equal only because he is a man" (emphasis in the original).[79]

Patsy's loss was devastating. Her husband observed, "Patsy has suffered the severest blow of her short life. Her faith in the integrity of the 'people,' their ability to see through the gloss . . . [and] into the issue, has been arrested. . . . No human being who held such fond belief in the people could survive such a telling disaster without the whole inner spirit being wrenched."[80] But, Patsy did recover emotionally. She also maintained her commitment to the Democratic Party, despite the local leadership. She reflected on the race and the party to a friend:

> I guess by now you have received all the gory news about the election. . . .
> I personally have no regrets with my own race—the tragedy is that those
> who contributed to my defeat—will not accept the responsibility for the
> mess. . . . From the headlines this morning, they still are trying to focus
> all reorganization attempts around Burns only. What the Party needs
> is the unification of all elements not around an individual, but around
> the Party figures as a whole. What they cannot accept is the sharing of
> the policies and not the dictation of it. Those who will accept dictation,
> are only those who desire personal gain in return for their pledge. Why
> can we not build a Party leadership based upon mutual respect and
> understanding?[81]

As a testament to Patsy's party loyalty, she spoke in support of Democratic candidates, even after her loss.

In the end, Democrats won two of the three new federal seats, Inouye the House seat and Long a seat in the Senate. Inouye became the first AJA elected to federal office. The second Senate seat went to Republican Hiram Fong, who became the first Chinese American US senator. The governorship went to a Republican, as well, with Burns defeated despite his role in gaining Hawai'i's admission to statehood. The Democrats also lost control of the new state Senate.

Beginning Again

As a result of the 1959 election, Patsy was out of office. The party leadership persisted in marginalizing her, but she had enough supporters at the Hawai'i Democratic Party State Convention to be elected as one of ten delegates to the 1960 Democratic National Convention. She also had enough political clout to be placed on the platform committees for the state and national Democratic Party. The reception that she received at the 1960 DNC, despite the mainland media focus on her exotic appearance, inspired Patsy to continue her political work. She returned to the Hawai'i legislature as a senator in 1962, and focused her political energies on educational issues. Two years later, Patsy gained another opportunity to represent the United States in Europe, and she finally succeeded in her campaign for the US House of Representatives.

Patsy arrived at the 1960 DNC in Los Angeles as a delegate for Adlai Stevenson and held Hubert Humphrey in equally high regard. She had reservations about John F. Kennedy, however, because of his international as well as labor politics. She expressed these concerns in a letter: "I am quite shaken by Kennedy's continued emphasis on the National Defense and Mobilization angle. I sure wish that he would talk about something else. . . . Also he made a very bad statement, from my point of view . . . on the ILWU and Teamsters endorsement or lack thereof. Though I may not care for them, he could have put it more palatably."[82] She was disappointed by Kennedy's nomination, but the accolades that Patsy received for her civil rights speech invigorated her.

Even as Patsy and the Democratic Party articulated their commitment to equality and inclusiveness, she received media coverage that focused on her appearance. The attention stemmed from an exotic fascination with Asian women. One commentator of the 1960 DNC recalled smiling "when Mrs. Patsy Mink, the lovely Oriental doll of a delegate from Hawaii, started a talk with 'My fellow Americans.'"[83] The writer highlighted Patsy's appearance to juxtapose her Asianness, femaleness, and slight stature with normative understandings of American citizens, particularly politicians, as white, male, and physically dominant.

The media focus on Patsy's physicality trivialized her and other women. In an article about the 1961 YDCA national convention in Miami, a journalist used the title "Mrs. Hawaii" to refer to Patsy.[84]

The article portrayed her as a beauty queen. The feature began by discussing her looks, not her politics: "The cutest senator you ever saw was in Miami Beach today. She has brown eyes, black hair, weighs 110 pounds and is five feet, one and a half inches tall. She wouldn't give her other dimensions."[85] The article eventually included information about Patsy's political career and views, but the journalist insisted on returning to her appearance, asking whether "her looks had anything to do with winning elections."[86] Patsy's dedication and political vision were irrelevant.

Patsy's origins in Hawai'i contributed to the gendered and sexualized image of her that circulated in mainland media. A picture of her feeding poi, a Hawaiian food eaten with fingers, to a visiting white, male politician appeared in two California newspapers in 1963.[87] One of the publications referred to Patsy, at the time a state senator, as a "hostess."[88] World War II and the Cold War led to the increased presence of American troops across the Asia-Pacific. The term "hostess" associated Patsy with other Asian women who worked as entertainers and prostitutes in rest and recreation sites that catered to the US military. Patsy considered suing the newspapers for their depiction of her. She wrote to a lawyer based in San Francisco, explaining, "I have debated many days over whether I should write you about the articles I have been receiving from friends carried by the Examiner in both S.F. and in L.A. . . . I am referred to as a 'Hostess,' to highlight the article's inference that the whole thing was purely a junket. My husband took great offense to this reference as he feels that such a title carries many connotations. He feels that I should obtain counsel and sue the newspapers for defamation."[89] In the end, after receiving advice from the lawyer, Patsy decided not to pursue a legal case.

Instead, Patsy focused her efforts on political mobilization. She gave talks to women's organizations about women's involvement in politics and the need to address gender discrimination. Patsy also challenged the gendered language that most Americans, including herself, tended to use. In a 1963 letter to the state chairman of the Hawai'i Democratic Party, she wrote, "Thank you for your memo on the Platform Committee. I wonder whether you intended it for me, though since I notice it was addressed only to 'Gentlemen,' of which I will never be. In the event you did not mean to discriminate against the women of the Democratic

Party, may I suggest . . ."[90] Patsy increasingly became outspoken about gender discrimination and demanded equality.

Patsy decided to run for the Hawai'i Senate in 1962. That year, Inouye left the US House, seeking instead the US Senate seat being vacated by Oren Long, who was retiring. Following the 1960 census, Hawaii was allocated two seats in the US House beginning with the 1962 election. Spark Matsunaga and Tom Gill (both World War II veterans and legislators) successfully ran for the open House seats. Patsy considered another run for the US House in 1962 but decided against it. Her 1959 campaign had been expensive, and she and John had mortgaged their house for her to participate. Since they were just paying off the loan, Patsy decided that the Hawai'i State Senate was a more feasible goal. In 1962, she again received the most votes of any candidate in the Fifth District. After a three-year hiatus, Patsy was back in elected office.

This time, Patsy chaired the Senate Committee on Education. She had emphasized educational issues in her campaign and developed a multipronged platform to improve K–12, technical, and vocational education. She also wanted to make college more accessible by offering a state version of the GI Bill that would provide low-interest loans for "all who desire to better themselves beyond high school."[91] Furthermore, reflecting her commitment to democracy, Patsy argued that the State Board of Education should be elected rather than appointed. Because Hawai'i has a unique statewide system of education, changes at the state level could alter the entire system.

Patsy was buoyed by her achievements during the 1963 Senate term, and Tom Gill's decision to run for the US Senate in 1964 reignited her interest in seeking election to the US House of Representatives. This time she decided to go for it. In the midst of planning her campaign, she was surprised by an invitation to join a US delegation to Germany. During John Kennedy's visit to Berlin in 1963, the West German government proposed that "100 American personalities from political and economic life as well as from all fields of science . . . visit the Federal Republic of Germany and especially the City of Berlin so that they can see personally what the German people has accomplished with the Marshall Plan aid."[92] The Americans who visited Germany in 1964 traveled in ten groups of ten people. Patsy was the only woman in her delegation, which focused on civic leadership. The other members of their study tour—businessmen, lawyers, and a labor representative—came from around the country.

Patsy shared highlights of her two-week tour of Germany with Hawai'i constituents through a published column as well as a "Friend of Mink" dinner when she returned. She reported on her group's visits to coal mines, shipyards, factories, and schools. She expressed admiration for how West Germany was reconstructing itself, taking special notice of how the government protected agricultural and green space, even as the country engaged in expanding its economic production. She spoke of this conservationist development approach in a speech to the Pan Pacific Real Estate Conference in Hawai'i: "I was privileged to visit West Germany this past summer as a guest of the Federal Republic of Germany. I was deeply impressed by the extent to which conservation practices have become the policy of the West Germany government. Parks, arboretums, and open spaces abound in the cities. . . . Careful planning of industrial centers so as not to pollute the fresh air of the residential areas and large agricultural plots outside the city gives [sic] one the constant feel of open space."[93] Patsy understood that the scale of societal reconstruction in Germany was not possible in the United States. However, she challenged her audience to consider what might be feasible in Hawai'i: "Free enterprise is a great tradition in our American society. It has achieved wealth and prosperity for our people. Can it also accept the challenge of preserving for America those things of ultimate beauty?"[94] These concerns about protecting the environment would be a continuing theme in Patsy's political career.

After three terms in the Territorial and state legislature, Patsy set her sights on federal office. The issues that she was concerned about—education, social welfare, global conflict, and the environment—all were tied to the federal government. She was particularly eager to support and expand Lyndon Johnson's War on Poverty through Great Society legislation. Patsy also had developed political credibility at the national level, as demonstrated by her leadership with the YDCA. And she had gained international exposure by representing the United States in Paris and Germany. Patsy was primed for national political service.

In the 1964 Democratic primary, Patsy's main opponents were Walter Heen and David McClung. The nephew of William Heen and a Chinese Hawaiian, Heen emphasized the need for a racially balanced slate of

Figure 2.2. John and Wendy join Patsy as she kicks off her barrier-breaking campaign for Congress in 1964. Source: *Honolulu Star Advertiser* Photo.

officials. In 1959, Inouye's campaign criticized Patsy for being a woman. In 1964, Heen indirectly criticized her for being AJA. McClung, another Democrat and a member of the Territorial as well as state House of Representatives, had the support of AFL-CIO unions. Although not favored, Patsy won both the primary and the general election. She came in second after incumbent Spark Matsunaga, but there were now two slots for the US House of Representatives. John Mink attributed this success "to a hard-fought campaign, working every minute. We did it on only $15,000; Heen spent about $40–50,000, McClung about 30–40,000; Matsunaga about 30,000."[95] Patsy and John did not have professional consultants, just each other and an enthusiastic yet inexperienced committee of volunteers. Their campaign strategy was focused on

what appeared to be an excessive effort on the neighbor islands, but this is where she won the election. . . . The peak of our strategy was the day before the election—she chose to charter a plane and to hit both the Kahalui, Maui, and the Kapaa, Kauai rallies rather than stay in Honolulu for the Democrat TV jamboree where she would be allowed at most 1 minute to speak amidst every other candidate. . . . The outer island rallies drew hundreds of people. She wowed them and the word got around.[96]

This campaign epitomized the politician that Patsy had become. She relied on her family for support and advice. She was not afraid to go against the grain and do something out of the ordinary. And, she had an ability to convey her political vision to voters. A dozen years after her return to Hawai'i, Patsy was ready for Washington, DC.

PART II

A Great Society at War

The only new woman member of the 89th Congress, Mrs. Patsy Mink (D-Hawaii) ranks second only to Lady Bird in the Capital's glamour gal spotlight. She is invited everywhere, and wherever she goes, flashbulbs pop, people stop her to talk and shake her hand. "It's more like Hollywood than Washington," said the first Japanese-American woman in Congress. "Somewhere this has got to stop. I can't keep up with my work—I don't think my constituents elected me to get my picture taken."
—*New York Sunday News*, 1965

It is easy enough to vote right and be consistently with the majority, but it is more often more important to be ahead of the majority and this means being willing to cut the first furrow in the ground and stand alone for a while if necessary.
—Patsy Takemoto Mink, 1975

Patsy Takemoto Mink arrived in Washington, DC, attracting publicity befitting a celebrity.[1] She was featured in local and national media, appearing in *Life* magazine and the Sunday syndicated news magazine *Roto*, as well as the television show *What's My Line?* Even in articles in which Mink was a minor subject, the news media tended to publish her picture. The attention reflected and generated popular fascination with the first woman of color congressional representative.

Mink was the only new woman elected to the 89th Congress, joining ten others in the House of Representatives and two female senators. At least initially, media attention tended to focus on Mink's physical appearance rather than her politics. She was featured in the fashion and social sections as a "glamour girl." Journalists commented on her clothes and social standing within Washington, DC, treating Mink as a celebrity

Figure II.1. Class photo for new members of Congress elected in the Democratic wave election of 1964, the freshmen of the 89th Congress. Source: Library of Congress/US House photo.

first and politician second. Even so, Mink and some pundits reflected on the significance of her election for women's political roles.

Mink also drew media attention for being Japanese American. Many of the articles used the term "Oriental" to describe her. Doing so emphasized her exoticness and foreignness, presumed qualities heightened by her origins in Hawai'i. One article even described the relationship between Patsy and John as a "happy ending of 'Madame Butterfly.'"[2] This famous opera by Giacomo Puccini tells the story of an ill-fated romance between a US naval officer and a young Japanese girl. The officer marries and eventually abandons his mistress, who becomes known as Butterfly. Years later, the officer and his second wife, a white American, take away the son that Butterfly had with the officer. She acquiesces to these demands and commits suicide. The reference to Madame Butterfly reveals how race and gender were central to the way this journalist perceived Patsy. Despite being a thirty-seven-year-old lawyer elected to the US

Congress, Patsy is compared to a vulnerable woman in Japan who gives up her child and life out of a hopeless devotion to a white man.

The media attention paid to Patsy extended overseas as well. She was interviewed by the Japanese press and featured in articles that lauded her achievements as a Japanese American congresswoman. The US government perceived the propaganda value of promoting Patsy. In February 1965, the United States Information Agency (USIA) featured her in an article that was circulated in multiple countries. Created in 1953 under President Eisenhower, the USIA helped fight the Cold War through cultural diplomacy. By featuring Mink, a Japanese American congresswoman from Hawai'i, the article broadcast the success of US democracy. Mink herself was invested in this portrayal. Introducing Hawai'i to audiences that regarded the state as exotic, or foreign, or backward, Mink proclaimed her home state a role model, arguing that "Hawaiians . . . have achieved racial equality while recognizing and preserving cultural

Figure II.2. Class photo of the women of the 89th Congress. Source: Library of Congress/US House photo.

differences."[3] Scholars and activists have critiqued this portrayal of Hawai'i as a multicultural paradise, given the social hierarchies and ongoing occupation in the islands. Mink evoked this representation to critique mainland forms of exclusion, but she also recognized and sought to address the inequalities that existed in her home state.

While flattered by the media attention, Mink also was eager to assume her legislative responsibilities. Before the new Congress convened, she visited Washington, DC, to attend orientation for new members. She learned about protocol and resources. She also met President Lyndon B. Johnson. Johnson had won a lopsided electoral vote one year after the assassination of President John F. Kennedy. The 1964 election also gave the Democrats a substantial majority in Congress, the largest since the Great Depression. The 89th Congress, particularly with the support of the thirty-six first-year Democrats, passed a series of Great Society measures designed to lessen inequality by promoting government responsibility for social welfare. The new laws in 1965 alone included the creation of Medicare, the federal health insurance program for senior citizens; the Voting Rights Act to protect racial and language minorities from disfranchisement, particularly in the South; the Elementary and Secondary Education Act, which provided significant federal aid to public education for the first time; and the 1965 Immigration Act, which ended the discriminatory national-origins quota system and limitations on immigration from the Asia-Pacific Triangle.

Patsy was an enthusiastic advocate for the Great Society. She believed in utilizing government resources to ensure equal access and social equality. Mink expressed in a commencement speech that "our government is now beginning to devote its mighty mechanism towards the solution of human misery in this country and the world. This program is the single most important ideal behind the move to build a great society."[4] Furthermore, Patsy was invested in improving education, which she described as "'the key that will unlock the doors' leading to the Great Society."[5] Creating equal opportunity in educational institutions would "stimulate a desire to seek more knowledge and creative thinking."[6] Education could cultivate the potential of individuals of diverse backgrounds; in turn, human creativity could improve the entire society.

Patsy connected the transformational impact of education with the struggles for racial equality. In a speech to the Japanese American

Citizens League, she argued that Japanese Americans had faced "displacement and social seclusion" but had subsequently "made giant strides in our assimilation in the total life and community of this nation."[7] She argued that they collectively "found education 'the best route to equality and social justice.'"[8] Elements of this speech previewed the emerging model-minority representation of Japanese Americans, which focused on their ability to overcome racial obstacles solely through hard work and educational success.[9] Yet Mink also communicated the need for political advocacy and the unfinished work of racial justice.

Mink requested and received the assignment to serve on the House Committee on Education and Labor. She played an important role in Great Society legislation through her involvement in crafting educational and labor policies, both of which were central to President Johnson's declared War on Poverty. It was through this committee that Mink also became involved in feminist legislation in the late 1960s and early 1970s, as she advocated for equal educational access for girls and women, federal funding to eliminate gender-biased curricula, and government-funded childcare.

Mink also served on the House Committee on Interior and Insular Affairs. This committee provided opportunities to focus on Indigenous and environmental issues. She persisted in her opposition to nuclear testing and critiqued US militarism, or how the valuing of a strong military pervades an entire society. She was particularly attuned to the impact of this mindset on the islands and waters of the Pacific. Even as Patsy left Hawai'i for DC, she brought a Pacific World perspective with her to Congress.

Patsy's congressional work day typically spanned twelve to sixteen hours. She devoted mornings to committee meetings and afternoons to congressional sessions. Evenings were spent reading and responding to correspondence; writing speeches; and preparing for the next day's committee work or floor debates. Mink assembled an office staff, some from among her supporters in Hawai'i, some already based in DC. They assisted in her responsibilities, but Patsy tended to pay personal attention to all the office work. She often opened letters herself; authored responses to supporters and critics; and rewrote her speeches. As in her campaigns, Patsy's political career in Congress was a collective family endeavor. John and Wendy assisted Patsy. John acted as adviser, sounding board, and human newspaper digest, and Wendy often helped in the office after school or during school breaks. Family dinners were devoted to discussing political issues.

As Patsy served six congressional terms from 1965 to 1977, she gained experience working both with and against the majority. Even as she helped mobilize legislative support for landmark policies, Mink often took positions that did not enjoy broad support. Her very first vote in Congress on January 4, 1965, demonstrated her willingness to stand on principle, regardless of the likelihood of success. In 1964, civil rights organizers had exposed and challenged the white-controlled electoral process in Mississippi as systematic racial disfranchisement. Locked out of the democratic process, local civil rights activists worked with volunteers from outside of Mississippi to form the Mississippi Freedom Democratic Party (MFDP). Together, they registered Black and white voters and conducted an integrated parallel primary. During the presidential nominating process, the MFDP contested the legitimacy of the all-white Mississippi delegation to the 1964 Democratic National Convention (DNC). The MFDP lost at the DNC in Atlantic City but did not give up its cause. On the first day of the 89th Congress, the MFDP protested the all-white congressional delegation from Mississippi and called on Congress to refuse them seats, because they had been selected in an unconstitutional process that excluded Black voters. Mink was among sixteen members of the House who called for withholding the oath of office from the all-white Mississippi regulars. Mink voted with 148 congressmembers to deny seats to the Mississippians. Not all Democrats did so, and the resolution was defeated. Spark Matsunaga, who introduced Patsy on the floor of the House of Representatives that first day of her first session, voted with the majority.

Mink's resistance to racism was both personal and political. When they moved to the Washington, DC, area, the Mink family first settled in Virginia. They arrived a few years before the 1967 Loving vs. Virginia Supreme Court decision banned antimiscegenation laws. Virginia school teachers observed to Wendy, then in seventh grade, that her parents' interracial marriage was likely illegal in the state, and therefore, she was "illegitimate." The Minks promptly relocated, first to Maryland, which turned out to have antimiscegenation laws on the books, too, and then to DC, where the Lovings had fled when Virginia courts declared their marriage a crime. These kinds of experiences fed Patsy's resolve to challenge racial inequality wherever it manifested.

Patsy's strong political stances frequently put her at odds with presidents, voters, and her party. Her opposition to the US war in Viet Nam, for example, pitted her against two presidents (Johnson and Nixon). Her advocacy for an end to military violence and a negotiated peace demonstrated her willingness to "cut the first furrow" and "stand alone" if needed. Her antiwar politics even led Mink to run for the presidency in 1972. As Mink observed, it was necessary, at times, to be "ahead of the majority" in order to advocate for what she believed was right and just.

"I SEE YOU HAVE APPOINTMENT WITH VIETCONG"

In August 1964, three months before my mother was elected to Congress for the first time, Lyndon Johnson secured from a compliant Congress broad authorization to use military force in Southeast Asia, even without a formal declaration of war. In the House of Representatives, the body my mother soon would join, no one voted against granting the president untethered discretion to engage militarily against North Viet Nam. In the Senate, only two members, Democrats Wayne Morse of Oregon and Ernest Gruening of Alaska, voted in opposition. Within six months of passage of the Gulf of Tonkin Resolution, Lyndon Johnson's escalation of US war making in Viet Nam was underway.

But in the fall election campaign, Johnson presented as the candidate who would promote peace and assure military restraint, at least in comparison to Republican nominee Barry Goldwater. On ABC's Sunday talk show on May 24, 1964, Goldwater had wondered out loud whether the United States should use nuclear weapons to defoliate forests and destroy infrastructure in North Viet Nam.[1] Campaigning in the summer, he had lambasted Johnson's stated caution in Viet Nam as "encourag[ing] the enemy to prolong the fighting."[2] Against growing fears that Goldwater's militance could lead to nuclear war, Johnson persuaded most voters that he was the "peace candidate," winning the largest presidential majority to date—in total vote, percentage vote, and margin of victory.[3]

By early March 1965, however—barely two months into my mother's first term in Congress—Johnson had launched a bombing campaign against North Viet Nam and sent in the first US combat troops.[4] My mother's first weeks as a freshman congressmember coincided with the initial US escalation of war in Viet Nam and with proliferating presidential feints and misrepresentations aimed at muting and mooting legislative opposition. One of just a handful of Democrats who challenged the terms of US military intervention in Viet Nam in 1965, my mother would spend her first years in Congress in dissent against her own party's war policy.

Mom criticized military escalation in Viet Nam from the outset, at first expressing opposition in public statements, letters to the president, and correspondence with constituents. As war persisted, she would collaborate with colleagues in sponsoring or supporting legislative efforts to attach end-the-war provisions to military spending measures. One of the first antiwar letters to the president she signed as a new member of Congress condemned the use of gas warfare by the United States in Viet Nam.[5] Letters to constituents in the winter of 1965 criticized the shift to offensive military engagement and argued the case for a negotiated peace. In May 1965, she spoke on the floor of the House of Representatives against the massive military buildup;[6] in August, in another floor statement, she called for a ceasefire and peace conference;[7] in September, she voted against another expansion of the president's war-making power.[8] Each of these steps away from her party's majority, and away from her party's president, mixed tortuous deliberation with buoying solidarity among the small group of sixteen or so representatives who were the first "doves" in Congress.

I was twelve going on thirteen when we arrived in Washington. My solipsistic preteen mind didn't pay close attention to my mother's professional struggles at the time, but in retrospect I am certain that Mom spent her first months in Washington anguishing over just how to follow her principles without sacrificing her effectiveness. The question for her was not whether to oppose US military intervention in Viet Nam, but how and when to express her opposition. The only woman of color in Congress, from a state not fully regarded as "American," she had to earn credibility in spite of who she was, where credibility was given to her white male colleagues because of who they were. She had navigated similar shoals back in Hawai'i, as a woman in the overwhelmingly male legal profession and as a woman in male-dominated politics. She also had survived the bullying and blowback meted out to advocates of unpopular views, especially about issues that magnetically attracted McCarthyite smears. But the transition to Washington added new challenges—adjusting to a new institutional culture; finding common cause among predominantly white and male strangers; winnowing blowhards from trustworthy allies; and learning to tolerate graciously Lyndon Johnson's efforts to charm complicity from the dovish new member of his congressional party, whom he informally referred to as "Miss Patsy."[9] Not only did she have to find her professional and political footing in a new context; she had to counter initial media attention that exoticized her and so jeopardized her standing as a serious policy maker.

Nineteen sixty-five was a watershed year for domestic policy, especially regarding civil rights and poverty mitigation. Although my mother was deeply involved in developing the Great Society programs that her Education and Labor Committee shepherded through Congress, the work she brought home—the work that troubled her most—was war policy toward Viet Nam. On weekdays, she often had late votes or late duties that kept her in her office until well after the conventional dinner time. When she got home, we usually chatted a bit about my day, my schoolwork, my adjustment to mainland winter and social fashions. But on weekends, when we cooked and feasted together (often inviting staff to join), family conversation always turned to Viet Nam.

My mother habitually insisted that "it's not enough to say what you're against, you have to say what you're for," and in keeping with that aphorism, our discussions usually wrestled with spelling out a policy alternative to US military intervention. I was reliably in the "out now" camp. My father—awarded the Distinguished Flying Cross and nine oak leaf clusters for his service as an Air Corps navigator in World War II—tempered my more extreme stance with "stop the bombing." My mother wondered whether the conflict between North, South, and the Viet Cong couldn't be turned over to the UN for resolution.

In the months following the initial escalation in March 1965, President Johnson put the question of support for his war directly before Congress. In early May, he requested a supplemental appropriation of $700 million to fund continued US military operations in Viet Nam.[10] In August, he asked for a $1.7 billion short-term appropriation for the war effort and to increase military personnel overall.[11] In September, he asked for blanket authority to combat communism in the Western hemisphere.[12]

Consideration of Johnson's requests by Congress focused our family discussions on what Mom would do or say in response. Would she vote against the supplemental $700 million, even though Johnson insisted he did not want to embroil us in war? Would she okay the $1.7 billion "emergency" appropriation based on Johnson's wink and nod to peace? Would she agree to further delegate congressional war power to the president, when delegation through the Gulf of Tonkin Resolution already had given Johnson carte blanche to expand the war?

Shortly before Johnson requested the supplemental $700 million, the first national protest against US military intervention in Viet Nam took place on the Mall in Washington, DC.[13] It was the day before Easter, 1965—cool but not cold, the cherry blossoms at their peak. My mother had gone home to Hawai'i for the holiday recess, but before she left had said, "You guys should go," referring to the peace rally and march. My father, habitually circumspect yet politically adventurous, plotted our itinerary—drive up to the Longworth House Office Building from our apartment across the Potomac in Arlington; park in my mother's underground stall; walk down Independence Avenue to the Washington Monument, where the rally would convene; then march up the Mall back to the Capitol with our fellow protesters.

It was my first political demonstration involving more than a hundred people. As a young child in Honolulu, I had tagged along to rallies for the *Golden Rule* and against the proliferation of nuclear weapons. So I was not a stranger to the idea of collective protest in general, or of advocating for peace in particular. But the rallies in Honolulu were small, assembling never more than fifty to a hundred participants. Rally organizers and leaders tended to be established in the community—clergy, professors, certain labor union activists. There was no student movement to speak of—or that I knew about—in Hawai'i when we left for Washington in December 1964, so I did not have an inkling of how politically impressive young people could be when they came together to make a point.

I can't say for sure that April 17 was a perfect day for a peace demonstration, but I remember it that way—sunny with blue sky and a bit of a breeze. As a thirteen-year-old girl from Hawai'i, I recall feeling slightly out of place among the twenty thousand mostly white college students. At the same time, I was exhilarated by the scale of the protest and felt a rush from participating in a just cause. I think it was then that I heard Phil Ochs for the first time.

My father had survived bombing missions over Germany in World War II and had supported Henry Wallace in his disappointing third-party progressive presidential candidacy in 1948. The combination of experiences set him apart from many of his fellow World War II veterans on issues of military intervention around the globe and anticommunist hypervigilance at home. It also set him apart from protesters, including me, who swelled with optimism that our collective action could end the war. Even as he participated enthusiastically in the rally and march, chanting "stop the war" and singing "We Shall Overcome," he darkened the moment with a dose of practicality: now that Johnson had committed to offensive military engagement against communism in Viet Nam, he mused, war policy would be difficult to reverse or defeat.

Looking back, I think my parents' political partnership benefited from my father's participation in that first mass protest against the war in Viet Nam. Even as he tried to cocoon my optimism about ending the war in his wet blanket of realism, my father was inspired by the energy and commitment of the twenty thousand protesters to redouble his own belief in the urgency of open opposition to US war policy. As my mother's resistance to presidential military initiatives intensified during late 1965 and early 1966, my father served as sounding board, interlocutor, and ally. He also served as screener for the hate mail that began to arrive, occasionally threatening but mostly just vicious, attacking my mother as "soft on communism" or "un-American."

Legislative resistance to military escalation proved difficult to register, as Congress's abdication of the war-making decision in the Gulf of Tonkin Resolution allowed President Johnson to commit hostilities before Congress had a say-so. During the first eighteen months of military build-up in Viet Nam, Johnson's requests for supplemental appropriations gave congressional doves opportunities to dissent against war policy, while simultaneously trapping them into officially approving the requests because anything short of full funding would not "support our troops" and, according to the president, would subvert the course toward peace.

Throughout 1965, congressional doves numbered fewer than two dozen. If they lacked influence due to scant numbers, they also lacked institutional power due to the rigid seniority system. Most of the doves, though members of the majority party, were relatively junior, so did not control committees of jurisdiction over military or foreign affairs. That honor went to conservative, anticommunist, racist southern Democrats, some of whom had served in Congress since the early 1940s.[14]

Although congressional doves had little direct leverage over Johnson's war plans, through public statements, through publicly announced letters to the president, and eventually through legislative assertion, they kept resistance to the war alive within the political establishment. Meanwhile, outside the hallowed halls, popular protest spread. Across the country, teach-ins, draft-card burning, resistance vigils, and street blockades were evidence of mounting opposition to US intervention in Viet Nam.[15] In Washington, the second antiwar mass mobilization in seven months saw twenty thousand protesters march around the White House in late November 1965.

Throughout my middle- and high-school years, the war in Viet Nam preoccupied—and frustrated—my family; the issue was ever present—at the breakfast table, on the drive to school, during weekend outings to the mall. An end to the war was elusive, as antiwar goals, both small and large, seemed incapable of securing legislative traction. I watched my mother agonize over what steps to take next—denounce the bombing? condemn support for the Ky regime? demand a ceasefire? cut off funds for continued war? insist on unilateral withdrawal? I listened to my mother and father discuss the unfriendly media coverage her antiwar position garnered in Hawai'i and the antagonism her position earned from Democratic state power brokers. I entered conversations about the horrors besieging the Vietnamese people that we saw on the nightly news.

We rarely talked about military operations. Our conversations about the war invariably flagged the war's implications for democracy and human rights: we talked of constitutional checks and balances; First Amendment protection of dissent; government secrecy; the public's right to know; ethnocentrism; racism; nonviolent protest. I learned civics in discussing Viet Nam over cocoa and coffee with my mother before dawn. I also learned a lot about racism, whether explicit or latent, in the US approach to war in Asia. The atrocities committed against Vietnamese civilians tormented my mother—most notoriously, the My Lai massacre. Acutely aware of anti-Asian racism in the United States, from the World War II internment of Japanese Americans to the United States' "Mere Gook Rule" in Viet Nam, my mother became convinced that racism was inextricable from the conduct of the war. Her perception that US war planners viewed Vietnamese lives as disposable and Asian Communists as another "yellow peril" stoked her opposition to the war.[16]

By the time the My Lai massacre was revealed to the public in the fall of 1969—it had been covered up for almost twenty months—the antiwar movement numbered in the millions and doves in Congress had developed strategies to foreground antiwar goals in the legislative process. In October and November 1969, antiwar forces mobilized protests, with teach-ins and rallies planned countrywide on October 15 and a mass demonstration of five hundred thousand accomplished in Washington, DC, on November 15.

I was a senior in high school in the fall of 1969 and not too keen on parental attention, as I was eager to stretch my wings and find my voice. So I did my own thing in preparation for the protests, mainly organizing antiwar activities in my high school. My organizing work included outreach to Vice President Spiro Agnew's daughter, a schoolmate, to whom I offered a black armband honoring the war dead to wear at October 15 events protesting her father's administration's war policy. To no one's surprise, this got her into a bit of hot water at home.[17]

At the demonstrations, I always seemed to have a parent as escort. My father accompanied me to the candlelight vigil in front of the White House in October, and my mother joined me for the march in November, with a few of her dovish colleagues in tow. We all sang along with Pete Seeger, in his ten-minute rendition of John Lennon's "Give Peace a Chance," from then on the anthem for the antiwar movement.

This was the end of the sixties, and lots of kids were in deep political and cultural rebellion against their parents. They worked hard to develop political analyses to buttress their antiwar opinions. Their family lives often were a terrain of conflict over values and life choices. My family life and my development as a political thinker followed a much easier course. While my father couldn't stand the way I dressed, and my mother chafed at my performances of independence, my parents and I agreed about fundamentals. With respect to Viet Nam, we had disagreements of degree and sometimes of method. My parents thought me more radical than they and more impatient to prevail. But our analyses tracked one another's, and we shared the goal of ending the war.

If we were ever out of step with one another, it was over feminism and the second-wave women's movement. As I approached the end of my teen years—during which I often had rebelled in mundane ways against my mother (think miniskirts and marijuana)—I was drawn more and more into a tight sisterhood with her that was sometimes about politics and sometimes just about living female. My father, while a wonderfully supportive spouse to my mother and loving believer in the limitlessness of his daughter's future, was nevertheless uncertain about feminism early on. Initially, he couldn't quite grasp why sisterhood was necessary, let alone powerful.

Yet it was the emergence of the women's movement in the mid- to late sixties, especially the antiwar actions and critiques by feminists for peace, that provided my mother tools for her boldest antiwar move. Advanced by the Jeanette Rankin Brigade in 1968 and the election of Bella Abzug to Congress in 1970, feminist antiwar appeals and arguments produced new allies and strategies for resisting the war. Most of Mom's antiwar work in Congress involved gender-free strategizing within a growing community of (mostly male) doves trying to end the war legislatively—typically by amending military appropriations bills to condition war funding on stopping the air war, or withdrawing troops, or declaring a ceasefire. But in April 1972, she decided to travel to Paris, France, with Bella Abzug, by then her best friend in the House of Representatives, to meet with parties to the stalled Paris peace talks, including Madame Nguyen Thi Binh, leader of the Viet Cong/Provisional Revolutionary Government delegation. Though not advertised as such, this was a feminist peace action, encouraged by Women Strike for Peace and engaging two feminist antiwar advocates in Congress in an effort to keep lines of communication open after President Richard Nixon suspended the peace talks and threatened never to reopen them.[18] The conversation with Madame Binh was not about women and war, per se, but was lubricated by common gender. Binh remarked, "As mothers, as women, you can understand profoundly the suffering of mothers and wives in South Vietnam. In any war it is the women who suffer most."[19]

I drove my mother to National Airport for her flight to New York, where she would connect with Abzug for their flight to Paris. I was home from college that weekend, an unusual break from school as no holidays or other scheduled vacations were on the calendar. I think I was recruited to come home to keep my mother company as she prepped for the trip and decompressed in its aftermath; my father was in the Kahana Valley on O'ahu, doing hydrology. Also, I was slated to speak on behalf of my mother at an Americans for Democratic Action banquet featuring candidates for the 1972 Democratic presidential nomination.

My mother returned from Paris inspired and uplifted by the mere fact of dialogue with wartime adversaries. She also returned with frustrations revived, as the American delegation to the peace talks behaved arrogantly toward the congresswomen and dismissively towards prospects of restarting negotiations, which they called a waste of time.[20] Back in DC, she was greeted by a euphoric daughter, thrilled at even a gesture toward peace. On the phone long distance to Hawai'i, her enthusiasm cooled as her despairing husband reported headlines such as "Reds 'Earnest,' Rep. Mink Says" and quoted news stories caricaturing her as radical, such as one claiming that she urged people to take to the streets to resist renewed escalation of the war.[21] In her Capitol Hill office only a couple of days after returning from Paris, the first trickle of hate mail arrived. One postcard read, "I see you have appointment with Vietcong and North Vietnamese while you were in Paris. Did you go there for 'instructions'?"[22]

3

A Dove among Hawks

Patsy Mink arrived in the US Congress as President Johnson escalated the US war in Viet Nam. The Gulf of Tonkin Resolution, passed in August 1964 on the basis of questionable evidence, authorized the president to use armed force, if necessary, to protect signers of the Southeast Asia Collective Treaty.[1] Beginning in 1965, President Johnson and his military advisors pursued bombing raids in both South and North Viet Nam and introduced US ground troops in substantial numbers. The conflict would escalate and worsen under President Nixon, despite his campaign promises of military success and plans for US withdrawal. Even after the Paris Peace Accord in January of 1973, Presidents Nixon and Ford lobbied the US Congress for additional funds to continue support for the Republic of Viet Nam (RVN), which finally fell in April of 1975.

The US war in Viet Nam, which spread throughout Southeast Asia, became the longest in US history at that time. It also was the first one that the United States "lost." Fearing an expansion of communism, the United States offered military, financial, and political aid to resist Vietnamese decolonization. The United States supported the French during the First Indochina War (1946–1954) and refused to sign the Geneva Accord that temporarily separated Viet Nam along the 17th parallel with the promise of a national election within two years' time. Presidents Eisenhower and Kennedy then backed RVN president Ngo Dinh Diem, a totalitarian and corrupt official who refused to implement political and economic reforms. Diem's presidency aroused the opposition of Buddhists, nationalists, and Communists. The National Liberation Front (NLF), commonly referred to as the Viet Cong, formed in 1960 and worked with the North Vietnamese to conduct military and political attacks against the southern political leadership. The resulting "Vietnam War," also known as the Second Indochina War, aroused a robust antiwar movement around the world. These critics questioned the legality, tactics, goals, and costs (both human and financial) of the US war in Viet Nam.

Patsy Mink, along with growing numbers of congressional members, engaged in legislative antiwar activism. During the Johnson administration, Mink initially gave the president the benefit of the doubt while also advocating for a diplomatic solution. Her peace politics, which motivated her early support of Robert F. Kennedy for the presidential nomination in 1968, aroused disapproval from Johnson and other members of the local and national Democratic Party. During the Nixon administration, greater numbers of Democratic and Republican politicians joined Mink to assert congressional responsibility for declaring war and limiting executive power.

In critiquing the US war in Southeast Asia, Mink foregrounded three main arguments. First, she called for the resolution of military conflict by upholding democratic principles of government. Second, she exposed the racism of US political leaders and military personnel in conducting and justifying war in Southeast Asia. Finally, she practiced feminist diplomatic leadership by traveling to Paris to negotiate peace and running for the US presidency in 1972.

A Democracy at War

Johnson had a close relationship with Hawai'i politicians generally, and he expressed a fondness for Patsy. He invited her to state dinners and bill signings and praised her legislative efforts. Mink matched Johnson's support with enthusiastic advocacy for his domestic programs, many of which were handled by the Committee on Education and Labor. A study by the *Congressional Quarterly* analyzed votes taken through August 4, 1965, and uncovered that Patsy "supported the President on 100 percent of 12 key votes and 91 percent of the 66 rolls calls."[2] Mink's backing of Johnson's Great Society initiatives was higher than that of most first-year congressional representatives.[3] Mink was a steady ally of Johnson's on the domestic front, but she expressed more ambivalence about his international politics.

In response to the US war in Viet Nam, Mink promoted democratic values of self-determination and humanitarianism on the global scale. She asked the US. government and its allies to set limits on military conflict and to prioritize diplomatic negotiations in order to achieve peace. Her most difficult congressional votes centered on how to support the president and the US military while also deescalating violence. Over her first four years in Congress, Mink became increasingly distant from Democratic Party establishment leaders due to her stance on war.

Mink cosigned letters and gave speeches that critiqued violence she found unacceptable to a democracy. Just three months into her term as a representative, and following the publication of a March 23, 1965, *New York Times* article, Mink cosigned a letter with fifteen other Democratic congressional representatives expressing concern about the use of riot-control gas in South Viet Nam.[4] The letter cited President Franklin Delano Roosevelt's statement that "use of such weapons has been outlawed by the general opinion of mankind."[5]

Similarly, Mink consistently called for an end to bombing in order to move forward with peace negotiations. In December of 1965, the chairman of the House Armed Services Committee (a Democrat) and former Republican presidential nominees Barry Goldwater and Richard Nixon advised President Johnson to expand the US bombing campaign to include Hanoi (the capital of the Democratic Republic of Vietnam [DRV]) and the nearby Haiphong area (a heavily populated industrial center and seaport). In response, Mink cosigned a letter, along with sixteen other Democratic House representatives, urging Johnson not to follow this advice. Initiated by Donald M. Fraser (D-Minnesota), Benjamin S. Rosenthal (D–New York), and Jonathan B. Bingham (D–New York), the letter attracted the support of Philip Burton (D-California), Mink's ally in the Young Democrats Clubs of America, as well as Edith Green (D-Oregon), Mink's fellow committee member on the House Committee on Education and Labor. Other signers included the earliest and most persistent critics of US policy in Viet Nam.[6] Their letter to the president stated, "We believe that such an extension would not bring an end to hostilities in Vietnam, but might lead to further escalations of an unpredictable character. Instead of saving lives, such a change in strategy might ultimately bring about vast increase in American casualties. In addition, the likelihood of massive civilian casualties in North Vietnamese cities would undoubtedly produce a world-wide reaction against the United States."[7]

Mink called for limiting violence by the United States and its allies to enable democratic governance. In March 1966, Republic of Viet Nam's premier, Nguyen Cao Ky, ordered the public execution via firing squad of a businessman accused of black market activities. Mink protested the barbarism and totalitarianism of the execution. In a March 15 statement in Congress, Mink criticized the "grave travesty on justice" that "has been perpetrated by the government of South Vietnam in the name of social and economic reform!"[8] She described the "senseless public execution" as "making a mockery of our whole system of justice."[9]

Mink emphasized the need for political reform in South Viet Nam again two months later. The proposed 1966 elections in South Viet Nam held the promise of a democratic state. Protesters in South Viet Nam, most notably Buddhists critical of religious persecution, also demanded the right to elect Parliament members. Given the stakes, Mink warned against potential violations against free elections, especially in light of comments by Premier Ky that "if the elections do not have the results desirable to the present regime, then the Directorate will fight!"[10] The threat of violence against undesirable electoral outcomes led Mink to argue for "the closest surveillance" possible.[11] Mink encouraged the president to "most seriously consider the proposal that either the United Nations or the International Control Commission [ICC] be called in to maintain a field surveillance of these elections." According to the 1954 Geneva Convention, the ICC was to supervise the ceasefire and the proposed national elections of 1956. Mink reminded the House and the president, "If our commitment truly is to freedom in Southeast Asia, then we have a solemn obligation to implement the conditions for that freedom."[12]

Due to the conditions of war, the parliamentary and presidential elections were postponed until 1967. Amidst charges of corruption, the election results confirmed the leadership of existing military leaders. Premier Ky became vice president, and General Nguyen Van Thieu, who had worked with Ky to orchestrate a coup of Diem in 1963, became president. They received approximately one-third of the votes, but the plurality was strong enough for an election that featured numerous candidates. Thieu would serve as president of the RVN until its downfall in 1975, and in exchange Ky became the primary behind-the-scenes military leader.

Ky, both as premier and as vice president, broadcast his desire to expand military activities. President Johnson and the US military advisors supported him, disregarding objections of congressional representatives like Mink. Beginning in 1966, the United States increased its military operations and expanded its bombing targets to Laos, Cambodia, and the demilitarized zone between North and South Viet Nam. The Ho Chi Minh Trail, which funneled people and supplies from the DRV to the NLF in the South, extended into these neighboring countries. The United States reported military successes but also admitted killing civilians in the North and the South. The incursions into Laos and Cambodia generated casualties among residents of those countries as well. The escalation of US military involvement led to separate announcements by the People's Republic of China and the Soviet Union that they would provide military and economic assistance to the North Vietnamese. In addition, the war drew increasing international criticism of the United States as Charles de Gaulle, president of France, called for US withdrawal. Even Pope Paul VI warned that "a settlement should be reached now . . . for (otherwise) it may have to be made later in the train of bitter slaughter and involve great loss."[13]

A Congressional Dove and a Presidential Hawk

Mink called for limits and conditions on US military and diplomatic support for the RVN. Given her loyalty to the Democratic Party and to soldiers in harm's way, Mink felt torn about her votes on funding authorizations. In addition, local Hawai'i interests were sometimes at odds with Mink's commitment to peace. The US military played a dominant role in the political, economic, and social life of the islands, as O'ahu was headquarters for the US military in the Pacific. Mink initially acceded to the White House claims but increasingly charted an independent political path.

In her first speech about Viet Nam in May 1965, Mink explained how she reluctantly decided to vote for $700 million in supplemental funds for the US military. President Johnson made the request as a vote of confidence, which led Mink to experience "a day that I shall long remember for the mental and emotional experience I endured."[14] Mink stated her "commitment to peace" and her belief that "peace can come to Viet Nam only through the conference table."[15] The president's public position was not unlike hers. He, too, criticized a policy of escalation and emphasized the need for negotiation in order to stabilize the political situation in Southeast Asia. Though they shared common goals, Mink expressed why she still held doubts:

> It is here at this point that I find myself in utter confusion. Without the facts and the full explanation of the strategy involved, which for obvious reasons cannot be revealed if the strategy is to work, I cannot disagree with the President purely on the assumption that my analysis is superior to his judgment.
>
> Had the President never stated that he was pursuing a course which he personally believed would permit the earliest possible convening of negotiations, I would have no choice but to vote against his actions thus far. But in the context of his avowed purposes, I believe that he is entitled to pursue his course with the support of the people of the state of Hawaii, as cast by my vote as one of its representatives.[16]

In essence, Mink supported the request for supplemental funding based on Johnson's words but with little evidence of how the US military was actually operating or planning. Mink cast her first vote on Viet Nam on the basis of faith in a Democratic president's commitment to a negotiated peace. Even so, Mink took pains to express her doubts and reiterate that a vote of confidence did not imply support for military escalation.

Mink voiced her critiques publicly in Congress, in the media, and increasingly at antiwar rallies. John and Wendy attended the largest protest to date, organized by the Students for a Democratic Society and held in Washington, DC, on April 17, 1965. There were approximately twenty thousand on hand, and the protest was clearly influenced by the civil rights movement. The antiwar rally leaders emphasized nonviolence, and the attendees sang the movement's anthem, "We Shall Overcome." Patsy did not attend, having left for Hawai'i the day before. However, she sent a statement to support a similar event, attracting much smaller numbers, at the Ala Moana Park in Hawai'i on July 4, 1965. Mink called for greater education among Americans so that they would be aware "of the grave implications that exist in the continued escalation of armed conflict in Vietnam."[17]

In addition to public speeches, Mink also privately communicated to President Johnson and his staff. In August 1965, Patsy contacted Larry

O'Brien, the special assistant to the president. Johnson cultivated relationships among Democratic congressional members by inviting them for special briefings. After Mink explained her position as a proponent of peace and her desire to gain some insight into the president's policies, O'Brien offered Mink a private briefing.[18] Eleven days later, Chester Cooper, the White House advisor for Asian affairs, met with Mink and suggested that she call for an end to the US bombing campaign and the beginning of negotiations in Geneva.[19] In John Mink's opinion, "Of course, the administration may be using her to sound out the public reaction and may abandon her if the reaction is bad."[20] Nevertheless, this meeting with the president's advisor encouraged Patsy to take a more vocal and pressing stance on the war.

One day later, she gave a rousing speech in Congress about the war. She expressed her conviction that the "President is earnestly doing everything within his power and resources to seek the peace in Vietnam."[21] At the same time, she asserted that "few are completely satisfied with the progress of our efforts."[22] Instead, Mink called for a stop to "this dialogue of war and more war preparations of blame and accusations" and argued that it was necessary, instead, to "begin in earnest our preparation for peace."[23] She requested that the United States send their best diplomats to Geneva to signal a desire for negotiation. She also demanded that the United States "promise now without reservations that the bombs shall cease to fall from the very instant that the negotiations begin."[24] Finally, she emphasized US responsibility for restitution: "Let us be prepared to match every military dollar that we have spent these past 11 years in Vietnam with a like dollar for peace, for the restoration of this war torn country, for its economic development, for education, for food and medical care for its desperately poor people."[25] Mink's vision of a Great Society for the United States extended to countries abroad.

Despite Mink's public appeal, which the White House privately encouraged, US involvement in Viet Nam accelerated. In addition to the bombing campaign, the United States introduced ground troops in March 1965, and the number of American soldiers assigned to Viet Nam escalated from 23,300 in 1964 to 184,300 in 1965; the numbers would continue to grow until 1968, the last year of Johnson's presidency, when the maximum number of 536,100 US troops in Viet Nam was reached.[26]

As Mink persisted in her antiwar statements, she learned that the president was becoming increasingly hostile towards her. In a hastily organized summit between Johnson and Ky held in February 1966, Hawaiʻi was chosen for the meeting site given its location roughly equidistant from Washington, DC, and Viet Nam.[27] Mink happened to be in Hawaiʻi at the time, hosting a business conference. She became part of the official welcoming party and as usual was featured in a photo with the president. However, he was less warm off camera. In the ride from the airport to the summit site, Johnson "was rather upset and sitting in the limousine with her asked curtly what her 'liberals' in Congress were up to."[28] The confrontation disturbed Patsy so much that she called her husband and debated whether to accept the invitation to fly back to Washington, DC, on the president's plane.

Johnson reprised the hostility at a White House briefing at the end of February 1966. According to John Mink, the president denied that he was a hawk, an advocate for war. However, he "stared at Patsy through the 1½ hour briefing," as he attacked "several eminent people who have testified before the Senate Foreign Relations Committee not in full accord with him."[29] As Patsy learned, Johnson often emotionally berated and intimidated his opposition. Johnson, "a tower of subdued rage," also "challenged those Congressmen there to repeal the resolution of Aug. '64," by which Congress gave the president authorization to proceed militarily in Southeast Asia.[30] An attempt to repeal the Gulf of Tonkin Resolution, led by Democrat Wayne Morse in the Senate, was easily defeated in early March 1966. Short of this step, Mink attempted to find political solutions beyond the Johnson presidency.

Seeking Solutions

Unmoored from the Democratic Party establishment leadership, Mink increasingly allied with more progressive members of Congress. Considered a dove, an advocate for peace, she became active in the Democratic Study Group (DSG). Founded in 1959, the DSG attracted 175 House members in the mid-1960s.[31] The group served as a progressive think tank within Congress, conducting research and promoting public policy. In addition, Mink also joined Members of Congress for Peace through Law (MCPL). This bipartisan study group, also founded in 1959, advocated progressive policies, such as disarmament and détente. Given official Democratic Party support for President Johnson, Mink explored alternative political paths.

Given Mink's abhorrence of violence, she worked with other legislators to propose a humanitarian response to the war. In late February 1967, Mink joined with twelve other congressional representatives, including one Republican, to propose a select committee to "investigate the plight of civilian casualties and refugees in South Vietnam."[32] The proposed Select Committee on Civilian Casualties and Refugees in South Vietnam would investigate the number of civilian refugees in South Viet Nam, the number of civilian war casualties resulting from military operations, and the availability of medical care facilities. It would have 120 days to make recommendations, including whether South Vietnamese civilian refugees or war casualties could enter the United States for medical care, as permanent residents, and as adoptees. And, the committee could recommend expenditures to provide adequate medical care in South Viet Nam. William F. Ryan (D–New York), a cosponsor of the bill, cited a "Senate Subcommittee to Investigate Problems Connected with Refugees and Escapees which stated that as of the end of 1965 there were nearly one million refugees in South Vietnam."[33] Although there "were no hard statistics available on civilian casualties," the "estimates show that since 1961 there were approximately 250,000 children killed in South Vietnam and another 750,000 injured."[34] As Ryan observed, "Even if these estimates are off by as much as two-thirds, the figure is truly appalling."[35] This humanitarian appeal, however, appeared to fall upon deaf years. The Senate would continue its committee on refugees and escapees, but the House would not create its own select committee.

In spring 1967, Mink had the opportunity to dialogue with international critics of the United States. She was an invited attendee of Pacem in Terris II, held in Geneva, Switzerland, in late May. The conference took its name, *pacem in terris* (peace on earth), and inspiration from Pope John XXIII's 1963 encyclical. The first Pacem in Terris held a conference in February 1965 in New York City.[36] A follow-up conference convened in Geneva, Switzerland, with sessions on Viet Nam, divided Germany, and the Middle East as conflicts intensified there during the spring of 1967. The US delegation included politicians, celebrities, and advocates for peace, including Martin Luther King Jr. Approximately four hundred people from eighty or more nations attended.[37] Despite the organizers' efforts, the Soviet representatives decided to pull out of the conference. Even with this critic of the United States voluntarily absent, Mink felt a sense of discomfort in hearing the barrage of anti-US criticism in relation to Viet Nam. She gave an impromptu speech, pointing out violence by both the United States and the Viet Cong. She also emphasized the constructive role that the international community could play in stopping the violence, particularly through institutions like the ICC and the UN. She concluded by emphasizing that "Vietnam offers the world an opportunity to come together in fierce determination to prevent a world war now before it is too late."[38]

Back in the United States, the presidential election season was emerging. Although the urgency of peace was always foremost among her thoughts, Mink at first acceded to endorsing Johnson for reelection as she initially did not see a viable alternative candidacy. However, when Robert F. Kennedy declared his presidential bid on March 16, 1968, she immediately joined his campaign. Kennedy entered the Senate the same year that Mink entered the House, and they had collaborated on political initiatives previously. Like Mink, Kennedy initially felt reluctant to disagree with Johnson, especially since his brother, John F. Kennedy, had escalated US involvement in Southeast Asia. A turning point for Robert Kennedy occurred after he held talks with the North Vietnamese and the NLF in Paris. Just over a month later, in March 1967, Kennedy proposed a three-point plan to end US involvement with the war in Southeast Asia. His plan, a more moderate version compared to the ideas proposed by the DRV and NLF, included a temporary end to bombing, as opposed to a unilateral end, in order to begin negotiations; a freezing of troop movements on both sides instead of withdrawal of US troops; and a democratically elected government in South Viet Nam that would allow the NLF participation as opposed to US recognition of the NLF and acknowledgment for the entire nation to determine its political destiny.[39] Kennedy's proposal was immediately dismissed by the Johnson administration, and his patriotism questioned. When Kennedy announced his presidential candidacy in March the following year, he was an outsider to the main leadership of the Democratic Party.

Patsy Mink's decision to support Kennedy, just a few days after his announcement, was a risky political decision. In January and February

1968, the Tet Offensive, a coordinated series of attacks on over one hundred cities and towns led by the NLF and the North Vietnamese army,
raised widespread doubts about US objectives in Southeast Asia. Even
so, John Mink observed that "very few congressmen have come out for
RFK. Patsy [was] one of only about 5 or 6. Much cowardice, especially
among those brought into the limelight by JFK. LBJ will try to destroy all
opposition. Already equating his opponent in Demo. Party to 'disloyal,'
'unpatriotic.'"[40] John described Patsy's decision as a possible "temporary
end of a glorious career for her."[41] Nevertheless, it was a "brutal decision"
made with a "clear conscience."[42] In contrast to Patsy's commitment to
Kennedy, House colleague Matsunaga and Senator Inouye pledged their
support for Johnson. But, Johnson announced on March 31, 1968, that he
would not seek, nor accept, the presidential nomination. The president
finally recognized the unpopularity of the war as well as of himself.

Following Johnson's announcement, Matsunaga, Inouye, and the
Hawai'i Democratic Party leadership switched their support to Hubert
Humphrey. Vice President Humphrey did not declare until April 27,
but he planned to continue pursuing Johnson's policies in Viet Nam.
Humphrey did not run in any of the primaries, which were only held
in thirteen states. Instead, he relied on attracting delegates from the
nonprimary states. In those locations, party leaders at the state level
tended to control votes in conventions and caucuses.

Another major contender for the 1968 Democratic primary was
Senator Eugene McCarthy (D-Minnesota). McCarthy originally voted
for the Gulf of Tonkin Resolution but became increasingly critical of
US policies. He was not a well-known national figure. In fact, McCarthy
initially lobbied Robert Kennedy to enter the presidential campaign.
McCarthy only entered himself as a peace candidate in November 1967
after Kennedy declined to do so. McCarthy's strong second-place finish in New Hampshire on March 12, 1968, behind Johnson, prior to his
withdrawal, led Kennedy to reconsider his decision. Over the next several months, McCarthy and Kennedy traded state primary wins.

Mink traveled to several states to campaign for Kennedy. One of his
biggest wins, the California primary, ended in tragedy. He was assassi-
nated in the early hours of June 5, after he gave his victory speech in Los
Angeles. Nineteen sixty-eight was a year of violence. Martin Luther King
Jr. was killed on April 4 in Memphis, shortly after he launched the Poor

People's Campaign. After his assassination, race riots broke out in more than one hundred cities across the United States. After Kennedy's death, the mourning was more sedate, yet still deeply felt. Just two months after marching in King's funeral procession in Atlanta, Patsy served as an honor guard for Kennedy's bier at St. Patrick's Cathedral in New York, along with Jacqueline Kennedy and civil rights leaders Ralph Abernathy and Andrew Young. Patsy also accompanied Kennedy's coffin on the eight-hour funeral train to Washington, DC, where he was laid to rest at Arlington Cemetery.

Originally scheduled to give commencement speeches in Hawai'i, Mink stayed on the East Coast for the funeral rites but telephoned to share her remarks. Speaking to graduates and their families at Kaimuki High School, Mink recalled the anguish that she experienced during both the Kennedy and King assassinations. She also reminded her audience to remain hopeful and dedicate themselves to pursuing their ideals. According to a newspaper article about the speech, "She asked how it could be right to go to war to liberate the poor of Asia sacrificing thousands of our own, and be unable to see the suffering in our own country. . . . The Hawaii Democrat said there is a desperate need for moral force in our lives, and she advised the graduates at this time of decision [to think] for themselves to make a sense of purpose their higher calling in life."[43]

In Hawai'i, Mink faced repercussions as the only major office holder who supported Kennedy. The state-level Democratic leadership denied her a position as delegate to the national convention in Chicago. In hindsight, Mink's absence might have been the best outcome. Antiwar protesters descended on Chicago to protest the Democratic National Convention, and violence erupted as the Chicago police, the US Army, the Illinois National Guard, and the Secret Service waged battle with activists.

Mink had a fight on her own hands in Hawai'i as she ran for reelection to the House. Neal Blaisdell, the Republican mayor of Honolulu, decided to enter the race. He called Patsy "a disgrace" and accused her of "being disloyal."[44] Some in the local Democratic establishment privately encouraged the Republican candidate. John Mink recalled that it was a "tough" campaign; "even the New York Times and Newsweek said Patsy would be defeated."[45] Though Blaisdell spent more than double on his campaign compared to Mink, she prevailed in the end, with almost double the votes.

Figure 3.1. Patsy and John (seen from the back) stand guard over Robert Kennedy's bier, with Ralph David Abernathy, Jacqueline Kennedy, and Andrew Young, at St. Patrick's Cathedral, New York City, June 8, 1968. Source: Library of Congress/ photographer unknown.

At the national level, the Democrats lost the presidency to Richard M. Nixon. The party also lost six seats in the Senate and five in the House. The Democrats still had the majority in both houses, but the gap was closing. One positive development regarding the war occurred, however—the United States and the Vietnamese finally agreed to negotiate. The United States, the RVN, the DRV, and the Provisional Revolutionary Government (PRG) that was formed by the NLF met in Paris in May of 1968. Initial discussions bogged down, though, like the war.

Race and War

When Richard Nixon campaigned for the presidency in 1968, he promised to bring law and order to US society. After his inauguration in 1969, Nixon announced a Vietnamization policy, one that withdrew US troops while training and funding South Vietnamese soldiers to fight the war. Mink was among the critics who argued that the president, despite his plans to withdraw US troops, actually prolonged and escalated the war. Without consulting or informing Congress, Nixon expanded bombing targets in Viet Nam, Laos, and Cambodia. He justified extending the war in order to guarantee the return of US POWs (prisoners of war) and other MIAs (missing in action). In response, congressmembers reasserted legislative authority over the declaration and funding of war to establish limits to executive power. Mink and others also expressed support for US POWs and MIAs, but indicated that their return would be hastened by the withdrawal of US troops and an end to the conflict in Southeast Asia.

Mink's critiques of the war increasingly focused on how the conflict fueled racism against Asian people. From 1969 to 1971, the US military and media covered the court proceedings against US soldiers for the 1968 massacre at My Lai. Following the Tet Offensive, a company of approximately 140 US soldiers entered what they believed to be a Viet Cong stronghold. By the day's end, the soldiers had killed more than five hundred villagers, including women, children, and the elderly. None of them resisted or shot at the soldiers. The US military covered up the story, before it was finally exposed almost twenty months later by reporter Seymour Hersch. He interviewed Ronald Haeberle, an army photographer assigned to Charlie Company. Haeberle wrote letters to military and government officials to expose the massacre, and he published the photographic evidence. Eventually, the US military charged over twenty men, including Lieutenant William Calley, with premeditated murder. Both the killings and the US public's reactions, however, raised disturbing questions regarding US policies in Viet Nam and American racial mindsets.

The Calley trial drew the most media attention. He was charged with murdering 109 individuals, including a two-year-old, by shooting them with a rifle.[46] He also ordered his platoon to kill everyone in the village. Court-martialed and found guilty of twenty-two murders by his peers of six military officers, Calley was sentenced to life imprisonment and hard labor on March 31, 1971. However, members of the US public and President Nixon criticized Calley's treatment as a form of political scapegoating. Jury members even received death threats and other forms of harassment. Nixon changed the sentence to house arrest and eventually pardoned Calley after three years.

The Calley case became a touchstone for debating the morality of the Viet Nam War. Soon after the exposure of the case, Mink called for an investigation of the My Lai massacre. In a letter to a military officer, who also expressed concern about the efforts to cover up the incident, Mink wrote,

> I agree fully with your concerns about a whitewash of the My Lai massacre. I am seeking a Presidential Commission to investigate this matter because I believe that as a nation we cannot allow this incident to be forgotten with the trial of only one man.
>
> There are all shades of opinion in the House. Some have spoken in a way that could suggest that the atrocities of the Viet Cong mitigate our own behavior. But this certainly does not represent the thinking of the whole Congress, as I know most members are as deeply shocked and horrified as you are.
>
> We cannot ever condone the murder of innocent women and children no matter how brutalizing war may be. If we do, as a nation we shall have lost our moral integrity to command the respect and honor of the world.[47]

Mink condemned Nixon for intervening in the Calley sentencing. She issued a public statement that emphasized the fairness of the judicial process and the necessity of prosecuting war crimes:

> How ever we feel about a specific decision by a court, the last hope for sanity in this country is our belief in our judiciary. It must not be subject to executive or legislative pressures. Least of all, by the President of the United States.
>
> . . . What the President should have told America is that Calley is not a scapegoat; that 59 other servicemen have already been tried and convicted of murder of unarmed prisoners or other defenseless Vietnamese civilians. The President should have pledged that America would not tolerate any violations of international law relating to the treatment of prisoners. The President should have remembered the 1,600 Americans who are being held by the enemy. The President should have reassured America that the rule of law prevails, and that through it justice is best served.[48]

Mink reminded President Nixon and the American public that their concerns about US POWs/MIAs should lead them to think more compassionately and fairly about Vietnamese civilians captured by US soldiers.

Mink underscored that racism explains why most Americans did not think of Vietnamese people as worthy of justice. In a speech given to the first national conference on Asian American studies, held in Los Angeles in April 1971, Mink connected the racism that led to the World War II incarceration of Japanese Americans with the My Lai Massacre. She noted that war against Japan justified mass detention, based on the "the belief that the 'inscrutable' Oriental could not be trusted. . . . The entire population of one national origin overnight became the enemy, stripped of property, rights of citizenship, human dignity and due process of law."[49] The Viet Nam War, in turn, reinforced these views of racial inferiority. In Mink's words, "All Vietnamese stooping in the rice fields are pictured as the enemy, sub-human without emotions and for whom life is less valuable than for us."[50]

Mink argued that Calley's defense rested upon the "Mere Gook Rule" (MGR). This informal US military code of conduct maintained "that the slaughter of women and children, our prisoners of war, was 'no big thing.'"[51] "The MGR says that life is less important, less valuable to an Oriental. Laws that protect other human beings do not apply to 'Gooks.' In a sense as William Greider of the Washington Post said before the verdict became known, the essence of the Calley case was to determine the validity of this rule."[52] Mink noted that even the indictment against Calley reflected the pervasiveness of the MGR outlook. He was charged with killing "Oriental" human beings. She pointed out, "The indictment made clear to me that the murder of 'Mere Gooks' was the issue, else why the special description of the victims as 'Oriental human beings'?"[53] The efforts to exonerate Calley validated the idea that the genocidal killing of Asian people, whom the United States was attempting to save from communism, was acceptable and justifiable.

In addition, Mink critiqued the racial implications of the Vietnamization policy. She described it as "a Madison Avenue soft-sell that this war can be won by us coaching the South Vietnam[ese] to do their own fighting and dying."[54] This coaching and substitution approach did not seek to end violence in Southeast Asia. Instead, the fighting and dying would be done by Asians, not Americans. Mink's racial critiques dovetailed with the emergence of an Asian American antiwar movement that condemned the racial mindset of most American policy makers as well as the US military culture on the battlegrounds.[55] In fact, these critiques of the Viet Nam War played a central role in the creation of an Asian American identity in the late 1960s, a pan-ethnic formation that proclaimed shared racial commonalities among people who traced their ancestry to diverse Asian countries and cultures.[56] The community activists who created and adopted the Asian American identity category primarily organized at the grassroots level, but they shared commonalities with Mink, who advocated in the national legislative arena.

Women's Antiwar Politics

By the beginning of 1972, Nixon and the hawks were on the defensive but still in control. The *New York Times* published the Pentagon Papers in June 1971. This secret study, prepared by the Department of Defense under Robert McNamara, examined the history of US involvement in Viet Nam through the Johnson administration. The papers "demonstrated, among other things, that the Johnson Administration had systematically lied, not only to the public but also to Congress, about a subject of transcendent national interest and significance."[57] The Pentagon Papers indicated that the true object of US policy in Southeast Asia was to contain China, not to promote democracy in South Viet Nam. The United States also systematically interfered in the internal affairs of Viet Nam and plotted to provoke North Viet Nam, before the Gulf of Tonkin incident. Even though the Pentagon Papers focused on events prior to his administration, Nixon attempted to block the publication. He also ordered the wiretapping of the psychiatrist of Daniel Ellsberg, the person who leaked the papers to the press. Nixon and his team wanted information regarding Ellsberg's mental state in order to discredit him. In 1972, Nixon and his supporters continued to resist efforts to set a firm date for troop withdrawal. Only 133,000 soldiers remained, but the US military continued to provide crucial air strike support. In fact, Nixon ordered the bombing of nonmilitary targets and the mining of Haiphong Harbor in spring of 1972. He also authorized the biggest bombing campaign yet over North Viet Nam during Christmas of that year.

Tired of the unending war, Mink allied with women to seek peace. She found a willing political partner in Bella Abzug.[58] A key activist with the organization Women Strike for Peace (WSP), Abzug entered Congress in 1971. Created in 1961, WSP was founded by women who self-identified and publicly proclaimed their roles as housewives and mothers. The organization fostered a grassroots political network among women to critique nuclear proliferation and global conflict. Prior to her election, Abzug, a lawyer and a labor rights activist, had lobbied members of Congress, including Mink, to end the war in Viet Nam. Once in office, Bella and Patsy became close friends, sometimes even wearing similar clothes and often sitting next to one another on the floor of the House of Representatives. They shared antiwar as well as feminist politics, and both were mothers of daughters.

Abzug and Mink proposed legislation to withdraw troops, end military funding by specific deadlines, and censure the president. In a January 18, 1972, speech, Mink contrasted Nixon's proclamation for "law and order" with his own behavior:

> Certainly the highest form of law in this country is the constitution, and the most important issue of order is war or peace.
>
> Yet we find the President of the United States in flagrant and admitted violation of the constitution. . . .
>
> By the adoption of the Mansfield Amendment in Public Law 92–156, the Congress made a decision that the Vietnam war should be ended at the earliest practicable date. The President was mandated to withdraw all our troops. . . .
>
> In his remarks on signing the bill the President stated flatly that he would ignore this provision of law. By so doing, he has usurped the constitutional power of Congress.[59]

This early attempt to censure the president only attracted thirteen other legislators, however.

Responding to the obstruction of the presidency and the impasse at the Paris peace talks, Mink and Abzug decided to travel to France to meet with representatives of the DRV and PRG. Journeys like these were organized on a regular basis by Women Strike for Peace. Cora Weiss, another key organizer for the group, facilitated the travels of US antiwar activists to North Viet Nam. Weiss believed in the power of citizen diplomacy, of the importance of political dialogue and friendship in bridging political divides. She had previously obtained the release of three American POWs and arranged the delivery of mail to POWs through the Committee of Liaison with Families of Servicemen Detained. Weiss met Mink at Pacem in Terris II and arranged the trip to Paris for Abzug and Mink. Amy Swerdlow, another WSP activist who became the organization's historian, was the third traveling companion in the group.[60]

Through Weiss's contacts, Abzug and Mink met with representatives of the DRV and PRG in April 1972. The US congresswomen sought out information to help solve the political impasse. They held long discussions with Madame Nguyen Thi Binh, foreign minister of the Provisional Revolutionary Government in the South. She was the only female leader to represent a major political interest at the Paris peace talks. One of the most visible Vietnamese women in the West for her role in fostering women's antiwar activism globally, Binh emphasized the connection that she had with Mink, Abzug, and Swerdlow as women and mothers. Despite these maternalist appeals, Binh, Mink, and Abzug also transcended traditional gender roles by being a head of state and congressional representatives.

In the end, Mink did not believe that the meetings generated any breakthroughs that could lead to peace. John Mink described both Patsy's excitement about this trip but also her pessimism. In his diary, he wrote,

> Patsy just called from New York, having landed a few minutes ago [from Paris]. . . . She is floating in euphoria. She spent a long time with the "plain" Mrs. Binh, and 2 hours with Xan Thuy, the North Vietnamese representative; also an hour with members of the U.S. negotiating team, who acted quite arrogant. . . . There appears to be little hope for a solution, however. There will be no negotiations on U.S.-POW's until the war is over. . . . Everyone is pessimistic about the future since the Paris negotiations were cut off by Nixon.[61]

Although the trip mainly confirmed the political impasse, Mink received highly critical media coverage for making the journey. John Mink observed that the press treatment of Patsy's trip "set off a heavy barrage

Figure 3.2. On a peace mission to Paris, Patsy Mink and Bella Abzug (D–New York) met with Madame Nguyen Thi Binh of the Provisional Revolutionary Government, April 21, 1972. Source: Library of Congress/photographer unknown.

of criticism, accusations, and denunciations by the papers, the radio, television, and worst of all, plain people. I can think of no other time, when one of her activities has aroused such reaction throughout such a spectrum of the public."[62] One constituent wrote to Mink, declaring that "until recently I have supported you, however grudgingly. . . . Your recent activities, however, have changed my mind."[63] Not only had Mink "trafficked with the enemy"; she also was accused of wasting "my tax money by your trip which I suspect was in part to allow you to shop in Paris."[64] As the correspondence indicates, the reaction to Mink's political journey was gendered. Her political goals, which were characterized as traitorous, were regarded as a cover for her "real" motivation of indulging in feminine consumption. Mink responded in a matter-of-fact tone: "I regret that you do not support an end of the war. I cannot change your views about that, and won't try. But, please be aware that many Congressmen and Senators have gone to Paris to discuss the prospects

In the Race Congresswoman Patsy Mink of Hawaii took this stack of petitions to the Capitol Friday to enter her name on Oregon's May 23 Presidential primary. It is the only one she will enter. (Statesman photo by John Ericksen)

Figure 3.3. Patsy reviews forms before filing her nomination papers as a candidate for US president in the Oregon primary, March 10, 1972. Source: USA Today Network/John Erickson photographer.

for Peace. I enclose two reports . . . which I hope you will read. Also, please be assured that I went at my own personal expense."[65]

Patsy responded to the political backlash about her trip, but she did not back off from her antiwar politics. In addition to running for re-election for the House of Representatives in 1972, she also agreed to campaign as a presidential candidate. A group of antiwar activists based in Eugene, Oregon, convinced Mink to do so. She always understood her limited campaign as a platform to end the war. She had committees only in Oregon and Hawai'i. Eventually, because of peculiarities of state election law, she appeared on the primary ballots in Wisconsin and Maryland as well.

Mink was not the only woman to run for the presidency in 1972. Shirley Chisholm also was a candidate.[66] The fact that both Mink and Chisholm, pioneering women of color in Congress, ran for the presidency in 1972 indicated how much the racial and gender social movements transformed US politics. Mink and Chisholm were allies, and the two of them agreed not to compete with one another.

Patsy campaigned vigorously in Oregon throughout the winter and spring of 1972. Her husband described one such campaign "swing. . . . They covered more than 1500 miles up and down the state, from Portland to Klamath Falls in one night, interrupted by a snowstorm in the Cascades, then back to Portland the next day."[67] Despite efforts like these, Patsy received "only 2% of the vote in Oregon—6400 votes."[68] As John observed, this was "an overwhelming defeat for the amount of time she spent there, for all of the optimism, which in the end was fantasy, that her supporters exuded."[69]

Patsy had to turn quickly from her disappointment with the presidential campaign to her local race. The Hawai'i Democratic leadership, with Johnson removed from the presidency, became increasingly critical of US policy in Southeast Asia. Inouye and Matsunaga as well as statewide and local Democrats began voicing their criticisms of Nixon's policy. Patsy's position, in other words, became more politically mainstream within the state. For the 1970 elections, the first time that the members of the House of Representatives were elected from districts rather than at large, Mink ran unopposed. In 1972, however, in light of her presidential campaign and trip to Paris, her own party put up a candidate against her. The Republicans also enlisted a female candidate, Diana Hansen.

The local media, which tended to ally with the GOP, fueled anti-Mink sentiment through editorials as well as misleading headlines. But in the end, Patsy won the election with 53 percent of the vote.

Legacies of War

On January 27, 1973, the Paris Peace Accord was signed by representatives of the United States, the Republic of Viet Nam, the Provisional Revolutionary Government, and the Democratic Republic of Viet Nam. By spring 1975, Viet Nam was reunified under communist leadership. The US war in Viet Nam had a profound impact on the peoples and governments in Southeast Asia and the United States.

Patsy Mink's political engagement against the war charted choppy waters of party politics. She challenged the eclipsing of Congress by the president on matters of war and peace, and she awakened attention to the racism that distorted morality in war. Mink was part of an initially very small contingent of doves in Congress, and her journey in opposition to the war was at times strategically challenging and personally risky. A staunch advocate for the social policies of her party's leader during her first two terms in Congress, she also was a critic of Johnson's war policy and the existential threat that war represented to a democratic government. Over time, her relationship to her party's president was defined by her opposition to his war. Her stance against his successor's conduct of the war grew to include stringent critiques of government secrecy, calls for greater accountability, and exposure of racialized disregard for Asian lives. Mink's antiwar work also engaged new allies, especially feminist antiwar advocates, and joined her in solidarity with emergent feminist political networks.

"YOU MUST BE A WOMEN'S LIBBER"

When my mother entered the national political scene in January 1965, our polity was on the brink of tectonic political change. As the first woman of color elected to Congress, my mother augured some of that change; her support for progressive causes helped advance it. But on my mother's first day in Congress, January 4, 1965, the brightest beacons of political change were not individuals but movements—not trailblazers who symbolized change but civil rights workers who made it happen. Lining Independence Avenue and the tunnels connecting the US Capitol to the House office buildings, Mississippi Freedom Democratic Party (MFDP) activists and their civil rights allies assembled in protest against the all-white Mississippi congressional delegation that had been elected in a whites-only political process.[1] Both a street-level demonstration and a parliamentary challenge, the MFDP mobilization to quash white democracy framed my first glimpse of official Washington. Support for the MFDP challenge and for voting rights across the nation determined my mother's first vote as a member of Congress.[2]

The MFDP's work was part of a propulsive struggle to democratize electoral processes. The MFDP shone a harsh light on the Democratic Party, pressuring it to become more accessible and more representative. Party reform would become an entering wedge for the full and equal electoral participation of people of color, young people, and women of all ages and races.

Following its 1968 convention fiasco, the Democratic Party committed to democratizing party governance. The party set up two commissions to devise mechanisms to promote those goals. My mother was tapped to serve on one of the commissions, the Rules Commission. Among the controversial changes promulgated by the Rules Commission was the promise that women would have parity with men on convention committees and in convention leadership.[3] In another step toward democratization, new rules also stipulated that people of color, young people, and women should be represented on state delegations "in reasonable relationship to their presence in the population."[4] State delegations that were not representative could be refused participation at the presidential nominating convention.

The inclusion of women in the Democratic Party's attempt to democratize marked a victory for feminists, who had been pressuring the party on women's issues since 1968, when women composed only 13 percent of the delegates to the presidential nominating convention. But even when the old boys were willing to let women in, they were not prepared to change their sexist and misogynist culture.

One of the more notorious examples of incorrigible sexism in the Democratic Party sizzled on the inside pages of the *Washington Post* and *New York Times* for a few days in the summer of 1970. In April, the Democratic National Committee (DNC) had invited my mother to testify about women's rights at a party conference on national priorities. Her testimony included an analysis of the multiple points of abject sex discrimination in policy and society, and a call to make women's rights an urgent priority. In rebuttal, one of the members of the party's National Priorities Committee, physician Edgar Berman, pontificated that "raging hormonal influences" disqualified women from leadership positions, especially the presidency.

Some weeks later, when the conference transcript became available, my mother sent the transcript to Hubert Humphrey, Berman's sponsor in Democratic Party officialdom. Her cover letter denounced the doctor's claims and demanded his ouster from the National Priorities Committee. Upon learning of my mother's demand, Berman proclaimed that the angry tone of her protest was proof of her own "raging hormonal imbalance."[5]

I described the ensuing brouhaha in some detail in phone calls and letters to my father, who was in Taiwan on an extended work project.[6] My father, who was reading Kate Millet's new book, *Sexual Politics*, while apart from his feminist wife and daughter, seemed to take the events I described in stride. He did worry, though, that my mother's insistence that the DNC remove Berman would attract another outpouring of hate mail, such as that which had followed her testimony against Supreme Court nominee G. Harrold Carswell a few months earlier.

In my letters, I expressed frustration that the male party establishment did not openly condemn or criticize Berman, even as leagues of women, including women physicians, took him to task. Still, the Democratic Party did eventually pressure Berman to resign his position in the DNC on July 31, 1970. Berman's departure did not signal his change of heart: on his way out the door he lambasted Mom and "women's lib." But it did augur an improved outlook for women in the Democratic Party. In the run-up to the presidential contest between George McGovern and Richard Nixon in 1972, the party pledged support for women's full incorporation into the party's decision-making apparatus. Yet official pronouncements did not automatically align with actual party practices. My mother continued to struggle against toxic behaviors and exclusions. Even I struggled with frustrations arising from the practice of simply adding in women without simultaneously rooting out sexism.

Early in the fall of 1971, soon after I began my sophomore year in college, the DNC called to invite me to serve on the Arrangements Committee for the 1972 presidential nominating convention. The national party handpicked committee members, usually a mix of big donors, party regulars, and elites from the state and city where the convention would be held. The committee was sort of an event-planning group, handling all manner of convention-related details such as hotel assignments for state delegations and candidates, transportation options, and extracurricular activities—pretty mundane stuff, though disputes over donor access and protest venues could send sparks flying.

My reaction to the DNC's invitation at the time was that the party was cheating by inviting me; I was a shortcut to diversity. I satisfied all demographic categories targeted for enhanced representation in the party—female, of color, and, at age nineteen, young. I also probably seemed like a safe bet—as the ostensibly well-behaved child of a congressmember.

An activist in my own right, I accepted the invitation to serve as the token young female of color on the Arrangements Committee. Because the committee charge included decisions about on-site facilities and amenities, some of our meetings took us to the planned location of the 1972 convention—Miami Beach, Florida. Upon arrival in Miami Beach for the first meeting, I was rudely awakened to the contradiction between the party's new democratic mission and its habitual business practices.

I was taken from the airport to the Playboy Hotel, where, to my shock and confusion, the DNC had booked rooms for Arrangements Committee members, including nineteen-year-old me. Although I was not a typical Playboy client, the Playboy staff did not miss a beat: upon check-in, I was assigned my own personal Playboy bunny, dressed in traditional skimpy costume with bunny ears and cottontail. She escorted me to my room, brought me chocolates and a flower, then turned down my bed. Later, she showed me to the hotel bar, where I joined other committee members, mostly men, as they ogled the many bunnies who floated around the lounge delivering cocktails. When I wondered out loud how the party thought it was advancing gender equality by patronizing a hotel whose essence was the sexual objectification of women, one puffy white man chortled, "You must be a women's libber." When I commented that being assigned my own Playboy bunny did not make me feel equal or welcome, patronizing snickers put me down.

The Arrangements Committee experience exposed me to sexist everyday practices inside the national Democratic Party, even during the heyday of party democratization. At the same time, my mother battled more serious misogyny in her own state party, as the Hawai'i Democratic Party was one of a handful of state parties that actively resisted gender parity.[7] The Hawai'i state party establishment was so retrograde, in fact, that it threatened to boycott the Miami Beach convention altogether to protest the new democratizing rules.[8]

As part of the democratization process inside the Democratic Party, more and more states were linking presidential preference contests with delegate selection through primaries or caucuses. Both processes diminished the rule of party bosses by leaving candidate choice to voters. The Hawaii Democratic Party clung to procedures that guarded boss power, following the least participatory route of candidate and delegate selection—the state convention.[9]

Choreographed by party elites, the Hawai'i delegate-selection process yielded an overwhelmingly male delegate slate: of the twenty delegates the Hawaii party slated for the Miami Beach convention, only four were women. One of those women—my mother, a sitting member of Congress—was given only one-half of a delegate vote. The half-vote designation deliberately belittled the highest-ranking Democratic woman in the state.[10] The disdain was familiar, as the party had denied her a delegate spot altogether in 1968.[11] As in 1968, punishment meted out in presidential delegate selection prefigured a broader swipe at my mother's very political existence: in 1968, some state party bosses reputedly went on to encourage a Republican challenge to her reelection to the US House; in 1972, bosses encouraged a primary challenge against her.

The governor's son, a political operative, explained to the DNC's Credentials Committee his plan to kneecap my mother:

> Because I am not happy with the way Patsy has been conducting herself as a person, as a Democrat, and as my Representative in Congress, I personally

initiated and led the move to have her elected but only as a one-half vote delegate. Having concluded that the way to do this was to reduce her vote totals in the 20th and 24th districts, I personally contacted various delegates from those districts and asked them not to vote for her. It may (but shouldn't) come as a surprise to Patsy, but I found the delegates very receptive to my request.[12]

My mother did not appeal her half-delegate designation to the DNC. But she did support and advise the Hawai'i Women's Political Caucus when it lodged a formal protest against the underrepresentation of women on the state's delegation.[13] The DNC Credentials Committee sent an investigator to Hawai'i to assess the situation. His Finding of Fact, delivered in late June 1972, began, "My over-all finding is that . . . the Democratic Party in Hawaii ha[s] . . . [a] notably inadequate understanding of what the Democratic National Committee has prescribed with respect to women's rights."[14]

Proving the investigator's point, the state party refused to name a gender-balanced team as its representatives to the Credentials Committee, sending two men and no women. When the DNC began preconvention deliberations, Hawai'i was refused participation across the board because of this masculine skew. The Hawai'i party responded by denouncing the gender-balance rule, but ultimately removed a man and added a woman to its Credentials Committee appointments, thus recovering a place in preconvention deliberations.[15]

As for the delegation challenge: it was killed off by tactical maneuvers at the national level, in the Credentials Committee. Remarkably, although Hawai'i had elected the first woman of color to Congress, the Hawai'i political establishment joined Alabama, Florida, and South Carolina to vanquish feminist complaints about gender imbalance in their delegations.[16]

If the politics of representation inside the Democratic Party disappointed many feminists, so did the politics of the party platform. In what was widely received by feminists as a betrayal, McGovern—on the eve of his presidential nomination—refused to support adding reproductive rights to the party platform and directed his delegates to follow his lead. Just six months before *Roe v. Wade* would be decided, McGovern's campaign believed that any mention of abortion rights would be fodder for Republicans. Other disappointments included rejection of the gay rights plank, as well as of the Poor People's Platform call for a sixty-five-hundred-dollar guaranteed adequate income.

The 1972 Democratic National Convention was the end point of the first national mobilization of feminists in electoral politics. Feminist wins were spotty, but feminists did accomplish enhanced visibility, both with increases in women's representation and with the presentation of coherently argued feminist positions on such issues as reproductive choice. Equally important, on the way to the Miami Convention, electorally minded feminists built what would become a lasting institution to promote the candidacies of women for public office—the National Women's Political Caucus (NWPC), founded in the summer of 1971. Putting the Democratic Party on notice about the need for gender parity at nominating conventions was the NWPC's first feat.[17]

Feminists also engendered the candidacies for president of two Democratic women. Hoping to normalize female aspiration to and service in high office, my mother accepted the invitation of antiwar Democrats in Oregon to wage a campaign in the Oregon presidential primary.[18] Seeking to coalesce the forces that eventually would become the Democratic base, Shirley Chisholm entered the presidential race in January 1972 and went on to campaign in fourteen states. My family spent many weekends in Oregon between September 1971 and the Oregon primary in May 1972, but my mother came up short. Shirley Chisholm's wider candidacy registered more successfully with some electorates, securing for Chisholm 151.25 delegate votes at the national convention.[19]

More women than ever before participated in Democratic Party proceedings in 1972, and some women reached higher levels than ever before. But women's issues and feminist agendas remained on the sidelines. In contrast, feminists had a pretty good year making policy in the Democrat-controlled Congress. Women in Congress were still very few in 1972, feminists even fewer. My mother no longer was the sole woman of color in Congress—Shirley Chisholm had joined her in 1969—but, still, there were only two. Bella Abzug had entered Congress in 1971, raising the profile of feminist advocacy within the hallowed halls. By 1972, though still struggling against the odds of low numbers, a half-dozen feminist activists in Congress successfully pressed for legislative innovations to give women legal tools to deploy on behalf of their own equality. Feminist advocacy inside and outside government secured results in March 1972, when the Equal Rights

Amendment passed Congress and advanced to the states for ratification. That same month, the Equal Employment Opportunity Act of 1972 became law, strengthening remedies available to the EEOC by giving it litigation authority, and also extending the reach of Title VII to include employees of educational institutions and the federal government. Then, on June 23, 1972, Title IX, shepherded through Congress by my mother and her colleague Edith Green, became law—and with it the possibility of gender equity at all levels and in all spheres of education.

4

A Feminist Legislator

When Patsy Mink joined the 89th Congress in 1965, she became one of thirteen female legislators, eleven in the House of Representatives and two in the Senate. By the time she left in 1977, female members in the House increased to nineteen, including four African Americans, but the number of senators declined to zero. Collectively, these women constituted a tiny percentage of the overall Congress, growing from 2.4 to 3.6 percent. They also differed amongst each other in terms of political beliefs, priorities, and party affiliations. Nevertheless, Mink worked with almost all of her female legislative colleagues, advocates in the growing feminist movement, and male allies in and out of Congress to pass bills to rectify or at least bring public attention to gender discrimination. Mink introduced childcare legislation, cosponsored and defended Title IX, argued for federal funding to support women's centers, feminist studies, and nonsexist curricula, demanded equitable economic rights for women, and called for women's political leadership in local, national, and international arenas. Mink collaborated with her congressional colleagues and activist allies to usher in a sea change in terms of gender policies and attitudes. Like all political revolutions, the feminist transformations of the late 1960s through the mid-1970s were incomplete and met with great resistance. Nevertheless, Mink's political leadership and collective approach deserve recognition. An analysis of her strategies and achievements reveals how an Asian American woman from Hawai'i fundamentally shaped feminist politics during the so-called second wave.

More recent scholarship of feminism challenges the schematic narrative of the history of feminism in the United States. The designation of second-wave feminism captures a range of political approaches and activist energies that emerged in the 1960s and 1970s that identified and challenged various forms of sexism and patriarchy. Within this period, different strands of feminisms describe divergent political approaches. Liberal feminists focused on obtaining equal opportunities as men, particularly in the economic and political realms. Radical feminists or women's liberation activists emphasized that the personal is political, that power and inequality shape all realms of life, including the division of household labor, sexual and gender norms, reproductive rights, and so on. They sought to transform social hierarchies, not just give women equal access to the existing society. Because both liberal and radical feminists primarily centered the experiences and involvement of white, middle-class, straight women, additional schools of feminism emerged. Lesbian feminists criticized heterosexuality as a compulsory form of male patriarchy.[1] Socialist feminists considered women's oppression as foundational to capitalist exploitation.[2] African American, Puerto Rican, Chicana/Latina, Native, and Asian American women formulated their own analysis of gender discrimination as intersecting with racial, imperial, and class oppressions.[3] This chronology and categorization of feminisms raise questions as to how to understand Patsy Mink, a woman-of-color feminist legislator who demanded both equal access and social transformation. She argued for feminist policies at the national legislative level in collaboration with grassroots, oppositional women's activism.[4]

Instead of the tendency to schematically divide feminism, scholars trace multiple origins and evolutions of women's activism that reflect the diverse identities, experiences, and political priorities of historical actors.[5] After all, activists tend to move between and combine multiple feminist approaches over an expanded period of time.[6] Mink's feminist legislative activism demonstrates this ability to adopt and utilize diverse political tools and approaches. In fact, she served as a "bridge" in two significant ways. She worked in tandem with grassroots advocates to effect legislative change.[7] Like Shirley Chisholm, Mink also "bridged" so-called liberal forms of feminism, with her focus on legislative change and equal opportunity, and feminism, with her call for intersectional political solutions that supported working and poor women, including women of color.[8] In other words, "liberal" approaches to political change also fueled transformative results that benefited women of diverse backgrounds. Mink's efforts to change the gendered political culture of Congress and enact intersectional feminist legislation illustrate these two forms of "bridge feminisms": collaboration between the grassroots and electoral politics as well as crossover among liberal, labor, and women-of-color feminisms.

Figure 4.1. En route to the Capitol from her office in the Cannon House Office Building, ca 1969. Courtesy of Gwendolyn Mink via Library of Congress.

Transforming Capitol Hill

Mink's very presence in Congress depended upon and further accelerated a change in the gendered nature of political culture. In comparison with her 1959 run for the US Congress, when Mink lost to Daniel

Inouye, her subsequent elections demonstrated her ability to persuade voters in Hawaiʻi that a male politician was not automatically a better representative for their state. Once Mink arrived in Congress, her political convictions helped to shift the way Congress and political parties operated. In fact, her double minority status as an Asian American and a woman provided a platform from which to reconsider the role of women in politics.

In early February 1967, near the beginning of her second term in the House of Representatives, Patsy Mink and two other congresswomen decided to stage a protest. As female legislators, they sought access to the House health club. Their ability to utilize the facilities, which included a "$500,000 20-by-60 foot swimming pool, heated to 80 degrees," was decidedly separate and unequal.[9] The health club granted women access only on Monday, Tuesday, and Friday, early in the morning from 7:30 to 9:00 a.m.[10] The limited times made it difficult for the female legislators to prepare for early-morning commitments. Aside from these designated hours, male members had the run of the facilities. The operators of the health club argued that women could not share the gym for two reasons: no separate changing rooms for women existed, and some male members of the House preferred to swim in the nude. To point out this disparity of treatment, Mink, Charlotte Reid (R-Illinois), and Catherine May (R-Washington) decided to respond to an advertisement for a late-afternoon calisthenics class that was sent to all members of the House. Bringing with them their exercise clothes and a female reporter, they demanded access to the gym and the class. The flustered staff called the director, who in turn responded that the course was for "members only," before "realizing his mistake."[11] The female congresswomen were in fact members of the House. Mink and her colleagues decided that they had made their point, and various newspapers around the country featured the story, often with humorous headlines such as "Gals Muscle In on House Gym" or "Patsy Seeking to Exercise Woman's Right to Exercise."[12] The committee that oversaw the operations of the health club offered to negotiate the terms of access by giving women two more hours every Monday to swim. However, Mink and others wanted full and equal access to facilities for all members of Congress, regardless of gender.

This episode illuminated how gender shaped the everyday interactions of Washington politics. As one newspaper article reported, among

Figure 4.2. Three congresswomen challenge the "men only" meaning of the "Members Only" sign at the entrance to the US House gym. *Left to right*: Charlotte Reid (R-Illinois), Patsy Mink, and Catherine May (R-Washington), February 6, 1967. Source: Library of Congress/US House photo.

the 424 male members of the 1967 Congress, many believed that "a woman's place . . . is in the home, not the House."[13] The physical infrastructure of the Congress, a male bastion, required alteration in order to create bathroom facilities for female members. Along with these building reconstruction projects, male legislators also had to adjust their interactions and attitudes towards their female colleagues. Edith Green (D-Oregon), a senior politician who served in Congress from 1955 to 1974, once "strolled into a huddle of congressmen who were deep in an animated discussion of current issues. Immediately, the conversation trailed off into a succession of polite compliments on how lovely she looked and how nicely she was dressed."[14] Rather than accept these remarks as expressions of gentlemanly gallantry, Green "grabbed the coat sleeve of one man and declared with elaborate sweetness: 'Ah, the weave is superb, the color sublime, and the match of the tie is exquisite.'"[15] Her mockery of their gendered performance pointed out how male members of Congress trivialized the intellect and political interests of female colleagues.

Described by Senator Mark Hatfield, a fellow Oregonian, as "the most powerful woman ever to serve in Congress," Green did not consider herself "a member of the so-called 'women's lib' movement."[16] Born in 1910, Green was at least one, if not two, generations removed from the women who became politically active in the US women's liberation movement, the so-called radical feminists, in the late 1960s and early 1970s. Green also opposed the "idea of a Women's Caucus for political pressure" as well as "quotas" for redressing gender discrimination.[17] In contrast, Green's colleagues, such as Bella Abzug, Shirley Chisholm, and Mink, collaborated with Gloria Steinem of *Ms.* magazine, Dorothy Height of the Council of Negro Women, and Fannie Lou Hamer of the Mississippi Freedom Democratic Party to form the National Women's Political Caucus (NWPC). Created in 1971, the NWPC served as the "only national organization dedicated exclusively to increasing women's participation in all areas of political and public life."[18] Despite holding the women's movement at arm's length, Green spearheaded some of the most important feminist legislation of this era, including the 1963 Equal Pay Act and Title IX. However, she also opposed the third pillar of feminist equality legislation, the inclusion of a ban on sex discrimination in employment in the 1964 Civil Rights Act.

Although Mink and her colleagues described the gym protest as a "gag with purpose," Mink took seriously her efforts for women's rights. In 1970, she called to remove Edgar F. Berman from the Democratic Policy Council's Committee on National Priorities (CNP). She also opposed the confirmation of G. Harrold Carswell for the Supreme Court.[19] In both instances, she emphasized their obstruction of women's rights as proof of their lack of fitness for these positions.

Mink's criticisms of Berman emerged as she testified before the CNP in April 30, 1970. In her speech, she emphasized themes that would recur in her gender advocacy: labor, education, and political engagement. Speaking to critics who believed "a woman's place is in the home," Mink emphasized that "42% of all adult women are working either by choice or out of necessity."[20] However, these women face the glass ceiling, earn less than men, and are still expected to assume the primary responsibilities of childcare. Mink also pointed out that these attitudes regarding women's assumed inferiority and economic dependence on men needed to be addressed through educational institutions. As she stated, "There are many fronts on which this battle must be fought. For instance, we must eliminate discrimination against women in our universities, which often impose quotas limiting admissions of women students and offer more scholarships to men than women. . . . In 1968 there were 4.5 million men entering colleges as freshmen compared to only 3 million women. . . . Women are systematically deprived of the educational tools they need for advancement. We must end this institutionalized deprivation."[21]

Mink further underscored that these inequalities existed not only due to men but due to women as well. This was a theme that she repeated in various speeches, as in these remarks from 1970: "Ironically many women themselves seem to share the view that women are not qualified for high office. . . . The attitudes of inferiority and guilt that have been inflicted on women have penetrated so deeply that many women themselves are convinced that they are second-class citizens."[22] Mink argued that "our nation can only benefit if we lift this depressing attitude from the minds of our citizens and give them the freedom and equality to participate fully in our democratic society."[23]

As Mink argued for the importance of giving "the cause of women's rights the highest priority" for the Democratic Party, Berman responded by pointing out women's inherent biological deficiencies. A member of the Committee on National Priorities, a close friend of Hubert Humphrey, and a medical doctor, Berman argued that women experienced "certain biological conditions that may be lunar, may be puberty, during pregnancy, and menopause."[24] He went on to point out that "in one of these phases you wouldn't—if you had an investment in a bank, you wouldn't want the president of your bank making a loan under these raging hormonal influences."[25] Berman also hypothesized, "Suppose we had a President in the White House, a menopausal woman President, who had to make the decision of the Bay of Pigs, which of course was a bad one, or the Russian contretemps with Cuba at the time."[26] In his opinion, "Anything can happen, knowing women, psychologically during this period, or during their lunar problem. Anything can happen from going up and eating the paint off the chairs."[27] Despite Mink's critiques of Berman's comments that reduced women's capabilities to their "raging hormones," he ended the committee meeting by joking with fellow male members of the priority council about female protesters, stating, "There were these five husky women in the back carrying placards ... As we left I said to Edward Bennett Williams, (a colleague on the commission), 'Would you want your brother to marry one of them?'"[28] A newspaper account of the interactions reported that Mr. Williams and chairman Joe Califano responded by laughing. Berman's comments on the appearance and lack of attractiveness of female protesters echoed commonly circulated critiques of women activists. For Berman and his male colleagues, the value of a woman lay in her physical attractiveness and ability to secure a marriage partner.

In response, Mink decided to take the situation into her own hands. She wrote to former vice president Humphrey with a copy of the hearing transcript, asking for his support to seek the resignation or ouster of Berman. She argued that "I am certain you will be appalled ... at Dr. Berman's disgusting performance in which he displayed the basest sort of prejudice against women, characterizing us as mentally incapable to govern, let along aspire to equality, because we are physiologically inferior."[29] Humphrey had worked closely with Berman during the 1968 presidential campaign and declined to intervene. Instead, he forwarded her correspondence to Berman so that the two could resolve their differences. Berman took the opportunity to insult Mink again, describing her letter as "emotionally charged" and "humorless"; he expressed mock sympathy for her "emotional outburst," since "women in your position are subject to more stress than they can possibly bear."[30] Berman refused to resign from the CNP. However, after their debate became public and newspapers reported on the conflict, condemnation of Berman created political pressure on the Democratic leadership. Eventually, Califano, cochair of the committee, suggested that Berman should step down.[31] Califano, who reportedly laughed at Berman's joke about the unattractiveness and unmarriageability of female protesters, publicly stated that "even if he (Dr. Berman) considers his comments as a laughing matter, I believe that they have gone far beyond the bounds of propriety and are an affront to the concept of equal opportunity and human dignity for the women of our nation."[32] Califano left the decision to Berman, and the physician resigned two days later.

Berman's departure reflected a collective achievement by Mink and the growing feminist movement. The *Honolulu Star-Bulletin* reported his resignation with the headline "Patsy Mink Wins Battle with Doctor over Hormones."[33] The media headlines and coverage tended to frame critiques of sexism as jokes. But Mink took seriously the need to remove from political leadership people whose views she regarded as inappropriate. As she expressed, Berman "was entitled to his opinion as an individual, but not as a representative of Democrats."[34] Just as importantly, a shift in public opinion motivated letter writers, many of them women, to condemn sexist remarks previously tolerated and enjoyed by an old boys' network. Mink's voice, in conjunction with many others, forced the Democratic Party leadership to publicly distance themselves from Berman, despite their personal connections to him, and declare support for women's rights.

A few months before the Berman controversy, Mink played a similar role in questioning the candidacy of G. Harrold Carswell for the Supreme Court. Nominated by President Nixon, Carswell faced scrutiny for a variety of issues, including a 1948 campaign speech he made in support of racial segregation and white supremacy while running for office in Georgia.[35] Carswell repudiated the views of his younger self as "abhorrent to my personal philosophy" and pointed to "his personal life," "six years as a United States attorney and 11 years on the federal bench," as proof that he could not "harbor racist sentiments or the insulting suggestion of racial superiority."[36] However, Carswell's membership at a segregated golf club, discovered after his statement, subsequently raised additional questions regarding his racial beliefs.

Mink was skeptical of Carswell's too-convenient, self-declared rehabilitation from racism but focused her critique on his recent role adjudicating sex/gender discrimination in employment. In 1966, Martin Marietta Corporation refused to admit Ida Phillips for an employment training program on the grounds that she had preschool-aged children, although the company selected men with similarly aged children.[37] Phillips filed a complaint with the Equal Employment Opportunity Commission (EEOC), which found the company in violation of Title VII of the 1964 Civil Rights Act. The law prohibited employment discrimination based on sex, as well as on race, color, religion, and national origin. Some historians suggest that opponents of the antidiscrimination law schemed to add "sex" to the banned categories of employment discrimination in order to undermine prospects for passage of the act. Others argue that Martha Griffiths (D-Michigan), who sponsored the Equal Rights Amendment (ERA) bill that passed Congress in 1972, purposefully and carefully planned the inclusion of this category in Title VII.[38] Once "sex" was added, Title VII served as one of the main avenues for women to contest employment discrimination against them. Following a favorable outcome of her EEOC complaint, Ida Phillips brought a class action suit against the Martin Marietta Corporation. The district court in Orlando, Florida, decided that the company had not violated Title VII. Phillips's treatment did not stem from one cause. She "was not refused employment because she was a woman nor because she had pre-school children. Instead, 'it is the coalescence of these two elements that denied her the position.'"[39] The Fifth Circuit Court of Appeals sustained the lower court. The chief judge requested a rehearing, but Carswell, who served on the three-judge panel for the court of appeals, voted to deny one.

Mink was the first person to testify against Carswell before the Senate Judiciary Committee, where she shared her views that "his appointment constitutes an affront to the women of America."[40] This was the first time sexism was proffered as grounds for opposing a Supreme Court

Figure 4.3. Mink testifying at Senate confirmation hearings against Supreme Court nominee G. Harrold Carswell, January 29, 1970. Source: Library of Congress/photographer unknown.

nominee.[41] Mink condemned Carswell's vote to silence the Phillips case, arguing that he "demonstrated a total lack of understanding of the concept of equality and . . . represented a vote against the right of women to be treated equally and fairly under the law."[42] She reminded the Senate committee that four million working mothers in this country have children under the age of six years. The decision of this Court which Judge Carswell sustained in effect placed all of these women outside the protection of the laws of this land. The decision stated that if another criterion of employment is added to that of the sex of the person, then it was no longer a discrimination based on sex. It ruled that Ida Phillips was not refused employment because she was a woman, but because she was a woman with pre-school age children.[43]

In critiquing Carswell's decision in the Phillips case, Mink foreshadowed what would be termed "intersectional" feminist thinking twenty years later. Rebuking Carswell, Mink emphasized the need to understand sex discrimination as both general and specific, sometimes affecting women in certain gendered life circumstances, sometimes affecting women on the basis of simultaneous class or race inequalities, and only sometimes affecting all women in the same way. In the Phillips case, Mink insisted that discrimination against mothers was sex-based discrimination and that the failure to recognize this compounded inequality.

Even another male judge recognized the implications of a narrow understanding of sex discrimination. In his dissent, Judge Brown offered the opinion that "if 'sex plus' stands, the Civil Rights Act is dead. . . . Free to add non-sex factors, the rankest sort of discrimination against women can be worked by employers. This could include, for example, all sorts of physical characteristics such as minimum weight, shoulder width, biceps measurements, etc. . . . without putting on the employer the burden of proving 'business justification' for such distinctions."[44] In essence, the appeals court "gave sanction to this employer's prejudices that mothers with young children are unreliable and unfit for employment."[45] Mink's attention to the connections between womanhood and motherhood also extended to race. As she stated, "Male supremacy, like white supremacy, is equally repugnant to those who really believe in equality."[46]

The hearings and deliberations dragged on for months. The opposition to Carswell included the National Organization for Women (NOW) and the Japanese American Citizens League. The collective pressure eventually led Republican supporters, including Hiram Fong, to vote against the nomination. Nixon persisted in his support of Carswell.

Nevertheless, his administration issued a statement calling for the Supreme Court to hear Ida Phillips's claim. Using a racial analogy, the government acknowledged that the corporation's practice and the lower court's ruling

> could promote job discrimination based on race, color, religion or national origin and "comprehensively impeded the government's efforts to insure equality of employment opportunities for all residents of the United States.
>
> "A practice of refusing to hire Negroes with preschool children while hiring whites with such children would apparently come within the rationale of the decision," the government said.
>
> Allowing the lower court decisions to stand "will cause unwarranted hardship to families in which the mother is the only available breadwinner."[47]

Mink regarded herself as a civil rights advocate for women, a decided minority in Congress but a majority of the US population. However, Mink, like Edith Green, initially declined to embrace the term "women's liberation."[48] While younger than Green, Mink was generally older than the feminist movement activists referred to by the term. She came of age following World War II, not in the 1960s. She expressed concern at the media representation of the "women's lib" movement, which "generalize public concern for women's rights by putting it all into our basket" and usually in a pejorative fashion.[49] She also described some activists as engaging in "absurd antics," although she herself engaged in protest activities. For Mink, the most valuable aspect of the women's movement stemmed from its consciousness-raising impact on other women; the movement represented "an educational effort particularly directed at women to make them better aware of the problems that other women are facing and thereby enlist their support in seeking correction."[50] Given their demographic majority, women held the potential to transform their minority political status. For Mink, women claiming political voice and building solidarity represented a natural and expected expansion of their social responsibilities and an expected civic duty in a democratic society.

Legislating Feminism

A year after Mink's successful protests against Berman and Carswell, she outlined three main political approaches to overturning gender discrimination in the legal system. In speeches and in a published law review article, Mink argued that "studies and discussions have evolved three general approaches for combating discrimination based on sex: 1) adoption of an equal rights amendment to the United States Constitution, 2) judicial expansion of the equal protection clause under the fifth and fourteenth amendments and 3) passage of federal and state legislation to prohibit overt discrimination and to eliminate situations which are discriminatory in effect."[51]

Not surprisingly, Mink supported the ERA, which stated that "equality of rights under the law shall not be denied or abridged by the United States or by any State on account of sex."[52] Introduced in each congressional session since 1923, the ERA drew more attention in 1970, when it finally passed the House but not the Senate. Attracting support from certain sectors of the women's movement, the proposed amendment successfully passed both houses in 1972. However, the ERA depended upon achieving ratification by three-quarters of the states, which did not occur within the mandated time limit. Also, the ERA would not be self-executing; its power would depend on interpretation by the Supreme Court. Although Mink supported the amendment, she also expressed concerns that it would not adequately or automatically resolve or end sex/gender discrimination. In terms of option two, Mink pointed out the repeated failure of the courts to "apply the existing equal protection clause of the Constitution to women."[53] The reluctance of the courts led Mink to find more promise in the third route: legislating equality, which fell into her purview as a congresswoman.

From the mid-1960s through the late 1970s, Mink played a crucial role in drafting, introducing, advocating, and promoting the implementation of key feminist legislation in relation to women's economic rights, childcare, and education. Although not always successful and not always fully recognized for her efforts, Mink worked with congressional colleagues and feminist activists to develop policy, influence the decision-making process, and monitor the implementation of significant legislation. In essence, Congress provided the platform for Mink to shape the broader political discourse of the United States. Three examples of Mink's engagement in intersectional legislative activism as a "bridge" feminist can be found in her advocacy for federally funded childcare, Title IX, and the Women's Educational Equity Act.

Early Childhood Education

In 1967, Mink introduced a bill to provide federal funding for early childhood education. Mink's proposal, which she advocated for during the next decade or so, departed in two significant ways from past childcare legislation. Previous programs either provided temporary services to recruit women for defense work during World War II or supported low-income parents as part of the 1960s War on Poverty programs. In contrast, Mink argued for federal government responsibility to provide childcare on a broader and more permanent basis. She believed that childcare should be available to all families, regardless of the income of the parents, and not just as an emergency measure. In addition, Mink advocated for quality early-childhood education that included meaningful learning experiences for children, not just "custodial care."[54] Her efforts to pass federal legislation held deep significance. As Mink argued, "The value of Federal legislation, as others before me have pointed out, is not only that it provides a specific program and specific amounts of money, but that it represents a national statement of purpose and support. It provides the inspiration for action and leadership at other levels of government, thus having an effect far beyond the simple provisions of law themselves."[55] Mink's attempts to pass federally funded childcare represented an effort to shape national values regarding gendered labor and governmental responsibility.

Patsy Mink's commitment to childcare reflected her personal experiences as a working mother and the collective needs of laboring women in Hawai'i. The racialized and gendered plantation economy of Hawai'i, where Mink grew up, fueled demands for maternity leave and childcare. Women, who were paid less than men, often carried their children on their backs while they worked. Some organized among themselves to share child-rearing duties. Older children watched over younger ones. And, unsupervised children sometimes suffered injuries or even death.[56]

This history of labor exploitation profoundly shaped Mink's political consciousness. Even though she eventually became a professional, Mink advocated for labor interests, along with women's equality. For instance, she testified on the need for childcare by referencing the daily challenges facing working women in Hawai'i:

> [Due to] the high cost of living in our islands, Hawaii has a higher than average proportion of working wives and mothers in the labor force. As in many areas, some of the children of these families where both parents work do receive good care from relatives or neighbours or from quality child care programs while mothers or fathers are away. But too many families are now forced to leave their children in understaffed and sometimes damaging environments because they can afford nothing better. The child care bill we have reintroduced addresses itself to this area of concern among others.[57]

The concern about adequate childcare was both a personal and a political issue. In response to a query about women's liberation, John commented, "Women's Liberation is nothing new in my life. Patsy and I have always abided by the principle of the absolute worth of the individual."[58] This belief in respecting each other extended to supporting one another in terms of household labor. John cleaned, cooked, and shared care of their daughter, Wendy. But both Patsy and John worked outside of the home and so needed reliable childcare for Wendy during the workday. They experimented with different forms of childcare, eventually settling on a patchwork of care and supervision that changed as Wendy aged. While Wendy was a baby, they relied on babysitters during the day; grandparents filled in if necessary in the evening. When Wendy was a toddler, they enrolled her in a care center that they belatedly discovered trained the kids according to gender stereotypes. Care options were so limited, though, that they had to stick with the toddler program for a time. A year later, they signed Wendy up for preschool at the University of Hawai'i lab school, which was linked to an aftercare program that kept her safe until her parents could pick her up. As Wendy grew a little older, they enrolled her in Japanese-language school and ballet, both after-school activities that kept her busy until the end of their workday. On many days, though, Wendy took the bus from

elementary school to her mother's law office, where she spent the afternoon with her grandmother in her grandfather's adjacent office. As an
adolescent in DC, Wendy regularly went to her mother's congressional
office after school, where she did homework while observing and engaging in political debates.

The Minks' struggle to assure Wendy's care while working outside the
home reflected broader trends in the United States. Despite the cultural
emphasis on domesticity after World War II, women, including mothers, increased their participation in the work force. According to Mary
Dublin Keyserling, an economist who headed the Women's Bureau during the 1960s, by 1967 "about 4 million working mothers [had] children
under 6 years of age" in the United States. However, "existing day care
facilities are available for only 310,000 to 350,000 children."[59] With a
longer history and greater participation in the labor force compared to
white, middle-class women, women of color were especially burdened
by the dearth of accessible, quality childcare. In response, a childcare
movement emerged during the 1960s and 1970s.[60]

The women's movement prioritized the need for childcare. As one
publication expressed, "Day Care is number one on the list of demands
of women's rights groups. . . . Child care is considered by some feminists
as the pivotal issue in determining the future course of women's rights.
Without day care to free women (and men), they say, you might as well
forget about equal pay, equal advancement, and *equal opportunity*."[61]
Childcare allowed mothers to more fully participate in economic and
political opportunities outside of the family. The availability of quality
care also lessened the guilt of many women, whose work responsibilities conflicted with their family duties. For some radical feminists, reas-
signing childcare could reconfigure the family and the community. They
advocated "universal child care" as "the responsibility of all society." For
them, "children are not private property" and "the nuclear family is ar-
chaic and stifling."[62] Childcare, for these individuals, allowed women
greater freedom and also challenged the hetero-nuclear family (breadwinner husband, domestic wife, and children in single-family households) as the basis of US society.

To lobby for federal legislation, Mink worked closely with various
organizations, including mainstream national feminist organizations
like NOW and those locally based, involving working-class women

and women of color. By the 1970s, Mink's childcare coalition included feminist activist groups and educational associations, as well as other legislators, both male and female. Once Shirley Chisholm, a former teacher who had managed childcare centers, joined Mink on the House Education and Labor Committee in 1971, they allied in the push for childcare legislation.

Mink worked closely with these advocates to enact childcare legislation in the early 1970s. But allies were fewer when she first introduced her childcare bill in 1967. In that year and again in 1969, she introduced bills to provide $300 million in funds for childcare. She cosponsored with twenty-four other legislators in 1967 and forty-nine others in 1969. Mink and her staff also organized public hearings about childcare in Washington, DC, and around the country. Then, in 1971, Mink partnered with Senator Walter Mondale (D-Minnesota) and Representative John Brademas (D-Indiana) to pass a $1.85 billion early-childhood-development bill in both the Senate and the House. Mink secured support from Republican officials for the 1971 bill, but President Nixon vetoed it.

The arguments against federally funded childcare reflected Cold War fears concerning the restructuring of the family and the increased role of the state. Nixon regarded government programs as antagonistic to family-based child rearing. In his veto message, he described the bill as "the most radical piece of legislation to emerge from the Ninety-Second Congress . . . [one that] would commit the vast moral authority of the national government to the side of communal approaches to child rearing over against the family-centered approach."[63] Although childcare advocates argued that these services would enhance family life, Nixon regarded the initiative as antifamily. Anti-childcare advocates wrote letters to congressmembers, expressing fears about the loss of parental authority and government intrusion into their lives. Mink and Mondale regarded these efforts as misinformation campaigns. Mink responded that the use of childcare is voluntary, not mandatory, and that parental involvement is welcome in such centers. However, opponents wrote and published inflammatory messages "to the effect that we are attempting to 'Russianize' our children."[64]

The charge of "Russianizing" American children resonated on multiple levels in the context of the Cold War. The phrase suggested that those who wanted to expand the US government into the "private" affairs of the family sought to control Americans, their children, and their collective way of thinking. Concerns about government totalitarianism and "Russianization" intertwined with religious concerns. Some parents wrote to Mink, worried that their children were not receiving adequate moral and spiritual instruction in secular, "godless," federally funded childcare institutions. Russianization of children also implied a Russianization of gender roles and American families. President Nixon, previously vice president under Eisenhower, engaged in the famous 1959 "Kitchen Debate" with Nikita Khrushchev, leader of the Soviet Union. Nixon showed off the gadgets of a middle-class American home to demonstrate how technology, consumption, and the nuclear family propelled US superiority. In the idealized nuclear family, the wife raised children and purchased goods. In reality, the economic demands of post–World War II society motivated housewives to enter the work force. And, the social movements of the 1960s and 1970s increasingly inspired women to demand an identity and standing independent from their family obligations.

Mink worked with feminist allies to advocate for federal resources for childcare throughout her first terms in Congress. She introduced and cosponsored legislation until she lost her senatorial campaign in 1976. She drafted and redrafted bills to provide federal funding for childcare programs, to ensure standards for early childhood education, and to support working parents, particularly mothers. While some elements achieved legislative success, Mink faced persistent and hostile opposition, particularly from those who feared fundamental changes in gender roles in US families.

The Mother of Title IX

In contrast to Mink's 1971 vetoed childcare bill, Title IX was signed into law in 1972 and was green-lit for implementation in 1975. Title IX was the brainchild of both Edith Green and Mink, encapsulating the commitment of both congresswomen to end sex-based discrimination in education. Each had worked for several years on legislative vehicles to achieve equal opportunity for women in education. Amending Title VI of the Civil Rights Act to add sex/gender to the ban on race discrimination in federally financed education programs was one thought that both women pursued for a while in separate bills. Comprehensive, free-standing legislation banning sex/gender discrimination in federal programs, from Social Security through elementary education, was another thought, spelled out in Mink's Women's Equality bill, which she introduced in the spring of 1970. In the end, the concept of gender equality in education was wrapped within Green's omnibus education bill, one of many programs sharing scrutiny on the way to becoming law.

Title IX bars discrimination against women in educational institutions that receive federal funds. It was a liberal feminist achievement, opening doors to women and girls; but also it was much more. Title IX supporters were motivated to demand these reforms in part because of their personal experiences of educational exclusion. The radical feminist mantra that the personal is political resonated with Title IX advocates who knew well how gender bias in school had circumscribed their opportunities. Mink's own educational experiences as a woman of color and a mother added to the nexus among her life experiences and policy commitments. For Mink and other feminist advocates, Title IX represented a tool for social change—letting women in, yes, but also expanding their dreams. With multiple bases for collaboration, Mink and feminist advocates forged a "bridge" partnership between movement organizations and congressional leaders that mingled overlapping feminist approaches to advocacy.

The gender ideology and patriarchal practices that precluded Mink's admission to medical school in the late 1940s persisted in US society into the 1960s and beyond. Mink witnessed the burdens of gender bias in her daughter's education. As a second grader, Wendy was denied standing to run for class president because a boy wanted the post. Her teacher advised that it would be more appropriate for her to be the boy's helper, as vice president. Ten years later, when Wendy applied to colleges, Stanford University turned her away, explaining that the school had reached its quota for female students.

Similarly, Bernice "Bunny" Sandler, a key force behind Title IX, came to her understanding of sex discrimination in education through her own experience with repeated rejections from graduate programs and teaching positions. As a woman, mother, and older student (she was born a year after Mink), Sandler experienced cumulative effects of discrimination. She channeled her rage by conducting a systematic analysis of the gender composition of university faculty. This data served as the basis for a class action suit against hundreds of colleges and universities for sex discrimination. Initiating the suit before the passage of Title IX, Sandler argued that the gender discrimination in hiring practices violated Executive Order 11246, which barred recipients of federal contracts from engaging in employment discrimination.[65]

Title IX, once enacted, awoke a raging opposition, particularly from male athletic programs. During the three-year period between passage and implementation, opponents of gender equity in athletic programs vigorously contested the new equality policy. They lobbied politicians to weaken, if not eliminate completely, the impact of the bill. Several members of the House and Senate repeatedly introduced amendments to curtail the scope of Title IX.

The defense and implementation of Title IX required vigilance and represented a collective feminist achievement. Sandler, her assistant Margaret Dunkle, and other feminist activists like Arvonne Fraser served as political watchdogs. The Women's Equity Action League (WEAL), created in 1968 as a spinoff of NOW, and the Project on Equal Education Rights, created in 1971 by the NOW Legal Defense and Education Fund, collaborated to offer research and advice for legislators. They worked closely with Mink, and other congressional allies, such as Green, Abzug, Chisholm, and Griffiths. Sandler, Dunkle, and Fraser also mobilized feminist constituents to engage in political lobbying.

This partnership fought repeated legislative assaults on Title IX. As journalist Kristina Chan has pointed out, "People have tried to change the law [Title IX] or abolish it completely. Title IX has gone back to Congress many more times than most other laws—24 times by 2007."[66] The Department of Health, Education, and Welfare (HEW), under Secretary Casper Weinberger, spent two years drafting implementation regulations once Title IX became law in 1972. After the draft version of the regulations became public, numerous educational institutions and associations, private citizens, politicians, athletic directors, and sports organizations (including the National Collegiate Athletic Association) lobbied for and against various aspects of the federal plan to apply Title IX to all levels of schooling. Responsive to the male athletics lobby, some legislators cycled a series of amendments to tie HEW's hands regarding gender equity in school sports and physical education, thus to cramp the reach of Title IX.

Sandler and Dunkle regularly contacted Mink and her legislative aide, Susan Kakesako. They strategized about which legislators to approach for support and who might take the lead on particular issues. One memo from Kakesako to Mink illustrates this dynamic:

[Margaret Dunkle] had come by last night to express her thanks (and that of Bunny Sandler and for the whole Education Task Force) that "without PTM['s] [Mink's] help it might have been lost." They knew of your behind the scenes work—phone calls and were really supported by your moral support. Also feels that you were the crucial person because of your ability and presence on Education and Labor Committee. The women now lobbying the Senate becuz they fear that resolution may still be shaken loose in House and go to Senate.[67]

This collaboration between Mink and feminist organizers made possible a critical revote in 1975 that saved Title IX as a robust and expansive equality policy. As HEW prepared its final draft version of the Title IX regulations, Representative Robert Casey (R-Texas) offered an amendment that initially had passed the House in April but had been rejected by the Senate. The House revived the amendment in July, just a few days before the Title IX regulations were scheduled for implementation. The Casey Amendment forbade HEW from enforcing Title IX by withholding federal funds from schools that maintained sex-segregated physical education programs, honorary societies, and social organizations. Mink opposed the amendment, in part because the issues already had been considered and disposed several times in prior months and years, and in part because the stakes were high as the amendment directly undermined Title IX.

Sex-segregated physical education was part of the system of unequal athletic opportunities limiting girls and women. In her speech against the Casey Amendment, Mink emphasized the importance of physical education classes as

part of the total educational experience of a child in the school system. . . . [As such] should not title IX apply to that child in physical education classes just as it applies in math classes or science and all of the other requirements under Title IX? . . . All we are talking about is an opportunity for youngsters to have physical education classes in which all of the activities are oriented to people as individuals, as human beings, not because they are girls or boys or men or women, but because physical education is an important ingredient in the entire educational experience.[68]

In addition, gender-segregated organizations in schools privileged and maintained old boys' networks, which reinforced unequal access to employment and academic opportunities. Finally, barring the federal enforcement agency from withholding funds from schools that violated the law would turn Title IX into an empty gesture. Mink cosigned a letter with seventy-seven other congressional representatives, warning, "The Casey Amendment will seriously weaken Title IX."[69]

Mink lobbied extensively against the efforts to dilute and repeal Title IX. She spoke against the Casey Amendment and other anti–Title IX efforts. She organized discussions and debated strategy with feminist organizers and congressional collaborators. Despite these efforts, the Casey Amendment passed again on July 16, 1975, this time by one vote (212 to 211). That day, Wendy suffered serious injury in a car accident and was hospitalized in intensive care. Patsy spoke against the amendment, but upon learning of Wendy's accident rushed to the hospital in Ithaca, New York, leaving the House of Representatives without casting her vote. One supporter commented, "How ironic it is that the demands of motherhood should come at a time when your vote could have kept defeated the unconscionable Amendment of Casey. How truly difficult to meet both private and public demands."[70]

Feminist supporters refused to allow the vote to stand. The *Washington Post* described how "several hundred" women roamed "the corridors" of Congress, "handing out literature, pursuing House members onto elevators, meeting in hallways and cafeterias to map tactics."[71] Casey himself described the mobilization as "the heaviest lobbying I've ever seen around here." The women "found enthusiastic backing among most women lawmakers and among congressional staff aides, particularly women." The lobbyists chanted "Give Women a Sporting Chance" to demand a revote. This collaborative political pressure led to a revote in the House on Casey's amendment. This time, opponents defeated the amendment (215 to 178). The number of votes against Casey increased a little, while a substantial number of Casey's supporters declined to vote. Still caring for Wendy in upstate New York, Patsy followed these developments while away from Congress. In her place, feminist activists worked collaboratively to block or at least politically embarrass some of the critics of Title IX. Some journalists describe Patsy Mink as "the mother of Title IX," now renamed after her. Mink's "heroism" represented a collective endeavor. Feminist activists inside and outside of Congress disrupted the regular work and power dynamics of Capitol Hill.

From the outset in 1971–72, the gender-equity mission of Title IX interacted with civil rights struggles focused on race as well as with economic-justice goals. In fact, more controversial than Title IX in the Higher Education Act of 1972 were an anti-busing initiative and a new provision for college financial aid. The critics of busing included Edith Green, who opposed the use of federal funds to support school integration through busing. Although the House-Senate conference committee that prepared a final iteration of the omnibus education bill adopted anti-busing language, Green considered it "pretense" rather than an actual ban. According to Green, she "actively participated in efforts to defeat" the House-Senate conference bill, and thus Title IX, also because she objected to need-based direct aid to college students, which she caricatured as an indefensible "entitlement."[72] She voted "no" on final passage of the bill that made Title IX law because of its provisions for students who were disadvantaged by economic status and/or by race.[73]

Mink strongly supported the college-access provision of the conference bill. About school busing, her thinking was more nuanced. She believed in integration and explained her position in a letter: "I am unfamiliar with the reasons for busing in your school district, but if it is to secure greater integration of black children then I am for it. It is regrettable that we have come to this point in our history where we have to use our children to accomplish what their parents have refused to do which is to live in harmony and not in segregation."[74] But despite Mink's support for racial integration, she believed that focusing on busing would lead to an impasse, not only legislatively but in society. She supported the final higher education bill neither in spite of nor because of its busing provision. Rather, she urged passage of the conference bill because it would carry Title IX across the finish line and because it would broaden federal support for college access through the first federal provision of financial aid grants directly to undergraduates. A vigorous proponent of racial equity in education, Mink simultaneously worked to increase funding for traditionally Black schools as well as educational programs and institutions in Puerto Rico, Hawaiʻi, and Alaska. Such education served Black, Latinx, Native Hawaiian, Asian, and Native Alaskan students.

After the passage of Title IX, its implementation became closely linked with the enforcement of civil rights laws. Legislators characterized Title IX as being modeled after Title VI of the 1964 Civil Rights Act, which banned discrimination on the basis of race, color, or national origin in programs receiving federal funding. In fact, the critics of both laws found common cause to attack them together. In 1974, Representative Marjorie Holt (R-Maryland) proposed an amendment to Title IX to prevent educational institutions from collecting data on race and gender. Without this information, schools lacked the ability to comply with either Title VI or Title IX. In other words, Holt advocated for a color- and gender-blind approach to prevent educational institutions from identifying and addressing ongoing inequalities.

Mink argued vehemently against Holt's proposal to the House of Representatives in December 1974: "Mr. Speaker, this is a most serious matter which we are considering. . . . This is a much more important and significant amendment. . . . Its net effect will be, in my estimation, to completely repeal the Civil Rights Act." While detractors and advocates debated busing, Mink believed that keeping statistical information held greater importance. She argued, "It is not simply a question of whether we are for or against busing, but whether we believe we are a nation dedicated to the concepts of equality." Mink invoked her own racial and gender identity in the speech, seemingly placing greater emphasis on the latter, to argue against the Holt Amendment:

> Now, I stand here before the House as a member of a minority race, as a member of a minority group in this country, really that should be the majority; the women of this country who have not ever been given their rightful entitlement to establish policies, to hold positions of responsibility, to compete for promotions, to hold professional positions in government and in institutions within our society. Of late, within the last

few years, the Congress has responded to the cries of discrimination by women all across our society. We have enacted laws whose effectiveness depends upon these statistics being available to enforce the law.[75]

Despite Mink's impassioned plea, the Holt Amendment passed the House. In a personal letter about the controversy, Mink observed about Holt that "being a woman does not by sex make one liberal."[76] In the end, as Mink entered into discussions with Republican HEW secretary Casper Weinberger to ensure that enforcement of civil rights law would continue, the Senate rejected the House measure. The federal antidiscrimination mandates of Title VI and Title IX survived the attempt to ban the collection of race and gender data necessary for enforcement.

Title IX transformed educational institutions, most famously school athletics. Just prior to its passage, "fewer than 295,000 girls participated in high school athletics, just 7 percent of the total number of athletes; fewer than 30,000 women competed in intercollegiate athletics, and women's sports received a scant 2 percent of overall athletic budgets."[77] In contrast, by 2016, approximately two in five girls/women played sports.[78] As historian Susan Ware argued in 2007, "While the playing field is still not totally level, women and girls now have far more opportunities to participate in organized athletic activities in their schools and communities than ever before."[79] In addition to these remarkable gains in athletics, including scholarships, Title IX shaped gender equity in education more broadly. Title IX's prohibition on sex discrimination by schools that receive federal funds spans a variety of issues related to the educational environment. These include admissions, financial aid, classroom climate, access for pregnant and parenting students, and sexual violence and harassment. Mink reflected on the significance of Title IX in 2002, on the thirtieth anniversary of the bill:

> The few pages of Title IX set a policy for the United States in all areas of education: elementary, secondary, higher education, graduate education; a policy that set forth explicitly that no institution should discriminate against girls or women in the courses and programs that they offered at these institutions. . . . In a very short period of time, . . . we began to see some very remarkable changes in our schools in the programs that were being offered, the number of women that were enrolled . . . Prior

to that, one could rarely ever see women students, especially in graduate programs. And they won fellowships and they had opportunities made available to them that were unheard of before 1972.[80]

Mink, a third-generation Japanese American who entered the legal profession and the realm of politics following her exclusion from medical school, fought to create these educational opportunities for all women.

Beyond Equal Opportunity

Although Title IX banned sex discrimination, it did not provide funding to transform educational institutions. As Mink and her feminist allies defended Title IX, they also introduced the Women's Educational Equity Act (WEEA). The bill allocated resources to develop new curricula, retrain teachers and counselors, and provide resources for girls and women to support their academic and professional interests. Members of WEAL and other women's organizations initially conceived and drafted the bill before enlisting the support of Mink. She agreed to sponsor WEEA in April 1972, reintroduced the legislation the next year, and held hearings to promote the bill. Walter Mondale introduced the legislation in the Senate and also held hearings. WEEA exemplifies how Mink worked collaboratively with activists to pass legislation and allocate federal resources to advance equity.

The supporters of WEEA who testified at both House and Senate hearings explained why such an act was necessary. Nancy K. Schlossberg of the American Council on Education testified, "From nursery school through graduate education, our educational system is guilty of fostering and perpetuating rigid sex roles for men and women which result in stereotyped self-images and career choices for both sexes."[81] Bernice Sandler, then serving as the executive associate and director of the Project on the Status and Education of Women at the Association of American Colleges, elaborated: "From the time a young girl enters school she learns more than just reading, writing and arithmetic. Her textbooks are far more likely to be written about boys and men; girls and women are rarely major characters. . . . When girls appear in books, they are passive; they watch, they read, they dream, and are incapable of solving the most elementary problems. About the most exciting thing that girls do in books is help mother with the dishes or take a trip to the supermarket."[82] These textbooks, reinforced by teachers and educational counselors, encouraged girls to pursue educational and career options in line with "feminine" roles, thereby creating "a pervasive pattern of sex discrimination."[83] While Title IX might prohibit more "overt forms of discrimination, . . . much of the discrimination that young girls and women face goes beyond the matter of official policies and practices."[84]

WEEA provided a federal mandate and government resources to go beyond banning de jure discrimination and address de facto structures and cultures of sexism. The bill proposed catalyzing curriculum reform in a variety of fields and supported emerging women's studies programs. The legislation also provided resources to retrain counselors and teachers. And, WEEA allocated funding for women's centers to help girls and women access educational and career resources. To maintain attention on these issues, the bill also proposed establishing a Council on Women's Educational Programs in the Office of Education. To advocate for WEEA's passage, Schlossberg emphasized that "any group which by numbers or image is seen as different from 'the majority' needs special visibility."[85]

Mink initially proposed up to $80 million over the course of three years to support WEEA. She also wrote to her contacts in women's and educational organizations to inform them of the proposed legislation and to solicit their feedback. In turn, women's newsletters and publications, like *Ms.* magazine, featured WEEA's significance. Even with this growing support, the bill met with indifference from many legislators. They did not attend the House and Senate hearings, even when they featured the testimony of tennis star Billie Jean King. The Nixon administration also opposed the legislation, since HEW resisted creating new categories of programs. In the end, Mondale proposed including the provisions of WEEA in an omnibus education bill under a "special projects" categorization that included six other new programs. Doing so protected the bill from scrutiny and potential elimination. Mondale, however, insisted on Mink's approval before he proceeded with this plan.[86]

The activists who worked closely with Mink expressed some reservations about this approach. They voiced suspicion that Mondale was trying to win "brownie points" with women for a possible presidential bid.[87] Mondale's commitment to feminist issues appears genuine, though, especially considering that he embraced WEEA despite garnering very little support from male colleagues in the Senate. Also, when Mondale ran for president in 1984, he selected Geraldine Ferraro, the first female vice-presidential nominee for a major party, as his running mate. In 1973, however, Mink's allies worried that Mondale's involvement detracted from her receiving credit for WEEA. In fact, she did have to correct the historic record when *Glamour* magazine only attributed the legislation to Mondale. Mink wrote to the editor-in-chief,

> I feel sure that a male must have written the editorial . . . about my bill, the Women's Educational Equity Act. . . . I gladly give Senator Mondale full credit for his perception of our problem, for his embracing my bill as an important step forward to women, for his leadership in having hearings on it in the Senate and for moving its inclusion in the Elementary and Secondary Education Act; but I do insist that the drafting of the bill and the genesis of the idea itself was all the work of the House.[88]

The media attention towards Mondale did not necessarily result from his efforts to exclude Mink from recognition. His legislative maneuver enabled her to serve on the conference committee to reconcile the bills between the Senate (which contained WEEA) and the House (which did not). Nevertheless, Mink and by extension the women activists had to demand credit for legislation that they proposed.

Mink underscored the importance of feminist advocacy that led to the passage of WEEA. The law passed in the summer of 1974 with a potential allocation of $30 million in its first year and up to $100 million over three years. In announcing WEEA, Mink publicly thanked the activists who marshaled the bill through the legislative process:

> During the four years of its life, my bill enjoyed the widespread and active support of numerous nationally known and respected women's groups and education associations, much of which could be attributed to the diligent and able work of Ms. Arlene Horowitz, a former Education and Labor Committee employee and activist in the women's movement. As the moving force behind the genesis of this bill, Ms. Horowitz was

instrumental in initiating the impetus for its consideration; her assistance was immeasurable and a large part of the success of this bill belongs to her.[89]

Mink's acknowledgment of the behind-the-scenes work by Horowitz brought into public view the collaboration between legislators and activists. Mink introduced WEEA as a result of conversations and lobbying efforts by women activists. She worked to expand the network of interested parties through her information dissemination and consultation process. Mink conferred with her allies over the course of the legislation. And, she and Mondale featured some of these individuals and organizations through hearings, thereby introducing these political voices into the official record and debates of Congress.

Passing legislation constituted only part of Mink's work as a congresswoman. As with Title IX, she and her staff kept a careful eye on the implementation of WEEA. They sought out public support in the appropriations process. In fact, WEEA, tucked into the special programs, only received a fraction of funds authorized. Also, Mink monitored the process of forming the Council on Women's Educational Programs and encouraged her activist networks to forward nominees. Mink herself served on the council for its first year. In addition, she sent letters, particularly to educational and women's organizations in Hawai'i to encourage them to apply for WEEA funding. The law, passed at the federal level, served as a platform for local educational institutions and organizations to rethink and revise their instructional approach. Mink's legislative activism was a true partnership between Capitol Hill feminism and grassroots activism.

This form of advocacy and "bridge feminism" can easily be overlooked. In the 1970s, Andrew Fishel, a researcher in the Department of Education, authored an assessment of the WEEA campaign.[90] He acknowledged that WEEA was "the first piece of legislation enacted by Congress which has exclusively as its aim the funding to improve the quality of women's education"; however, he also decided that the bill "cannot be considered of vital national significance," given the eventual budgeting allocation, which turned out to be $6.2 million instead of the larger amounts initially requested.[91] Fishel argued that what made WEEA "interesting" was that it demonstrated "how a few dedicated individuals, supported by special interest groups and a few members of Congress can get a relatively obscure piece of legislation considered and adopted by Congress."[92] While Fishel acknowledged women's activism in initiating and advocating for WEEA, he characterized Mink as a moderate in her support, unwilling to bring the legislation up for debate and not "regarded as a feminist."[93] When Fishel shared his research with Mink to ask for accuracy, she refused to respond but hand wrote on his draft, "I consider this article insulting. . . . Who 'dared' call me a moderate on women's issues!"[94]

Rethinking Feminism

Mink advocated for gender equity on a range of issues. She co-led with Margaret Heckler (R-Massachusetts) the first all-women congressional delegation that traveled to the People's Republic of China in the mid-1970s. Mink also played a leading role in sponsoring legislation for the National Women's Conference (NWC) of 1977.[95] This gathering was inspired by the United Nations' declaration of International Women's Year (IWY) in 1975 and the World Conference on Women held in Mexico City that summer. The 1977 NWC brought together two thousand official delegates from the fifty states and six territories to discuss, debate, and vote on a national platform of women's issues.[96] The event also attracted an additional eighteen thousand observers from across the nation and representatives from fifty-six countries in Asia, Africa, the Caribbean, Eastern and Western Europe, Latin America, and the Middle East. Mink worked with feminist allies like Abzug and Chisholm to convince Congress to allocate $5 million for this unprecedented event, an amount that translated to only four cents for every woman in the United States. Mink also envisioned the conference as a partnership between the grassroots and the federal government. She insisted that the national gathering had to be preceded by pre-conferences held in each state and territory. In conducting outreach and selecting delegates, local conference organizers were mandated to involve diverse women, those with low incomes, homemakers, rural women, lesbians, and people of different religious faiths and ages, as well as women of color.

Figure 4.4. Patsy and Bella Abzug were linked by common struggles for peace and equality. They became good friends and allies. Photo circa 1977. Courtesy of Gwendolyn Mink.

Patsy Mink's political contributions to feminist legislation of the 1960s and 1970s expand our understanding of feminism. First, her involvement demonstrates that an Asian American woman was at the center of these pioneering initiatives. Her life experiences as a woman of color shaped her intersectional understanding of injustice and motivated her efforts to change federal legislation. Second, Mink worked collaboratively with grassroots activists at the local and national levels. Finally, Mink combined her advocacy for legislative change with the goal of profoundly transforming US society.

Mink advocated both for "negative" rights of equal opportunity, commonly understood as "liberal feminism," and for "positive" rights of state redistribution of resources, demands associated with more radical social movements.[97] Some Asian American revolutionary women activists during the 1960s and 1970s criticized Mink for being "200% American" and having false hope in the "American system."[98] Committed to political liberalism, Mink participated in representative government, because she believed democratic advocacy could change the nation. She worked from within to transform the system, utilizing the master's tools to significantly renovate and reclaim the master's house for herself and others traditionally left out in the cold.

MAUCH CHUNK

One of the ways daily life changed dramatically when we moved to Washington was the loss of routine encounters with nature, both visual and tactile, for pleasure and to nurture it. From our home on O'ahu, we had feasted on ocean vistas and mountain rainbows on the drive to and from school each day. Evenings had begun with a stroll around our yard, raking stray leaves from plumeria, mango, or papaya trees, then watering thirsty birds of paradise and red ginger that lined the walkway to the front door. On weekends we had spent hours watching the horizon from the beach, hiking muddy central O'ahu trails, or pampering the many orchids nestled in my grandmother's greenhouse.

In Washington, we lived in apartments and eventually a townhouse. While the city offered many parks and curated groves of beautiful flowers in springtime, daily life mostly involved encounters with various forms of concrete—sidewalks, roads, and buildings. We had to work a bit to find ways to be immersed in greenery, to witness wildlife, to honor nature's challenges and splendor.

I often wondered whether my father felt straitjacketed by urban life. Professionally and personally, he thrived in forests and on mountains. When I was a young child, there was nothing that thrilled him more than "having to" climb high in the Ko'olau to explore groundwater sources when his job required it. It worried my mother when he was isolated in the mountains, usually with only one colleague, defenseless against wild boar and far from help in the event of an accident. But he flourished in the wild, perhaps because adventures in wilderness had provided his only taste of freedom during the six years he spent in a Pennsylvania orphanage. In DC, the closest he regularly came to a forest was from the confines of a car traversing the Baltimore-Washington Parkway, a trip he made several times a week for a couple of years to fulfill a fellowship at Johns Hopkins.

My mother's relationship to the natural world was less immersive than my father's, and more reverential. She had scientific curiosity in the biology, chemistry, and etiology of living things, as well as spiritual engagement with nature's intricacy and beauty. She was drawn to understanding the interweaving of the natural world and human history, for good and for ill. She was especially attentive to the ways the experience of nature knitted into cultural practice and identity, a disposition influenced and heightened by Native Hawaiian cosmology. As for many in her time, reading Rachel Carson's *Silent Spring* focused her thinking about environmental health, justice, and protection.

If life in Washington was bereft of the natural wonder we were used to in Hawai'i, my mother's work and my father's family introduced us to environmental, cultural, and sociological issues that we had not yet paid much attention to when we arrived on the East Coast in December 1964. One set of issues coming into focus during the mid-1960s involved coal mine health and safety standards, as well as provision for miners who had been disabled by black lung disease contracted in the mines. My mother's Education and Labor Committee had jurisdiction over these matters, and so she began to develop a degree of expertise on the subject of coal mining, especially working conditions and compensation for the injured.

On occasional weekends, we took road trips to coal country so that my mother could acquaint herself with mining communities and the lay of the land. Once, we explored a mining area of West Virginia in advance of official visits her committee would make as it weighed legislation. We also explored mining areas of Pennsylvania, where I learned the distinct geologic trajectories and economic histories of bituminous and anthracite mining. On the interstates, my father taught me to recognize various rock formations, especially the pink-red-gray bedrock known as Mauch Chunk shale.

One of the pluses to life in Washington was that we were only a four-hour drive from my father's mother, Grandma Helen, who had lived her entire life in a small anthracite-mining town in northeastern Pennsylvania. I had met Grandma Helen only once before our move to DC: in 1958, when I was six years old, I spent two weeks with her while my parents traveled to a "young political leaders" NATO conference in Paris. My grandmother lived in a town known by old timers as Mauch Chunk, but which had been renamed "Jim Thorpe" at some point in the 1950s. Born in Nesquehoning, Pennsylvania, my father and three of his five siblings had been removed to an orphanage soon after my grandfather died in 1930, so I can't quite say that he grew up in Mauch Chunk. But he did go to high school there (he and his siblings were returned to my grandmother in 1937) and considered it the town he was "from."

Mauch Chunk was the county seat of Carbon County, in anthracite country. It had been a railway crossroads for shipping coal back in the day. During the 1870s, labor organizers known as the Molly Maguires were tried, jailed, and hanged there. Once mining exhausted the anthracite coal supply, the town, which sits at the edge of the Poconos, adopted the moniker "Switzerland of America" to attract winter tourists interested in Pocono skiing. When that didn't create a tourist economy, the town decided to rebrand itself altogether by purchasing the remains of the legendary Native American athlete Jim Thorpe of Oklahoma from his widow. Although Thorpe had never set foot in the town and had no relationship with it, Mauch Chunk renamed itself "Jim Thorpe" and built him a prominently situated mausoleum. That didn't improve the economic prospects of the town either, but the town stuck by its new name and fought his heirs when they sought return of his remains to his home lands in Oklahoma.[1]

The town of Jim Thorpe was excited when the wife of one of its high school star graduates was elected to Congress. The isolated, depressed, all-white town did not embrace women's rights or integration, but nevertheless embraced its connection to the Japanese American congresswoman from Hawai'i. In early May 1965, just months after my mother's first term began, Jim Thorpe hosted a "dinner-dance" in her honor.[2] Aspects of the event were cringeworthy, what with ticky-tacky, touristy nods to somebody's idea of Hawai'i—a hula girl on the invitation,[3] plastic lei for all, Tommy Dorsey's "Hawaiian War Chant" in the background. But it was otherwise a respectful welcoming of the daughter-in-law of one of the town's citizens.

On the drive to Jim Thorpe for the event, we detoured through several adjacent anthracite counties before entering the Lehigh Valley, where Jim Thorpe rests. We saw depleted mines, some of them stripped. Near Shamokin, guides walked us into an underground mine. I still have the piece of anthracite that a local official gave me as a memento.

On this and on other trips to visit Grandma Helen, we drank in the history of coal mining and witnessed the intense cultural and economic despair of a coal community that had no more coal to mine or ship. The downtown area went through a facelift of sorts in the late 1960s, when Hollywood arrived to film *The Molly Maguires* starring Sean Connery and Richard Harris. Still, the spruced-up storefronts did not conceal the town's apparent economic defeat. Geographic isolation built cultural walls around the dead economy, as "the Chunk" became increasingly suspicious of major breakthroughs happening elsewhere, such as integration, women's rights, and student activism. Five decades later, this would be Trump country.[4]

My mother did not represent a coal district and did not have first-hand knowledge of work and life in a mining community. But she made learning about coal part of her job from her first days in Congress, and through my father's roots in a coal community she came to understand the history of labor relations in mining, the ongoing struggles of workers, and the anxiety of life in a coal economy with no apparent future in coal.

Although it was not her first choice, she was prepared to assume leadership of the Subcommittee on Mines and Mining by the early 1970s, when she had accumulated enough seniority on the House Interior Committee to serve as a subcommittee chair. Her subcommittee became one of the engines of legislation to regulate and curb the strip mining of coal on environmental grounds.

The prospect of environmental regulation of strip mining aroused angry and incessant opposition from coal mine owners. They attacked my mother, often ridiculing her leadership on the issue not only because she was Asian American and a woman but also because she was from Hawai'i, where there obviously is no coal. In one Capitol Hill demonstration against strip mine controls, a protester carried a sign that read "Patsy Mink is a fink," while Senator Harry Byrd denounced "the bill written by coal mining experts from the beach at Waikiki."[5] Eventually, some coal industry groups called for boycotts of Hawaii travel, pineapple, and cane sugar.[6] While most of the hostility directed at Mom arguably was part of the rough-and-tumble of (sexist, racist) politics, at the extreme it was life-threatening. In October 1975 the FBI received what it considered credible information that the head of a Virginia coal company had taken out a hit on her, or tried to (the hit man initially was offered ten thousand dollars for the job; he upped the ante to one hundred thousand dollars).[7]

In the season of the Patty Hearst kidnapping, there was some concern that I might become a target as well. The police in Ithaca, New York, where I was a graduate student, as well as the Cornell University Safety Division, were notified of the threat and asked to check on my well-being periodically, which I found both preposterous and embarrassing.[8] But when a burly stranger showed up on my doorstep with what looked like a shotgun, I panicked, fleeing into the house before thinking to lock him out. He followed me inside, but seeing other occupants, hightailed it back outside. I would not have been more frightened if Freddy Krueger were after me. Even though it was improbable that a shooter or kidnapper would come a-knockin', the episode, by now bemusing, at the time triggered irrepress-ible fear.

Despite this brush with coal industry violence, my mother hunkered down and continued to work towards strip mine regulation until her first tour of service in Congress came to an end in December 1976. The legis-lation she promoted, versions of it vetoed by President Gerald Ford, was signed into law by President Jimmy Carter in 1977. One of Mom's most prized keepsakes was a pen used by Carter to sign the Surface Mining Control and Reclamation Act into law, which he sent with a letter com-mending her advocacy and leadership.

As my mother's first career in Congress drew to a close, I carried the torch for coal miners and mining into a new iteration. I found myself drawn to the late-nineteenth-century history of mine labor, especially in the an-thracite region, which sometimes claimed to be the birthplace of the sec-ond industrial revolution in the United States due to the conjuncture of railroad development and mining. Especially interesting to me were the po-litical effects of the desperation coal bosses structured into the lives of their workers. My dissertation was inspired in part by the politics awoken among working people of Mauch Chunk and surrounds at the turn of the twen-tieth century—immigrants and nativists, Slavs and Anglos, workers and bosses, unorganized and organized. I launched my dissertation research in 1977 with a trip to Mauch Chunk to remember one set of labor activists, the Molly Maguires. I aimed to visit the Mauch Chunk jail, where one of the imprisoned Mollies allegedly had imprinted his hand in the concrete wall of his cell while awaiting execution by hanging. But although these were heady days for women's rights elsewhere, not so in Mauch Chunk. I was not allowed to step foot into the jail—I was not allowed across the threshold—because I am female.

example #1
p4

5

A Pacific Environmentalist

As Patsy Mink spearheaded antiwar and feminist initiatives, she also engaged in environmental politics. Mink's worldview reflected a Pacific sensibility. She wrote to a political colleague to share that living on "an island state, I feel the people of Hawaii clearly recognize the importance and value of our natural resources."[1] Mink's newsletter further explained, "Those who have lived in an island environment where the interaction of the elements is perhaps more readily apparent than elsewhere, have a greater awareness of the interdependence of man and his surroundings."[2] Residents and visitors to the islands lived surrounded by the ocean, beaches, dramatic mountains and canyons, lush greenery, and changeable tropical weather. However, Hawai'i's main economic activities centered on agribusiness, the US military, and tourism. All three industries furthered settler-colonial processes that sought to vanquish Native peoples in order to possess Native lands. These industries also tended to overuse, pollute, and even destroy the surrounding natural resources. Mink recognized these ecological dangers. Her roots in Hawai'i shaped her political approach, motivating her to challenge the US security state and the excesses of modern capitalism. Along with burgeoning social movements, she sought to redefine what is essential for life and whose lives are worth protecting.

During the Cold War, Pacific islands and waters served as laboratories for weapons testing. Although militarism and economic production impact the environment on a global scale, those traditionally marginalized by the US polity experience the detrimental effects more acutely. Environmental racism, a concept that recognizes how racialized individuals and communities are at greater risk of regular exposure to pollutants, toxicity, and other hazards, is pronounced in the Pacific.[3] Elizabeth M. DeLoughrey points out how the US government, most notably the Atomic Energy Commission (AEC), utilized Pacific Islands for nuclear testing, based on the false belief that their geographical

ı the United States and their island topography might
ıte" the impact of radiation.[4] Such a belief in ecological
nes that only land matters, not the air and water that con-
ılate among the islands. In addition, these "remote" is-
ᶦact home to Indigenous peoples. Pacific Islanders, Native
d Native Alaskans, along with others who occupied these
ame militarized laboratories were exposed to radiation,
s, and other toxins. In turn, they served as test subjects
clear-medical complex. Also, nonhuman life forms that
ıir, and water environments ecologically link the human
n.

very important →

Mink's environmental politics focused on both the particular and
the universal impacts of militarism and capitalism. She recognized that
Indigenous peoples, especially those in the Pacific, tend to be at greater
risk of environmental danger. Mink argued that their lives, lands, and
waters mattered and needed to be protected and valued. At the same
time, she marshaled humanistic arguments based on science and ratio-
nality to emphasize that environmental hazards inevitably transcend
their locales, that they defuse and spread and have an impact on the
entire world. As a woman of color warning against militarized and economic destruction, she both listened to and sought to amplify voices
traditionally marginalized in the US polity. As a result, she faced hostile
criticism for stepping out of her place by challenging the twin engines
that dominated US society in the context of the Cold War: free enterprise
and national security. Nevertheless, Mink sought to bring the ecological lessons of the Pacific to the rest of the United States and to advocate
for limiting the power and purview of the military-industrial complex.
She did so by strengthening the educational and regulatory role of the
federal government and by supporting the demands for Indigenous autonomy and reparations.

Pacific Lives

From 1965 to 1975, Amchitka Island—described as a "remote and
windswept" place off the coast of Alaska—served as the site of three
underground nuclear tests.[5] The 1963 Limited Test Ban Treaty among
the United States, the Soviet Union, and the United Kingdom eliminated

nuclear testing above ground and under water. Subsequently, these Cold War enemies found new locales in which to detonate weapons underground. Nestled in one of the most seismically active regions in the world, Amchitka, one of the Aleutian Islands and a national wildlife sanctuary, became the test site for the 1965 "Long Shot" detonation, an eighty-kiloton bomb with five times the power of the atomic bomb dropped on Hiroshima to end World War II. The AEC set off "Long Shot" purposefully "after a nearby magnitude-8.7 earthquake . . . to determine whether monitoring techniques could differentiate between natural seismicity and nuclear explosions."[6] In 1969, scientists detonated the much larger one-megaton bomb called "the Milrow," followed by the 1971 Cannikin test, which detonated the largest underground bomb ever exploded by the United States. The five-megaton weapon held four hundred times the power of the Hiroshima bomb. These planned nuclear tests drew a firestorm of protests in the context of the 1960s and 1970s, when critics of the Cold War and advocates for protecting the environment coalesced into mass social movements.

Mink's protests against underground nuclear testing in Alaska in the 1960s and 1970s reflected her long-standing concerns about Cold War militarism. In the midst of this global conflict, the Pacific Islands served as bases for training and deployment, as sites for rest and recreation, and as locations for testing weaponry.[7] Mink's challenges to the Amchitka nuclear tests were an extension of her earlier protests against open-air nuclear tests in the Marshall Islands. She also connected her antinuclear campaign to efforts to prevent conventional and chemical testing in Hawai'i. To understand the Pacific as an interconnected oceanic and land region, various scholars emphasize the importance of a Pacific World framework.[8] Just as an Atlantic World perspective connects Europe, Africa, and the Americas, a Pacific World viewpoint brings together the peoples, lands, and waters in and bordering the Pacific into a common analytical lens. Mink's lifelong connection to Hawai'i and her identity as a Japanese American influenced her understanding of nuclear testing and militarism as a Pacific World issue. Her political vision illuminated how the US government engaged in necropolitical projects that utilized colonized islands as sites of destruction. In response, she argued for an ethical recognition of Pacific lives, lands, and waters.

The Atomic Energy Commission's selection of Amchitka Island for nuclear testing reflects a viewpoint that discounted Pacific islands and life forms as remote and expendable. The AEC explained that it chose Amchitka "after an extensive survey of many areas throughout the world."[9] The island's "remoteness" constituted a key factor in its selection, despite its status as a national wildlife refuge. Amchitka's primary inhabitants consisted of animals, notably sea otters and birds. The island's residents included the bald eagle, ironically the symbol of the US nation. To counter the protected status of a wildlife refuge, the AEC obtained presidential and secretary of the interior permission to embark on nuclear testing. Government scientists considered the geology of the island, located in "an active earthquake area," as an asset for the experimental design of nuclear detonation. They expressed some concern, since similar nuclear testing in Nevada also generated seismic activity. However, the study determined that the Nevada aftershocks had little likelihood of affecting the San Andreas Fault, located under the more populated state of California over two hundred miles away.[10] Consequently, the report minimized the possibility of widespread damage due to earthquakes in the Amchitka region, despite its location at another trigger point of the San Andreas Fault.

Mink and other critics of nuclear testing on Amchitka refuted the official arguments about "containing" the impact of detonation on a "remote" island. Instead, she emphasized the ecological and environmental connections between the Aleutian Islands and the rest of the Pacific. Mink lobbied extensively by writing letters, giving speeches, generating publicity, and presenting arguments in Congress. She included in the *Congressional Record* a letter by the president of the Hawai'i State Federation of Labor AFL-CIO, which stated,

The island lies at the crux of an earth fault and, as you are well aware, runs all the way down the Pacific Coast to California. Even the slimmest chance that a nuclear blast could trigger ground motion along the San Andreas Fault should be enough to preclude such tests. Such an earthquake could very well devastate areas of dense population!

Here in Hawaii, we are painfully aware of the frightening consequences of such earthquakes. In recent history, we recall two huge tidal waves (tsunamis) caused by earthquakes in the Aleutians. The one in 1946 killed 173 of our people and caused damages of over $25 million on the island of Hawaii alone. Tsunamis set off by earthquakes in the Aleutians could destroy areas of Alaska, California and other islands in the Pacific as well as Hawaii.[11]

Media coverage and correspondence about Amchitka portrayed the AEC as gambling with the lives of people in and bordering the Pacific. *Science* magazine published an article about the proposed detonations entitled "Earthquakes and Nuclear Tests: Playing the Odds on Amchitka."[12] Mink also received a telegram from the president of the American Federation of Teachers in Hawai'i, stating simply, "Amchitka Test on site edging San Andreas Fault is playing Russian Roulette with America."[13]

In addition to the possibility of environmental disaster, Mink raised concerns about the political fallout from the Amchitka tests, particularly from Pacific Rim countries. As she noted in a letter to President Nixon, "The governments of Canada and Japan have registered official protests with the Department of State concerning the tests. It is also worth noting that Amchitka Island is very close to Russia."[14] Mink, and other Japanese American congressional leaders from Hawai'i, also highlighted that the detonation of the largest nuclear bomb would occur just as the Japanese emperor visited the United States for the first time. In fact, this unofficial meeting with President Nixon took place in Alaska. In addition, Mink expressed concerns that in the Cold War context, nuclear testing, not just the military deployment of nuclear weapons, constituted acts of aggression. Mink reminded US policy makers that the very geological interconnectedness of the Pacific World could aggravate political tremors. The Amchitka tests held the potential to detonate both seismic shifts and political rifts.

Mink raised the sense of Pacific-wide endangerment and also argued for the specific importance of Amchitka Island, its wildlife, its environs, and the people connected to this land. In a letter to the secretary of the interior, Mink argued, "As the test is in a National Wildlife Refuge, other functions entrusted to you, by statute, are also being violated by the Cannikin blast. . . . Please answer each of the following questions: Is it permissible to use a .22 rifle on Amchitka? Is it permissible to use a slingshot against wildlife there? Is it permissible to throw rocks at the wildlife there? Is it permissible to detonate a five-megaton thermo-nuclear bomb there?"[15] In this series of questions, Mink reminded a federal official of conservation of his responsibilities for the wildlife on Amchitka. She also underscored that nuclear bombs are not exceptional weapons, deserving of exemption from federal regulation.

Mink highlighted how nuclear testing on a remote island had the potential to poison the Pacific Ocean and the life forms that the water sustains. In a 1971 letter to President Nixon, asking him to stop the Cannikin test, Mink warned, "We are already polluting our oceans and damaging our fisheries and even the microscopic oxygen-producing sea organisms that sustain all life on this planet. It is acknowledged that the Amchitka blast will introduce radioactivity into the ocean—the only question is how soon, and how much. The peril of miscalculation is too great to permit such a risk."[16] The impact on sea life, in turn, could have an impact on human beings, who depend upon the ocean for their sustenance.

Alaskan Natives also expressed this concern. The Association of American Indian Affairs (AAIA) joined in a court case to block the 1971 Cannikin test. The organization explained its apprehension that radioactive "seepage could contaminate the salmon that pass through Alaskan coastal waters on their spawning migration and seriously threaten the health of thousands of Alaska Natives who depend on salmon as a major source of food."[17] The AAIA noted that it had attempted to stop nuclear testing before: "In the early 1960s the AAIA played a major role in halting Project Chariot, a series of proposed nuclear blasts near the Alaska Eskimo village of Point Hope that threatened to contaminate Eskimo food sources."[18] Nonwhite people and nonhuman forms of life inhabited the regions of the world deemed "remote" and hence bombable. Their geographical and cultural distance from the normative citizens of the continental United States resulted in their designation as expendable collateral damage.

To highlight the importance of these locations designated for military experimentation, Mink emphasized the historical and anthropological significance of places like Amchitka. She brought attention to an archeological project by the University of Alaska to excavate a "prehistoric settlement," consisting of eighty to one hundred sites on the Aleutian Islands.[19] These research locales, near the Bering Strait, potentially offered information about the early origins of humankind and the migration of Asian peoples to the Americas. Nuclear testing, not surprisingly, dramatically disrupted these endeavors. In an interview with a Fairbanks, Alaska, newspaper, the researchers explained, "If the blast does not occur, they will most certainly go back to the site for extended digging. And if the test is run they'll go back too, 'Just for a day to see what's left.' Th[ere] won't be houses on the hill, they're fairly sure. In fact the hill may also be missing after the megaton blast goes off."[20]

Mink recognized the militarized mindset, because her home state of Hawaiʻi also served as a site of conventional and chemical testing. Mink repeatedly demanded that the US Navy and Department of Defense stop using Kahoʻolawe Island as a bombing practice site. The smallest of the eight major Hawaiian Islands, Kahoʻolawe neighbors Maui, the third most populated island in Hawaiʻi and the location of Mink's childhood home. The navy used Kahoʻolawe on a regular basis as a bombing range.[21] In her protest letters, Mink pointed out the negative impact of this practice: "Residents of nearby Maui are understandably outraged by the noise and tremors caused by these explosions, and they are concerned with the danger to their lives and property."[22] These fears included the possibility of being bombed themselves. The navy denied this by stating, "In over 25 years of bombing Kahoolawe, there is no recorded instance of stray ordnance striking Maui as a result of an attack on the desolate island."[23] However, in 1969, Mink's former high school classmate and then mayor of Maui County, Elmer Cravalho, discovered "an unexploded 500-pound bomb" on his property. Mink conveyed this to the secretary of the navy, explaining that "the bomb was manufactured six or seven years ago but dropped within the past two or three months. It was found by its impact crater, and its brand new condition gave positive proof that the bomb was dropped recently and was not the result of a test years ago."[24] The US military conducted similar tests on Kaʻula Rock Island and also inadvertently bombed the nearby, populated Niʻihau Island.[25] In fact, US pilots sometimes mistakenly targeted locals who fished near bombing sites.[26] A comparable incident in the Philippines in 1976 resulted in a "Navy practice bombing" that "killed six Filipino fishermen."[27]

Mink and others condemned the dangers of conventional and chemical testing. The United States utilized a range of weapons in the Viet Nam War, including napalm and Agent Orange. The military experimented with these and other weapons first in the United States and in locales controlled by the government. In response to a query from Mink, the US Army initially denied any testing, but then qualified its response: "The Army has not tested either chemical or biological munitions in Hawaii. The Army has conducted limited chemical tests under strict safety precautions to obtain defense information."[28] When pressed for information, a spokesperson subsequently revealed that "four chemical tests were conducted on the Island of Hawaii at an Army jungle environmental test site in the Waiakea forest reserve."[29] In essence, the US military tested chemical weapons in the open air.

Mink's exposure of testing in Hawai'i reveals the interconnectedness of the Pacific and Southeast Asia in the practice of war making.[30] Historian Simeon Man reveals how the US military practiced war games in the fiftieth state, casting racialized individuals on the islands to play the role of the US enemy.[31] Various sites of the Asia-Pacific served as interchangeable locales to stage and make war. For example, Mink and her political collaborators connected Hawai'i's predicament with that of the Philippines as well as Culebra, an island in Puerto Rico also designated as a target-practice site. In 1974, after extensive and widespread protests, the US Senate barred the military use of Culebra. In lobbying for a similar bill regarding Kaho'olawe, Mink offered the opinion, "I believe Hawaii deserves as much consideration as Puerto Rico."[32] The United States incorporated Hawai'i, Puerto Rico, and the Philippines all in the 1890s, and their status as colonized and militarized sites continued well into the twentieth century. Only in 1990, after extensive protests and political pressure, particularly from Native Hawaiian activists, did the US Navy agree to stop using Kaho'olawe as a bombing practice site.

Mink's arguments against militarized testing in the Marshall, Hawaiian, Philippine, Caribbean, and Aleutian Islands foregrounded the mutual dependence of human beings on animals and the environment. She highlighted the intrinsic importance of land and water in sustaining life. Her geographical base in Hawai'i, ancestral connections to Japan, and political affinity for other Pacific islands shaped Mink's worldview, such that she valued the farthest, least visible portions of the United States. This perspective directly challenged a US Cold War mentality that divided the geopolitical world and prioritized national security needs, military preparedness, and weapons deployment. *destroyed them*

The Energy Crisis as Environmental Crisis

Patsy Mink's concerns regarding the ethical uses of the environment expanded beyond the militarized Pacific. She foregrounded the excesses of modern technology and capitalism throughout the United States. In late October 1975, as Patsy and John prepared to travel to Japan, the director of the US Federal Bureau of Investigation contacted the legal attaché, based in Tokyo, to request additional security. The FBI had received information, after some delay, of an alleged assassination attempt against Patsy, ordered by the coal company president James Brown.[33] As the chair of the Subcommittee on Mines and Mining, under the jurisdiction of the Committee on Interior and Insular Affairs, Mink regularly received hostile attacks that questioned her political legitimacy. She became a target because of her efforts to pass legislation regulating strip mining, an environmentally damaging method of extracting coal. She and her collaborators succeeded in passing bills twice in 1974 and 1975. Both times, Republican president Gerald Ford exercised his veto privileges after intense and well-financed lobbying by the coal industry. Only after Jimmy Carter became president, when Mink was no longer in Congress, did the legislation finally become law. In a letter to Mink, Carter shared, "I want you to know how deeply I appreciate your tireless efforts on behalf of this legislation and your commitment to preserving the beauty of our land."[34]

Mink's attempts to regulate strip mining provoked intense resistance. These debates reveal dichotomous understandings of the environmental regulatory role of the federal government in the midst of an energy crisis. Also, the conflicts delineated who constitutes a citizen and has the authority to claim rights and protections. Mink's critics claimed racial, gender, class, and regional privileges to question her ability to speak on behalf of the nation. Specifically, the coal industry evoked provincialism to protect white, male, Appalachian miners and their breadwinner roles. Using similar logic, they denigrated an Asian American female politician from islands far removed from their coal mines. In response to charges of greed and destruction, the coal mining industry argued that they sustained the livelihoods of those who truly matter to the polity: laboring white men and their families.

The US mining industry became a treasured national resource in the midst of the global energy crisis of the 1970s. A key turning point occurred in late 1973 as the Organization of Petroleum Exporting Countries (OPEC) announced an oil embargo against countries that supported Israel in the Yom Kippur War. Fuel shortages and inflated gas prices rocked the global economy. In response, the United States turned towards alternative and domestic sources of energy, including nuclear and coal.[35] Critics who opposed the regulation of coal mining repeatedly pointed to the global context of the energy crisis and the need for domestic energy sources. As President Ford stated when he vetoed the 1975 Surface Mining Control and Reclamation Act, "I am unable to sign this bill because . . . the Nation would be more dependent on foreign oil— when we are already overly dependent and dangerously vulnerable. . . . Coal production would be unnecessarily reduced—when this vital domestic energy resource is needed more than ever."[36]

In contrast, Patsy Mink and other environmental advocates argued for the need to monitor uncontrolled economic and technological development. A long-time critic of nuclear testing and militarized uses of the Pacific, Mink emphasized the importance of creating a sustainable environment for all. She authored the Environmental Education Act to promote public education on environmental issues. In a 1970 speech to support the bill, Mink observed,

We know that our air and water have been despoiled by pollution. Lead, mercury, sewage, and other contaminants have been poured into our rivers and streams. Auto exhausts and smokestacks befoul the air we breathe. DDI and other pesticides are working their way through lower life forms toward the advanced species. Our seas are being rendered lifeless by nuclear waste and chemical warfare agent disposals, and the blue sky itself is threatened by the advent of the SST [supersonic transport].

Certainly man now has the technological means of destroying all that nature has created. It will not take any new advances. All we have to do is maintain our present course and the inevitable collapse of the world ecology will result.

We can and must take drastic actions to prevent the pending disaster to our environment. Stepped-up programs to combat pollution are essential, but a necessary parallel is better education of our citizenry to the importance of this peril. Only through a fully informed and concerned public can we hope to reverse the course of destruction and turn toward beneficial policies.[37]

In contrast to Ford, Mink called for federal intervention, both to regulate industry and to better educate the citizenry. She also argued for a much more expansive understanding of national responsibility and resources. Although the context for this speech preceded the energy crisis, Mink's remarks nevertheless offer an important contrast to Ford's. He focused on coal and energy as essential resources, given the danger posed by foreign control over oil. In contrast, Mink identified unchecked modern technology as the chief threat to human life. She proclaimed a clean environment as necessary for the well-being of the nation and of humanity more generally.

The opponents of strip-mining regulation questioned the role of the federal government in intervening in their livelihoods and made personalized attacks against Mink. She received some thoughtful and respectful letters from both supporters and opponents of her proposed legislation. However, her papers also indicate a substantial amount of hostile correspondence that directly questioned her character and fitness to make policy. The attacks underscored Mink's gender and race as contributing to her lack of legitimacy. Claiming a tradition of social uplift, economic independence, and male-headed households, the opponents of mining regulation proclaimed themselves the true representatives and deserving citizens of American society.

The legislation that passed in 1974 and again in 1975 under Mink's leadership focused on similar issues, although attempts were made to address the concerns of President Ford after he pocket-vetoed the first bill. The proposed law attempted to "establish a series of minimum federal standards: To protect the environment from coal surface mining and surface impacts of underground coal mining; To insure restoration and reclamation of surface-mined land to its pre-mining condition; and To protect water resources, particularly in the West where the expected boom in energy development could strain the area's scarce water resources and ruin its agricultural productivity."[38] Advocates for these protections argued that federal standards and the creation of a reclamation fund were necessary. Given the expense and dangers of underground mining, surface mining—conducted by removing earth to expose coal—became and was projected to become an increasingly important sector of coal production. The *Washington Star* newspaper reported that surface mining only generated 9.4 percent of the nation's coal supply in 1940 but increased to 48.9 percent by 1972.[39] To expedite the process of surface mining, operators tended to dump the earth that they exposed "over the hill," thereby spreading "the destruction of the mine face in the most brutal way, creating unearthly slides of jumbled slate, rock and mud which crush trees and often slump across roads, into streams and even homes."[40] In addition to creating unsightly and unstable surfaces as well as debris pollution, strip mining created long-term water pollution: "Blasting loose the overburden, or the material on top of the coal seam, often destroys underground watercourses, or cracks the bedrock allowing acid mine water to seep into the groundwater. . . . The river runs yellow and acid because of the water running out of old coal pits. . . . Water spouts down from the mines, its sulphurous content quickly turning into sulphuric acid in the presence of air."[41] Strip mining literally poisons the environment, directly affecting the people who live near mines and frequently work for the mining industry.

Opponents of federal regulation ignored environmental issues and focused primarily on economic impacts. The coal company owners spearheaded and financed the campaign, but they enlisted (some claimed coerced) their employees and subcontractors to serve as the faces and voices of the campaign. Mink and other political leaders received numerous letters, some obviously form letters and others written meticulously by hand, blaming federal regulation for potential job loss. The owners emphasized that passing the strip-mining law would inevitably lead to decreased production, lower wages, and layoffs. Mink pointed out that these threats of financial disaster were not based on reliable industry studies. While a decline in coal production might occur, the requirement to restore and reclaim land could increase job opportunities. Also, tax breaks given to coal companies offered financial incentives to practice land stewardship. Mink posited that it was the refusal of coal companies to be environmentally responsible that threatened both their workers and consumers economically. Nevertheless, individual miners and their families emphasized that she and the federal government would be directly responsible for their financial woes. One letter writer stated, "I very much object to Federal intervention called democracy and properly labeled communism."[42] Others warned that legislators who passed the strip-mining regulation must be ready to increase welfare payments, since they were forcing economic dependency on those who were finally achieving some financial benefits in the midst of the energy crisis.

Federal regulation of mining was interpreted as an economic threat targeting white men and their families in Appalachia. Perceived as outcasts left behind by modernity, these miners defended a US tradition of white working-class masculinity. The *Washington Star* offered a portrayal of mining communities: "City people come to a place like Garrett County and it takes them a while to understand they're in a foreign country with foreign ways: Miners are men, women stay home; segregation is still practiced openly, with bars in a town like Westernport having a small backroom where 'colored' are served."[43] Critics of strip-mining legislation claimed the defense of white masculinity as their prerogative.

In early April 1975, most likely around the time when James Brown allegedly arranged Mink's assassination, coal mine owners instigated a truck caravan protest in Washington, DC. Numerous participants stated that the owners financed the trip, paying for hotels and travel expenses; others claimed that they attended at their own expense; and still others reported that participants were threatened with economic retribution if they did not support the caravan. Together, the protesters drove an estimated seven hundred coal trucks and other vehicles from Appalachia to Washington, DC, rumbling through the streets of the capital and honking their horns. They lobbied President Ford to veto the strip-mine bill, visiting political leaders and displaying signs that read "Strip Mines or Welfare Lines," "Cut Us Off—Cut Off TV," and "Our Black Coal Lights the White House."[44] This muscular display of vehicles and workers sought to intimidate political representatives and to target Patsy Mink.

While other congressional officials, such as Representative Morris Udall (D-Arizona) and Senator Henry Jackson (D-Washington) also spearheaded strip-mining legislation, Mink aroused intense hostility from opponents of federal regulation. They questioned her fitness to devise regulations on mining, claiming that she had likely never visited a mine, given her origins in Hawai'i. Prior to her appointment on the

Subcommittee on Mines and Mining, Mink did gain familiarity with the culture and industry of mining. Her husband had grown up in mining country in Pennsylvania, and his mother still lived there. In addition, the paternalistic economy of mining towns, with workers indebted to and dependent upon big financial interests, resonated with the plantation economy in Hawai'i. Also, Mink majored in scientific fields in college, given her interest in becoming a medical doctor. Furthermore, her husband specialized in groundwater geology. Even more important, Mink was a diligent legislator, holding hearings and arranging field trips to investigate a variety of mining practices and policies. However, her critics assumed her ignorance, focusing on the lack of mines in her state.

Following the truck caravan protest in Washington, DC, critics of strip-mine legislation launched a boycott of Hawai'i pineapples. Personalizing Mink's call for regulation as a direct economic affront to Appalachia, they responded by financially threatening what they perceived as a quintessentially Hawai'i product. The boycott effort sought to pressure Hawai'i voters and threaten Mink's chance of reelection. The *Kentucky Coal Journal* even published a political cartoon, portraying Mink as a muscular hula dancer, throwing "the Hawaiian Punch!" at Coal. In contrast to Mink's presumed aggression, coal is described as the "Heart of America's energy" and an innocent victim of her attack. The lump of coal appears puzzled and hurt but still protests, "Hey Lady! I'm trying to Help."[45] Mink's critics portrayed her as irrational and aggressive, transgressing expectations of exotic Asian/Hawaiian womanhood.

Opponents of federal strip-mine regulation maintained that their identities, communities, and economic livelihoods ran to the core of the nation's values and underpinned the nation's well-being. They also argued in contrast that Mink, as an Asian American woman from the middle of the Pacific Ocean, had no legitimacy to influence the national polity. Environmental advocates and defenders of Mink disputed the premise that individual legislators could speak only to their narrow regional interests. As one Honolulu journalist commented, "The questioners are placing preposterous limits on congressional initiative. It's like saying that congressmen from Idaho or Kansas, for instance, should concern themselves only with the future of potatoes and corn and forget about the use and abuses of off-shore drilling.... As an American, a congresswoman and as chairman of the mines and mining subcommittee,

Mrs. Mink has the moral, civic, and constitutional obligation to promote legislation apt to set limits to a process that is increasingly devastating American landscape and soil."[46]

In the debates regarding strip-mining legislation, Mink drew from her experience as a racialized woman from the Pacific to offer broader lessons for the national polity. She pointed out that "the issue of strip mining is almost a classic one of short-term gains versus long-run costs."[47] Mink urged congressmembers to ask themselves, "Must we waste the land so that we may waste the electricity?"[48] Mink asked Americans to consider the long-term impact of their personal decisions, to rise above individual interests and think of the broader implications for the entire society for generations to come.

De/Gendering Liberalism and Decoloniality

In the efforts to stop military testing in the Pacific and prevent destructive strip-mining techniques in Appalachia, Mink's political approach reflected her commitment to political liberalism. She believed in the power of the federal government to limit the destructive reach of the US security state and regulate the excessive practices of capitalism. To advocate for these policies, Mink adopted a gender-neutral humanist approach. She assumed the status of universal human citizen-subject, a role usually reserved for white men within the Western political tradition. Mink ran for the US presidency on an antiwar platform in 1972, recognized her groundbreaking role as a woman, and advocated fiercely for women's issues. Nevertheless, she chose strategically not to frame antimilitaristic critiques and pro-environmental politics in explicitly gendered ways.

Even as she adopted this approach, Mink amplified the voices on the bottom of US social hierarchies. For example, her emphasis on humanistic political liberalism differed from the perspectives of some Native Hawaiian activists, who articulated decolonial and Indigenous gendered worldviews to demand a more ethical relationship among land, water, and life. Nevertheless, they formed a political partnership in which Mink demanded US responsibility and supported Pacific Islander/Indigenous sovereignty. As a representative, she understood her role as introducing the concerns of her constituency (defined broadly) into congressional deliberations. Mink did not always agree with these perspectives but believed in the representative and deliberative process of democratic governance.

Mink's relationship with Native peoples and Pacific Islanders provides an opportunity to examine critiques of Asian Americans as settler colonialists in Hawai'i.[49] Jodi Byrd characterizes racialized people, "forced into the Americas through the violence of . . . colonialism and imperialism," as arrivants, a category distinct from settlers and Indigenous peoples.[50] Yet, Dean Itsuji Saranillio also warns us to "not mistake 'arrivant' as an invitation to 'innocence.'"[51] As someone who recognized and experienced a history of discrimination and marginalization, Mink strove to gain full citizenship rights within the US nation-state. In doing so, she advocated for a liberal vision of the American polity. She campaigned for statehood and advocated government responsibility for guaranteeing racial and gender equality and protecting the environment. Consequently, she worked with Indigenous groups in Alaska, Hawai'i, and the Trust Territories to bring attention to their concerns and demand equal treatment within the US nation-state. Nevertheless, Mink recognized that her advocacy for political inclusion at times departed from the goals of her Native and Pacific Islander allies, some of whom wanted independence. In turn, Mink championed the principle of self-determination to set limits on the US state and support calls for Indigenous sovereignty. Tensions and distinctions existed between Mink's political liberalism and some Pacific Islander calls for sovereignty. She attempted to reconcile these differences through her commitment to democracy and justice.

Mink used the language of science and civil liberties to advocate for stopping military testing and practicing environmental stewardship. After all, her intended audience was the executive branch of the US government. The president of the United States, in consultation with leaders in the armed forces and the Department of Energy, made the ultimate decisions regarding national security and military preparedness. Members of the US Congress, particularly the Senate, could declare war, fund defense spending, and influence international diplomacy. However, both Congress and the US public deferred to executive leadership in times of global conflict. Over the course of the US war in Southeast Asia, elected officials and members of the public began asserting their rights to politically monitor the conduct of war and the US presidency.

Initially, though, the commander-in-chief held more authority and lee-way. For example, environmental advocates and Hawai'i elected officials like Senator Daniel Inouye and Representative Spark Matsunaga, both former veterans, at first engaged in protest over US military exercises on Ka'ula Rock Island, especially in the aftermath of a 1965 acciden-tal bombing of Ni'ihau. However, as the United States began its ground war in Viet Nam under President Johnson, these protests transformed into cooperation. Military and political leaders persuaded residents and elected officials of Hawai'i to regard these exercises as essential for the success of the US war effort. Mink persisted in her critiques, though, because of her concerns about militarization and her antiwar politics.

Mink represented a distinct minority in Congress due to gender, race, and political beliefs. She clearly operated in a white, male-dominated political space. By necessity, she formed political alliances with men and women, whites and people of color. She made arguments for unpopular positions that challenged the US security state. To do so, she utilized frameworks that generated greater political traction. She cited scientific studies to warn against nuclear testing and unregulated strip mining. She articulated civil liberties arguments that critiqued secrecy as antithetical to democratic forms of government. In fact, in order to obtain US exec-utive branch documents on the Amchitka tests, Mink organized a group of thirty-three representatives and senators to sue the Environmental Protection Agency (EPA). Former attorney general Ramsey Clark, Mink's law school classmate, argued the case, *Mink v. EPA, et al.* (1973), which led to the strengthening of the Freedom of Information Act. By setting a precedent piercing executive branch secrecy, *Mink v. EPA* pro-vided justification for the release of President Nixon's secret Watergate tapes. In these efforts, Mink demanded the political authority normally reserved for the white, male subject.

Nevertheless, skeptics dismissed Mink due to her gender. A 1965 editorial in Kaua'i Island's newspaper, the *Garden Island*, initially char-acterized Mink's concerns about the transfer of Ka'ula Rock from the Coast Guard to the navy as premature and unwarranted. Entitled "Let's Not Holler before We Are Hurt," the editorial indicated that "Mrs. Mink probably got alarmed over the idea that perhaps the Navy was plan-ning to use Kaula for target practice . . . [but] there has been no no-tice on the part of the Navy regarding what use is being considered for

Kaula if and when it is transferred."[52] The writers gave obvious deference to the navy, while characterizing Mink as crying wolf, giving alarm without evidence. One week later, however, the editors retracted their position. They only did so, though, because "Kauai's commercial and amateur fishermen" informed the editors "how wrong we were and we got quite a few details on how the Marines have been bombing the rock almost regularly."[53] Even though the editors corrected their opinion about Ka'ula, the newspaper only reversed its position due to reports provided by male fishermen, not a female congressional representative. Mink even wrote to various media sources and constituents in Hawai'i, who credited the Asian American male congressional leaders for leading the charge against military testing. In reality, she had been one of the earliest and most consistent critics. In a note to her staff, Mink requested that they "pls always take the time to educate these guys."[54]

While Mink fought these gendered aggressions through rational debate and correcting the historical record, Native Hawaiians, or Kanaka Maoli, articulated their critiques of militarism through a gendered Indigenous epistemology.[55] The movement to end bombardment and gain access to Kaho'olawe played a central role in forming the Hawaiian sovereignty movement from the 1970s onward.[56] The concept of "Aloha 'Āina," roughly translated as "to cherish and care for the land," emerged from the efforts to reassert Kanaka Maoli sovereignty.[57] The demand to stop bombing Kaho'olawe and create an alternative relationship among humans, land, and water mobilized Native Hawaiians to revive their cultural, political, and spiritual values and reclaim land rights. Kaho'olawe represented an important locale from which to stage these protests. The island served as a "spiritual center," the physical incarnation of the sea god Kanaloa, "born of the union of Papa, earth mother, and Wakea, sky father."[58]

In January 1976, thirty Native Hawaiian activists attempted to land on Kaho'olawe. Inspired by Indigenous protesters on Alcatraz Island, they sought to protest military testing and reclaim the island.[59] Mink had lobbied the US military to allow access to Kaho'olawe for Indigenous activists. In a letter to the commander-in-chief of the Pacific in December 1975, Mink stated, "I am writing to support the request of" Gail K. Prejean, director of the Hawaiian Coalition of Native Claims, "for entry to the Island of Kaho'olawe for research purposes."[60] Mink framed Prejean's query in terms of "research" and Prejean himself as a "representative of a group of people of the States," because those were the terms upon which the US military might allow admission onto Kahoʻolawe. Mink also explained that Prejean's "research" included inspecting "the extent of devastation and waste and the condition of sacred areas of Hawaiian heiaus [temples], fishing shrines and burial places."[61] Mink stated that the visit would help determine "whether the trust relationship that the State and the Federal government have to Native Hawaiians has been properly executed."[62] The navy and air force both denied the request, so Indigenous activists engaged in civil disobedience to gain access to their historic lands. Of the thirty who attempted to land on Kahoʻolawe, only nine arrived on shore. The Coast Guard picked up most of the protesters, but two men evaded capture. Walter Ritte Jr., chair of an activist organization, Hui Alaloa, and Dr. Emmett Aluli eventually left voluntarily after two days. During that time, they surveyed Kahoʻolawe.

In a press conference following their return, Ritte and Aluli spoke of the island's beauty, the desecration of land via war games, and their gendered relationship to the environment. Their accounts challenged military depictions of Kahoʻolawe as useless land, only fit for bombing exercises. Ritte said in tears, "I'm 30 years old and for 30 years, I thought Kahoolawe was a rock they bomb, but it's a beautiful island."[63] He testified to the destruction of sacred shrines that the US military had wrought. Ritte compared the negative impact of the military to the commercialization of Hawaiʻi, saying, "I always thought it was the hotels that desecrated our islands, but now I know that the bombing is the desecration."[64] He pointed out how the environmental damage constituted spiritual damage for Native Hawaiian people: "The river beds were full of silt. You could see where bombs had hit and had created new valleys. . . . We saw huge boulders—you know Hawaiians worship boulders—split. If our grandparents had seen that they would have cried."[65] Neither Ritte nor Aluli brought food or water with them. When asked how they survived for two days, Aluli claimed that "they were watched over by the goddess Hina," who "made it rain to wet their backs, and blessed them with water when they were thirsty."[66] Although both Ritte and Aluli were experienced hikers, and one was a hunter, they did not speak of their survival skills, more commonly associated with masculinity.[67] Instead,

Aluli evoked the protective powers of Hina, a powerful moon goddess who represents the natural process of healing, growth, and transformation. Just as the island of Kahoʻolawe represented a union between sky father and earth mother, so the male activists spoke of the gender complementarity of Indigenous epistemology. Samuel Crowningburg Amalu, another activist who joined the Aloha ʻĀina movement, explained that "we love that soil—It is part of the living flesh of Papa who was our ancient mother."[68]

In contrast to the life-giving force of Hina and Papa, the protest organizers associated the bombing of Kahoʻolawe with the devastating impact of "white man's churches" on Indigenous belief systems.[69] The protesters quoted in the local newspaper, all of them male, critiqued the destruction created through the collusion of commercialism, Christianity, and militarism as extensions of white masculinity. Instead, they evoked Indigenous deities and worldviews that foregrounded their connections to and ability to survive on Kahoʻolawe as a spiritual and gendered connection to the land. This initial landing inspired a series of additional occupations as well as the Protect Kahoʻolawe ʻOhana (PKO) movement. PKO, through protest and negotiation, forced the US Navy to enter into a consent decree in 1980, which allowed "a right to visit and care for the island."[70] Another decade after the decree, the military finally agreed to stop bombing the island.

As part of the movement's efforts to hold political leaders accountable, Native Hawaiian female activists also appealed to Mink to gain access to Kahoʻolawe. In March 1976, five kupuna, or honored elders, from Molokaʻi, four female and one male, wrote to Mink and other government representatives in Hawaiʻi to ask for assistance. They wished "to touch the aina [land] of Kahoolawe before [their] eyes close for the final time."[71] They appealed to Mink and authorized political leaders, because "the Navy has granted you and other politicians, permission to go onto Kahoolawe."[72] The kupuna enlisted Mink as a representative of Hawaiʻi to represent them to the US Navy. Like Ritte and Aluli, the elders regarded Kahoʻolawe as "being sacred lands of our ancestors containing our heiaus [temples], . . . sacred pohaku [stones], sacred puu (where the piko [center or umbilical cord and/or placenta] of the new born were buried)."[73] They asked to "experience the ʻaina' of Kahoolawe, to feel the mana [spirit] which radiates from it's [sic] sacred soil."[74] In their appeal to Mink, the kūpuna emphasized a genealogical/reproductive connection to the land. Their human ancestors lived and worshiped on the island; the piko of their people, or the originating materials of life, were buried there; and the land itself represented the descendant of their spiritual mother. The kūpuna asked Mink to translate their desires and worldviews to the US Navy. Their letter pointed out, "The values we speak of are foreign to the ears of the Navy, but are at the roots of our Hawaiian culture."[75]

Mink respected their desires and understood their request in gendered ways. She forwarded their letter to the rear admiral and commander in charge of Pearl Harbor and asked for permission to personally escort "the six women mentioned in the attached letter."[76] The five kupuna did name an additional female escort to accompany them. One of the letter writers, listed last, was male. Mink apparently assumed that all of them were female, perhaps because of their appeal for spiritual and ancestral connection to Kahoʻolawe.

Not surprisingly, the US military refused Mink's request. They rejected these gendered Indigenous ways of understanding and interacting with the island of Kahoʻolawe. The navy had previously, on February 13, allowed a group of kūpuna on the island, where the elders conducted a ceremony to "restore mana to the island."[77] "Mana" is roughly translated as "a power that . . . can only be manifested through correct and responsible actions"; the kupuna sought to recognize "that the island—a living and breathing entity—had been defiled through misuse and neglect, and they sought to restore Kahoʻolawe's mana by calling the ancient gods back to the island."[78] In his study of the PKO movement, Jonathan Osorio argues that the presence of the kūpuna and their religious ceremonial role transformed the movement to reclaim Kahoʻolawe by signaling "a deeper commitment to Hawaiian values and traditions."[79] Perhaps recognizing this more profound claim to Kahoʻolawe that the kūpuna evoked, the navy denied the request to visit the island. The violence against the lands of Hawaiʻi mirrored the epistemological rigidity of the US armed forces.

The gendered and spiritual values that Native Hawaiian activists articulated differed from the values of others who supported the return of Kahoʻolawe. Native Hawaiian desires to touch the ʻāina and experience the mana of the island contrast with the motivations of those who wanted to gain recreational access to the island and its surrounding waters or who wanted to protect their property values. Coalitional work against military destruction could exist, but political distinctions also persisted. Mink attempted to bridge these divides and to demand accountability from the US military. While she chose a gendered strategy that privileged Western humanism, she also recognized and respected alternative epistemologies.

Mink understood that her proposed solutions to US militarism could differ from those of Native Hawaiian activists. In the case of Kahoʻolawe, Mink repeatedly submitted bills to demand its return to the state of Hawaiʻi. In contrast, the Aboriginal Lands of Hawaiian Ancestry (ALOHA) requested that she "abstain from taking part in any move to return military lands to the State of Hawaii until our Hawaiian people have had an opportunity to present a legislative bill in the next Congressional Session. As you are aware, our primary objective is to seek lands and/or money reparations from Congress for the aboriginal and part aboriginal Hawaiians."[80] Returning land to the state of Hawaiʻi did not fulfill the goal of Native Hawaiian sovereignty. Mink understood this incommensurability. In a letter to a constituent, she wrote, "Those who wish to take over the island do not want it to revert back to either the County of Maui or the State. They wish it to be declared an asset of ALOHA or part of their aboriginal claims of the native Hawaiians."[81] Federal control meant military control. State control likely would end militarized testing, given the unpopularity of these exercises in Hawaiʻi. However, state jurisdiction did not necessarily lead to land reclamation by Native Hawaiians.

Understanding this distinction, Mink respected the call by ALOHA to demand the return of land to Native Hawaiians or compensation from the federal government for the illegal act of deposing Queen Liliʻuokalani. Mink began working with the group closely in 1973, soon after ALOHA was formed. At times, she withheld federal legislation until receiving the organization's approval in order to follow the group's political lead. As she expressed to the leadership of ALOHA, "May I congratulate each of you for your willingness to undertake so profound a task as that of seeking ultimate justice and fairness for the descendants of Ancient Hawaii. Much patience will be required, but perseverance will bring success."[82] To bring attention to land reparation, Mink offered advice, organized hearings in Hawaiʻi, and arranged meetings with federal officials, including members of the Committee on Interior and Insular Affairs. Mink did not always agree with the goals and strategies of ALOHA, as she explained to a Native Hawaiian constituent:

> I am informed by my staff of your phone call telling about your reservations on the ALOHA bill. I share those reservations, but I do feel that these people have a right to pursue their goals in the Congress and have therefore agreed to help them. We will try, and perhaps if . . . they do not succeed in enactment of their bill, they may be more willing to go the route of seeking greater benefits under [another avenue] which was my initial suggestion. They asked me not to go this route and to give ALOHA a chance, and I agreed.[83]

Mink went on to explain that as someone who was not Indigenous, she sought to respect and support Native Hawaiians. She also encouraged the letter writer to make clear her concerns to other members of her community. Mink stated that "I hope that you and others, who are the ultimate beneficiaries, will speak up. . . . I am deeply committed to do all that I can to help the Hawaiian people. And, so, we must depend upon all Hawaiians to arrive at their true feelings and to express them. . . . Now is the time to say what you think is right and what ought to be done."[84] Mink believed in the process of democracy, both within the Native Hawaiian community and in the US nation.

In response to those who questioned the idea of land reparations, Mink asserted the importance of a full congressional hearing and the political legitimacy of compensating Indigenous peoples for land. She pointed out the similarity between Hawai'i and Alaska, the two newest states of the union: "One hundred and six years ago Russia sold Alaska to the United States. The natives of Alaska did not receive any monetary consideration for this taking of title to the land. Despite the long time interval the Congress recently voted $1 billion to these natives of Alaska because of this taking."[85] This compensation inspired Native Hawaiians who "believe that their cause is of greater justice than [that of] the Alaskans because they were taken by conquest. The Hawaiian monarchy was overthrown by U.S. soldiers and the Queen was imprisoned. Crown lands were taken and the natives were not compensated."[86] In 1920, the Hawaiian Homelands, lands held in trust by the state for Native

Figure 5.1. Patsy helps Hawaiʻi visitors celebrate King Kamehameha in Statuary Hall of the US Capitol on King Kamehameha Day, ca 1970. Source: Library of Congress/US House photo.

Hawaiians, were created to help redress this loss. However, lack of funding as well as the restrictive criteria used to qualify Native Hawaiians for homesteading led to questionable policies that did not fully acknowledge Indigenous claims.[87]

Mink disagreed with those who criticized using tax dollars to compensate Native Hawaiians. In a letter to one such critic, she asked why certain government initiatives are more readily embraced and others regarded with suspicion: "When the Alaska natives got their $1 billion did you cease to pay your taxes? Or when Nixon gave away the White House helicopter, or the villa to the Arab ruler Sadat, did you throw away your card? Or when the Pentagon asked for $2 billion for just one nuclear sub, did you gasp in disgust?"[88] Mink's queries emphasized that government allocation of resources and citizen reactions to these expenditures reflect their political priorities. She suggested that critics of Indigenous land compensation are more likely to accept military-related expenses, despite their greater cost. Mink concluded by emphasizing that "the bill the Hawaiians wrote by themselves does not envision one dime going directly to any person. . . . No Don Ho or rich Hawaiian will get anything out of this fund. It is to go in trust for the welfare of the people as a whole."[89] After considering all of these factors, Mink emphasized that "I do believe that it is worth at least a fair hearing in the Congress."[90] Mink's conception of democracy recognized both individual rights and the collective rights of the disfranchised.

Mink's approach to political representation reveals the complex relationships between Asian Americans and Pacific Islanders. She navigated between political liberalism and Indigenous sovereignty. She fought racialized patriarchy through humanistic neutrality while also uplifting a Native Hawaiian gendered decolonial imaginary. In a letter to the Council of Hawaiian Organizations, she indicated that "you may be assured of my support, and that I will do everything I can to bring about our common goal of a halt to the bombing and a return of the island to the people of Hawaii."[91] Mink's conception of the "people" of Hawai'i included Native Hawaiians as central members of her constituency, even as their demands for land return conflicted with the desires of other residents who benefited from their dispossession.[92]

Lessons from the Pacific

The environmental politics articulated by Mink and Native Hawaiian activists offered alternative political imaginaries. Instead of the deathscape created by the US security state in the Pacific and unchecked economic growth nationally, Mink evoked an interconnected world that linked ecology to human life. Her broad vision of the world challenged both uncontrolled militarism and capitalism. She represented an outsider to the US polity due to her ethnicity, gender, connection to Hawai'i, and political beliefs. However, in relation to the Indigenous people of the Pacific, Mink represented an influential insider. While she advocated for full inclusion and government accountability, some of her Indigenous allies demanded an end to militarized violence and also political and cultural autonomy. In essence, some Native Hawaiian activists offered a transformative Pacific imaginary. They articulated and practiced a spiritual connection among people, land, and water to counter the white patriarchal confluence of the US military, nation-state, and Christianity.

Mink's commitment to political liberalism constrained some of her strategies and solutions. In light of the gendered and racialized hierarchies of the US military state, Mink strategically occluded gender in her political presentation. Although she foregrounded women's issues and perspectives for other issues that she advocated, Mink utilized gender-neutral discourses to claim political authority regarding the environment and military testing. Even so, she experienced marginalization as an Asian American woman within the US polity. She also responded to and supported gendered and Indigenous appeals for accountability and spiritual connection.

The differences between Mink and some Native Hawaiian activists reveal tensions between political liberalism and Indigenous sovereignty. Yet, opportunities for coalition formation and mutual support reveal possibilities for Asian American and Pacific Islander alliances. Their respective calls for an end to militarism and a return of occupied land during the Cold War still resonate strongly throughout the Pacific World today. The ongoing occupation and violence of the US militarized state and its allies is visible in places like Standing Rock, Okinawa, Guam, and Jeju Island. Such repression continues to inspire resistance and alternative political imaginaries that demand an ethical consideration of the lands, waters, and lives of those on the margins of empire.[93]

PART III

Oceans and Islands

In its 200-year history, only 11 women have served in the U.S. Senate. And nearly every one of them was first appointed to fill the unexpired terms of a member who retired or died, often their husbands. Today, all 100 Senators are men. To put it bluntly, we have moved from tokenism to total segregation. . . .

As one woman member recently put it, "There are three times as many whooping cranes as Congresswomen . . . but nobody seems concerned about our being an endangered species."
—Women's Campaign Fund, 1976

Her career defies conventional political wisdom. She fights when others rush to conciliate. She speaks out when others think it much wiser to remain silent. She stands on principle when others opt for expediency. Moreover, she is a woman in a human enterprise dominated by men. . . .

In a political universe whose fundamental laws of behavior call for compromise and backroom bargaining, Mink all too often treats politics as though it were a high-minded debate conducted on a purely rational plane. She believes strongly in altruism. "I'm not here to be a weather vane for party opinion or party leadership. . . . I think my job is to reflect what I think to be the best judgment I can put to any issue regardless of whether or not it is popular."
—"Patsy Mink: A Farewell to House Work," 1976

The US bicentennial year of 1976 encouraged national reflection.[1] The country faced the challenge of "celebrating" its national heritage. Mass social movements from the mid-1950s onward exposed systematic exploitation, violence, and inequality in US society. In addition, economic recession and high unemployment during the 1970s generated anxiety and resentment. And, political scandals, most notably the lingering aftermath of Watergate, revealed widespread corruption at the highest and lowest levels of electoral leadership. One strategy that bicentennial organizers adopted, according to scholar Natasha Zaretsky, was to foster local and private celebrations, distanced from the federal government.[2] In contrast, Patsy Mink doubled down on her commitment to national service. Nearing the completion of her twelfth year of service as one of 435 representatives in the House, she ran for the US Senate, a hundred-member body, an all-male bastion.

Mink's campaign faced notable challenges, systemic to female candidates and specific to her commitment to political independence. Created in 1974, the Women's Campaign Fund (WCF) represented an electoral arm of the women's movement. The nonpartisan organization was "formed for the sole purpose of raising funds to elect progressive women to political offices."[3] The lack of financial support constituted a deep gender gap. As WCF explained, "Women candidates simply do not receive the same financial support as male candidates when they seek higher political office. No matter how impressive their legislative records or demonstrated vote-getting ability, the myth persists that women candidates are less electable and potential contributors want to back a winner. Like most myths, this one is self-perpetuating. Contributors don't contribute to women because they want to back a winner and women don't have a chance to win without these contributions."[4] The WCF attempted to break this cycle by narrowing the gender gap in fundraising, and the organization selected Mink as one of four women candidates to help integrate the Senate in 1976. Mink needed this support, because her primary opponent, Spark Matsunaga, was out-raising her.

The financial disparity between Mink and Matsunaga reflected their political base, the gendered dynamics within the Hawai'i Democratic Party, and their approach to leadership. Matsunaga's house district centered around Honolulu, the political and financial capital of the state. Mink's district constituted the rural communities on O'ahu and the outer islands. While both attracted similar numbers for their campaign kick-off fundraiser dinners (with Mink slightly ahead), Matsunaga charged one hundred dollars per person, and Mink charged fifty.[5] These differences compounded over time, allowing Matsunaga to purchase more air time on media and present himself as the winnable candidate.

The old boys' network in Hawai'i also influenced the Matsunaga-Mink primary. Both Democrats, they campaigned for the opportunity to replace Republican Hiram Fong, who was retiring. Hawai'i's other senator, Daniel Inouye, initially warned that a Matsunaga-Mink campaign would result in "blood running in the streets."[6] Inouye eventually decided to remain "neutral" in the campaign. Other leading Democratic leaders, however, warned that a hostile primary and the decision of both representatives to run for the Senate could lead to party losses across the board. The implication was that Mink, who had declared her intentions before Matsunaga, should not run for the Senate. Matsunaga claimed that "most Democrats want him to run . . . and would prefer that Mrs. Mink stay in the House. 'I hope she will see the picture as most people in Hawaii see it.'"[7] Matsunaga's statement conflated "most Democrats" with "most people in Hawai'i." The Democrats who spoke out publicly about the Senate race were men, many of them Japanese American. As Mink noted, "The state Democratic Party has taken sides in the Senate race through the governor, the titular head of the party. . . . Gov. George Ariyoshi has come out with a slate of candidates that he favors for election, but . . . this ticket does not include me."[8] Matsunaga, a 442nd veteran from World War II, drew from the same network of male political patronage that supported Inouye during his 1959 victory for the House of Representatives against Mink.

By 1976, the Hawai'i Democratic Party had additional ammunition to charge Mink with excessive political independence. Matsunaga's campaign argued that he and Mink had similar political records. Matsunaga, however, overstated how the League of Women Voters characterized his votes. He apologized, but only a day before primary election.[9] Matsunaga emphasized that he primarily differed from Mink in his political approach: he cultivated connections and had the right temperament to network with members of Congress. He, his staff, and even their Republican opponent also indicated that Matsunaga used his influence to help Mink gain an important committee position, and she promised in return not to run for the Senate.[10] Mink refuted Matsunaga's allegations. In a handwritten press release, which it is not clear she released, Mink wrote, "It's time Spark admitted his lie. . . . He knows I did not seek membership on the Appropriations [Committee] in 1975. He knows I was elected by the whole House to the Budget Committee."[11] In addition, Mink pointed to distinct differences in their political record. The Americans for Democratic Action, a progressive watchdog organization cofounded by Eleanor Roosevelt, supported Mink's contention that she distinguished herself politically from Matsunaga. The organization "judged Mink and Matsunaga and other House members according to their votes on 19 issues, including oil decontrol, food stamps, aid to New York City, the B-9 bomber and CIA funding. Mink followed liberal lines on 95 percent of the issues."[12] Matsunaga "showed liberal tendencies on 68 per cent of the issues."[13] In the Senate, Inouye demonstrated "only slightly liberal leanings" with "56 per cent," and Republican Hiram Fong came in at "22 per cent."[14] Between Mink and Matsunaga, these differences tended to surface in international issues, with "Mrs. Mink vot[ing] repeatedly against military aid . . . , and Matsunaga consistently support[ing] it."[15]

Additionally, what Matsunaga described as a weakness, Mink characterized as her strength. Throughout the campaign, Mink emphasized her political independence. She did not play it safe politically; rather, she was willing to be "ahead of the majority," a phrase she used to declare her senatorial campaign.[16] She criticized the US war in Viet Nam during the Johnson administration, not only after Nixon came to power. She challenged executive privilege and secrecy in withholding information about nuclear testing on Amchitka. Mink sided with Robert Kennedy in 1968, when the Hawai'i Democratic Party leadership backed Hubert Humphrey. In 1972, she ran for the US presidency and traveled with Bella Abzug to meet Madame Binh in Paris to explore whether female diplomacy might end the war in Viet Nam.

Being a trailblazer was not necessarily a comfortable position, since those spearheading change also faced significant headwind. According to the *Hawaii Observer*, "She did not enjoy the opprobrium her critics heaped on her during the war. 'It isn't pleasant to take the verbal abuse . . . [,] but when an issue is important enough and involves the lives of other people, it is a deeply moral question. I took that position in the belief that it was right. . . . [And] the fact is that I was right and they were wrong."[17] Political observers also noted these distinctions between Matsunaga and Mink. One article described Matsunaga working "his way as a deputy whip partly by cultivating some of the mainstays of the old, encrusted establishment of committee chairmen and other senior House figures"; in contrast, "Mrs. Mink has generally sided with the vocal bloc of liberal Democrats who now have come into power."[18]

The distinction between Matsunaga and Mink was even apparent to high school visitors. John Lau, a student from Maui High School, wrote about his impressions of the two politicians during a Washington, DC, trip that he won through the 4-H organization. Matsunaga arrived first to a joint meeting and "tried introducing the four of us to her [Mink], but he had forgotten our names and had to read them off our name tags"; in contrast, Mink had already met the students earlier in the day "and she knew us all, including our names!"[19] Although both candidates promised to send materials on criminal reform for their high school debate team, only Mink followed through with the commitment. She also met with the group at the end of the day, telling the students that they "were the first people ever to receive 'Mink for Senate' buttons."[20] Lau subtitled his article "Cat Meets Dog," and in his opinion, "The cat had won!!"[21]

Mink took seriously the role of responding to her constituents, including those not yet of age to vote. Her opponents charged that she overlooked the interests of islanders. Mink indicated, though, that she and her office staff "spent at least 90 percent" of their time "devoted to individual ombudsman service to the people of Hawaii. I have helped literally thousands of people confront their government over injustices, errors, and inequities, and have helped to give meaning to the concept of equal justice."[22] Mink believed in service to the people, insisting on "reading every piece of correspondence that leaves her office."[23] She regarded politics as a form of public education, which entailed "verbaliz[ing] . . . issues in common terms in order to help crystallize public opinion."[24] As Mink noted, the public felt at times confused on difficult issues, like the war in Viet Nam: "Nobody had all the answers, but the fact that I was willing to take a strong position and explain it was appreciated by the people who opposed my views."[25]

Despite Mink's efforts and belief that she could prevail, Matsunaga, with his political connections, his larger campaign chest, and his base in the more concentrated urban area of Honolulu, received 51 percent of the vote to Mink's 41 percent.[26] The results were not as lopsided as Mink's loss to Inouye in 1959 but still left her out of federal office. Daniel Akaka, a Democrat and the first Native Hawaiian representative, won Mink's House seat. At the age of forty-eight and after twelve years of service as an elected representative, Mink was without a political job. She was not alone. None of the female candidates for the Senate prevailed in 1976. Ironically, Congress authorized the National Women's Conference during the bicentennial to reflect on the past, recognize continuing challenges, and chart a path forward. As the election results indicated, much work remained for women to achieve equality.

For the next fourteen years, Mink continued to pursue her political passions. In recognition of her leadership on environmental issues, the newly elected Democratic president, Jimmy Carter, appointed Mink the assistant secretary of state in charge of Oceans and International Environmental and Scientific Affairs (OES). Her purview literally encompassed the entire world, but she also was motivated by the realization that experiments in the name of science as well as calls for environmental protection could both deeply harm already-marginalized groups, particularly women and Indigenous communities. Finding the executive branch more restrictive compared to elected office, Mink resigned within a year to serve as president of Americans for Democratic Action. From that vantage point, she advocated moving the center of the Democratic Party and the nation towards more progressive politics. With the election of Ronald Reagan in 1980 and the ascendancy of conservatism at the federal level, Mink decided to return to Hawai'i. She ran for Honolulu City Council and focused on issues to improve the quality of life on the islands. As Mink entered middle age, she persisted in her political explorations. Characterized and criticized as a "chronic dissenter," Mink pursued her passion for politics, continuing to create "more waves" as she explored the oceans and islands of her home world.[27]

VIOLATED

Threaded through my mother's professional and political career were various challenges motherhood posed for women of her day who defied gender prescriptions while also raising young children. Early on, law firms turned her away from jobs because she was the mother of a young child. As she made her way in politics, opponents and critics whispered about how her child needed her full attention. Wondering how she juggled lawyering, politics, and mothering, my teachers periodically suggested she was less of a mother because of her public notoriety. After a "duck and cover" drill, my third grade teacher lamented that I was plumb out of luck of ever seeing my mother again in the event of a nuclear attack during school hours because she was so busy. Some of Mom's friends policed her motherhood by routinely asking me questions about my home life. One friend repeatedly opined that I was lucky to have a grandmother who could guide me into adolescence as my mother's plate obviously was overflowing with professional obligations.

By far the most profound—and most cruel—challenge to my mother's sense of her worth as a mother arrived in the US mail on March 5, 1976, the day before my twenty-fourth birthday. Sent by a medical researcher at the University of Chicago, where my mother had attended law school, the letter disclosed that I might have been damaged in utero as the result of a medical experiment my mother had been enrolled in unwittingly during her pregnancy in 1951–52.[1] The letter arrived twenty-four years too late for my mother to thwart the medical abuse of both her body and mine. Anguished upon learning that a third party had used her body to transmit carcinogenic poison to her fetus, my mother was inconsolable.

I was in DC on a weekend break from graduate school when the letter arrived. Dated January 1976, it had been addressed to my mother at a location she had not inhabited since 1953. On the verge of being returned to sender, the letter eventually had been forwarded to her congressional office. The delay in receiving the letter poured salt in the wounds inflicted by its contents, as the University of Chicago knew perfectly well how to find her: she was one of the most visible members of its 1951 law school class (along with then-congressmember Abner Mikva and former US attorney general Ramsey Clark). What's more, she had participated in alumni events; engaged the university and its faculty on numerous issues over the years; and sent her daughter to college there.

The letter's delay was symptomatic of a far more dangerous delay. Twenty-five years passed before University of Chicago maternity patients were notified that they had received diethylstilbestrol (DES) during pregnancy as part of a medical experiment about which they had not been informed and for which they had not given consent. The purpose of the experiment had been to test claims that DES prevented miscarriage, premature labor, and related problems. The head of OB-GYN at the University of Chicago, suspecting that DES was not useful, conceived the experiment to test his negative hypothesis.[2] Compounding the delay, the university continued to withhold notice about DES exposure for four years after the Food and Drug Administration issued a warning about the carcinogenic dangers of DES for the daughters of women who had ingested it during pregnancy.[3] In fact, the university itself never told mothers about the secret DES experiment, or that their daughters were at risk of vaginal and cervical cancer, as well as other reproductive complications. But for a five-hundred-thousand-dollar National Institutes of Health grant received in 1975 by a University of Chicago researcher to track adverse effects of DES on offspring from the 1951–52 experiment, we might never have been informed. It was the researcher, not the university, who sent the letter. In a meeting with my father, the researcher reported that the university was miffed with her for "stirring up concern" about the experiment among people who otherwise would not have known they were involved.[4]

The four paragraphs that arrived in an innocuous envelope on the eve of my birthday deranged my world and devastated my mother. The paragraphs did not include any instructions or exhortations as to what kind of precautionary or diagnostic care DES offspring should seek. The interest expressed in the offspring of the experiment regarded not our well-being but our whereabouts. Apparently, the point of informing the mothers that they had been in the DES experiment was to secure contact information for the offspring, so that we could be examined by an expert selected by the researcher. We were data points, not patients.

We spent the next day and a half in tears, wrenched by sobs of both despair and anger. We were each jumbles of overlapping emotions. My mother felt violated, her body invaded by a toxic chemical unbeknownst to her. She felt tricked, having obediently ingested "vitamins" that turned out to be DES throughout her pregnancy. She was horrified that her body was the conduit for the carcinogenic endangerment of me. She was frightened for my future. I, too, felt violated—invaded and battered by strangers who impaired my life choices before I was even born. I, too, was scared of what I might have to deal with medically going forward. I was angry that I had spent two years embracing the University of Chicago as a college student, all the while unaware that the university had damaged my insides without forewarning and with apparent impunity.

I calmly had assimilated the epilepsy diagnosis I received in 1968 and in 1975 had survived a head-on auto collision while riding shotgun. My mother was adept at navigating my medical crises, and I adapted to their chronic consequences without fuss. We habitually pushed through adversity, resolute and resilient, practical and persistent. We could not push through the news from the University of Chicago. It was a gut punch from which we could not easily recover. We were apprehensive about the medical jeopardy I incurred from DES exposure. And we also were horrified that the university had stolen our bodily integrity, trammeled my mother's right to withhold consent, and robbed me of reproductive health and choice going forward.[5]

In the wake of receiving news of the DES experiment, I extended my stay in DC to secure medical evaluation. I knew I did not want to be evaluated by University of Chicago experts—I didn't want anyone affiliated with the university to touch my body. Yet I was about to enter an unfamiliar gynecological landscape of colposcopes and cancer risk assessment. In the dark about which doctor best suited my situation, my mother turned to a law school classmate who recommended someone with great enthusiasm. We visited the recommended gynecologist, who dismissed the concerns we presented—DES exposure, cancer risk, reproductive complications—as "typical women's hysteria." We left without an examination; I didn't want this guy to touch me any more than I wanted the university to. As we reached the exit door he opined, "You're not going to find a physician willing to second guess the work of a colleague in the profession, especially one from the distinguished University of Chicago faculty."

As my mother searched for appropriate gynecological care, my father flew to Chicago to meet with the researcher who sent the letter, as well as to procure my mother's medical records. The records clearly indicated that my mother had been one of the thousand women who had been given DES throughout her pregnancy (another thousand had been given a placebo). Meanwhile, my mother identified a trailblazing gynecological researcher-practitioner at the Columbia Hospital for Women in DC, who determined that my reproductive tract bore the telltale signs of DES exposure.

A lawyer and a feminist, my mother decided that both the university and the drug manufacturer needed to answer for violating her body and inflicting injury on mine. After discouraging demurrals from mainstream attorneys, she sought advice from Dr. Sidney Wolfe of the Public Citizen Health Research Group. She explained the elements of the legal claim she wanted to make in a letter to Wolfe in September 1976:

> 1) failure to advise me at the time of the experiment in 1951 that I was in this group; 2) lying to me that I needed "vitamins" to help the fetus; 3) failure to keep records of the "dosage" and number of pills I was issued and over what period of time; and 4) failure to notify me when the general medical world became alerted to the hazards discovered in daughters whose mothers took DES (in my case, they cannot get by with the excuse of "no address" because of my general notoriety as a politician).[6]

Wolfe directed us to the Public Citizen Litigation Group, which agreed to manage the case.

Joined by two other mothers, my mother sued the University of Chicago and Eli Lilly, the manufacturer and distributor of the DES, on behalf of the class of mothers who had been unwittingly enrolled in the 1951–52 experiment. A judge refused to certify the class, so the three mothers proceeded as the only parties to the claim. During the course of litigation, the mothers' case against Eli Lilly was dismissed. But breaking legal ground, a toxic battery claim against the University of Chicago was allowed to proceed.[7] In his ruling on a motion to dismiss, the district court judge held, "Battery is defined as the unauthorized touching of the person of another. To be liable for battery, the defendant must have done some affirmative act, intended to cause an unpermitted contact. . . . We find the administration of a drug without the patient's knowledge comports with the meaning of offensive contact."[8]

In the end, the university settled with the mothers. Under the settlement, university hospitals and clinics offered free diagnostic examinations until 1988 and subsidized treatment for DES injuries until the offspring reached age seventy.[9] Each mother received seventy-five thousand dollars before legal expenses. I was not impressed with the settlement but understood that the assurance of care for the offspring as a class, even though the court had not recognized the mothers as a class, would be valuable to sons and daughters who chose care from the University of Chicago. I did not trust the university to be guided by my best interests and so did not plan to avail myself of its medical services, ever.

Alongside the mothers' litigation, several of the daughters pursued legal claims against the University of Chicago and Eli Lilly. Like our mothers, we were not certified as a class. Each of our complaints alleged battery, malpractice, and product liability. My case went to trial early in 1983.

My trial was sordid, painful, and infuriating. Not only did I endure public description and depiction of my reproductive anatomy; I withstood misogynist interrogation while in the witness box. The jury, populated in part by antichoice suburban Chicago homemakers, was put off by the person opposing counsel made me out to be. Cross-examination revealed that I had been sexually active for several years prior to my first DES-related colposcopy; I was epileptic; I was unmarried and childless; I was a "career woman." They flipped the script and put me on trial. According to defendants' attorneys, I was to blame for the injuries I had incurred as a fetus: they suggested that promiscuity could have caused my reproductive anomalies; that epilepsy medications could impede my ability to bear healthy children; and that being unmarried at age thirty-one showed I was not actually interested in motherhood, as did my professional commitments and aspirations. The fact that I was the lone Asian American in the Chicago courtroom compounded the effects of gender shaming. The jury found in favor of the University of Chicago and Eli Lilly. I felt savaged.

Although it did not win vindication, our litigation fertilized emerging legal terrain. The mothers' case raised the issue of toxic battery, asserting that involuntary, nonconsensual, toxic dosing of a person's body is "an offensive invasion of their persons" to which existing legal theories and remedies can be applied.[10] The daughters' cases raised the thorny question of third-party fetal battery of an eventually born child. Outside the courtroom, the mothers' claim contributed straightforwardly to the developing law of environmental and product accountability. The daughters' claim of fetal battery was vexed, causing controversy even on my legal team. The chief danger was that my claim of battery *in utero* by third parties might be conflated, in another context, with claims of "fetal rights" or "fetal protection" and deployed against pregnant or potentially pregnant women.[11] Also controversial was how the fetal battery claim affected jury selection. My attorneys used the jury-selection process to suss out attitudes toward reproductive choice with the aim of selecting likely antichoice jurors who might lean sympathetic to fetal interests. But patriarchy bites back: jurors with antichoice profiles tend to be those most committed to policing gender conventions and least empathetic to young feminists like me.

The experience of medical and pharmaceutical abuse, along with the bruising battle for legal vindication, cast a long shadow over our lives. I tried to bury both the legal and the medical ordeals in the far recesses of my memory, never speaking about either trauma and rarely reporting my medical status even to my closest friends and family. Ever the activist, my mother made the personal political. Drawing from her own experience of toxic battery, she made it her obligation to advocate against toxic environmental exposure while in local politics during the 1980s. Upon her return to Congress in 1990, she became a legislative activist for women's health, for gender equality in medical research, for DES research and education, and against the Republican effort to restrict tort litigation remedies available in product liability cases.

6

A Progressive Political Vision

Patsy Mink left the House of Representatives at the end of her six terms, but she stayed in Washington, DC. No longer a legislator, Mink redefined her role in a shifting political landscape. The election of Jimmy Carter after the era of Nixon and Ford allowed Democrats cautious optimism. In his inaugural address, Carter emphasized human rights, not just Cold War alignment, as the cornerstone of US foreign policy. His secretary of state, Cyrus Vance, defined human rights to include social welfare, "the right to fulfill vital needs such as food, shelter, and education."[1] Furthermore, this political vision was directed both outward towards other countries and inwards within the United States. The Carter administration, however, inherited an economic recession with high unemployment rates and rising costs of living, particularly due to escalating oil prices that resulted from US–Middle East conflicts. The new Democratic political leadership deployed a contradictory mix of federal spending to stimulate the economy, deregulation to empower the private sector, and roll-backs on government expenditures to strive towards a balanced budget. While the Carter presidency asserted commitment to human rights, it increasingly adopted neoliberal approaches of scaling back regulation and investment in social welfare.

In this context, Mink worked both inside and outside the federal government. Initially, she moved from the legislative branch to the executive, becoming an assistant secretary of state in charge of OES, the Bureau of Oceans and International Environmental and Scientific Affairs. Her scope of work covered approximately 70 percent of the earth's surface and focused on issues that impacted the entire planet.[2] She operated within a governmental bureaucracy with a labyrinth of units, each with its own alphabetical identification, seeking to address issues related to environmental protection, international cooperation, and human rights. Mink's understanding of the "human" encompassed marginalized groups such as women and Indigenous peoples.

Just over a year later, Mink decided to resign her position and became, instead, a critic of the Carter and then Reagan administrations from the outside. From 1978 to 1981, she served as the president of the progressive organization Americans for Democratic Action (ADA). Mink collaborated with labor, education, women's, civil rights, and peace groups to combat the rising tide of conservativism. Instead of working from the inside, Mink felt more at home exerting leadership and pressure from the outside. No longer an elected official, she experimented with finding an appropriate platform in Washington, DC, that allowed her to raise her political voice.

Becoming an Assistant Secretary (of State)

Mink joined OES with the belief that her environmental and political commitments could influence policy and diplomacy. The emphasis that President Carter and Secretary of State Vance placed on human rights aligned with Mink's goals. As an assistant secretary of state, she supervised a domestic staff of over 130 and another one hundred internationally, with attachés located in about twenty embassies around the world. The bureau had a broad charge to promote nuclear nonproliferation; develop alternative energy; delineate water, fishing, and shipping rights; foster responsible uses of the environment; and encourage population-control practices.[3] The office fostered US relationships with other "developed" nations and with the United Nations. OES also participated in East-West conversations between socialist and nonsocialist countries. In addition, the office developed North-South agreements between "developing" and "developed" nations. And, OES served as the official country director for the Arctic and Antarctica, with oversight in the antipodes of the world. As one newspaper article reported, "Mink's new job literally covers the earth from pole to pole and from the skies to the seas."[4] But despite the bureau's expansive role, Mink discovered that its location in the State Department, the master's house, was quite confining. A (mis)match between Patsy Mink and OES stemmed from institutional and cultural factors, in large part due to gender and race.

Mink received the State Department appointment as a result of feminist advocacy. When she lost the senatorial primary to Matsunaga in 1976, she confessed experiencing "frustration and anxiety and deep depression"; she recalled that after all her efforts, "It was difficult to avoid a gloom and doom feeling, like the end of the world."[5] Despite the "let-down," Mink "decided she was not going to be a quitter."[6] The feminist advocates who supported women in politics did not quit either. Mink explained, "If it were not for the efforts of women in Washington, a coalition of 40 or 50 women's groups who began intensive activity after the 1976 election and submitted hundreds of names of qualified women for government posts to the president and his committees, I doubt that I would have had the opportunity to be considered."[7] After a decade of women's social movement advocacy, President Carter and Secretary of State Vance both publicly stated their support for affirmative action to address persistent racial and gender inequalities. Feminist and racial advocacy groups pressured them to follow through on their pronouncements.

The diversification of the upper echelons of the executive branch was far from comprehensive. A *New York Times* editorial characterized "picking President-elect Jimmy Carter's Cabinet" as "this city's favorite guessing game."[8] In speculating about who would fill cabinet positions, the writer asserted, "Some ground rules are reasonably clear."[9] The overall power structure, "the really big jobs," would remain in the hands of "senior experienced men."[10] Cyrus Vance, for example, "was no surprise."[11] A Yale graduate, Vance had a political pedigree; his uncle had been an ambassador to the United Kingdom, and Vance himself had previously served as secretary of the army under President Kennedy and deputy secretary of defense under President Johnson.

In addition to these seasoned white male politicians, the *Times* editorial predicted the token inclusion of women and people of color in the Carter Democratic administration: "two women, one black, and one Republican."[12] The flippancy of the journalist revealed the superficiality of affirmative action efforts. Feminist lobbyists agreed. They pointed out the delay in appointing women and the pattern of hiring them in positions "less senior than those given to loyal male workers of this and previous administrations."[13] Mink, they protested, should have been appointed secretary of the interior, given her legislative committee experience in this area, rather than assistant secretary of state. If Mink had been selected, the author of the "Guessing Game" editorial argued, she would have been "a triple 'first'—the first woman to head Interior, the first Hawaiian and the first Japanese-American to serve in the cabinet."[14]

Newspaper coverage in Hawai'i also speculated that Mink's racial background and home state likely factored into her eventual appointment in the State Department; nevertheless, the island press also emphasized that these representational considerations provided Mink with a significant platform. The *Honolulu Advertiser* argued, "Politically, of course, it will not be lost that Mink is Oriental, a favorite of women's groups, and a deserving Democrat from a western state that went for Carter. But it's much more significant that she is an outstanding person with a combination of drive, vigor and experience that would be an asset in many positions."[15] The editorial continued that Mink brought with her "what might be called a special 'Pacific perspective,' a feel and sympathy for not only the peoples and places of this area but of Third World problems and attitudes in general. That will be especially important in a time when major emerging foreign policy issues involve relations with the Third World."[16] Over the next sixteen months, Mink attempted to bring her Pacific World perspective, an ecological concern for water, land, and people living on the margins, to the State Department, a bureaucracy rife with power hierarchies.

Environmentalism and Human Rights

In 1973, Congress created OES to formulate and implement a coherent national policy regarding environmental and scientific issues that crossed national boundaries. The concept of environmental diplomacy "acquired currency" during the same year "after the formation of the United Nations Environmental Programme."[17] This new State Department bureau, the only one imposed by the legislative branch, overlapped with a plethora of other offices and agencies inside and outside the State Department. Aware of the challenges of her new position, Mink nevertheless found the opportunity appealing. OES signaled an approach to foreign policy that aligned with her own. In her Senate confirmation statement, Mink pointed out that "in an era, less dependent on a more traditional military-defense role in U.S. diplomacy, and more dependent on an economic, and moral suasion, U.S. technological leadership is key to a successful U.S. foreign policy."[18] As a long-time critic of US militarism, Mink preferred to promote international and educational cooperation, to use persuasion and negotiation rather than force.

As head of OES, Mink intended to weigh in on pressing issues related to technology, diplomacy, and human rights that had long interested her. Mink offered distinctive insight to the bureau's division on Environmental and Population Affairs, which promoted international cooperation to protect the natural environment, including endangered species. In this realm of her work, Mink foregrounded a definition of environmentalism that included human welfare and human rights. As she explained in a speech to members of the Japanese American Citizens League in San Fernando Valley, "The whole concept of international environment . . . has been redefined under the Carter Administration. Rather than presenting a 'negative kind of concept of just preventing pollution,' environment has been described as the total condition people find themselves in."[19] In other words, environmentalism represented a way to advocate for human rights, conceptualized as "improving the quality of life, medical care, access to the benefits of technology."[20] Mink cited Carter and Vance to support these statements, but she also understood that she was forging new ground in insisting on connecting environmentalism and human rights. She explained to one of her assistants, "OES needs to develop its own paper on human needs—Our 'Bible' to convert the unbelievers."[21] This conception of a "total human environment" required "1. Water," including drinking water and water for farming, "2. Food—land & ocean resources," "3. Health," including birth control and addressing infant mortality and inadequate nutrition, "4. Housing," and "5. Energy Needs."[22]

These concerns regarding human welfare had economic, regional, and gendered impacts. In a speech given in Hawai'i, Mink reminded her audience, "We know that at least one billion people still live in poverty or near poverty. Of the poor, women and children suffer the most. . . . Of the world's illiterate, three-quarters are women."[23] At another talk in Nairobi, Kenya, where Mink addressed the fifth meeting of the United Nations Environment Programme, she emphasized the importance of advancing "the human condition so that all peoples can share the bounty of the earth to enjoy good nutrition, safe water, and a healthful environment in which to live."[24] These changes had a significant impact on women: "Women suffer the worst nutrition and are in the poorest health as they struggle to keep their children alive. A diminished economic, social and political role for women stifles rightful aspirations which instead, if nurtured, could help to double the capacity of a community."[25] Mink's understanding of environmentalism did not seek solely to "protect" the environment from human beings. Instead, she foregrounded how the environment could sustain human life and enable women to fully thrive.

Mink's office oversaw "population control," which has been characterized as a code word for eugenics. Feminists of color have critiqued predominantly white women's organizations for their focus on controlling fertility while ignoring eugenic practices of forced sterilization that targeted poor, disabled, and nonwhite women. The term "reproductive justice" was coined in the 1990s to demand a broader range of reproductive rights that pivoted on safeguarding women's choices about whether, when, and how to bear children. In the late 1970s, Mink's commitment to birth control for women emphasized their autonomy and agency. Her own experience as an unwitting subject of a DES medical experiment reinforced her belief that all women should have sovereignty over their own bodies.

Mink's political commitment to Indigenous communities similarly shaped her understanding of human rights and environmental politics. In the realm of fishing rights, most notably whale hunting, she navigated between calls to save endangered species and demands to respect Native cultural practices. In 1946, the United States established the International Whaling Commission (IWC). The agency fostered international cooperation to promote conservation and regulate commercial whaling. In the 1970s, Greenpeace, an organization founded to protest nuclear testing on Amchitka, launched the "Save the Whale" campaign. It did so by confronting whaling ships and promoting public awareness of how the industry exploited natural resources. Mink supported their overall goal. The OES staff drafted President Carter's opening remarks for the IWC meeting in June 1977. He commented that "whales have become symbolic of our environmental problems as a whole. No longer are they viewed as a product from the sea available to those with the technology for their harvest."[26] Carter promised a US commitment to a "ten-year worldwide moratorium on commercial whaling." At this meeting, the IWC recommended a drastic reduction of the commercial quota worldwide and a complete moratorium on hunting of the bowhead whale.

This quota reduction and moratorium, however, raised complicated issues. Whale hunting constituted a significant commercial practice for some countries, most notably the Soviet Union and Japan. Together, they accounted for over 85% of the commercial whaling industry.[27] In response to the IWC recommendations, Japanese industry leaders contacted members of the US government to express their opposition. They explained that given the limited land for farming and animal stock, Japan relied heavily on seafood "as a source of animal protein"; in fact, "We Japanese have consumed whale meat for more than 1,000 years."[28] The reduction in whaling would have a tremendous impact on their economy, if the quota were instituted.

In addition, Indigenous peoples in the United States, most notably Alaska Natives, also protested the ban on bowhead whaling. S. Lynn Sutcliffe, as legal counsel to the Alaska Inuit community, expressed these concerns to Secretary of State Vance and copied Patsy Mink. Sutcliffe reminded them that "the Alaskan Eskimo's cultural and nutritional well-being is dependent upon their ability to continue to hunt the Bowhead whales as they have done for thousands of years."[29] The issue of Indigenous peoples' hunting rights differed from the claims of other nations. First, Alaskan Natives focused on subsistence, not commercial hunting. In fact, Sutcliffe argued that Inuits were "dedicated to the preservation of the bowhead whale species," given its significance to their culture; they would willingly collaborate "to accumulate scientific information to judge what further internal restraints on their own activities or what external restraints on other persons [sic] activities might be necessary to preserve both the bowhead and their own unique culture."[30]

Failure to respect Indigenous peoples' hunting rights, in contrast, raised issues of "dereliction of duty" on the part of the United States. The nation held a trust relationship with Native peoples, which was subject to international scrutiny for potential violations of human rights. The United States had a long history of such violations, but Indigenous activists mobilized globally during the 1960s and 1970s to bring visibility to these injustices and to demand retribution. Mink appeared to concur with their perspective. Despite repeated requests from the media, Mink declined to give public statements regarding the bowhead whale controversy, but she communicated privately with various members of the State Department. In one such telephone conversation, which Mink documented in a memo, she pointed out that "the civil disobedience potential which could give us international publicity . . . could be harmful to our human rights position. . . . that all nations should defend their rights of native minorities and their subsistence ways."[31]

Some political leaders and environmental organizations dismissed Indigenous claims, fearing that if the government did not follow through on international agreements, then other nations also would challenge the IWC. Don Fraser, representative from Minnesota, argued that "the Bowhead is mainly hunted in US waters by Alaskan Eskimos" and that whereas in the past, they hunted for subsistence, "as Eskimo culture has changed, Eskimos have come to use high-powered guns to hunt and kill and they do so now more for sport than subsistence."[32] A more callous whale advocate remarked to Mink "about the importance of the whale in the Eskimo culture. . . . He could not accept that view. . . . He said he thought that they could find something else to hunt or eat."[33] Similarly, environmental activist groups, most notably Greenpeace, also disregarded Indigenous rights claims. In fact, the organization publicly attacked Mink, charging her with condoning the murder of innocent animals.

Other political and environmental advocates sought to honor Indigenous rights while promoting conservation. Environmental organizations, such as the Friends of the Earth and Rare Animal Relief Effort, emphasized the importance of "full Eskimo participation" in developing an international conservation policy.[34] In fact, involving Indigenous peoples in these commissions was crucial, because "Eskimos . . . are thought of as members of a special world community rather than U.S. subjects."[35] As Inuit peoples, they shared cultural and political commonalities with Indigenous peoples in "Greenland, the Soviet Union, Canada and the United States"; the issue is vital "to the survival of subsistence aboriginal cultures around the world. Without their cooperation, the whales can hardly be saved. With it, they can be."[36] This perspective recognized Alaska Natives not as a minority group subsumed within the US nation but as part of a global Indigenous community across the Arctic.

Mink also sought Indigenous representation and advocated for respecting Native ways of life. After much deliberation and consultation with various executive branch departments both inside and outside the State Department, Mink announced a collective decision. The State

Department, with concurrence from Commerce and Interior, would not challenge the IWC moratorium on whale hunting. However, she noted that the ban stemmed from the fact that "the U.S. government, not the Eskimos, failed to comply with the expressed wishes of the IWC since 1972."[37] In other words, Indigenous peoples were not the root cause of the overexploitation of the whale population. In addition, Mink announced that "native aboriginal hunting of endangered species was always exempt" from IWC regulations, which only applied to commercial whaling.[38] This politically astute move both acknowledged Indigenous rights and positioned the United States as a willing participant in and enforcer of international conservation agreements. In a newspaper interview in which Mink finally felt free to express her views after the State Department had issued its position, she underscored both of these positions: "She rejected a description of Eskimos hunting whales in 'a sportive chase with snowmobiles, walkie-talkies and long-range harpoon guns.' [Instead, Mink stressed that] they use a shoulder gun adapted from the weapon 19th-century whalers used. . . . In the spring hunt—which produces most of the annual take—they go out in traditional kayaks."[39] In line with Mink's belief that environmental protection needs to go hand in hand with sustaining human life, including the lives of those often regarded as marginal within the United States, Mink pointed out, "The Eskimos' ability to hunt whales is the very heart or spirit of their culture. . . . If we have an opportunity to save a culture from extinction, this is as important as saving the whales."[40]

The State of Bureaucracy

These efforts to expand the goals of environmentalism and human rights gave Patsy Mink a sense of accomplishment. However, these "wins" were few and far between. To oversee OES, Mink had to acquire a thorough grasp of diverse issues, develop timely and appropriate responses to advance her political vision, and assert her leadership within OES and beyond. As she discovered, she inherited and operated within an institution that resisted her leadership due to her identity as a political appointee and a woman of color. She had to navigate the work culture of a complex organization that normatively practiced gatekeeping.

The political origins of OES along with its topic encroachments into other agencies' jurisdictions created challenges for anyone in the assistant secretary role. In March 1976, during the confirmation hearings of Mink's immediate predecessor, Senator Claiborne Pell pointed out that "the State Department . . . has had your position filled less than 20 percent of the time."[41] Pell, who helped to establish OES, noted that "the office had been established for 29 months and vacant for all but 5."[42] Former vice president Hubert Humphrey added that "unless the Secretary of State and the President of the United States are going to give you backing, you will be in an office that is set off in the corner."[43]

The difficulty of leading OES and the broader ineffectiveness of the bureau were captured in a December 1976 study, "Technology and Foreign Affairs."[44] Its author, Dr. T. Keith Glennan, was the first director of NASA and a former commissioner of atomic energy. After conducting interviews with 140 people, including experts on science, technology, and the environment both in and outside of the bureau, Glennan concluded that the bureau was hampered by its "lack of 'clout'" and in its limited ability to attract staffing talent, since a position in OES was perceived as a "dead end" assignment.[45] Glennan emphasized that "strong leadership cannot assure an effective Bureau, but its absence will almost certainly guarantee an ineffective one."[46] He identified a series of ideal traits for the assistant secretary: "He must be a respected scientist, a capable administrator and a skilled diplomat."[47] Mink, arguably highly qualified as an administrator and diplomat, was neither a scientist nor a male. On the three pages in which Glennan elaborated on his vision of leadership, Mink circled all the male pronouns associated with the ideal assistant secretary and proclaimed in the margins, "But I am a She!"[48] Given the overwhelmingly male world of scientific, technological, and political circles as well as the history of institutional neglect for OES, being a she would prove challenging.

Operating within the bureaucracy of the State Department was new for Mink. As a legislator, she could identify issues to address, dialogue with constituents, and develop alliances to advocate for change. During her terms in Congress, Mink supervised a staff, both in Washington, DC, and in Hawai'i, but she selected these individuals and trained them to support her work. As an assistant secretary, Mink inherited a much larger bureaucracy. As a short-term political appointee, she faced the challenge of coaching career members of a civilian diplomatic corps whose terms would outlast hers.

Her files reveal numerous efforts to train staff and transform the work culture. She outlined commonsense office routine procedures and also tried to foster a collective practice of debate and analysis. She sent memos that included instructions to staff on how to answer, record, and respond to phone calls; how to write reports that thoroughly analyze issues so that she and others had all the information necessary to develop opinions and recommendations; and how to document significant decisions rather than rely on memories of verbal interactions. As Mink explained to one of her key assistants, Tom Reynders, "I want to give everyone a sense of participation. . . . We need to create a climate of our willingness to hear. . . . We will then only get the strongly held and well-thought-out views."[49] To foster a more cohesive work culture and community, Mink advocated the relocation of the multiple departments under OES into one office suite, located on the same floor of the State Department. Given the lack of sustained leadership and the size of the bureau, the staff drifted into patterns of work that did not rely upon an overall leader. Instead, each subunit, particularly those led by ambitious staff, sought to gain political attention. Mink tried to right the OES ship to assert her leadership and strengthen the bureau's role within the State Department.

Mink's efforts faced challenges from within and without the OES. A month after Mink began her work as acting assistant secretary, she wrote to a friend, "My days are already full of paper pushing and I feel tortured by the immobility that these techniques impose upon the bureaucracy. My hope is that these first impressions will fade as the real tasks of policy formation become more evident."[50] As Mink imposed her work standards and developed recommendations for hiring and staffing, she began to feel more at ease with her position. Almost nine months into her role, Mink wrote, "As in any new job, it took quite a while to learn the system, and to begin to feel a master of it rather than a slave."[51]

Nevertheless, difficult internal dynamics, especially related to gender and race, persisted within OES. In one memo addressed to her assistant in late October 1977, Mink provided extensive details about her interaction with a troublesome male staff member. He claimed that Mink didn't communicate with him yet vociferously disputed her views when she did. He refuted her interpretation of past conversations but also refused to write down key points of their conversation. He also undermined her in public settings and only grudgingly accepted her views when male authorities also articulated the same perspectives. Mink concluded, "Brown's problem may be that he has never worked for a female. . . . and being the military type . . . can't take orders from a woman."[52]

Within OES, Mink was a distinct minority in terms of gender and race. In response to affirmative action mandates issued by Cyrus Vance, Mink noted that her bureau "is quite bad—not counting the secretaries—there are only 4 women paid more than $20,000—whereas there are 50 men paid more than $20,000. Are there any minorities at all making more than $20,000?"[53] Her assistant responded in the negative. This racial and gender hierarchy reflected the OES job classifications. White men occupied positions of leadership for foreign service and technical expertise. Women concentrated in the general civil service category and clerical roles.

Mink's challenges also arose from outside of OES, including from another woman. The day that Mink received confirmation from the US Senate, Lucy Benson also was appointed under secretary of state, becoming the highest-ranked woman in the State Department. Civil rights activist Andrew Young also became the United States ambassador to the United Nations during the same confirmation. Mink reported to Benson, a white woman who had previously headed the Massachusetts League of Women Voters. Although the two women appeared to share similar commitments to women's political leadership, Mink commented on the narrowness of Benson's gender politics. In a casual conversation before a volatile meeting, which Mink documented in a memo to one of her staff members, she noted that Benson "only cares for the ERA! What a mixed-up person."[54] In contrast to Mink's intersectional and expansive concerns about women's educational, economic, reproductive, and political rights, Benson only focused on whether women had the same legal rights as mandated by a constitutional amendment. Mink's memos further noted Benson's many attempts to interfere with appointments and assert direct oversight in OES. In the December 1977 meeting, Mink stated, "It's time you know that unless I have complete autonomy in selecting my own deputy, I quit, and you may so inform the Secretary."[55] When Benson passive-aggressively asked if Mink did not want her help, Mink declared, "I must make the selection myself. These people are accountable to me and to me alone. If that's not acceptable, I quit."[56] Although Mink did not declare her resignation until April 1978, her difficulties with Benson persisted. All of OES's memos had to receive Benson's approval in order to be forwarded to other sections of the State Department. In other words, Benson served as the gatekeeper of Mink and OES.

In Mink's resignation letter to Vance and her departure announcement, she reiterated these frustrations. Mink expressed support for the overall mission of OES and identified a list of fifteen significant accomplishments in environmental diplomacy under her leadership. One category of achievements included responding to emergency situations, such as foreign fishing vessels entering US ocean space or the unexpected reentry of a Soviet satellite. A second group of accomplishments highlighted Mink's and OES's role in working across governmental agencies. OES collaborated with the National Security Council, the Council on Environmental Quality, and the Department of Commerce on a range of issues. These included projects related to Antarctic marine resources, weather experiments, transborder data flow from computer technology, environmental impact statements in foreign jurisdictions, and Trust Territory political status. A third category consisted of negotiating agreements between countries. These discussions included American Indian and Alaskan Native fishing rights. Finally, OES prepared significant reports, such as the Panama Canal Treaty Environmental Impact Statement, and developed policies on issues related to oceans, environment, and technology.[57]

Despite these feats, Mink warned of structural obstacles that impeded OES's full potential. She pointed out that "oversight as practiced in the State Department" was rather stifling. Mink cautioned, "Unless the State Department accepts the need of the Assistant Secretary for OES as a policy maker with all the essential prerogatives of a Presidential appointment, then the job should not be filled."[58] The current arrangement essentially meant that "the Department of State has chosen to have it [OES] run by a seventh floor principal instead of an assistant secretary."[59]

As a political advocate who prided herself on independence, Mink was ready to leave OES but not necessarily Washington, DC. She floated

Figure 6.1. In this 1979 photo, Bella Abzug, *left*, and Patsy Mink stand with Gloria Steinem as she speaks in Washington, DC. They warned presidential candidates that vague promises for women's rights would not be enough to get their support in the next election. Source: AP Photo/Harvey Georges photographer.

the idea of a Civil Rights Commission posting, but she may have burned her political bridges with the Carter administration. After all, the president was under pressure from conservative Democrats, especially those from the South. In January 1979, seven months after Mink's departure from OES, Carter fired her close friend, Bella Abzug, from the National Advisory Commission on Women's Issues due to her criticisms of his gender policies. The feminist coalition that helped land Mink the position in the State Department clearly had declining influence on the Carter administration.

Asian American advocates also expressed concern upon learning of Mink's resignation. Both Mink and David Ushio, a deputy assistant secretary of the interior, resigned in April 1978, which led the Japanese American Citizens League to point out, "The Carter administration has nobody to 'look out for Asian-American interests.'"[60] The previous year, legislation was introduced to designate the first ten days of May Asian

Pacific Heritage Week. The effort failed, but after "the departure of two of the Carter administration's top Asian-American appointees," the bill passed upon reintroduction, and the president agreed to celebrate Asian Pacific Heritage in May 1979. The symbolic recognition of Asian American and Pacific Islander heritage was politically useful in light of the upcoming 1980 elections and the departure of significant Asian American political leaders from the Carter administration.

Within a month of her resignation, Mink landed at the helm of Americans for Democratic Action. Progressive advocates with close connections to leading politicians created the organization to promote liberal policies. Rather than seeking to influence power brokers from within a bureaucracy, Mink found the freedom to critique and openly promote alternative ideas from the outside. She did not possess an official role in the government, but she had the freedom to express her political voice.

Democratic Action

Americans for Democratic Action as an organization was diametrically opposite of the State Department. Established in 1946, ADA attracted members of the political elite who sought to assert progressive leadership. Former first lady Eleanor Roosevelt, economist John Kenneth Galbraith, labor leader Walter Reuther, historian Arthur Schlesinger, and theologian Reinhold Niebuhr founded ADA, and the organization's past presidents included former attorney general Francis Biddle and Senator George McGovern. Mink became the group's first female president. Based in Washington, DC, ADA also was a grassroots organization but with elite political contacts that promoted individual as well as chapter memberships across the country. ADA forged coalitions with progressive organizations, particularly civil rights, labor, peace, and women's groups. A handful of paid staff, whom Mink characterized as "sorely overworked and underpaid," oversaw daily operations.[61] The presidency, however, was a volunteer position. Within one month of Mink's resignation from the State Department, she moved from a large, stifling bureaucracy to an advocacy group. Instead of behind-the-scenes negotiations, Mink traveled around the country, speaking to the public, mobilizing grassroots organizations, and lobbying political leaders.

Through ADA, Mink promoted a liberal agenda against a rising tide of neoliberalism.

When Mink assumed the ADA presidency in June 1978, Jimmy Carter was still in office. His policies, with the support of Democratic leaders, increasingly resembled Republican agendas. Facing rising unemployment and fiscal fears, Republicans led a tax revolt, targeting government spending on social welfare programs as a primary culprit for the country's economic woes. George McGovern, the 1972 Democratic Party presidential nominee and the immediate predecessor to Mink as ADA president, warned in his outgoing address, "California has voted overwhelmingly to approve Proposition 13 [to reduce property taxes]. In New Jersey a rightwing extremist has taken a Senate nomination by pledging to cut taxes and to gut government. In Ohio a general rejection of bond issues may close down schools in Columbus and Cleveland. Across the country politicians are chasing and fanning the popular whirlwind. They are seeking a mandate to govern by running against government itself."[62]

The coordinated attack against government spending was selective and racially coded. McGovern pointed this out by asking, "If government has the money to bail out Lockheed [a company known for its central role in developing technology for the defense industry] . . . , why is it powerless to help older people, neglected children and average Americans—including those with black skin?"[63] McGovern expanded upon this charge of the conflation of racial and economic resentment:

> While the tax revolt expresses profound and legitimate anger, it also has undertones of racism. . . . A news weekly quoted one California voter: "It's those social services that annoy . . . me—social services for the colored, the Mexican, and so forth." It is unfashionable now to worry about the poor and minorities and to defend the idea that they, too, deserve an opportunity. Perhaps property taxpayers ought to remember, if only for a moment, how many of them would never have owned a home without a government loan and a mortgage tax write-off.[64]

It might be expected that McGovern as head of ADA would criticize a Republican agenda that prioritized defense spending, corporate welfare, and whiteness. What concerned him and Mink was how much the Democratic leadership caved in to these political pressures and abandoned a vision of a liberal and activist government. McGovern cited Carter's 1978 State of the Union address, in which the president insisted that "government cannot solve our problems . . . define our vision . . . eliminate poverty . . . or reduce inflation."[65] This "despair of democracy" created "inaction."[66] McGovern dismissed this approach by asking, "If Franklin Roosevelt had assailed the needy and the old as shiftless and thriftless, could he have passed unemployment compensation, rural electrification and social security?"[67] Instead of less government, McGovern called for political vision and compassion, not just efficiency. Patsy Mink took up this mantle, asserting the need for an activist government to promote peace and protect working people, racial minorities, and women. It would prove to be an uphill battle as neoliberal agendas increasingly gained traction.

Stormy Political Seas

Just as Mink's work in the State Department encompassed almost the entire planet, ADA had expansive political interests. The organization held an annual convention at which the president, numerous honorary vice presidents, and board members were elected. ADA also held regular national board and executive board meetings. Elected at the June 1978 national convention, Mink attended the national board meeting that month, in which twenty-six substantive topics were discussed. ADA was concerned about international relations, such as the military budget, human rights, the United Nation, US-Soviet relations, South Africa, international trade and investment policy, détente, and US-China policy.[68] ADA also addressed environmental issues and slotted time to discuss alternative energy, environmentally beneficial public works, and air quality. The group focused on economic issues such as full employment, tax reform, housing, urban policy, a national healthcare system, and national health insurance. ADA also prioritized racial and gender issues such as the ERA and the Wilmington Ten (an almost-all-African American group falsely accused of inciting a riot to promote educational integration). And, the organization discussed how to facilitate democratic participation by reforming political funding, promoting voter initiative, and bringing attention to the political status of Puerto Rico.

Mink's notes indicate that some of these issues were tabled or deferred for future discussion, but the scope of ADA interests was vast. Mink regarded this breadth of ADA as its strength. In her first article in the organization's publication, she pointed out,

> I have embarked upon the rather stormy seas where the political climate is stirred by a backlash against government programs, government spending, and government regulation. . . . Like most other organizations, we have been swept into one fight after another in one-issue campaigns. I do not suggest that these efforts were not needed or that the issues were not important to ADA. . . . But, having expended our efforts on these single battlefronts—abortion rights, gay rights, gun control, school busing, the Panama Canal treaties, Proposition 13, ERA, labor-law reform, the Humphrey/Hawkins jobs bill, nuclear power plants, Bakke, South Africa, and so on and on—we have had little time left over in which to organize against the attack upon the entire liberal approach towards government and its responsibilities.[69]

Mink believed that ADA as a comprehensive organization was well situated to build relationships with other liberal and progressive groups that might only focus on particular issues. Together, they could form a broad and effective coalition. Mink issued a challenge to "enlist all who share our outlook to join forces and save America from the ruin of the selfish I-me-my politics of 1978."[70]

The organization's primary domestic priority became the fiscal policies and national budget under Jimmy Carter. One of Mink's first statements focused on the Revenue Act of 1978, passed by Democrat-controlled Congress and signed by Carter. Characterizing the tax bill as containing "a litany of regressive provisions," Mink highlighted "the capital gains tax cuts and the corporate tax reductions" that would "seriously undercut the interests of low and middle income taxpayers."[71] These critiques of Democrat-endorsed fiscal priorities continued for the remainder of Carter's administration. Leon Shull, the national director for ADA, declared in a memo to the organization's officers, board members, and chapters that "it now appears certain that ADA's principal domestic concern during 1979 will be the Carter Administration's proposed Fiscal Year 1980 Federal Budget. . . . The new budget will be $20 billion below the needed monies to simply keep human needs programs (education, health, jobs, etc.) at present levels. Only the military will be spared and they will get a 3 percent real increase—meaning a total 10 percent dollar increase. These Carter policies will be disastrous for the 'quality of life' for all."[72]

In response, Mink, Shull, and others created an ad hoc coalition, one that they would continue to grow under the presidency of Ronald Reagan to approximately 150 civil rights, environmental, labor, and women's organizations. ADA issued press statements, held public hearings, and lobbied its political contacts in the federal government. It sought to "win adequate funding for all effective human needs programs, to cut back the military budget, and to make clear our view that the federal budget is not the prime culprit in causing inflation."[73] ADA responded to the calls for efficiency and cost cutting but demanded accountability from "President Carter and other elected officials [who] seem to have chosen to lead the Democratic Party on a course away from that party's strong and compassionate progressive tradition."[74] As Mink expressed in an ADA press release, "Human needs and national priorities have been sacrificed to political expediency. . . . The President has betrayed the majority of Americans who wish to have a government that is both efficient and yet generous enough to use its powers affirmatively for the common good."[75]

ADA's efforts met with limited results. In an organizational memo, Mink reported that "*the Senate budget committee recommendations for the first budget resolution are a travesty*. The committee has taken nearly every human needs program and cut it down to the barest bones. . . . [Also,] *the House committee recommendations made a bad Carter budget even worse*" (emphasis in the original).[76] Nevertheless, she believed in the importance of their efforts, since the House committee did recommend a cut in military spending. Mink characterized this as "an important victory although it does not go far enough. We have convinced the members of the House budget committee that no area of the budget is immune to cutbacks."[77]

Regardless of the obstacles ahead, Mink believed in the need to offer an alternative political vision. In a letter to ADA membership and friends, she expressed the belief that "Americans today are not less compassionate than they once were. But the burdens of inflation and grossly unfair taxation are heavy, and those who profit from these inequities have fabricated a mythology—which some voters have accepted—which blames the poor, nonwhites, government programs and regulations, and the environmentalist for high prices and high taxes. *This mythology must be rebuked and refuted. . . . ADA believes that human beings are not expendable.*"[78]

Recentering Political Priorities

To recenter the national political agenda, ADA foregrounded the concerns of those traditionally marginalized in the US polity due to race, gender, and class. The organization, under Mink's leadership, endorsed the campaign seeking redress and reparations for Japanese American incarceration during World War II. ADA also authorized a second local chapter in Puerto Rico and a Hispanic caucus to foster national collaboration among Latinx organizations across the United States. ADA advocated for political representation for Washington, DC, a city with a significant African American population. Despite serving as the nation's capital, the District of Columbia remains disfranchised in the federal government. In addition, the Hawai'i ADA group issued a statement in support of Native Hawaiian groups, demanding that President Carter stop bombing exercises on Kaho'olawe and return the island to the peoples of Hawai'i.

The cross-racial alliances that ADA sought to build were reflected in the organization's choice of speakers for the crucial election year of 1980. The ADA national convention that year featured Cardiss Collins, the chair of the Congressional Black Caucus. The first African American woman elected in the Midwest, Collins had previously traveled to China with Mink as part of a congresswomen's delegation. In a letter thanking Collins for addressing ADA, Mink shared her observations of the Democratic Party: "I must conclude that our Party has abandoned its traditional role of having as its first priority the concerns and needs of the poor. It has become very much a middle class–oriented Party wedded to a balance the budget attitude. It was a disappointing experience."[79] To combat this orientation, Mink expressed her "hope that the Congressional Black Caucus will continue to press hard for all the minority planks which will be taken to the floor of the [national] convention."[80] Together, they "could well write the course of this nation for the next decade."[81]

Mink also prioritized women's issues within ADA. She attended rallies for the ERA and lobbied for extending the state ratification deadline. She promoted the concept of comparable worth as a strategy to address the wage gap between men and women, a gap that actually increased after the 1963 Equal Pay Act. Mink pointed to the structural inequality within the economy that consigned women to lower pay, because they "work in 'women's jobs' that are undervalued and underpaid"; she sought instead to go beyond equal pay for equal work to equal pay "for work of comparable value."[82] This call for comparable worth entailed recognizing and paying equally when women and men "do work which requires the same skill, effort and responsibility," even if they are not of the same job classifications.[83]

Very importantly, given the efforts to restrict abortion access and funding for impoverished women, Mink continued to emphasize reproductive rights. After the Supreme Court upheld the 1976 Hyde Amendment, which barred the use of federal funds for elective abortions, ADA issued a statement declaring its opposition to "any anti-abortion legislation."[84] Mink stated that "only by actively supporting publicly-funded abortions, can we make sure that every pregnant woman (regardless of her economic circumstances) receives at least a minimum standard of health care. . . . For the sake of social justice, equity and the health of mothers and children, every woman must be guaranteed the right to decide, together with her doctor, whether to carry a pregnancy to term."[85]

ADA's efforts to bring together multiple interest groups and issues under one umbrella organization faced challenges. A member of the Women's Lobby, a group that had previously worked with Mink to pass feminist legislation, wrote to criticize ADA for featuring Jesse Jackson at the organization's national convention.[86] The author criticized Jackson, "Dick Gregory and other swinging male blacks . . . [for] telling folks that the abortion issue is a 'white woman's' issue and 'genocide' for blacks"; they "are not serving the cause of liberalism in this country well."[87] ADA did not retract the invitation to Jackson, an African American minister and civil rights activist. As a religious leader who grew up in a single-female-headed household, Jackson believed in family planning but also the sanctity of life.[88] He eventually changed his stance from anti-abortion to pro-choice over the course of the next decade as he ran for the US presidency.

The hostility expressed by a member of a predominantly white female organization, the Women's Lobby, against an African American male leader illuminated racial and gender tensions that existed between ADA allies and within the organization. One of Mink's colleagues characterized ADA as "mainly appeal[ing] to middle class haoles across the country."[89] Mink's response indicated that she did not believe transforming the composition of ADA members was necessarily the only solution. She emphasized working with a wide coalition of organizations so that those "who we do not include, be included somewhere else . . . women's movement, civil liberties group, gay groups, Hispanics, Blacks, Asians and American Indians."[90] Mink envisioned ADA's role as helping to "make these groups more akamai," a Hawaiian creole or pidgin term that means "savvy and smart."[91] By working together, which at times required political compromise, they could be more effective.

Whenever possible Mink emphasized how her political priorities on so-called special-interest issues translated across social boundaries. In a speech given in Illinois, Mink congratulated "Chicagoans for electing a woman Mayor" and reminded them of the work of ratifying the Equal Rights Amendment. She also shared how her own experiences with reproductive injustice connected to ongoing political dangers.[92] She recollected her time in Chicago, where she spent four years of her life, earning a law degree and starting a family: "I have a lot of pleasant memories about this city. My only pain comes from my need to have had to file a class action law suit against the University of Chicago because while I was pregnant, I together with 800 other women were administered DES without our knowledge or consent in a [sic] experiment to determine the drug's effectiveness to prevent miscarriage. Twenty-four years later I was notified, not because they were concerned about my health or my daughter's, but because they wanted to have follow up data."[93] Mink, who seldom shared such intimate information in her speeches, emphasized that her "personal tragedy . . . could have happened to almost anyone."[94] Mink's insights resonated for other women concerned about reproductive rights.

In addition, she connected her status as a medical guinea pig to the commercial and scientific experiments that all human beings experienced:

> We live in a frighteningly impersonal world. Decisions are being made for us which have far reaching effects on our lives. We are seldom ever consulted. We are pawns set in orbit in this technological world. We are constantly being experimented upon in the marketplace with foods and commodities which later turn out to be harmful to our health. Chemicals are being used in the manufacturing of goods which are adding toxic residues to our environment. Workers are expected to go to work, unquestioning, in unhealthful environments. PCB's, asbestos, aerosol sprays, saccharin, methapyrilene, many many more found after the fact to be injurious to our health.[95]

This political pivot from reproductive health to human safety to environmental protection reveals how Mink understood these issues to be interlinked. The personal and the gendered revealed systemic political-economic forms of inequality and injustice. Rather than be immobilized by the enormity of these issues, Mink believed that a proactive federal government could regulate commercial, technological, and scientific practices to protect human beings from harm.

Receptivity and Resistance

Mink's efforts to persuade the hearts and minds of the American public and political leaders met with a mixed response. When she decided to step down from the ADA presidency in the summer of 1981, she had served for three years, one more than most other presidents. Since the position was not paid, Mink commuted from Oʻahu, where she taught courses at UH starting in fall 1978. She and John maintained their home in Washington, DC, given that her work with ADA frequently brought her to the nation's capital. As early as the previous year, Mink expressed interest in passing on the political torch. She was popular as an ADA president but thought that the organization could benefit from new leadership.

Her efforts to articulate a progressive political vision, to influence policy makers, and to motivate the grassroots received recognition from the ADA leadership. Shull, who worked closely with Mink, described her as "ADA's prime organizer, prime ambassador, prime lobbyist, and prime fund raiser."[96] John Kenneth Galbraith, the influential economist as well as a founder and previous past president of ADA, expressed, "Nothing in my years in ADA has made me happier than my acquaintance and, I hope I can say, warm friendship with you."[97]

Despite these accolades, Mink also received letters that reflected the political mood and priorities of the electorate that differed drastically from hers. One individual, who described himself "as a dedicated political liberal," nevertheless criticized ADA for "spawn[ing] multiple generations of welfare 'addicts.'"[98] Another recipient of ADA letters wrote to express racial resentment of white Americans:

> You in Washington may not know what it is like here. Los Angeles has been described as "Little Mexico" and most of us are afraid to go to that city and walk on the streets, even in day time. Another part of Los Angeles is loaded with Asiatics, and a friend of mine had to leave his job in that section because of these foreign strangers.
>
> Maybe you want to call me a bigot but it seems to me that if we, the white people do not agree with everything the "strangers" want and do, we are bigots. . . . In other words, we are no more bigots than anyone else is. Senator Hayakawa called the U.S.A. the "melting pot" of the world. The scum always rises to the top of a melting pot, leaving the good things at the bottom.[99]

Mink could not change the minds that harbored these racist attitudes.

The 1980 elections dealt a major blow to progressives and liberals. ADA did not initially endorse Carter, because of its opposition to his policies. However, once he received the Democratic nomination, the organization had to back him as an alternative to Ronald Reagan. The Republicans won the presidency and also regained the Senate. They had not achieved a majority in either chamber of Congress since 1954. Even though the Democrats held onto the House, they lost progressive advocates. In handwritten notes, Mink estimated that "51% of the House are regarded as conservative."[100] This political development, characterized as a "Reagan Revolution," was not a sharp departure from what ADA faced in the Carter administration. Rather, Reagan continued and accelerated existing trends.

True to her fighting spirit, Mink offered these words of encouragement to ADA constituents and progressive advocates: "We're dismayed by the consequences of Nov. 4. . . . But by no means are we going to allow ourselves to waste a moment weeping over the consequences. The stage has been set for us, not to lie back nursing our wounds, but to examine where we must go."[101] Having worked from within the State Department and also as a leader of a grassroots political-advocacy organization, Mink was ready to shift the stage of her political battles. She and John decided to pack up their home in Washington, DC, on a more permanent basis and resume her political and electoral work in Hawai'i. It was time to go home and reconstruct what home meant from the ground up.

BACK HOME IN WAIPAHU

My parents resumed living full-time in Hawai'i soon after Ronald Reagan's first inauguration. They settled in Waipahu, in the small house we had lived in before my mother was elected to Congress. My parents had maintained strong ties to the community throughout their Washington residency so, aside from the stresses of moving their belongings and twelve-year-old dog five thousand miles, the transition from Washington to leeward O'ahu was seamless. Once home, they surrounded themselves with cats, kittens, and the elderly dog, then dove headlong into local political issues such as the siting of a power plant. Local advocacy swiftly drew my mother into local politics, leading her to run successfully for the city council in 1982.

In Waipahu, daily life began before dawn when chickens started clucking in somebody's back yard. Chante, the dog, joined the cacophony for a while. Hawai'i's mandatory four-month rabies quarantine for all inbound pets had knocked the wind out of him, though. My parents visited him at the quarantine station every day, but precious moments of familiar human company did not dispel the trauma of solitary life in a kennel cage for a prolonged period. Eventually liberated, Chante joined my parents in Waipahu, happy to be reunited with his best friends. He survived in his new digs for barely a year.

Except for the clucking chickens and the occasional clatter of dishes in neighboring houses, my parents' Waipahu neighborhood was peaceful before dawn. The neighborhood sat on lowlands near sugar cane fields, so sometimes the bittersweet, caramel scent of harvested and crushed sugar cane would cling to the morning air. Waipahu was on the dry side of the island, rain-wise, but the air was humid so scents hovered for a long while. If the smell of sugar cane carried a hint of ashiness, my father would wander the house to close all the jalousies and sliding doors as the ashy aroma meant either that production was underway at the sugar mill or that burning had begun in the fields, both activities quite odorous and polluting. Although signs of the cane harvest were less nauseating in the early 1980s than in my childhood, the challenges of humidity and fumes revived old discussions about the need for air conditioning.

Morning routines in the Waipahu home began with coffee and more coffee for my mother; coffee and a cookie for my father. Both parents lingered over the morning paper until a neighbor's ancient car motor coughed and sputtered around 6:00 a.m., signaling that it was time to get ready for the long commute into town for work. Waipahu, an old sugar-plantation community, was a semi-suburban, semi-rural separate world about twelve miles from Honolulu. In rush hour traffic, it could take well over an hour to traverse those miles.

One of the great pleasures of early morning for both my parents was the seemingly guileless attention they received from the family clowder. Guru, a tuxedo, often sat in my father's lap while he read the morning paper. Big Whig, a tabby, preferred my mother's company, often sprawling on the table beside her cup of coffee. Quester, an inky mixed breed, spent a good thirty minutes scratching his back across my father's toes. Sophist, very beige, sat serenely on a chair beside my mom. My mother named the cats after characters I had encountered in my travails with sexism in academia.

Soon after returning to Waipahu, my parents became custodian, benefactor, and friend to many cats, some a bit feral, some gifted, all of whom were extremely devoted to them. They especially enjoyed raising kittens until each was ready to make another household its own. Occasionally, a neighbor or nearby friend would adopt from my parents' clowder. My grandmother, also a cat fancier, took Sophist and one of her kittens. Even I took one, in a trans-Pacific adoption as I lived twenty-five hundred miles away in California.

Life in Waipahu during the early 1980s with the cats and the plants and the early morning clucking was normal life, which had been on hiatus for the sixteen years my mother spent working in national government and politics. Once back in Waipahu, my mother had the best of two worlds: in Waipahu, an unassuming lifestyle on the same island as her mother, brother, and extended family; and on the city council, a platform for public service and political engagement.

My mother juggled many priorities in the restored normalcy of her 1980s life in Hawai'i. Although her responsibilities were local—to constituents, neighbors, and family—her advocacy included national issues such as bilingual education, comparable worth and wage equity, and progress toward women's equality. In local government, she worked on mass transit, developer accountability, and environmental protection. In national politics, she continued working with Americans for Democratic Action as well as with feminist groups to promote women candidates and women's issues in the Democratic Party.

Whatever the focus of her attention on any given day, always uppermost in her mind was the well-being of her aging mother, Mitama Takemoto. My grandmother, widowed since 1972, was resolutely independent, still living alone in her own home near Kaimukī, though increasingly frail.

Eventually, my mother decided that being a phone call away was not good enough to meet my grandmother's care needs. So with the design and construction help of one of her cousins, she had a mother-in-law cottage built next to her mother's house that she and my father would live in, with cats. Thus ended life in Waipahu.

My grandmother passed away in June 1987, shortly after the cottage was completed. Mother and daughter didn't have a chance to enjoy adjacent living. But my parents moved into the cottage anyway, where my mother could be near my grandmother in spirit. By then the clowder had been winnowed to a pair, Big Whig and Quester.

Big Whig and Quester did not appreciate the thirty minutes they spent on the road when they moved from Waipahu to Kaimukī. But they loved discovering their new domain, finding lots of places to hide, trees to climb, and screen doors to destroy. They retained their Waipahu predawn habits and developed new quirks, like watching TV.

In 1988, as my mother was about to embark on a mayoral bid, one of her opponents in the race gave her a kitten. The two candidates had bonded over cats, discovering their common affection when my mother mentioned that Quester had passed away. Knowing Quester's markings, the opponent gave my mother a tiny black kitten, saying she hoped it would mend her heart. The kitten was feisty, random, and destructive at first, cuddly one minute and on attack the next, shredding screens and drapes and furniture. He earned the name Kid Vicious, though the thought did cross our minds to name him after an electoral foe.

Kid imprinted primarily on my father, demanding lots of morning lap time in exchange for good behavior. My father became Kid's personal chef, concocting a raw diet before raw diets were a thing. My mother became his stylist, providing grooming on demand. Both my parents adored him.

Following the 1988 electoral loss, my mother settled into the role of citizen activist. Especially prominent on her daily schedule was detail work for the *Public Reporter*, a government transparency project she launched in late 1988. Published as a hard-copy newsletter in a pre–World Wide Web era, the *Public Reporter* announced the policy doings of the state legislature, including the contents of proposals and the role played by elected officials in promoting or opposing them.

In the spring of 1990, my parents took their first-ever travel vacation, taking time away from all work-related obligations. They traveled to Slovakia, still part of Czechoslovakia, where my father hoped to uncover his maternal roots. Their destination was the city of Kosice in the east, sixty miles from both Budapest and the Ukraine border. My father's brother Jim had ascertained that a distant relative resided there and that Grandma Helen's forebears hailed from the surrounding area, where they had been miners. The expedition was an equivocal success. My father did not find his distant relative, but found someone who had known her. He also tasted indigenous pierogis, *hrudka* (egg cheese), and sauerkraut soup, triggering memories of his mother's holiday cooking. Although the search did not yield genealogical revelations, it provided opportunities for my father to soak in the history and culture of eastern Slovakia enough to project his mother's family's pre-emigration story. A Slovakian student befriended my parents on the train from Prague, annotating the view and enriching their appreciation of the region. At the end of the journey, they left with him a copy of my first book, which dealt in part with nativist responses to Slavs who emigrated to the United States in the late nineteenth century, as my great-grandfather had done.

Kid the cat was thrilled to welcome my parents home. They wouldn't be home for long, though. Shortly after their return from Slovakia, Senator Spark M. Matsunaga passed away. Matsunaga had been my mother's colleague in the House of Representatives before defeating her in the 1976 race for the US Senate. Then congressmember Daniel Akaka won appointment to Matsunaga's vacant US Senate seat, opening the congressional spot my mother had once filled. A special election was called to fill the US House seat for the remainder of Akaka's term; and as this was an election year anyway, the House seat in the new Congress also was up for grabs. The trajectory of my parents' lives changed in a flash. My mother decided to run.

7

Practicing "We" Politics

Close to the age of fifty-five, Patsy Mink restarted her public life. No longer in office, she also did not possess a political appointment nor a national position of leadership. She nevertheless pursued her passion for making change. Patsy and John returned to their home in Waipahu, a rural community created on a former sugar plantation. Located in the ʻEwa District, Waipahu was technically within the city and county of Honolulu, since all of Oʻahu was considered the county of Honolulu. However, Waipahu was twelve miles away from the hustle and bustle of downtown and the tourist district of Waikiki. When Patsy and John first purchased their home in the 1950s, she was just starting her political career in electoral politics in the territorial House and Senate. Due to the relative isolation of Waipahu, the house was affordable and still closely connected to the plantations. Patsy found the small rural community familiar to her. She recalled that "everybody worked for the plantation"; as a result, it was "a very tight, small community. We who moved in the ʻ50s were sort of looked at as outsiders."[1] Over time, though, the Minks discovered a sense of home and community belonging. Even when they rented out the house during Mink's terms in the US Congress, she remembered that "I never really psychologically left Hawaii. Even though I worked in Washington, . . . I always had felt that my home was in Waipahu."[2] Seventeen years after she left Hawaiʻi, Patsy was back home, reassessing what she wanted to do with her life.

Instead of going into retirement, Patsy began a new phase of her political career. Outraged by the proposal to locate a rubbish-to-energy plant in her neighborhood, which Mink believed would have detrimental effects on air quality and ground contamination, she led a grassroots campaign to protest the decision. This petition drive, in turn, led Mink to run for city council. Not many politicians, as many media commentators indicated, would pursue this trajectory of going from federal to local office. However, in the mid-1980s, Honolulu City Council grappled with essential quality-of-life issues. The council made decisions and recommendations regarding the allocation of water and land, economic development and affordable housing, and social services. City council was an arena in which Patsy could make a difference and have a direct impact on the residents of Honolulu.

The microcosm of the local held important political implications. First, Patsy's approach to governance revealed her fundamental belief in government transparency, collective deliberation, and democratic access. As the chair of the Honolulu City Council, she articulated and practiced a vision of government antithetical to power and machine politics. Second, Patsy held political leaders accountable to a liberal vision of government responsibility, which entailed allocating state resources and making policy decisions to support those traditionally marginalized in the political process: women, the elderly, the impoverished, and the rural. Third, these approaches to governance placed Mink in a position to critique Reagan Democrats, i.e., Democrats who supported Republicans. Her battles on the city council responded to political developments that resonated beyond the local.

Grassroots Politics

Patsy Mink did not plan to leave politics, but her return to elected office via a grassroots local campaign was nevertheless surprising. Scholars of US politics noted the shift towards conservatism in the 1970s and 1980s as coinciding with a "Not in My Back Yard," or "Nimby," mentality. The focus on protecting self-interest and local communities justified protecting the privileges of predominantly white neighborhoods and the turning away from a national collective good. The prioritization of the "local" and of the politics of me-ism detracted from a liberal vision of government in which the state used its authority and allocated resources to advocate for equality, offer a safety net for the economically vulnerable, and protect the environment. Mink's political career in the 1980s revealed an ability to engage with the local and foster a collective vision of government accountability and common good.

Mink was drafted into the Waipahu community effort to protest a proposed energy recycling plant. The impulse behind establishing H-POWER (Honolulu Program of Waste Energy Recovery) stemmed from environmental and land-use concerns. The proposed plant was intended to burn solid waste, thereby reducing land fill and simultaneously generating steam energy. Given the limited land available on O'ahu and the need to manage human-generated waste, the Honolulu City Council decision to green light the project made sense. However, the mandate to locate the plant in Waipahu ignited community concern. The residents were presented with the plan with minimal opportunities for input. The city council likely selected Waipahu for the energy plant because the community was predominantly working-class with little political power.

Despite the concerns of some Waipahu residents, it took effort to generate a collective community response. As Mink recalled, some people supported the H-POWER plant, because "it was projected as something beneficial for the plantation and for the union and the workers."[3] Others, however, expressed concern about the environmental impact of collecting and burning garbage in their community. Given these differences, Mink worked with the residents to develop a united response: "When we were engaged in preventing H-POWER from coming into Waipahu, we mobilized the community based upon what was good for Waipahu—not who was closest to, or farthest away, or who would get the most soot or pollution, or the smell from the garbage. The total community said this is not good for the community and they mobilized to defeat that proposal."[4] This collective "we" helped distinguish this localized effort from a "me-centered" approach. Mink explained this Waipahu ethos: "When you live in Waipahu, you're a part of the community. The people . . . relate to the community concept. . . . They think in terms of their community, not themselves. *My* street, *my* bus stop is the mentality downtown. That's all you care about—*my* parking problems, *my* shopping center, my, my, my, my. . . . It isn't *our* community. But when you live in a place like Waipahu, your thoughts are not for yourself, for your own convenience or satisfaction. Your concepts are community-wide."[5] It took this collective effort to change the minds of the Honolulu City Council. The members finally agreed to reconsider the decision in 1982, after a lengthy educational and lobbying campaign. Mink described it as "'hard work. We organized and we testified. It was a 24-hour-a-day ordeal for the community. So when we finally won it, some people said, 'Hey, the city is so important to the well-being of all communities.'"[6]

Mink also gained insight into the importance of the city council and decided to run for a seat. She would become the representative of the district that encompassed Waipahu and the nearby agricultural, small-town outposts to the big city of Honolulu. Patsy recalled that it was her husband, John, who encouraged her to enter the race. Basically a legislative body for the island of Oʻahu, the council met twice a month throughout the year. In contrast, the state legislature was in session only for certain months out of the year. John encouraged Patsy to take on the regular work of governance. In bringing her political energies and vision to the city council, Patsy attempted to bring the "we" rather than "me" approach to the island.

Into the Sunshine

When Patsy Mink assumed office on the city council, she helped transform its political culture. As the *Honolulu Star-Bulletin* editorialized, "Five new faces on the nine-member Honolulu City Council are little short of a revolution—a clear voter demand for a fresh start."[7] The previous council, chaired by old-school Democrat Rudy Pacarro, had a reputation of being "clannish, closed and hostile" to many of Democratic mayor Eileen Anderson's proposals.[8] While Anderson sought to approach economic development more cautiously, the old "majority in cooperation with developer-oriented lobby groups treated her proposals on Development Plans for the island with something akin to contempt."[9] The new majority, which was more progressively Democratic, with seven Democratic members and two Republicans, was not necessarily antidevelopment. However, they were more inclined, as the newspaper editorialized, to balance development needs "with concern for the environment, the future, and the general public interest—and that's what we think the voters were saying in this election."[10]

Mink became the chair of this new city council after some political negotiations. She had the most overall political experience of all members, but not the most seniority on this governmental body. Pacarro, in a bid to retain more influence, attempted to persuade the two Republican members, as well as some of the more centrist Democrats, to support Marilyn Bornhorst for council chair. Bornhorst had served on the city council since the mid-1970s and became the council's first chairwoman

Figure 7.1. Mink was sworn in to the Honolulu City Council on December 1, 1982. Courtesy of Gwendolyn Mink.

in 1977. However, she had been politically isolated by the "clannish" men, often offering the lone dissenting vote against their decisions. Previously responsible for marginalizing Bornhorst, Pacarro thought a council chair offer to her would appeal to the incumbent Democrats and the new, more progressive council members. Instead, Bornhorst, who had more experience on city council than Mink, decided to side with the five other Democrats to support Mink as council chair. These political maneuvers, not uncommon as new terms begin, would hold long-term ramifications in the ensuing battles.

In Mink's inaugural speech as the new city council chair, given a few days after New Year's in 1983, she signaled her commitment to open government. She encouraged "all of the people to exercise their rights of petition. No one group will be given greater weight than another."[11] She also reminded the other members of the city council that their authority to govern rested on the public trust and that they must listen as well as exert strong leadership. After all, "The mandate from the people is not to quiet controversy or limit debate or to write weak consensus legislation, but rather it is to conduct our business in a way that allows for maximum public input and after that input has been made, to be deliberate and decisive."[12] Mink also encouraged the council members to regard their responsibilities as individuals rather than factions. She articulated her belief that "until a decision is actually made and the votes are taken, I have the distinct impression that this council will be made up of nine individual points of view on most of the critical subjects. . . . Whatever the outcome, what counts is that the vote is taken fairly and openly, with all sides of the issue having an equal opportunity to be heard."[13] Honolulu, which had strict "sunshine" laws to ensure transparency and accountability, had not in fact operated in such a manner. In her first speech as city council chair, Mink signaled that she was planning to practice "open government," a government open to all members of the public, not just those with money or influence. Decisions would be made after public debate and rational deliberation, rather than through back-room deals.

Mink reallocated resources and personnel in order to assist council members in their fact-finding and decision-making process. She did so to bolster the overall status of the council. She advocated for each council member to appoint at least one research staff member. That way, the council could obtain information and develop assessments independent of the Office of Council Services, whose personnel was mayor appointed. As Mink argued, "A legislative body cannot function in an efficient, effective, knowledgeable way without adequate staff. And, it's not only because we need to respond to the city's executive branch, but the entire private sector and public sector. If you don't have staff to look at what we're being told, you have to accept on faith."[14] Mink understood research staff as essential to an independent legislative branch of city government. In addition, the salary given to council members presumed that they would work part-time on governance. In contrast, Mink emphasized that "if the Council is to have a legislative role as co-equal branch of the city government, then it cannot be served by people whose jobs and responsibilities have been defined as part-time."[15] Honolulu was the eleventh-largest city in the United States, and Mink believed that council members needed to take their work seriously and to be taken seriously.[16]

The sharing of power and resources did not eliminate disagreements regarding policy or approaches to governance. The council discussed difficult and important issues that had a direct impact on the quality of life on the island of Oʻahu. As a *Honolulu Star-Bulletin* editorial pointed out, "To voters, the issues of local concern are just as important. The problems of streets, garbage, water, planning, zoning and parks affect the every-day life of residents."[17] Mink's priorities as a member of the city council encompassed three main sets of issues. First, she focused on environmental issues. She identified among her top ten priorities the need to protect "our natural environment," ensure a "fair and equitable distribution of our water supply," and safeguard "our agricultural areas."[18] The use of the word "our" underscored Mink's belief that these were collective goals. They also were controversial topics, since instituting and enforcing land- and water-use policies ran counter to investors eager for development and plantations that relied upon pesticides.

Second, Mink emphasized the importance of affordable housing. One journalist who profiled Mink explained how this issue reached a crisis point in Hawaiʻi:

In 1981, when the average fee-simple home on Oahu was selling for $191,597, and mortgage rates were 16 percent, less than one percent of Oahu residents could qualify for a conventional mortgage. Even back in 1975, when the average sale price was $83,797, and mortgages were a "low" nine percent, a full 86 percent of Oahu residents couldn't qualify.... Some buyers found a solution—they bought less expensive leasehold homes, or settled on a townhouse or condo outside the city, or turned to parents or relatives for help in financing the down payment or co-signing the loans.

Others were simply frozen out of the market, particularly lower income families. And without government intervention, they promise to remain outside the market.[19]

In fact, the housing crisis in Oʻahu led a group of predominantly Native Hawaiians to "squat" on beach land over an extended period. Critics of Democratic mayor Eileen Anderson claimed that she allowed these shanty towns to grow, but it was the election of Republican Frank Fasi that brought these conflicts to a head in 1985. Mink advocated for long-term development policies that mandated a certain percentage of affordable housing units. Otherwise, only wealthy residents, visitors, and investors from outside of the islands could afford to buy a home there. Mink sought various strategies to create emergency alternative housing for the beach protesters. She queried the US military to access and convert their unused facilities. She also proposed building temporary housing on land set aside for real estate development. Fasi dismissed her efforts but offered limited alternatives himself. He did have the power of the police and threatened to evict the homeless beach families, unless they agreed to relocate to camp facilities.

Third, Mink sought to mandate equal opportunity and lessen economic burdens on Hawaiʻi residents. She believed that the government should assure "equal employment opportunities regardless of race, ethnic background, sex or sexual preference, age or disability."[20] She also promised to enact "fair and reasonable rates of taxation." In a move not popular with the tourist industry in Oʻahu, Mink sought to increase hotel taxes to lessen the financial burden on residents.

Finally, she believed that government should provide "essential services such as health, recreation, transportation," and childcare. As reported in *Ka Huliau*, Mink argued that

America's strength . . . is in its ability "to garner its national resources to help people who are disadvantaged or lacking in opportunities—whether it's in the field of health, social services, education, jobs, housing or whatever." . . . She [believed] that those who have made it should be willing to help those who haven't until such time when those who haven't are in a position to help themselves. Afterall, those who have made it, haven't done it by themselves Mink points out[.] "If they've made it, it's because society provides the general support and opportunities to get them where they are going. They should look after their brothers and sisters."[21]

While some of Mink's ideas received support from other council members, others did not. As Fasi (a former Democrat who converted to the GOP) entered the mayor's office in 1985, Mink increasingly became embattled and marginalized by his administration.

Putting on the Gloves

Multiple political pundits characterized Mink as a "fighter," as "scrappy," as someone who stood up for what she believed to be right. One journalist even used the boxing metaphor of Mink "putting on the gloves" and "com[ing] out fighting."[22] Mink had to do just that as she came head to head and toe to toe with Frank Fasi. She also confronted three city council Democrats who decided to switch political parties in order to ally with the new mayor. The "defections" of the Democrats created a new Republican majority on the city council and forced Mink out of her position as council chair. She, in turn, began an unprecedented recall campaign against the three new Republicans, arguing that they did not give voters the opportunity to endorse or reject their political decision. At stake was not just their battle for control of city council but also the fate of the Hawai'i Democratic Party. Given the national ascendancy of the Republican Party, the Democratic base and leadership had to mobilize for the recall campaign. Otherwise, the highly publicized switch in political affiliation of three officials could easily accelerate into a groundswell of defections, particularly by those less committed to Democratic Party principles and more inclined to align themselves with the party in political power.

Fasi was a brash and colorful political leader. The longest-serving mayor of Honolulu, he helmed the city for a total of twenty-two years. Fasi had a big personality. One newspaper described him as a "near-genius at attracting media attention. His white cowboy hat, his pipe—and lately—his dog Gino have all become immediately recognizable public symbols of the man and the administration."[23] Fasi laughed at and refused to respond to criticisms raised by Mink and described political opponents as "stupid."[24] Mink in turn characterized Fasi and his managing director, Andy Anderson, as "the two 'cowboys.'"[25] The phrase captured their masculine comradery, their confrontational posturing, and what she believed was their shoot-from-the hip attitude towards governance. Mink, who had political differences with Mayor Eileen Anderson, nevertheless supported her reelection. When Fasi won instead, Mink expressed that she "was shocked."[26] As the mayor and head of city council, Fasi and Mink, with their diametrically opposed political approaches, personalities, and agendas, were on a collision course.

In the early months of 1985, they sparred with one another, criticizing each other's proposals and decisions. Fasi castigated Mink's approach towards addressing homelessness as well as her efforts to create childcare services through the public parks. Mink challenged Fasi's decision to fire the staff members of neighborhood commissions. These boards offered a local forum in which residents could engage in political processes, and Mink believed that the staff should not be patronage appointees but civil servants. Echoing her commitment to an independent city council, Mink stated, "The neighborhood board should be under the control of the neighborhood commission. No one else—not the mayor, not the managing director, not the council—should have the right to fire the neighborhood board employees. . . . The charter calls for a balanced government—not one run autocratically by the mayor."[27]

The increasingly visible impasse led some council members, more sympathetic to Fasi, to support replacing Mink as chair. Three of the Democrats, George Akahane, Toraki Matsumoto, and Rudy Pacarro, all had previously worked with Fasi when he had last been in the mayor's office. Pacarro, the previous city council chair, jubilantly welcomed and literally embraced Fasi upon his return to the mayoral office. Fasi had offered Matsumoto and Pacarro cabinet posts, which they turned down. All three also allied themselves politically at times with the two Republicans on city council. According to a local newspaper, "None of them, however, was willing to take Mink's seat and the political heat a coup would bring."[28] In addition, one of the Republicans, Tony Narvaes, indicated that "he was unwilling to be the 'swing vote' in ousting the former congresswoman from her corner office."[29] The paper reported, "5 Give Up on Bid to Oust Mink," but their efforts actually escalated in the coming months.

In early June, as Mink traveled to the mainland, Fasi held a televised press conference in his mayoral office. The three Democrats, Akahane,

Matsumoto, and Pacarro, announced that they were switching parties, giving the Republicans a 5–4 advantage on the city council. They explained that "they were disappointed with the Democratic Party and unhappy with council operations."[30] They decided this collectively and announced publicly, even signing their Republican membership cards on television. Bornhorst offered the opinion that their decision was about "power. . . . The boys have never liked for a minute having a bunch of wahines [women] lead the council."[31] The state Democratic Party chair, James Kumagai, found their decision "appalling" and also indicated that he believed it "was strictly done for the gain of power."[32] The new Republicans did not disagree. When asked why he did not change political affiliations by himself, Akahane said, "There'd be no majority," and Matsumoto pointed out, "With three or four Republicans, you don't have the power."[33] Mink learned about these developments on a stopover in San Francisco and returned immediately to the islands. The next day, she demanded a recall election for the three new Republicans.

Mink believed that the recall went beyond the issue of who had control over city council. Since Akahane, Matsumoto, and Pacarro had been elected as Democrats, she believed that constituents had the right to determine whether they should stay in office. In addition, the public nature of their announcement and the location of the televised press conference all indicated that Fasi had planned this maneuver to broadcast his political power. As part of the sunshine laws, council members were not supposed to meet in groups of more than two to discuss policy and proposals. If more members planned to meet, then an announcement had to be circulated to allow for public input. Although somewhat cumbersome, the sunshine laws sought to minimize factionalism and the preplanning of votes. With five Republican members in city council, Fasi could call party meetings and circumvent the intent of the sunshine laws. As Mink argued, "Fasi and the GOP council majority will 'run this city as a closed institution with five people meeting in a partisan caucus. . . . I really think not only is the [Democratic] party in jeopardy by this turnover and switch, but that the whole respect and integrity of the political democratic—small 'd'—process is being threatened.'"[34]

If the defections by Akahane, Matsumoto, and Pacarro went unchallenged, then the Democratic Party as a whole became vulnerable. The GOP was in the ascendancy nationally, but not locally, at least not until these political changes occurred. While members of both parties had switched previously, they did so before an election. They announced their party affiliation and ran as a member of the new party. In contrast, the three council members made their switch in the middle of their terms and publicized their decision as a statement of support for a Republican mayor. The obvious effort by Fasi to court the council members and announce their party switch indicated that he expected to assert his authority and influence on city council, a legislative body that Mink believed should operate independently and serve as a check on executive power.

In contrast to Mink's efforts to share power, the new Republicans communicated clearly who was in charge. Now the minority, the Democrats predictably lost their committee chairmanships. Previously, Mink had even created new committees in order for the Republican council members to have leadership opportunities.[35] Under Republican leadership, the Democrats also lost the staff support Mink had secured for each council member. Only the committee chairs (all Republican) received staffing support. The nonchairs (all Democrats) had neither formal positions of leadership nor research personnel. The changes were announced as a cost-cutting measure and justified on the basis of leadership positions. However, the impact was decidedly partisan.

Mink's demand for a recall resulted in a long campaign that lasted for the remainder of the calendar year. She and her supporters gathered names on petitions in order to initiate the electoral vote. Suits and countersuits were filed to determine whether the recall process was legal, whether there was fraud involved in gathering signatures for the petition, whether the electoral districts for the recall vote were legitimate based on shifting demographics in the state, and eventually whether recalled officials could be appointed to government positions or had the right to run in the special elections to succeed themselves. The media revealed a pitched political battle for the hearts and minds of voters.

Recall critics pointed to the cost involved in the process, argued that the Democrats had a case of sour grapes, and, most of all, asserted that Patsy Mink was to blame. Her critics revealed the depth of their vitriolic feelings against her. One letter published in the local newspaper was entitled "arrogance of power." The individual pointed out, "Ordinarily I steer clear of politics but when Patsy Mink is using my money to try to re-gain her position in the 'arrogant clique' I rebel."[36]

The recall supporters included the highest political leadership in the Hawai'i Democratic Party. They emphasized what was at stake politically. Mink always occupied a marginal status within the Democratic Party, particularly locally. She was a political maverick who stood by her principles and did not follow the dictates of the party leadership. But, the recall campaign that she initiated eventually generated support from George Ariyoshi, the governor and titular head of the Hawai'i Democratic Party, as well as Daniel Inouye, the most senior political official from the state of Hawai'i. Ariyoshi and Inouye donated money and contributed their considerable political clout to recall Akahane, Matsumoto, and Pacarro. Mink initiated the recall through grassroots organizing and petitioning, but the leaders of the party did their best to ensure the recall's success.

Although Mink disagreed with members and leaders of the Democratic Party, she believed in the broader principles of being a Democrat. She also affirmed that elected officials should be accountable to their constituency. She explained in interviews and to voters, "The principle is that when people run for an elected office, they have a certain kind of responsibility of trust that they bind themselves to their electorate. We believe that when you run for office and you're elected as a member of a political party, that means something. . . . Membership in a political party says you uphold the principles and policies and program of that party and therefore you commit yourself to that membership for the term of office for which you are elected."[37] If someone does decide to switch, particularly in "this instance [when] we feel that there was such a collective conspiracy involved[,] . . . the people ought to decide whether they should remain in office . . . or not."[38] Mink fought to give voters the chance to decide. In response to charges of wasting tax dollars, Mink pointed out, "The essence of the issue here is beyond the price of money. You cannot put democracy on the table for a few pieces of gold."[39]

The recall was a mixed success for Mink. She was uncertain as to how people would vote. Akahane, Matsumoto, and Pacarro were seasoned politicians who had served multiple terms in office. The three also boasted of loyal constituencies who supported them as individuals, not as members of a particular party. However, as the recall campaign gained momentum, and as the Democratic Party heavy hitters came to bat, Fasi called on Ronald Reagan himself to offer a radio endorsement for the three council members. In fact, Akahane and Fasi had attended a White House reception to recognize Democrats who switched to the Republican Party. In the end, though, all three lost their positions, thereby entering "Hawaii's political books as the first politicians thrown out of office by recall."[40] Akahane, the new council chair and based in a heavily Democratic district, "was smashed by a nearly 2-to-1 margin"; Matsumoto also "lost the seat he has held since 1968" by approximately one thousand votes.[41] Pacarro had a strong base within the Filipino community and lost by less than one hundred votes. Akahane accepted his defeat; Matsumoto and Pacarro refused to yield. Pacarro pursued legal channels, claiming that there were more than one hundred blank recall ballots, which could change the results of his race. Both decided that they would run in the special election to replace themselves. All three incurred considerable debt to run their recall races. Without the possibility of another campaign, they could not generate funding to alleviate their debt. So, in addition to wanting to regain their offices, Matsumoto and Pacarro needed to get their financial coffers out of the red.

Mink, who felt vindicated by the outcome, nevertheless was subject to political backlash. Rather than allow Matsumoto and Pacarro to run for office, after they had been recalled, she and Bornhorst pursued a legal challenge to determine whether recalled candidates could run again to replace themselves. The court eventually decided that they could not, due to the existing statutes. However, the statutes also were eventually deemed unconstitutional for abrogating the political rights of individuals. While Mink and Bornhorst persisted in these legal battles, the Democratic Party leadership and candidates for the open positions were ready to move on. They believed that they could defeat Matsumoto and Pacarro and resented the delay that resulted from the court challenges. Mink received more blame than Bornhorst. When the new city council was constituted, with Democratic victories in all three seats, Mink was not reelected council chair. After multiple meetings and protracted negotiations, Bornhorst became the new leader instead.

The recall campaign that Mink launched exemplified her political beliefs and practice. She embraced and advocated for an open government in which constituents could hold elected representatives accountable. She believed in the principle of independent branches of government and the practice of checks and balances. She did not back down from a fight, or as one of her supporters stated, "Patsy don't take no shit from nobody."[42] Mink was both the igniter and the lightning rod, the person who attracted the emotional ire of opponents and Democratic Party members. The hostile targeting of Mink was no doubt connected to what political commentator Dan Boylan observed: "She's always stood one click to the left of her party's mainstream and well beyond the reach of those who think elected officials can be managed."[43] As a result, "Patsy Mink's remained very much her own woman."[44]

A Tale of Three Elections

In the aftermath of the recall effort, Mink ran two losing campaigns before winning back her old seat in the US House of Representatives. These efforts reveal Mink's revered status as an independent political voice with a substantial voter base in Hawaiʻi. However, she never held nor sought the backing of big donors, and she never had the full support of the Democratic Party leadership. In addition, her progressive politics also meant that she would not draw from the more moderate and centrist voters and definitely not from conservative ones. These factors hampered her efforts to run for governor of the state as well as the mayor of Honolulu.

Mink had been a rumored candidate for the governorship long before she decided to run in 1986. Ariyoshi, due to term limits, could not serve again. Speculations circulated widely as to who would enter the race and become the leader of the Democratic Party. In the end, the three primary candidates included Mink, Cecil Heftel, and John Waihee. Heftel, a wealthy entrepreneur, replaced Matsunaga in the US House of Representatives when he went to the US Senate. Heftel had a record of high absenteeism, however, and Mink highlighted his lackluster political career in Congress. Even so, Heftel led in the polls through most of the campaign, bolstered by his $2 million campaign fund, which included a $1.4 million loan of his own money. Waihee was lieutenant governor under Ariyoshi and inherited the latter's political machine. Waihee spent seven hundred thousand dollars on his primary campaign, loaning himself two hundred thousand dollars of these funds. With fewer financial resources than Heftel but more political capital, Waihee eventually won the primary and the overall contest, becoming the first Native Hawaiian governor of the islands. Mink trailed the other two both in fundraising and in votes. She spent $270,000, less than a seventh of Heftel's campaign expenditures and just over one-third of Waihee's. Of the three, she was "the only candidate to agree to voluntary state spending limits," which made her eligible to receive public funds to support her campaign.[45] Mink needed the resources, and she also believed in bringing "under control the excessive spending on our campaigns."[46] Otherwise, the victory would default to the wealthiest, and those who received substantial contributions were subsequently expected to provide political favors in return. Reflecting her political base, Mink's campaign funds came "in small amounts, no great big ones."[47] Nevertheless, she passionately believed that she could win "by discussing the issues," by forcing "dialogue on the big issues as she sees them—education, health, housing and environment."[48] Mink's idealism did not translate into electoral victory though.

A different dynamic characterized Mink's bid for the mayoral office in 1988. The primary contender in that Democratic race was Bornhorst, who supported Mink as council chair in 1983 and then reassumed that role after the recall campaign in 1986. The two women shared similar politics and allied with one another on multiple occasions. Mink positioned herself in the race as the one with most federal experience, someone who could build bridges with the state and federal governments and bring in resources for the city of Honolulu. Bornhorst presented herself as the local choice, since her entire political career focused on governing the city and county of Honolulu. As she stated, "I'm a city specialist in an era of specialization. I've spent 13 years learning to be mayor."[49] Although both women offered progressive voices, Bornhorst nevertheless characterized herself as more "pragmatic," "more moderate than Patsy," and less inclined to solve "a problem by throwing money at it than she is."[50] Mink may have disagreed with this characterization, but Bornhorst succeeded in persuading the Democratic Party leadership and more voters that she was the better choice. Opinion polls indicated that Bornhorst received approximately double the support compared to Mink. Bornhorst, a white woman, led "handily among Caucasian voters."

However, she also ran "a close second to Mink among voters of Japanese ancestry."[51] Bornhorst was also "particularly strong among men voters and among Mainland-born voters."[52] She even received the endorsement of the Hawai'i Women's Political Caucus. The caucus president commented that the decision "was a 'painful' choice since . . . Mink [was] one of the group's founders."[53] Mink's base derived from "labor union members and lower-income families."[54] A similar poll published three days later described the "typical voter" for Bornhorst as "Caucasian, man, Mainland-born, Republican or politically independent, over 45, non-union, upper-income."[55] In contrast, Mink's typical voter was a "woman of Japanese ancestry, Hawaii-born, Democrat, under 35, union member."[56] Bornhorst as a white woman had crossover political appeal. Mink, given her race, gender, and political commitments, stayed solidly within a certain sector of the Democratic base.

Bornhorst won the primary against Mink but lost in the general election against Fasi. As with the governor's race, Mink believed she had the ability to win the primary. She criticized the polls for influencing the outcome of the mayoral race. The published data, she believed, instilled a sense of hopelessness among her potential supporters and thereby discouraged them from voting.

However, Mink was not yet done with her political career. In an extensive interview about her passion for politics, Mink discussed the asymmetrical relationship she had to the Democratic Party. As a reflection of her party loyalty, she "never attempted to unseat an incumbent Democrat."[57] It was more difficult to campaign against an incumbent, but Mink also made these decisions based on principle. Despite her commitment to the party, the interview pointed out that "some consider Mink a party rebel, somewhat of an 'outsider,'" and asked if this status bothered her.[58] Patsy answered "without so much as a flinch. 'I think the party has to have people like myself who are the conscience of the party. They may not like it, but they're a whole lot better off having people like me, and not just go-alongs to get along. A reputation that is built upon principles is a good reputation to have.'"[59]

In 1990, at the age of sixty-two, Mink decided on one more campaign. Daniel Akaka, who succeeded Mink in the House of Representatives, was appointed to the US Senate following the death of Senator Matsunaga in April 1990. Mink's former congressional seat became open. There was

Figure 7.2. Election night festivities, September 22, 1990. Mink won two elections that night: the special election to fill the vacant second congressional district seat for the remainder of the term and the primary to choose the Democratic candidate for the next Congress. Family, friends, and political allies crowded the terrace of the Oʻahu YWCA, where Mink often celebrated election returns during the 1990s. Courtesy of Gwendolyn Mink.

no Democratic incumbent in the race. Mink had the experience of an incumbent, however, as she had served six terms previously in the US House of Representatives. Also, Mink had remained active in national politics, even as she engaged with the local. She advocated and collaborated with national allies throughout the 1980s on progressive politics generally but especially for women's rights. In 1984, the Americans for Democratic Action promoted Mink as a vice-presidential candidate. Mink had joined with other feminist political leaders to lobby Walter Mondale to choose a female vice-presidential candidate, and he eventually selected Geraldine Ferraro. Rumors also circulated that Mink might be appointed to the Supreme Court, had Mondale been elected. Mink attended the Democratic national conventions and was thrilled by Jesse

Jackson's runs for the presidency in 1984 and 1988. After Mink lost both the governorship and the mayoral office, she established a watchdog organization to report on local as well as national political developments. In fact, she offered political analysis and commentary on a regular basis in 1989 on the Hawai'i National Public Radio station. In an interview entitled "The Political Animal in Patsy Mink," she responded to the question of whether she would ever get out of politics. She said "Never. . . . I enjoy it too much."[60]

After almost a decade immersed in the local politics of Hawai'i, Mink was ready to return to Washington, DC. Her leadership on city council, the recall campaign, and failed electoral efforts reveal a fundamental political consistency about what she believed and practiced. She built a career and life based upon principle, receiving both loyal support and hostile derision for not being a go-along. As she explained, "You have to carve your path and strike out for a goal."[61] Mink's passion for making political change led her back to the US House of Representatives.

PART IV

A National Reckoning

I consider Title IX to be one of my most significant efforts as a Member of Congress, and I take special pride in honoring its contributions to changing our view about women's role in America. . . . However, it is even more important that we not become complacent about Title IX. . . . Title IX must be protected and defended to ensure that equal educational opportunities for girls and women are preserved for all generations to come.
—Patsy Takemoto Mink, 2002

I've run many, many times, and I've lost many times, but I've never given up a feeling that I as an individual and you as an individual can make the difference.
—Patsy Takemoto Mink, 1992

In 1990, Mink reentered Congress at the age of sixty-two, resuming the office that defined her career.[1] She served in the House of Representatives until she passed away in 2002. Throughout this second tour of service in the Congress, Mink offered steadfast advocacy for social justice, particularly for women, the poor, immigrants, and racialized communities.

The last twelve years of Mink's life were marked by global as well as domestic conflict. War was the most critical international issue: her terms in office were bookended by the first Gulf War (1990–1991) and the beginning of the War on Terror following the 9/11 attack in 2001. On the home front, antiracist and antisexist forces fought persistent racism and misogyny. The 1992 acquittal of four white police officers who assaulted Rodney King sparked an uprising in Los Angeles, an explosive protest against police violence and racism. Compared to the 1965 Watts Rebellion, the 1992 conflicts revealed the depth and volatility of multiracial conflicts, not just between Black and white but also with Latinx and Asian American communities. New issues flashed in some quarters during the decade, as well, as marginalized communities marked significant anniversaries that raised awareness of the United States' history of settler colonialism and imperialism: the 1492 so-called discovery of the new world, the 1893 illegal overthrow of the Hawaiian monarchy, and the 1898 Spanish-American War that significantly expanded US empire overseas. Throughout the decade, the so-called gender war intensified, mobilizing women against sexual harassment and gender violence and in defense of reproductive rights. Accompanying and underlying these conflicts was the broadening reach of neoliberal policies, which defined the ideal role of government as one that enabled free market capitalism and "personal responsibility."

Mink rejected neoliberalism, even when dressed in Democratic garb. Having grown up during the Great Depression and entering Congress during the Great Society, she believed that government should intervene to protect workers and the poor from exploitation and the vagaries of market forces. Committed to civil rights and equal opportunity, she advocated bringing women, people of color, and Indigenous communities to the center of national dialogue and enacting policies to promote equity and social justice. Mink's policy and political commitments put her outside the mainstream of the Democratic Party of the 1990s, which had bent toward neoliberalism since the late 1970s.

Mink's political efforts were wide-ranging during the last decade of her life. Among her many initiatives, she spearheaded legislative feminism. She collaborated with movement advocates to address issues central to women, particularly in the realms of education, health, sexual harassment, welfare, violence, and immigration. A woman of color, she pursued intersectional lawmaking, which always asked how a given policy would affect marginalized or disadvantaged women. This approach considered how race, gender, class, and immigration status interacted to shape women's lives and sought to deploy government resources to address women's diverse needs.[2] Mink pressed for policies to aid women who bore the worst consequences of inequality, even when victory was not likely. She made political compromises, as well, hoping to eke out some gains for ignored or marginalized communities. Despite the vice grip of antiprogressive paradigms during the 1990s, Mink fiercely believed that the legislative battle was worthwhile. As she stated, "I've never given up a feeling that I as an individual and you as an individual can make the difference."[3]

"NOBODY AROUND HERE IS INTERESTED"

On September 22, 1990, voters in Hawai'i's second congressional district sent my mother back to Congress after nearly fourteen years away. Because she was to fill a vacancy, she was sworn in within days of the special election. Speaker Tom Foley, who first entered Congress with my mother in January 1965, assembled a full chamber of House members to greet her with a thunderous welcome. On the House floor, my mother, bedecked in lei, beamed for several long minutes as she basked in her colleagues' bipartisan aloha.[1] My father and I watched from the members' family gallery, eyes glistening with pride and delight.

Following the swearing-in, we gathered with friends in my mother's temporary office in the Longworth Building. Anthuriums, red ginger, and maile from Hawai'i brightened the worn congressional décor. Pink telephone log slips carpeted my mother's desk with messages of congratulations. Well wishers dropped by to celebrate by enjoying pineapple, pipikaula, and chocolate-covered macadamia nuts, some of my mother's signature treats from Hawai'i. When the new Congress took over in January 1991, Mom would host another celebration to kick off her first full term since 1977, this time in a more permanent office in the Rayburn Building with family from Hawai'i bringing and preparing even tastier treats.

A lot had changed since my mother's first tour of service in Congress. Some changes were mundane, but notable. The technology of office work transformed radically between 1977 and 1990: the fax machine replaced the telex; desktop computers replaced typewriters; intranet email replaced telephonic voice messaging from House leadership; and broadband television piped House business and twenty-four-hour news into every office via C-SPAN and CNN. Over the course of the 1990s such changes would proliferate, as Congress connected to the Internet, legislative documents became accessible online, and members embraced cell phones. Presumably these changes improved efficiency and smoothed communications. They also subtly changed the characteristics of staff (more legislative aides, fewer typists) and the accessibility of members to their publics (more case work and faster feedback from constituents regarding pending legislation).

Some changes were laden with promise, but inevitably limited. Such was the Congressional Caucus for Women's Issues, founded as the Congresswomen's Caucus in 1977, after my mother's first tenure had ended.

My mother wholeheartedly embraced the caucus and applauded the sisterhood it affirmed as well as the visibility it could bring to certain legislative initiatives, most famously family leave and domestic violence. At the same time, she was ever aware that the women's caucus was not necessarily a feminist caucus and that its emphasis on bipartisanship and consensus foreclosed championing certain women's issues that divided liberals and conservatives, especially the issue of reproductive choice.[2]

Other changes were altogether inauspicious. Defensive battles against Reagan-era initiatives to curb rights and remedies guaranteed by the federal government seemed to deplete optimism and boldness among Democrats in Congress. Relentless barrages of invective from advocates of patriarchal family values, often mobilized in white evangelical churches, cramped progressive policy imagination. Meanwhile, the rise of center-right Democrats—"New Dems" associated with the Democratic Leadership Council—skewed mainstream policy debates away from the antiracist, feminist, and economic-justice advocacy that had animated my mother's previous congressional service. Consolidating this retrenchment, advances toward diverse representation had stalled since my mother left Congress in 1977, especially for women. The number of African American women had dropped from four to just one when my mother arrived in 1990.[3] Only one Latina served in the 101st Congress. Women of all races in Congress numbered twenty-nine in 1990, an anemic increase from nineteen at the end of the 94th Congress in 1977.

My mother returned to a Democratic congressional majority and Republican White House, a partisan division of power descriptively similar to most of her first tenure in Congress. But with the exception of white southerners, congressional Democrats during the Nixon years sustained a feisty opposition to Republican assaults on the Democrats' New Deal and Great Society policies and had even forged ahead with a few new democratizing policies such as Title IX. By 1990, however, many Democrats had ceded the domestic policy template to Reagan Republicans, acquiescing to the terms of Republican policy discourse even while fighting to preserve or improve funding levels for this or that program the Republicans put on the chopping block. Such was the case with welfare state policies, with many Democrats guarding only those welfare state benefits that were perceived as "earned" (such as Social Security), not those that were stigmatized as "handouts" (such as Aid to Families with Dependent Children, or welfare).

By the early 1990s, many Democrats spoke like Republicans, lamenting poverty as "a way of life" caused by "irresponsible" sexuality, single motherhood, and the decline of the patriarchal family.

Despite the pervasiveness of the Reagan Republican paradigm by the early 1990s, Democrats did muster a resolute defense of one policy arena associated with the democratizing achievements of the 1960s and early '70s: the Civil Rights Act. In 1989, under the impact of conservative judicial appointments by both Nixon and Reagan, the Supreme Court gutted Title VII of the Civil Rights Act of 1964, the provision barring discrimination in employment.[4] Democrats in Congress responded with legislation to override the Court by specifying manifestations of discrimination prohibited by Title VII, as well as some technical elements of Title VII enforcement. The legislation primarily aimed to restore, not expand, the Title VII framework that governed jurisprudence before the Supreme Court savaged it with its decisions in 1989.

Restoration of the disparate-impact standard established in *Griggs v. Duke Power Company* in 1971 was the foremost goal of the civil rights bill.[5] The Supreme Court had dismantled the *Griggs* standard, a framework for addressing racially skewed effects of employer policies, in *Wards Cove v. Atonio*, a case that challenged the hiring scheme of a salmon cannery. Alaska Native and Asian Pacific seasonal workers raised a Title VII claim because the cannery's hiring practices privileged white workers for year-round jobs. The 1990 civil rights bill codified *Griggs*, thus invalidating *Wards Cove*. Alleging that the restored *Griggs* standard inevitably would pressure employers to adopt racial quotas to fix demographic workforce disparities, President George H. W. Bush vetoed the bill on October 22, 1990, barely a month after my mother's return to Congress.[6]

As a member of the House Education and Labor Committee, one of the committees with jurisdiction over the civil rights bill, my mother immediately engaged the struggle to strengthen Title VII, not only with regard to the *Griggs* standard in disparate-impact cases, but also with regard to the discriminatory treatment of women. Although the 1990 civil rights bill focused on restoring pre-1989 applications of Title VII, it also added a new remedy for victims of discriminatory treatment that was especially significant for women plaintiffs—money damages. As enacted in 1964, Title VII did not allow monetary damages for discrimination. But challengers to race-based discrimination under Title VII could simultaneously invoke Section 1981 of a still-valid nineteenth-century civil rights statute,[7] which allowed money damages to remedy race-based discrimination. Title VII's failure to provide any money damages at all in effect created separate tracks for race- and sex-discrimination victims. Along the sex-discrimination track, remedies were limited to such "equitable" relief as reinstatement and back pay. The inadequacy of equitable remedies was especially galling in sexual harassment cases, where winning the right to one's old job alongside a harasser was a hollow victory for any harassed worker. The 1990 civil rights bill worked to fix this by adding the possibility of compensatory and punitive damages to all types of discriminatory treatment covered by Title VII.

As Congress contemplated overriding Bush's veto, Mom and colleagues Patricia Schroeder (D-Colorado), Barbara Boxer (D-California), Nancy Pelosi (D-California), Marilyn Lloyd (D-Tennessee), and Nita Lowey (D–New York) called a press conference to draw attention to the unequal treatment of women in employment discrimination law.[8] The vetoed Civil Rights Act of 1990 did offer a step toward justice, in that it permitted successful sex discrimination claimants to recover money damages. However, the bill capped punitive damages available to victims, singling out sex discrimination for lesser remedies.

The 101st Congress could not override the Bush veto, so Democrats revived the civil rights bill at the outset of the 102nd Congress in January 1991, triggering a new round of legislating. The issue of capped damages for victims of intentional sex discrimination continued to arouse controversy. The Bush administration insisted that unlimited damages would open the floodgates to ("frivolous") sexual harassment claims, while feminists demanded equity for women under the Title VII framework and underscored the stark hardships imposed on sexually harassed workers under then-current law, especially sexually harassed women in low-wage jobs.[9] Mom reproved the Education and Labor Committee during hearings early in 1991, noting, "Women . . . have gone to court, won their cases, suffered unspeakable humiliation and degradation and yet because of the limitation of remedies under Title VII have been unable to recover compensation for their losses. After nearly 20 years of experience under Title VII, it is fully appropriate, indeed long overdue, Mr. Chairman, that we reevaluate and reinstate common sense, common law concepts of equity in applying all of the laws with regard to discrimination in the workplace."[10]

In early June 1991, the House passed a civil rights bill that disappointed feminists, including Mom, because it applied a cap to punitive damages in intentional sex discrimination cases.[11] The Senate was poised to move its

Figure 8.1. Congresswomen's press conference to protest the unequal treatment of women in Title VII's remedial scheme, October 24, 1990. *Left to right:* Nancy Pelosi (D-California), Patricia Schroeder (D-Colorado), Barbara Boxer (D-California), Nita Lowey (D–New York), Marilyn Lloyd (D-Tennessee), and Mink. Source: Library of Congress, CQ Roll Call Photograph Collection/R. Michael Jenkins, photographer.

own bill forward, but was interrupted by the retirement of Supreme Court justice Thurgood Marshall, an African American and civil rights hero, on June 27. Within days, Marshall's announcement was followed by the nomination of Clarence Thomas, a reactionary African American judge, to fill the Supreme Court vacancy.

During the summer and fall of 1991, the Clarence Thomas nomination, coupled with a threatened second veto, delayed Senate progress on a civil rights bill. While the House awaited Senate action on civil rights, the Thomas nomination drew the focus of Mom and other congressional feminists. On the basis of Thomas's record as chair of the EEOC and appellate judge, they knew that as associate justice he would add to the wing of the Court that had cramped Title VII jurisprudence and that threatened reproductive rights, centrally *Roe.*

A political science professor and a feminist scholar, I wrote about racialized gender inequality in social policy and taught courses on women and the law as well as on American politics. With more than a passing interest in the mobilization against Thomas, I involved myself in the background of my mother's work against his confirmation.

By 1991 my mother and I had become political and professional counsel to one another. We spoke by phone a couple of times a day. Between phone calls, we faxed one another enthusiastically, sharing news clips or reports we each thought the other should not miss. Although I lived and worked twenty-five hundred miles away in California, my mother was privy to my every encounter with racist misogyny and discrimination, from the sexual harassment I endured in graduate school to the bullying and disparagement from male colleagues I still had to steel myself against on the job. In turn, I was a sounding board when she needed to debrief and decompress, a scholarly guide to research and expertise about social policy and women's issues, and an occasional speechwriter who brainstormed first drafts, as I did for her testimony against Thomas.[12]

From October 7, 1991, until her death in 2002, my mother kept a small note from a telephone message logbook taped to the bathroom mirror in her personal congressional office. The note was so meaningful to her that when she moved offices in the late 1990s, from one hall of the Rayburn Building to another, she moved the note and posted it prominently on the mirror in the new bathroom. She first posted the message slip upon receiving it, so it was up when I visited at Thanksgiving in 1991, five weeks after Clarence Thomas was confirmed to the high court. I asked why she decorated her bathroom with such an ugly piece of perforated note paper. She said, "I keep it there as evidence of how bad things are and how much we have to do."

The note was the record of an incoming phone call from a US senator's chief of staff. My mother had called the senator after Nina Totenberg of NPR reported charges of sexual harassment from a former employee of Clarence Thomas, Anita Hill. Totenberg's October 6 interview with Hill was the first public airing of a sexual harassment claim against Thomas, though his behavior had been intensely rumored, and perfunctorily considered, behind the scenes for a month.[13] When Totenberg's story about Hill broke, the Senate Judiciary Committee had already cleared Thomas for consideration by the full Senate. My mother phoned the senator as part of several congresswomen's efforts to drum up support within the Senate to reopen the Judiciary Committee's confirmation hearings, specifically to investigate the sexual harassment allegations. The senator's chief of staff returned my mother's call, leaving the message, "Nobody around here is interested."

The next day, October 8, several feminist congresswomen, including Mom, took to the floor of the House of Representatives in a series of one-minute speeches supporting Anita Hill and calling on the Senate to hear Hill's testimony. When a first-term congresswoman, Rosa DeLauro (D-Connecticut), was chastised during House proceedings for transgressing an arcane rule that barred House members from commenting on Senate business, a group of congresswomen decided to speak to the Senate leadership directly. Their action coincided with an uprising among DC feminists, who flocked to Senate corridors to make the same demand. An iconic photograph of the congresswomen's march to the Senate hit newspapers across the country the following morning, sparking widespread mobilizations in solidarity with Hill, and with sexual harassment victims generally.[14]

Anita Hill's experience struck a nerve among women.[15] In living rooms and classrooms and auditoriums all around the country, women expressed their outrage and solidarity in speakouts that foreshadowed the #MeToo movement more than a quarter-century later. At the University of California at Santa Cruz, where I chaired the Status of Women Committee, we organized a speakout a few weeks later, featuring one graduate student and three faculty, including me. We each shared painful stories, mostly about sexual victimization by professors, but in my case also about the misogyny I encountered when I filed a grievance. The details of each of our experiences were unique but the pattern was too familiar. We hoped our disclosures would add to the multiplier effect of Anita Hill's courage, inspiring more women to come forward to challenge sexualized and gender-bound unequal treatment by mostly male powers.

Clarence Thomas was confirmed to the Supreme Court following an abusive hearing at which Anita Hill was demeaned, dismissed, and disparaged by the all-male Senate Judiciary Committee headed by then-Senator Joseph Biden (D-Delaware). Although Hill's testimony described a misogynist temperament unworthy of high office, Thomas's confirmation was a foregone conclusion. Chair Biden, eager to show how he could work across the aisle, had promised his Republican colleague John Danforth a speedy confirmation process for Thomas when they were together in the Senate gym.[16] He kept his word, even after Hill spoke her truth. On October 15, 1991, just four days after Anita Hill's stunning testimony, the Senate approved Thomas's nomination. If women were empowered by the example set by Anita Hill, they also were demoralized by the treatment she received from the Senate. As my mother remarked to her hometown paper, "If Professor Hill could not get her day in court without character assassination, a secretary, a woman in a factory, will think 'What chance do I have?' That is the sad outcome of the confirmation."[17]

On the heels of Clarence Thomas's confirmation, the Senate revived consideration of the civil rights legislation that had been stalled since Thurgood Marshall's retirement. The uproar sparked by the Hill-Thomas controversy heightened concern to enhance civil rights in the workplace, or to appear to do so. Even President Bush, who had vetoed the first iteration of the civil rights bill, indicated a willingness to compromise to get a bill through. But the price of compromise was women's second-class status in the framework of remedies for discrimination, including sexual harassment—through caps on both compensatory and punitive damages. Worse, the caps on damages were calibrated by size of employer, not even by degree of injury. Under the damages scheme, the recompense available to a victim of sex discrimination would depend on the size of her employer's workforce.[18]

Feminists, my mother among them, were incensed by the deliberate legislating of inequality under the rubric of "civil rights." Senate allies promised to undo the remedy scheme in future legislation, if only women's advocates would go along with the compromise legislation. Most did, though not without remark. Patricia Schroeder, for example, attested that she had "an awful lot of trouble with the civil rights bill, because it really has treated women as second-class citizens."[19] The civil rights compromise passed with overwhelming Democratic majorities in both House and Senate. Mom was the lone feminist who would not go along.[20] She voted "no" on final passage both because of the caps on damages for women and because the *Wards Cove* plaintiffs, mostly Alaska Native and Asian Pacific Americans, were uniquely barred from litigating under the new civil rights law.[21]

The spontaneous and vigilant mobilization of feminist congresswomen did not block the confirmation of Clarence Thomas or stop the Congress from legislating the unequal status of sex discrimination under the Civil Rights Act. But it did remind my mother of the power of collective voices, even a small number, in bringing visibility to causes she cared about. The congresswomen's intervention on behalf of Anita Hill, though scorned by the male Senate leadership they addressed, did successfully ignite pressure on the Senate to reopen hearings to receive Hill's testimony. In turn, Hill's testimony and public ordeal awakened women politically, leading more women to run for office and to win in the unprecedented "Year of the Woman" election of 1992.

In the next Congress, convened in January 1993, my mother set about applying some of the lessons she drew from the long struggle over civil rights legislation and the brief but explosive battle against Clarence Thomas. Her key takeaway was the importance of organizing, not only in the grassroots but in the Congress itself. Some of that organizing could be formalized through creation of congressional caucuses. An active inaugural member of the Progressive Caucus, which formed in 1991, Mom worked toward forming an Asian Pacific Caucus, which got off the ground in the spring of 1994. As there were only three Asian Pacific Americans in Congress at the time (five counting the nonvoting delegates from Guam and American Samoa), the new caucus sought critical mass by inviting any member with Asian Pacific constituencies in her or his district to join.

Other organizing within Congress was more about developing a common discourse to shine a light on issues that tended to receive scant attention, such as poverty and social justice. As a complement to the bipartisan Congressional Caucus for Women's Issues, Mom brought together Democratic congresswomen, now numbering thirty-five, in informal monthly lunches or coffee klatches where they could hash through issues. Shifting subsets of Democratic women attended for a time, building camaraderie across the many institutional forces of separation, from jurisdiction (committee assignments) to geography (location of offices). The aim, here, was to provide congressional women Democrats a place to deliberate, even mobilize, as feminists—at a time when the Women's Caucus position on controversial women's issues was either neutral or attenuated.

Throughout her public life, my mother was willing to stand alone, if necessary, as she did in voting against the compromise Civil Rights Act of 1991. But she preferred organizing, mobilizing, and figuring out ways feminists and progressives could make change notwithstanding the strength of conservative majorities. Legislative politics always involved coalition, often required compromise, and sometimes required holding one's nose just to make that first step toward something better. She engaged all of these legislative dynamics across fifty years of public service, never more so than during the 1990s, when neoliberalism, racism, and patriarchalism gripped policy discourse and constrained policy choices.

8

The Third Wave

On October 8, 1991, Patsy Mink marched to the US Senate with six other Democratic women members of the House of Representatives. It was a radical act of protest to demand full consideration of Anita Hill's allegations of sexual harassment against Supreme Court nominee Clarence Thomas. When Representative Rosa DeLauro (D-Connecticut) was censured by the House and her words stricken from the record because she dared to criticize Senate deliberations, seven women of the House of Representatives decided to interrupt a meeting of Senate Democrats to deliver their criticisms personally. Twice blocked from entering the meeting room, they were eventually allowed to speak to the Senate majority leader, Democrat George Mitchell, in his office. The seven congresswomen demanded a delay in the confirmation vote for Supreme Court nominee Clarence Thomas until Anita Hill's allegations of sexual harassment could be fully weighed.

The congresswomen's persistence, along with extensive face-to-face and phone lobbying by women's organizations and outcry from women constituents, made an impression on senators. Senate aides recalled that aside from the Persian Gulf War, they had not received so many calls in such a short amount of time. Faced with widespread outrage, all one hundred members of the Senate agreed to postpone the confirmation vote for a week. The Senate Judiciary Committee agreed to conduct hearings featuring in-person testimonies from Professor Hill and Judge Thomas. The televised proceedings generated heated debates across the nation about sexual harassment.

The Hill-Thomas hearings launched the third wave of feminism, and Mink played a central role in creating a legislative wing of this movement. Rebecca Walker, daughter of writer Alice Walker, coined the phrase "the Third Wave" in a *Ms.* magazine article after witnessing the spectacle of the hearings. In response, Walker called for a movement to transform "outrage into political power."[1] In particular, she identified the

Figure 8.2. The day after Anita Hill indicated her willingness to testify about sexual harassment by Clarence Thomas, seven congresswomen marched in sisterhood from the House chamber to Senate caucus rooms on October 8, 1991. *Left to right*: Louise Slaughter (D–New York), Barbara Boxer (D–California), Eleanor Holmes Norton (D-Washington, DC), Nita Lowey (D–New York), Patricia Schroeder (D-Colorado), Patsy T. Mink (D-Hawaiʻi), and Jolene Unsoeld (D-Washington). Source: AP Photo/ Marcy Nighswander photographer.

need for a feminist politics that does not prioritize race over gender but rather foregrounds intersectional analysis, a method of advocacy and activism that begins with the recognition that women's inequality varies with their race, class, sexuality, immigration, and disability statuses and experiences.

Beginning with her first tour of service in Congress, Mink had promoted analyses and policy perspectives that were intersectional, though not named as such. The Hill-Thomas hearings fueled Mink's intersectional feminist activism in the 1990s and gave visibility to new cadres of allies both inside and outside Congress. In the House and Senate, record numbers of women joined incumbent feminists following the 1992 wave election. Women of color did not win election to Congress in large numbers, but their total did increase by a few. Together, feminist congresswomen began working more consistently as a coordinated political force through the Congressional Caucus for Women's Issues (CCWI). With roots dating back to the late 1970s, the CCWI was a bipartisan group, its members disproportionately white and economically privileged. Caucus members had to navigate political and social differences, often avoiding controversies that might disrupt comity. Nevertheless, after the Clarence Thomas hearings, the CCWI became decidedly more activist, and some members became more intersectional. The caucus developed comprehensive legislative agendas, where they could agree, and synchronized political efforts to bring attention to women's issues. Mink worked closely with the CCWI to address sexual harassment, women's health, and educational equity.

Implicit Intersectionality

Mink was no stranger to opposing Supreme Court nominees, given her unprecedented challenge to the 1970 nomination of Judge G. Harrold Carswell as an "affront to the women of America."[2] Mink's critique of Carswell had centered on his lack of understanding about how gender discrimination operates against women who are mothers of young children. Similarly, in opposing Clarence Thomas, Mink emphasized some of the distinctive inequalities endured by different groups of women. Her concerns emerged in three stages. First, she offered testimony against Thomas on September 20, 1991, prior to public knowledge of Anita Hill's allegations. Mink's criticisms focused on two issues: Thomas's track record of limiting government enforcement of antidiscrimination policies and his lack of transparency concerning reproductive rights. During the second stage, Mink's opposition escalated as she learned of and witnessed Anita Hill's testimony regarding sexual harassment. Finally, Mink joined other feminists in demanding women's political empowerment as the best way to prevent a repeat of the Hill-Thomas hearings' misogynist dismissal of women's experiences.

These three phases of Mink's critiques were rooted in intersectional thinking, which informed her advocacy for civil rights, understanding of sexual harassment, and demand for women's political power. Kimberlé Crenshaw introduced the term "intersectionality" in the late 1980s and early 1990s. The emergence of this body of thought coincided with Mink reentering federal policymaking and the Hill-Thomas hearings. In her critiques of Thomas, Mink often articulated an implicit rather than explicit form of intersectional analysis regarding gender discrimination. She did not invoke the term, but she channeled its essence.

Mink's initial opposition to Thomas focused on his failure to enforce antidiscrimination policies, especially with respect to sex/gender. In 1981, Thomas led the Office for Civil Rights (OCR) of the Department of Education, and in 1982 he became chair of the Equal Employment Opportunity Commission (EEOC). In testimony she submitted to the Senate Judiciary Committee in late September 1991, Mink argued that Thomas's record in both jobs "reveals his disregard for women's legal rights to equal treatment in education and in employment."[3] During his time at OCR, Thomas narrowed and weakened "Title IX guarantees of non-discrimination and equity in education." He sought permission to "repeal regulations," defied a court order to enforce compliance, and restricted the possible remedies for discrimination in education.[4] Similarly, Mink described Thomas's record at the head of EEOC as "a legacy of neglect for women's wage and job discrimination."[5] The US Government Accountability Office found in 1988 that the EEOC "typically closed cases without adequately investigating employees' claims."[6] Under Thomas, the commission "weakened women's Title VII protections by expanding employer defenses."[7] Thomas also undermined affirmative action by banning "the use of goals and timetables in any settlements in which the EEOC was involved."[8]

While Thomas's hostility to antidiscrimination law was known and criticized by both women's and civil rights organizations, his views regarding reproductive rights were murkier. Mink spotlighted Thomas's evasiveness during the confirmation process, during which he claimed never to have discussed *Roe v. Wade* and not to have an opinion about the case and related issues. Four years prior, Robert Bork, a Reagan nominee for the Supreme Court and Mink's law school classmate, faced extensive questioning because of his well-known conservative views. Taking a lesson from Bork's experience in his failed confirmation process, Thomas's supporters coached him to be noncommittal about legal issues. Mink argued that "the confusion Judge Thomas has deliberately created about who he is, about what he thinks, and about how he thinks, ought to disqualify him from ascent to the High Court."[9] The confirmation process, in Mink's eyes, necessitated honesty from the nominee: "The public has a right to know how a prospective Justice approach[es] rights, how he interprets the Constitution, and how he relates both to gender equality."[10] This transparency is especially important for women, since "women's health and women's lives depend on continued protection of reproductive decision-making as a realm of fundamental liberty."[11] Mink's concern about reproductive rights stemmed from long-standing interests in these issues. However, the focus on *Roe v. Wade* during confirmation hearings also reflected the intensification of legal challenges to reproductive rights.[12]

In her critique of Thomas, Mink affirmed women's rights in education and employment, as well as in reproductive decision making. The crucial category for her argument was gender. Mink's opening remarks highlight this, as she stated, "I come before you as a woman, legislator, and a citizen to ask you to consider the implications of Judge Thomas' appointment as Associate Justice of the Supreme Court for women's equality and women's opportunities."[13] Mink emphasized sex/gender in her testimony, because she recognized that many of the rights jeopardized by Thomas's confirmation were foundational for all women. At the same time, she emphasized rights that were of heightened importance to women most burdened by inequality—economically insecure girls and women whose dreams and futures depended on equal educational opportunity; women workers in low-wage jobs characterized by exploitation and abuse; and women whose decisions about motherhood deserved support. Discussing rights clustered around childbearing, Mink used the language of reproductive choice (more commonly associated with a white-led movement) rather than reproductive justice (a framework associated with women of color but yet to emerge in the mid-1990s). Yet, Mink advanced principles that later would be axiomatic for reproductive justice advocates, such as the right to reproductive health care and the right to resources necessary to access that care. In her testimony against Thomas, she argued that "women's full equality and personhood depend on our ability to make reproductive choices" and that women who choose to have children need to be protected from discriminatory practices such as so-called fetal protection policies that regulate women on the basis of pregnancy and restrict pregnant women's rights to work.[14] Linking the conditions of childbearing to the right to choose not to, Mink offered an approach to reproductive rights that paid attention not only to how motherhood inflected gender but to how other circumstances of gender—e.g., race, class, sexuality, age—inflected women's reproductive priorities.

During the second phase of Mink's advocacy against Thomas, her opposition intensified due to Anita Hill's allegations and the Senate's inadequate response. Hill charged that Thomas had sexually harassed her between the years 1981 and 1983, when he was her supervisor at the OCR and EEOC. Ironically, these government offices were responsible for addressing sexual harassment complaints in employment and educational settings. The Senate Judiciary Committee became aware of Hill's allegations long before they became public. The committee queried Hill, who initially requested anonymity but then asked the committee to take up her account on a confidential basis. Future president Joseph Biden, then head of the Senate Judiciary Committee, chose not to directly engage the Hill accusations. In early September he asked the Bush White House to authorize an FBI investigation during which both Hill and Thomas were interviewed. Thomas denied the charges. Despite Hill's allegations, or because of Thomas's denial, the committee did not take up Thomas's alleged sexual harassment of Anita Hill. At the conclusion of routine confirmation hearings on September 27, the committee cleared the nomination for consideration by the full Senate. At this point, the public did not know Hill's story. On October 6, two days before the scheduled confirmation vote, two news sources leaked Hill's allegations. Hill held a press conference the next day. Even then, only after the visible protests by congresswomen and the general public did Biden proceed with hearings to more fully investigate Hill's charges.

The televised Judiciary Committee hearings, which lasted three days beginning on October 11, 1991, sparked national interest in the allegations of sexual harassment. Hill shared details of Thomas asking her out for a date and then harassing her by making remarks regarding pornography, bestiality, sexualized body parts, and even pubic hair on his can of Coke. Biden attempted to underscore that the hearings were not a trial. However, the all-white male members of the Judiciary Committee, particularly those who supported Thomas, treated Hill as if she was a hostile witness to be cross-examined. They dwelled repeatedly and salaciously on humiliating details. They questioned Hill's credibility by asking why she took so long to come forward and why she continued working with Thomas. The viewing public served as a jury, making determinations as to the guilt and innocence of Hill and Thomas and their respective corroborating witnesses.

Hill and Thomas offered a study in contrast. Hill, a woman of color and law professor, presented herself with decorum throughout the hearing process. In contrast, Thomas, a man of color accused of sexual impropriety, expressed emotional outrage, demanding that the Senate and the public respect his privacy and dignity. He presented himself as the victim, the subject of a "high-tech lynching" whose humiliation was compounded by network television. This incendiary charge caused considerable discomfort and effectively silenced the critics of Thomas on the Judiciary Committee.

Thomas's defense was ultimately effective for many of the viewing public and the other members of the Senate. Some people reacted strongly for or against Hill or Thomas, deciding that one was clearly lying and the other telling the truth. Others found both Hill and Thomas to be credible but still sided with Thomas. Many viewers and commentators expressed anger at Biden, the Judiciary Committee, and the Senate for publicly airing what they voyeuristically witnessed. In the end, some of the Democratic senators who initially supported Thomas, including Joseph Lieberman, decided to vote no. Thomas was still confirmed as Supreme Court justice, though by the narrowest margin to that date (52–48). Democrats who continued to support Thomas tended to come from the South, a region and a party known for condoning the actual lynching of Black men.

Mink both marched to demand that the Senate take the charges of sexual harassment seriously and sat in on two of the three days of the hearings. She pointed out to her supporters that, as a House member, she could not take part in the confirmation debates. She also could not vote, a Senate responsibility. There were thirty-four female representatives in the House in 1991, constituting nearly 8 percent of the House, and only two in the US Senate.

Mink shared the lessons that she absorbed in listening to Hill and observing the hearings overall. She wrote to her constituents, some of whom expressed admiration for Mink and others of whom denigrated her "flaming" liberalism. Mink stated simply, "I believed Professor Anita Hill."[15] Hill was not politically motivated, since "she is a Bork-conservative."[16] In addition, "She had four (4) witnesses who testified she told them contemporaneously about the harassment," and "she passed a lie-detector test."[17] Mink asked, "How could anyone not believe her?"[18] In fact, Mink argued that the senators who voted for Thomas likely believed Hill as well. They might have publicly stated that they disbelieved Hill, but "it must be because in their eyes, they favor him regardless of his sexual harassment of Anita Hill. . . . It is not that they don't believe Anita Hill. They conclude notwithstanding her charges, that Judge Thomas is qualified."[19] Patricia Schroeder, another of the demonstrators who marched on the Senate, commented, "It's a male bonding thing. . . . They all think of themselves as potential victims, thinking, 'We need to stick together or all these women will come out and make allegations setting us up. We've heard this kind of thing before.'"[20] Or, in the words of feminist scholar Catherine Stimpson, "Professor Hill was a victim of a low-tech gang rape, meant to humiliate and control her."[21]

Pervasive stereotypes of Black womanhood contributed to the Judiciary Committee's treatment of Hill and the broader society's willingness to disbelieve her. The all-white male senators had limited understanding of what constituted sexual harassment. One of the key standards of proof focused on whether the sexual advances and sexualized comments were "unwelcome." Both African American men and women tend to be hypersexualized as part of the ongoing legacies of slavery. African American men are commonly racialized as sexual predators; African American women tend to be perceived as always already sexually available. Between Thomas and Hill, the all-white and male senators wanted to believe Thomas, given their shared gender. Even the national audience sided with Thomas two to one, according to one poll.[22] As an African American woman, Hill was doubly removed from the standard bearers of US citizenship, white men. Mink even received a letter from an Asian American woman who experienced sexual harassment but nevertheless supported Thomas. These responses foregrounded how women needed to educate one another about sexual harassment. Mink expressed, "We have a hard road ahead of us, to convince WOMEN . . . about sexual harassment and to make them understand that it is a serious offense against their own dignity."[23]

Following Thomas's appointment, Mink and other feminist critics engaged in a third phase of political opposition. They promoted understanding sexual harassment as a serious and ongoing obstacle for women's equality, and they demanded political power. As Mink wrote to a supporter in Santa Cruz, California,

> Currently, there are six women nominated for the Senate, and eight other states have women running for the nomination. In California alone, 18 women have been nominated to run for the House, and more than 150 are running nationwide. The media is saying that this is the backlash to the Clarence Thomas Hearings. In part this is true, however, women are tired of taking a backseat, and we are tired of being patted on the head, the only way to gain equality is to gain power. We must teach the establishment that we will not take sexual harassment and inequalities lying down. That we will stand up and fight for our rights and what we believe in.[24]

Following the Hill-Thomas hearings, 1992 culminated in a wave election, dubbed "the Year of the Woman." Record numbers of women ran for and won electoral office, ushering in new possibilities for feminist lawmaking.

The Hill-Thomas confirmation hearings were a watershed moment in US history. The nomination of a conservative African American man to the Supreme Court, the visibility of an African American woman in educating the national audience about sexual harassment, and the inadequacies of the all-white and male Senate Judiciary Committee revealed the deep political divides that existed in US society. Mink's efforts sought to disrupt the status quo, demanding that those in power take seriously the concerns of a woman of color. Her statements tended to address "women" as a collective category, even though she implicitly recognized how intersecting forms of inequality and identity shaped women's lives in particular ways. Her vision for female empowerment, though, did not just focus on the most elite women but included those marginalized by the political process.

The Women's Caucus

Created in 1977, the year that Patsy Mink left the House of Representatives and the year of the National Women's Conference, the Congresswomen's Caucus served as a bipartisan forum. Women in the House of Representatives had previously collaborated across the political aisle. However, coming together in an official caucus formalized their interest in exchanging ideas and formulating policies affecting women. The group subsequently renamed itself as the Congressional Caucus for Women's Issues (CCWI) to include male members who wanted to join. By the time Patsy Mink returned to Congress in 1990, the cochairs were Patricia Schroeder, who assumed the position in 1979, and Olympia Snowe (R-Maine), who did so in 1981. They eagerly welcomed Mink, known for her advocacy of women's issues. In the early 1990s, the caucus launched coordinated efforts to package related legislative initiatives into coherent political agendas. In partnership with women's organizations, members of the CCWI asserted their collective political will to challenge deep-rooted forms of exclusion and subordination.

In the early months of 1991, the CCWI decided to reintroduce the Women's Health Equity Act (WHEA), a collection of twenty-two bills to address women's health care and close gendered disparities in medical research. Originally introduced in summer 1990, the new package included a specific piece of legislation sponsored by Mink after her return to Congress. She called for $30 million for ovarian cancer research. Described as the "silent" cancer, the disease "kills three out of every five [diagnosed] women" due to the lack of an early-detection test.[25] The legislation mandated a substantial increase in funding, compared to the $7.9 million allocated in 1989 primarily for treatment. Also, Mink's bill, cosponsored by seventy-five members of the House, focused on research to foster detection and prevention. The proposed legislation was part and parcel of a broader series of initiatives to advance health research, support more robust services, and focus on prevention of diseases for women.

The overall approach of WHEA emphasized that women as well as "minorities" faced unique health challenges due to their gender and race.[26] Researchers tended to focus on male subjects and diseases more common among men, particularly white men. To correct this bias,

WHEA sponsors and women's health advocates argued that women-targeted approaches needed to be mandated and financially supported. Mink, who had a personal investment in raising awareness about the medical misuse of Diethylstilbestrol (DES), was deeply committed to transforming the healthcare system to address women's needs.

The CCWI mobilized women's organizations and feminist allies to support WHEA. For example, the National Women's Health Resource Center (NWHRC), founded in 1988 to bring awareness to women's health issues, convened a two-day symposium in December 1990. The gathering attracted "more than 100 national experts . . . to assess the state of knowledge on women's health concerns, how research is affected by the inadequate representation of women in clinal trials and the need for more coordinated interdisciplinary research."[27] These women's health experts worked in conjunction with the introduction of WHEA. As the chair of the NWHRC stated, "This symposium has set the stage to determine the course of the women's health agenda for the coming decade."[28] Similarly to the 1970s, the bridging of nongovernmental and governmental feminisms served as a powerful political force.

The legislative category of "womanhood," as articulated by WHEA, encompassed women of diverse racial and class backgrounds. Cardiss Collins, an African American congresswoman from Illinois, served as secretary for the caucus, a position traditionally held by the second most senior woman in the caucus.[29] She authored three of the twenty-two bills, with two of the proposals focused on Medicaid coverage to ensure healthcare access for impoverished women and children. Other bills focused on stigmatized medical conditions, such as mental illness, alcohol abuse, AIDS, and sexually transmitted diseases. WHEA sought to offer a comprehensive package of bills to address a wide range of health conditions that affected the lives of women of diverse backgrounds.

Given the bipartisanship of the caucus, there were limits to what was politically feasible for it to endorse. Collins, a Democrat, also proposed a bill to establish school-based health clinics. However, Snowe, the co-chair and a Republican, "felt that the bill might be too controversial because it would allow such clinics to offer family planning services."[30] In response, Collins agreed to reintroduce the legislation "without the family planning provisions"; the summary for the "Adolescent Health

Demonstration Projects" emphasized that "no funds under the legislation could be used to pay for an abortion."[31] Collins did point out,
though, that there should be flexibility at the local level, if schools decided that they wanted to introduce family planning.

Not including abortion and family planning as part of WHEA did not
prevent Collins, Mink, and others from advocating reproductive choice
on other platforms, including the proposed Freedom of Choice bill designed to codify *Roe v. Wade*. As Mink explained in a letter to critics
of her position, "Abortion is a deeply personal issue that involves one's
religious beliefs, personal ethics, individual circumstances and a host
of other emotional and moral considerations. I firmly believe that no
government, state or federal, should have the authority to take this decision away from a woman, and have maintained this position throughout my political career."[32] The CCWI bipartisan collaboration was not
a complete match for Mink's beliefs, but nevertheless was an important
mechanism to advance certain women's issues.

Although the group included Republicans, the CCWI agenda overall
found more support among Democrats. For example, during his last two
years in office, President Bush consistently rejected requests to meet with
the caucus.[33] President Clinton's election in 1992 improved prospects
for presidential cooperation. Clinton's election in fact made possible the
enactment of the Family and Medical Leave Act (FMLA), a measure
introduced repeatedly since 1985.[34] Designed to provide employees with
unpaid leave for up to twelve weeks due to birth, adoption, or the serious health condition of an immediate family member, the FMLA recognized the changing workforce. As the draft report for the legislation
indicated, "The typical worker is no longer a man supporting a wife who
stays at home, with the woman caring for the children and tending to
other family needs."[35] Instead, women, including women with young
children, were increasingly the norm in the workplace. Furthermore,
"as our population ages, many working people are becoming responsible
for the care of their aging parents."[36] To catch up to other industrial-
ized as well as developing countries, the FMLA proposed a minimum
threshold to protect workers and their families. Introduced initially by
Patricia Schroeder, the bill eventually passed both houses of Congress in
1992 only to be vetoed by President Bush. When President Clinton was
elected, his staff notified Congress that the administration prioritized

the passage of the law.[37] In fact, the FMLA, cosponsored by Mink in 1991 upon her return to Congress, was the first bill introduced into the House of Representatives in 1993. In recognition of her role, she attended the White House signing of the law the next month.[38]

Although male Democrats were likelier allies than were male Republicans, the Thomas confirmation process showed that male Democrats could not be counted on to advance women's political goals. The unreliability of male allies compounded the frustrations of bipartisan consensus that governed CCWI policy advocacy, limiting legislative breadth and success. Even so, the combined political efforts of congressional women brought visibility and attention to some women's issues. Following the Hill-Thomas hearings, CCWI mapped out an agenda that addressed sexual harassment and educational access.

How Schools Shortchange Girls P6

On April 21, 1993, Mink spoke to the House of Representatives to introduce the omnibus Gender Equity in Education Act (GEEA). Mink and her legislative director, Laura Efurd, played a central role in bringing this collection of initiatives together. Mink served as chair of the CCWI's Economic and Educational Equity Task Force, and GEEA represented the "first time the congressional caucus for women's issues has developed a comprehensive legislative package to address the educational inequities girls and women face in our school system."[39] In the 1970s, Mink led the charge for gender-equity initiatives, like Title IX and the Women's Educational Equity Act (WEEA). Two decades later, she had the opportunity to reinvigorate these programs and address persistent gender barriers. As Mink stated, "My involvement in this issue goes back many years, and I am very excited about this renewed enthusiasm in Congress, among education and women's groups, and in schools all across this Nation, to rid our education system of the barriers girls and women face in striving for educational, economic, and social equity."[40]

Similar to past feminist legislative efforts, the proposed legislation resulted from a partnership between community and legislative allies. The previous year, the American Association of University Women (AAUW) reached out to Mink as well as African American congresswoman Maxine Waters (D-California) about the organization's goal of "developing comprehensive legislation to promote equity for women and girls in the education system. They envisioned a package of bills to be introduced by members of the Women's Caucus, much like the Women's Health Equity Act."[41] The AAUW had recently released a study, *How Schools Shortchange Girls*, documenting the various ways that girls experience unequal opportunities in education. The findings noted that "at all classroom levels, from preschool to university, with male or female teachers, . . . boys receive more instructional time and more teacher attention than girls."[42] In addition to this pedagogical gender bias, girls tend to "have fallen sharply behind their male classmates in key areas such as mathematics and science, as well as in measures of self-esteem."[43] Finally, the report emphasized that "sexual harassment is epidemic in America's schools. . . . 85% of girls reported being harassed in school, often with severe consequences. 33% of girls who were harassed reported not wanting to attend school, while 32% did not want to talk as much in class as a result of the harassment and 28% said that the experience has made it harder to pay attention in school."[44] This research was cited to support legislative reform. The AAUW collaborated with other feminist organizations, like the National Coalition for Girls and Women in Education—which represented over fifty national organizations advocating for gender equity. Together, they worked closely with Mink and members of CCWI to respond to gendered crises in schools. They developed legislation, generated public interest, and held national conferences and hearings to advise policy makers.

The memos and notes in Mink's papers reveal close collaborations as well as occasional moments of dissonance. The AAUW and other feminist allies expressed interest in working with Mink, given her robust track record. One memo, written by Efurd to document a meeting with the WEEA advocates from the National Coalition for Girls and Women in Education, indicated that "they are very excited about PTM being back in Congress and are enthusiastic about working with PTM on WEEA and women's equity."[45] Mink had lobbied the same groups to join her efforts to save WEEA, the legislation that she originally proposed in 1974. In 1991, the Bush administration whittled the allocation down to five hundred thousand dollars a year. This represented a 95 percent decline from the allocation's highest amount of $10 million in 1980, when

President Carter was still in office.[46] WEEA eventually became enfolded into the Gender Educational Equity Act (GEEA).

At the same time, the AAUW decided to enlist Dale Kildee (D-Michigan) as a primary sponsor for the legislative package. Efurd complained that this "is not the original agreement that was made with the Women's Caucus—can you believe they did that (I can)."[47] CCWI frequently worked with Kildee, since he served as the chair of the House Subcommittee on Elementary, Secondary, and Vocational Education; Kildee was a powerful ally. But while Mink and other female legislators did the heavy political lifting, the AAUW gave Kildee credit for the concept and the work as "the principle sponsor."[48]

Like the women's health initiative, GEEA bundled separate pieces of legislation sponsored by CCWI members. Collectively, the package addressed educational challenges experienced by girls and women. Mink and her staff coordinated these efforts, and Mink herself proposed the creation of an Office of Women's Equity in the Department of Education to focus federal attention on these issues. She also sought to expand funding specifically for WEEA. The proposals strengthened Title IX enforcement, including against sexual assault and sexual harassment. In essence, GEEA added new provisions and enforced existing ones so that schools could go beyond "equal-access" policies to identifying and eliminating "inequitable practices."[49]

The proposed programs fell into three categories. First, the laws promoted more equitable learning and extracurricular opportunities. These included developing programs to fund equity training for teachers and schools, promote girls' achievement in math and science, and require disclosure of athletics spending for men's versus women's sports. Second, GEEA attempted to change the culture of educational institutions by penalizing gender discrimination and offering support for young women. The legislation proposed prevention education to address sexual harassment, supported programs for pregnant and parenting teens, and encouraged coordinated health, education, and social services in schools. Finally, the legislation sought to mandate federal accountability. The proposed Office of Women's Equity in the Department of Education could focus attention on gender-equity issues, given the weak track record of the Office for Civil Rights. In addition, GEEA stressed the importance of federal data collection and federally funded educational research to address gender equity.

CCWI members were clearly concerned about sexual harassment in the aftermath of the Hill-Thomas hearings and the military Tailhook scandal. In September 1991, eighty-three women and seven men were sexually harassed and assaulted during an aviators', or "top gun," convention sponsored by the Tailhook Association in Las Vegas.[50] Similarly to other sexual harassment and assault cases, it took some time for the victims to come forward and for the military brass to respond. The incident occurred shortly before the Supreme Court confirmation hearings, but it took two-plus years before the military resolved the scandal. In the opinion of a Hawai'i newspaper, there were clear inequalities of treatment: "Those who spoke out were subjected to intimidation and scorn. The woman who first took the Tailhook charges public, Lt. Paula Coughlin, has since resigned from the Navy after repeated verbal abuse and humiliation."[51] In contrast, "Admiral Kelso is allowed to retire, with his pension and dignity intact, thanks to a vote from the male-dominated Senate."[52]

Mink invoked both Thomas and Tailhook to emphasize the urgency of passing GEEA. The prevalence of sexual harassment in politics, in the military, and in schools collectively reinforced the "notion that somehow women are second class citizens."[53] Gary Peller, a law professor and a father, agreed. He authored an editorial for the *Washington Post* entitled "For Girls, High School Sometimes Feels like Tailhook." He pointed to "the reality that sexual harassment by some teachers and many male students *does* exist in high school, denying female students their rights to equal educational opportunity."[54] To challenge this second-class status, Mink and others tackled multiple arenas of gender inequality. She gave high priority to education, though. As she stated, "We continue to believe that the process of eliminating inequalities begins in our education system."[55] Mink fundamentally believed in the role of the federal government in mandating equity, which in turn allowed public institutions at the local level to challenge discrimination. As she concluded in her introduction of GEEA, "It will determine the future success of our daughters, granddaughters, and many generations to come."[56]

The CCWI won enactment of most elements of GEEA, which were incorporated into the 1994 Elementary and Secondary Education Reauthorization Bill. Mink told Schroeder, a good friend and ally, that she considered reauthorization of WEEA the cornerstone of GEEA/

ESEA legislation.[57] But, as with other legislative efforts, compromises eventually were required to assure passage. One such compromise affected the proposed Office of Women's Equity in the Department of Education. Faced with Republican women's opposition to the new agency, Mink agreed to the lesser designation of a single position as special assistant for gender equity, instead.[58] The bipartisan method of the CCWI often diluted feminist prescriptions but also permitted the advance of some feminist goals.

Backlash

Feminist bridging between lawmakers and nongovernmental organizations, as well as across the partisan divide, was necessary to bring attention to pressing issues facing girls and women. These allies faced strong headwinds. Susan Faludi's award-winning book, *Backlash*, detailed the groundswell of resistance to feminist politics that emerged in the 1980s. The backlash continued in the 1990s, constricting feminist opportunities to secure robust legislative goals, even those embraced by the CCWI, such as GEEA.

Beverly LaHaye, president of the conservative group Concerned Women of America, described GEEA as "Patricia Schroeder's radical" act that needed to be stopped. It constituted "one of the most frightening assaults on parental authority" and a product of "militant feminists" seeking to overturn their defeat of the Equal Rights Amendment.[59] In a manner recalling the "family values" concerns that Olympia Snowe articulated to Cardiss Collins in WHEA, LaHaye fanned fears that gender-equity programs in schools would degrade sexual norms. She believed that GEEA would "authorize the Department of Education to 'de-program' what children learned in their homes," and thereby encourage promiscuity, promote birth control, teach radical feminist theories of child abuse, erase differences between boys and girls, undermine family values, and substitute government for parents.[60] These charges replicated similar alarmist arguments utilized in the late 1960s and 1970s to prevent government funding of early childhood education and to stop the ERA.

Conservative arguments against GEEA also echoed arguments that targeted WEEA. In January 1981, as Ronald Reagan became president, the conservative Heritage Foundation described the WEEA program as "more in keeping with extreme feminist ideology than concern for the quality of education."[61] A year later, the *Conservative Digest* published an "exclusive" expose, entitled "Feminist Network Fed by Federal Grants: Insider Exposes Education Department Scandal."[62] The article criticized WEEA and its director, Leslie Wolfe, for funding various feminist initiatives. These included NOW's efforts to train "community leaders . . . on using press to promote sex equity [and] develop strategies to cope with racism and sexism."[63] Another program deemed dangerous by *Conservative Digest* was led by United Farm Worker labor leader Dolores Huerta, who sought to train "Hispanic farmwomen in 'citizen advocacy and community organizing.'"[64] These and other projects led the *Conservative Digest* to describe WEEA as "a money machine for a network of openly radical feminist groups."[65]

This 1982 conservative call for "a swift dethronement" of Wolfe led to a reorganization of WEEA within weeks and her eventual departure a year later. As one editorial remarked, "Under the guise of a reorganization, Reagan appointees have downgraded the Women's Educational Equity Act program from its place near the top of the Education Department bureaucracy to one near the bottom of it. Five of the seven staff members who worked in the . . . program have been RIFfed [reduction in force], including Dr. Leslie Wolfe, the program director who was the target of a particularly virulent attack in the Conservative Digest. All five were women. The two people who were not RIFfed are men."[66] After the purge, WEEA needed to be resuscitated in the 1990s.

Critics of GEEA maintained that women did not need targeted educational interventions. They questioned the validity of the AAUW study and indicated that the CCWI was misled and crying wolf at nonexistent issues. Christina Hoff Sommers, who gained recognition throughout the late 1980s and early 1990s for her attacks against feminist politics, published an editorial in the *Wall Street Journal* just as Congress was deliberating GEEA. Sommers argued that "the focus on 'bias' and 'gender equity' diverts attention and resources . . . towards the gender-bias industry," which was seeking to solve a nonexistent problem.[67] Mink was well aware of these critiques, as the documents appear in her papers.

Mink countered that discrimination still existed against girls and women. As she wrote to a constituent, "I do not share Christina Hoff

Sommers' view that discrimination against girls in our education does not exist. . . . There are many other studies on bias in textbooks, standardized tests, math and science scores, drop-out rates, etc . . . that all demonstrate elements in our school system which discriminate against girls."[68] In her September 30, 1994, statement calling for passage of GEEA, Mink reminded legislators that comprehensive educational reform was needed to address the intersectional needs of students. After all, "Pregnancy is the most common reason girls give for dropping out of school and almost half of teen mothers who drop out never complete high school."[69] In addition, "Many schoolchildren today are struggling with a host of social problems—including poverty, poor nutrition, drug abuse, family violence, and inadequate health care—that prevent them from achieving their full academic potential."[70] Mink and other members of the CCWI sought to address these "basic needs" to allow students from diverse backgrounds with diverse needs to turn their "full attention to schooling."[71] On educational equity issues as on other issues affecting women, Mink centered the equality and resource needs of the most disadvantaged women and girls in conceiving policies to advance gender equality.

WELFARE IS A WOMEN'S ISSUE

When Democratic leaders in Congress pushed aside feminist calls to end women's inequality in the enforcement design of the 1991 Civil Rights Act, they practiced "topic extinction," a form of erasure that denies women's authoritative claims to correct their own inequality.[1] To be sure, Democratic leaders appreciated the increasing gender skew that made women an ever-larger share of their core constituency. And they certainly welcomed the electoral "Year of the Woman" in 1992, which introduced twenty-four newly elected women to the House in 1993 and brought the total number of congresswomen to forty-seven—thirty-five of whom were Democrats.[2] But Democratic leaders largely celebrated women as additional foot soldiers for established causes, as interlocutors within established paradigms, and as votes for established agendas. When women members sought to shift the political frame on the basis of perspectives earned as women, they often were marginalized. When they raised issues based on their expertise as survivors of gender inequality, they often were ignored. When a women's issue proved salient, women's leadership often was sidelined.

Women of color in Congress were especially vulnerable to topic extinction, more so when they advanced legislative ideas that centered the experiences, needs, and dignity of economically precarious women of color. In her brilliant exegesis of the policy innovations pursued by women of color in Congress during the mid-1990s, Mary Hawkesworth describes episodes of silencing, discounting, demoralizing, and devaluing reported by congresswomen of color during interviews.[3] Not all episodes told the same story. Sometimes, an idea proposed by a congresswoman of color was hijacked by a white (usually male) power broker, rendering the idea successful but the congresswoman's role invisible. At other times, an agenda advanced by congresswomen of color was dismissed or ignored, rendering the congresswomen and their ideas eclipsed and not heard.

The dynamics of topic extinction were nowhere more relentless than in the policy arena of welfare reform. From the 1960s through the 1990s, the call for "welfare reform" was a race card, code for disciplinary policy aimed at Black women in particular.[4] Advocacy for welfare reform trafficked in racial stereotypes of lazy, loose, and irresponsible mothers for whom public benefits were a moral hazard. Campaigning to "end welfare as we know it," Bill Clinton rode those stereotypes to a presidential election victory in

1992. When he took office in 1993, my mother led the legislative resistance to ending welfare, closely tracking development of Clinton's welfare reform proposals and offering policy alternatives that would simultaneously enhance the economic security and self-sovereignty of mothers in need of welfare.

By the time my mother returned to Congress, I was an established scholar working on racialized gender inequality in US poverty policy. When Bill Clinton launched his bid to cure teen pregnancy, single motherhood, and welfare participation by overhauling the Aid to Families with Dependent Children program, my scholar-activist path converged with my mother's legislative one. In the late spring/early summer of 1993, as the president's interagency task force on welfare reform got underway, my mother enlisted my collaboration in convening a forum on welfare reform to give visibility to feminist research on mothers' poverty. Much of the Clinton welfare reform agenda was dressed in social science findings attested by male researchers, findings that in every way affected mothers and judged them, without concern for their equality and self-sovereignty.[5] Mom's ambition was to shift the frame, centering the welfare question on what low-income mothers required to be economically independent and secure. For this she needed to spotlight research that began by understanding that "welfare is a women's issue," as feminist welfare-justice advocates repeatedly asserted, and that produced findings that advanced poor mothers' economic well-being by prioritizing their equality.

We reached out to Heidi Hartmann, groundbreaking feminist economist and founder of the Institute for Women's Policy Research. Together, we assembled feminist scholars from a range of academic disciplines whose work we thought would awaken policy makers to the fact that welfare policy was a gender policy, that antiwelfare politics was racist misogyny, and that mothers' poverty was a manifestation of intersectional gender inequality. The scholars convened on Saturday, October 23, 1993, in the packed Cannon Caucus Room for an all-day conference to "break myths and create solutions."[6] Cochairing the event with my mother were congresswomen Maxine Waters and Lynn Woolsey, both Democrats from California, and congressman Ed Pastor (D-Arizona). As a first step in topic extinction, C-SPAN declined to cover the conference.

The 1993 Women and Welfare Reform Conference nurtured the collective activism of feminist policy advocates and scholars to thwart punitive welfare reform. Nonfeminist progressive allies joined episodically to express opposition to Clinton's key welfare reform ideas—stringent work requirements for welfare participants and time limits on cash assistance. In a June 1994 letter signed by ten congresswomen of color, twenty men of color, and eleven white progressive allies, congressional critics of Clintonian welfare reform axioms declared, "We believe that welfare initiatives should focus on improving prospects for poor parents to support their children through work rather than penalizing people for falling on hard times."[7]

My mother introduced a welfare bill in June 1994 to stake out the position that welfare policy should support low-income mothers and their children with a safety net as well as with opportunities. A few months earlier, she had rejected an invitation to sign on to the Congressional Women's Caucus statement on welfare reform because it did not center the economic security and opportunities of low-income mothers. In a memo to her legislative director, Laura Efurd, Mom rejected the Women's Caucus's bipartisan nostrums as "a nothing position" that paid insufficient attention to ending mothers' poverty and defending poor mothers' right to care for their own children.[8]

The election of 1994 put Republicans in charge of the future of welfare reform, with the Republican "Contract with America" foretelling doom for mother-respecting and justice-regarding poverty mitigation through social policy. In July of 1994, I attended the first Ways and Means Committee hearing on the Clinton bill. Still in the minority party at that point, Republicans tempered approval of the punitive elements of the Clinton bill with calls to push poor mothers harder and further. Witness for the administration Health and Human Services secretary Donna Shalala cleared the path to bipartisan welfare reform by adopting Republican ideas. To the consternation of every feminist in the room, Shalala foregrounded the "problem" of unmarried motherhood, thus enlisting in the Republican mission to deploy patriarchal family values in the reform of welfare. "I don't think anyone in public life today ought to condone children born out of wedlock, . . . even if the family is financially able," Shalala said during questioning that followed her testimony, which included calls for abstinence-based programs in schools and governmental messaging to teens that unwed motherhood is a "mistake."[9] The die was cast, even before the Republicans took over.[10] The question for feminists was whether advocacy could make welfare reform less mean, less anti–poor mother, and less disciplinary.

In the spring of 1995, a group of influential women academics, some of whom had participated in the 1993 conference my mother and I organized, declared their opposition to the welfare bill that was beginning to make its way through the new Republican Congress. Their action inspired the formation of a scholar-based mobilization we called the Women's Committee of One Hundred, an aspirational name expressing our initial hope to enlist a hundred social science researchers, public intellectuals, and activists in the cause of feminist welfare justice. We developed a pledge that enumerated our reasons for opposing the welfare bill while also stipulating the elements of a welfare policy we believed would redress mothers' poverty and assure them the same rights available to nonpoor women.[11] We insisted that any welfare bill should protect the reproductive and family rights of low-income mothers, including the right to parent alone. We responded to the call for compulsory wage work by single mothers with a call to provide childcare, offer education and training, and recognize caregiving within families as work.

The pledge was the basis for recruiting members to help build a campaign to shift the welfare debate. My mother was an adviser and exponent, enrolling some of her colleagues as members, including Maxine Waters, Nydia Velazquez (D–New York), Nancy Pelosi (D-California), Carrie Meek (D-Florida), and Zoe Lofgren (D-California). Drawing on social science expertise available through our network, my mother organized special order events during which she and her congressional allies spoke facts about mothers' poverty against the racist-misogynist myths behind punitive welfare reform.[12] The Women's Committee of One Hundred worked separately but in tandem, responding to legislative developments and anticipating opportunities to make a difference. We allied with the National Organization for Women and the NOW–Legal Defense Fund (NOW-LDEF) to mount lobby efforts, beginning with a Mother's Day legislative campaign in May 1995.

At the core of my mother's work, my own work, and the Women's Committee's work was a commitment to awakening understanding that the targets of welfare reform were women—low-income mothers, disproportionately of color—and that plans to withdraw their safety net reverberated inequalities across the spectrum of "women's issues," from reproductive rights to intimate associational liberty to domestic violence to educational access to unequal pay to childcare. During the summer and fall of 1995, the Women's Committee worked doggedly to mobilize the grassroots and to intervene in policy discourse, distributing teach-in packets, connecting with welfare-rights groups, organizing call-in campaigns to members of Congress, and taking out full-page ads in the New Republic and New York Times.[13]

Meanwhile, my mother introduced and advocated a substitute bill, which she offered initially as an alternative to the Clinton bill, then as an alternative to the Republican bill, once the Republicans took over in January 1995. The bill was cosponsored by seventy-five Democrats, including most congressmembers of color and progressive white allies.[14] Although the bill won ninety votes, none of its provisions were incorporated into the official Democratic substitute—an example of intersectional feminists and progressives being humored but still discounted.

As the Republican-helmed, bipartisan welfare reform bill crawled through Congress, all who fought for a welfare policy that made paramount the economic and equality needs of mothers and their children intensified resistance to the brutal legislation agreed to by House and Senate conferees. When the conference report was announced in November, Women's Committee members flocked to Washington to lobby against the conference bill. From my mother's apartment and office, we fanned out across the Hill to remind as many members as possible that there was a better way to reform welfare. Around this time, too, the Women's Committee joined with the National Organization for Women to stage a demonstration in front of the White House against the bipartisan antiwelfare legislation that would soon land on the president's desk. Ever victims of topic extinction, our White House action was ignored by the press, which was more interested that day in the Hooters Girls March on Washington to protest an EEOC ruling that Hooters engaged in sex discrimination by hiring only women as Hooters Girls.[15]

A very bad welfare bill passed Congress, but a veto campaign waged by the antipoverty policy community stopped it from becoming law. In 1996, the welfare reform legislative process began all over again, a bill ushered into law by summer. Enactment of the Personal Responsibility and Work Opportunity Reconciliation Act did not close the books on our opposition to welfare reform, however. For the remainder of the decade, supporters of the policy in both parties introduced legislative fixes, adumbrations, and funding clarifications to enhance administration of the new law. An especially anti–poor mother innovation arose in the form of fatherhood-promotion legislation, advanced by some Democrats as well as Republicans. Various fatherhood-promotion bills emerged to supplement the marriage promotion enshrined in the 1996 law, the goal being poverty alleviation through the formation of heteromarital, patriarchal families.[16]

My mother and I exchanged some pretty operatic screams about the proliferating privileges awarded to fathers as poverty solvers in latter-day welfare legislation. Stalwart intersectional feminist that she was, she fought hard against the fatherhood bills, typically by offering amendments to remove sex-based discrimination in favor of fathers or to extend the favors promised to fathers to mothers as well.[17]

As the decade ended, the first installment of the welfare program created by the 1996 law also drew to a close. The 1996 law required that the new Temporary Assistance for Needy Families (TANF) program be reauthorized after five years. Late in 1999, I convened the executive committee of the Women's Committee of One Hundred to consider whether and how we might engage the TANF reauthorization process to restore the safety net, invest in mothers' opportunities, protect rights, and recognize the care work performed within families. As we had in 1995, we once again drew up a statement of principles, along with proposals to overhaul specific provisions of the 1996 TANF statute.[18] We struck a policy alliance with the emergent Welfare Made a Difference Campaign, which assembled welfare rights advocates from across the country, and with NOW-LDEF, which focused on feminist policy.

Following her strategy of trying to amend the life out of bad welfare bills, my mother embraced the idea of an omnibus TANF reauthorization bill that would turn anti–poor mother, antiwelfare TANF on its head. She envisioned a bill that would amend TANF point by point: changing its purpose from rewarding patriarchal family formation to ending poverty; circumventing time limits by stopping the clock when participants were in compliance with the law; defusing the punishment of work requirements by counting caregiving, education, and overcoming barriers to employment as work; and restoring reproductive liberty. These ideas formed the core of legislative proposals proffered by the Women's Committee, Welfare Made a Difference, and NOW-LDEF (later renamed Legal Momentum). In October 2001, my mother introduced HR 3113, a feminist intervention in TANF reauthorization that garnered ninety-three cosponsors but no hearing in the legislative debate.[19]

My mother and I crossed paths on other issues, but the quest for a feminist welfare policy was our only arena of sustained collaboration. As an educator, I regularly encountered Title IX, perhaps the most renowned second-wave policy achievement, for which my mother was principle legislative champion. As chair of the Status of Women Committee on my campus, I fought to improve Title IX enforcement, especially with respect to sexual harassment and sexual assault. I joined a Title IX class action against my university for its negligent handling of multiple rape and assault allegations.[20] In addition to grieving a specific instance of gang rape, our complaint spelled out the ways a school's dereliction toward survivors created a hostile environment for women on campus. This work brought me to the edges of my mother's ongoing efforts to strengthen Title IX enforcement and to enact GEEA, though we deliberately did not engage each other about it. The Office for Civil Rights of the Department of Education (OCR) adjudicated our claim that the university's shoddy execution of its Title IX obligations created a hostile environment for women on campus. OCR found the university in violation of Title IX and stipulated remedies, vindicating our complaint on the merits.[21]

Occasionally, Mom and I skirted collision with one another, as when I published two op-eds in the New York Times taking to task a phalanx of feminists for cramping sexual harassment law in defense of Bill Clinton, who stood accused of lying under oath in Paula Jones's sexual harassment suit against him.[22] My mother took pride in every word I ever published, including the op-eds. She got a kick out of my brief notoriety, which attracted a few radio and television invitations. She even shared my analysis, up to a point, especially that the viability of sexual harassment law depended on the reliability of its advocates. But she also understood the Clinton scandal as fundamentally a political one, though waged on the backs of potentially sexually harassed women. She saw complexity where I was laser-focused on the implications for victims of inconsistent feminist applications of sexual harassment legal standards.

As interlocutors and each other's fiercest defenders, my mother and I grew our feminism where we intersected. By the turn of the twenty-first century, when we converged behind a feminist plan to reform welfare reform, we were more closely aligned than ever before. She had a more

Figure 9.1. The Women's Center at the University of California–Santa Cruz, where Wendy was a professor, invited Patsy to speak on women's issues, ca. 1993. Source: Annie Valva photographer.

urgent sense of the need to disrupt habitually white, middle-class, and masculine poverty discourse and policy, as well as a more ferocious commitment to honoring and empowering low-income mothers as agents of their own lives. Willing to be iconoclastic, as needed, but careful to resonate with congressional allies, Mom invested her whole legislative self in advancing the cause of feminist welfare justice. Wiser for having weathered policy and political struggles, by 2000 I readily appreciated the need to argue radical shifts in accessible terms, because in all probability we would have to live to fight another day. Dismounting my high horse, I met my mother on the terrain of intersectional feminist principle, where together we waged one last fight for women's equality.

example #2
p 4

9

Battling Poverty

In March 1994, Patsy Mink rose before the House of Representatives to engage her colleagues in "a discussion of the whole welfare reform issue."[1] Two years after Bill Clinton was elected president on the basis of a promise to "end welfare as we have come to know it," and two years after the unprecedented electoral gains during the "Year of Woman," Mink spoke before the still predominantly white and male political body of Congress.[2] She wanted to remind the policy makers of the country that the brunt of their political attacks on welfare "is being heaped upon women in this society."[3] Women were disproportionately poor, earning "at the level of 60 cents to 70 cents on the dollar, based upon equal educational background and equal experience when it comes to men holding the same position."[4] This gendered poverty also was racialized, as economic disparities increased when compounded by race.

The skewed demographics of poverty were readily apparent in Aid to Families with Dependent Children (AFDC), the welfare program that drew the most political ire despite the fact that its expenditures constituted only 1 percent of government spending.[5] Almost all the recipients of AFDC were impoverished mothers and their kids. Those who were poor in the United States in the mid-1990s included 22 percent of all children. While more than one in five children were poor in the country, one in every seven was enrolled in AFDC. Furthermore, women and children of color were disproportionately poor and therefore were disproportionately represented on welfare rolls.

Mink's political opponents recognized the gendered and the racialized configuration of poverty, but they espoused fundamentally different solutions. In their minds, the lack of heteronormative households— what they perceived as the foundation of the middle class—led to poverty and all the attendant social ills. They believed that women-headed households, especially women of color–headed households, led to child neglect, crime, and drug use. In their eyes, these families socially reproduced the underclass. Clinton and many Democratic Party members also espoused a belief in the panacea of middle-class normativity. Clinton ran for the presidency as a "new Democrat." He rejected the Republican charge that Democrats supported irresponsible government spending. Instead, he centered his political identity on advocacy for the "'deserving' middle class—people who 'played by the rules.'"[6]

The political symbolism of dismantling welfare preyed upon and ignited popular perceptions of the poor as undeserving, as not playing by the rules. Stereotypes of the poor held that they lacked the drive and character to lift themselves out of poverty and off government reliance. Given the disproportionate percentages of women of color in poverty, particularly African American women and Latinas, the neoliberal Democratic critique of welfare was drawn by racialized misogyny. In addition to invoking racialized tropes to justify policy proposals, Clinton and the New Democrats advocated a version of welfare reform that subordinated the needs of racial minorities, immigrants, and vulnerable women in order to distance Democrats from association with "big government." After twelve years of Republican presidencies, first with Ronald Reagan and then with George H. W. Bush, the "new" Democrats embraced neoliberal values of privatization and the individual ability to ascend the financial ladder.

Mink staked her ground in the legislative battle. She challenged fundamental neoliberal assumptions that were widely shared among Republicans and Democrats. Instead of blaming the poor for being poor, Mink and other welfare-rights advocates identified the need for structural solutions that targeted the problem of poverty, not the perceived overuse of welfare. Working with antipoverty and feminist allies, Mink advocated for educational opportunities, job training, employment options that paid beyond minimum wage, universal health care, and government-funded childcare. In essence, Mink believed that the government should help alleviate social inequality.

Mink's approach to welfare offered a gendered understanding of what constituted valuable labor. As she stated in a subsequent speech, "The current effort to reform welfare begins by assuming that work for wages is the end goal of reform. I disagree strongly. There is value to society in a mother's care for her small children. Being on welfare does not negate that value."[7] Coinciding with the emergence of the term "reproductive justice," first coined by Black feminists, Mink advocated for the right of poor and racialized women to make reproductive choices and be mothers.[8] She challenged the patriarchal logic of heteronormative families as the solution to poverty. She questioned the neoliberal prizing of paid work as determining the ultimate worth of human lives. And, she called for a form of government that valued the dignity of poor people.

The fights to overhaul welfare policy unfolded over two stages in the early to mid-1990s. During the 103rd congressional session (1993–1994), Mink was aware of Clinton's promise to fundamentally transform welfare and alarmed by reports from his appointed task force. In response, she worked with allies to assert political leadership on welfare reform. Competing factions among Republicans and Democrats, including Mink, proposed legislation to define the goals and parameters of welfare. They did so before the Clinton White House finally proposed its bill in June 1994, introduced too late for passage by the 103rd Congress. The political debates in Congress, the media, and broader society became increasingly fractured during the historic fall election. In what was described as a "Republican Revolution," the GOP recaptured both the House and the Senate, for the first time since 1952.

The Republican political victory launched phase two of the welfare debates. During the 104th Congress (1995–1996), Newt Gingrich (R-Georgia) became speaker of the House and led the implementation of the party agenda entitled the "Contract with America." Republican legislative engineering ultimately culminated in 1996 with the replacement of AFDC by the Temporary Assistance for Needy Families (TANF) program. The new policy negated the idea of welfare as a legal entitlement, defined as "a guarantee of access to benefits."[9] For poor people, an entitlement affirmed the principle that government has a responsibility to assure the survival of those with few or precarious means.

Three main touchstones emerged in these welfare debates: mothers, children, and immigrants. Each of these groups is viewed as different and apart from normative rights-bearing citizens in the United States. When being a mother, child, and/or immigrant intersects with racialized otherness and poverty, that outsider status is even more pronounced. In the welfare debates of the mid-1990s, Mink advocated for the humanity, dignity, and political rights of impoverished women, children, and immigrants, many of whom were people of color. She was joined by a broader network of community advocates and intersectional feminist scholars who believed that the government should play an important role in alleviating poverty, particularly for those who experience structural exclusion and inequality.

Mothers in Poverty

As the chair of the CCWI (Congressional Caucus for Women's Issues) Economic and Educational Equity Task Force, Mink planned to introduce a Women's Economic Equity Act comparable to the health and education equity acts. The issues of welfare and poverty, however, fractured the bipartisan CCWI, just as it did the Democratic Party and to a lesser degree the GOP. Nevertheless, as welfare became a political symbol that ignited the fury of politicians and voters, Mink consistently emphasized the need to identify structural reasons for the feminization and racialization of poverty. She also sought to create policy solutions that did not punish but instead supported mothers living in poverty.

The call to reform welfare was a popular political issue during Clinton's campaign for the presidency, but it was placed on the back burner as the new administration focused its initial political attention on reforming health care. Bill and Hillary Clinton collectively used their political capital to craft and advocate for universal health care. They developed a plan mandating that individuals purchase insurance, the government subsidize those with lower incomes, and businesses provide coverage. The two-year fight, ultimately unsuccessful, took precedence over welfare reform.

Senator Daniel Patrick Moynihan (D–New York) threatened to obstruct healthcare legislation, which had to pass through his committee, if the White House did not fulfill its promise to propose substantive welfare form. Moynihan, previously an assistant secretary of labor under Lyndon Johnson, had authored the controversial 1965 report entitled "The Negro Family: The Case for National Action." In response to the series of urban riots in the mid-1960s, Moynihan attempted to understand the roots of Black poverty. He identified the high rates of single mothers as a primary cause for creating a culture of poverty. This lack of heteronormative families among African Americans, particularly the absence of male breadwinners and family patriarchs, would resurface as a causal explanation for poverty in the late twentieth century.[10]

The AFDC program drew the most political vitriol, even though the government supported diverse welfare initiatives such as subsidies to farmers and health insurance for the elderly. Launched in 1935 in the midst of the Great Depression, Aid for Dependent Children (the predecessor to AFDC) was fundamentally shaped by gendered assumptions about labor. Almost all (88 percent) of the initial recipients "were needy because the father had died. AFDC benefits were intended to enable the widow to care for her children at home."[11] This welfare program regarded the male head of the family as the primary breadwinner, with wives and children as economic dependents. This was a structurally created dependence, as married women were discouraged from working. Despite the economic hardships of the Great Depression, jobs were primarily reserved for men. Aid for Dependent Children preserved this heteronormative family structure by allowing widowed mothers to take care of their children through government support.

New Deal funding to support gendered dependence did not extend to men, women, and children of color. They were disproportionately poor and more likely to work. Racialized women and children could not necessarily depend upon the wages of a male breadwinner. Also, like other welfare policies of the 1930s, AFDC was primarily intended for the "deserving poor," most notably for white Americans. These racial exclusions were embedded in policies and practices. For example, Social Security did not cover farm labor and domestic work, occupations that people of color tended to fill. State, local, and city administrators also buttressed white privilege by not qualifying people of color for benefits. Finally, one of the most spectacular examples of racial exclusion during the Great Depression was the forced deportation of approximately four hundred thousand to two million Latinx people, regardless of citizenship.[12] The government allocated funds primarily to support white deserving widows.

By the end of the twentieth century, the women and children served by AFDC and the cultural understanding of poverty shifted drastically. Welfare recipients still consisted predominantly of mothers and children, with approximately five million parents (95 percent of them women) and 9.6 million children.[13] However, mothers were increasingly portrayed not as deserving but as predatory. First, in contrast to the earlier focus on widows, the Congressional Research Service (CRS) reported that "AFDC now serves primarily divorced, deserted, and never-married mothers and their offspring."[14] Welfare recipients were no longer virtuous widows, whose experiences of single motherhood resulted from the deaths of their husbands. Instead, single motherhood arose from perceived questionable choices. They may have decided not to marry but still have children. These women may have contributed to the dissolution of a heteronormative relationship. These women were no longer the victims of circumstances beyond their control but the willful perpetrators of immoral behavior.

Secondly, gendered expectations regarding paid work shifted. AFDC was originally intended to allow mothers to care for their children without working for wages. However, over the course of the twentieth century, women increasingly entered the labor force. When the Equal Pay Act passed in 1963, about 36 percent of women were employed compared to 57 percent by the 1990s.[15] Cultural wars ensued as antifeminists lambasted the feminist movement for trying to take away women's privileges as housewives and mothers. However, the same conservative critics denigrated poor mothers for neglecting to work and lift themselves and their children out of poverty. As sociologist Lynn Fujiwara points out, this demand for poor women to work stemmed from a "racial project" that designated immigrants and "women of color as workers rather than mothers."[16]

Finally, and very importantly, women and children of color were disproportionately represented among welfare recipients. The *New York Times* reported that the top three racial categories among mothers who received welfare in 1991 were Black (38.8 percent), white (38.1 percent), and Hispanic (17.4 percent).[17] In comparison, the 1990 census reported that African Americans constituted almost 12 percent of the overall population, and Hispanics comprised approximately 9 percent.[18] The higher percentages of Black and brown women on welfare reflected the greater instances of poverty within these communities. Also, since the 1960s and 1970s, the welfare-rights movement had demanded access to government social welfare programs for people of color.[19] The changed racial profile of welfare recipients, shifting family structures, and race-based expectations of women's labor all combined in widely circulated representation of the welfare queen. Popularized by Ronald Reagan beginning in the mid-1970s, the welfare queen trope posited that the stereotypical welfare recipient was an irresponsible woman of color who repeatedly had children and yet was unable to care for them. To survive, such women allegedly "sponged off" government resources. The idea that welfare recipients were parasitic "queens" rallied support for curbing or ending welfare and collateral elements of the social safety net.

Given the overdetermined representations of welfare recipients as women of color and as inadequate mothers, welfare-reform proposals tended to involve punitive measures. Four main legislative factions emerged in Congress during the mid-1990s—moderate and conservative Republicans as well as moderate and liberal/progressive Democrats. The conservative Republicans, including Newt Gingrich, predictably offered the most extreme proposals. They advocated cutting off "benefits to unmarried mothers under the age of 21 and turn[ing] over the savings to the states for programs to care for the children, such as orphanages and group homes."[20] Charles Murray, a social scientist who led this call, explained, "Some children would be better off in orphanages than with single welfare mothers. 'The dirty little secret is a very large number of them are rotten mothers.'"[21]

The justification to separate children from their parents and place them in institutions evoked past practices of racial and cultural removal. Indigenous children were separated from their families and communities, forced into boarding schools from the mid-nineteenth century onward in order to "kill the Indian, and save the man."[22] Also, the practice of removing Black children from their families ran counter to the National Association of Black Social Workers' stance against transracial adoption. In a 1972 position statement, the association "affirm[ed] the inviolable position of Black children in Black families where they belong physically, psychologically and culturally."[23]

Despite the extremism of conservative Republicans, they shared political commonalities with moderate Republicans and many Democrats. A proposal, first introduced in November 1993 and endorsed by 160 of 176 House Republicans, sought to cut off benefits to mothers under age eighteen. In addition, mothers who gave birth while on welfare would not receive additional funds, even though the average increase consisted of "less than $75 a month."[24] Moderate Democrats, enthusiastic supporters of Clinton's plan, responded to harsh Republican proposals with tough talk of their own. Their proposal included a requirement that teenage mothers establish paternity and live with their parental family in order to receive benefits. Both parties also instituted work requirements that forced welfare recipients to engage in work, job training, and job searches for specified hours each week in exchange for benefits. And, both Republican and Democratic plans set an expiration date for benefits, most commonly two years. Previous welfare policies, enacted during the last big reform in 1988, offered exceptions to work requirements for mothers with children younger than three. In contrast, the 1994 proposals imposed work requirements on mothers with children just over six months old.

The overall thrust of these proposals threatened the removal of benefits to ensure that poor mothers, especially young mothers, behaved responsibly. They had to first resort to privatized sources of support, such as partners and parents. If poor women received government benefits, then they were expected to give up choice—choice over whether to have children, where they could live, and what they did with their time and lives. The practice of fingerprinting welfare recipients by some states, justified by government officials to prevent fraud, reinforced the idea that to be poor and to receive government aid was akin to being a criminal.

Valuing Motherhood and Childhood

Mink's welfare approach and legislative proposal challenged the underlying assumptions and goals of the other bills. She wanted to utilize government resources to solve poverty, not primarily to reduce the number of welfare recipients. Mink first emphasized the need for more accurate representations of welfare recipients. Working with antipoverty advocates and feminists who recognized intersectional forms of oppression, Mink designed a series of government programs to enable the poor.

Mink's papers contain multiple reports, prepared by the nonpartisan CRS based on her requests, to understand who received welfare. Vee Burke, who worked in the Education and Public Welfare Division of CRS, authored many of these papers. In one memo, she explained that mothers who were younger than twenty-four when they first received AFDC tended not to stay on welfare long term. More than four out of ten (43 percent) were "short-term cyclers" who used welfare for fewer than twenty-four months. In other words, these individuals (an estimated 2.275 million out of five million families) were already leaving welfare by the cut-off date that was being proposed by Congress. Another one-third stayed longer, between twenty-four and fifty-four months (two years to four and a half years), but they were not lifetime users of welfare. The long-term users of continuous welfare (between fifty-five and sixty months) constituted approximately a quarter (24 percent) of the recipients.[25] In sum, close to half of the welfare recipients stayed on AFDC for less than two years and three-quarters of the total left before four and a half years.

The actual size of welfare families also challenged popular depictions of irresponsible reproduction. As Mink explained, "The average number of children on AFDC is two, that is the typical family size. So we are not facing a situation, as some have suggested, that people go on welfare to have children because that can lead to additional sums of money."[26] Mink reiterated this point about family size to her congressional colleagues and constituents, many of whom wrote angry letters demanding welfare reform. In one exchange, Mink questioned the presumption of the letter writer that he had the right to pass judgement on the reproductive decisions of welfare recipients. She queried him, how many children do you have?

Mink's understanding of welfare mothers shaped her policy proposals. The other bills targeted young mothers, seeking to discipline their behavior and wean them off government assistance. Mink focused instead on older recipients, who tended to have older children, had attended or graduated from high school, and had some job experience. In May 1994, Mink introduced her Job Start for America Act to target "welfare recipients who have the greatest potential for success in the workplace for job training and education programs in order to move them quickly into the workforce."[27] She explained that "over one half of adult welfare recipients cycle on and off welfare [and] actually work while receiving AFDC."[28] In other words, for these recipients, it was not the lack of employment or lack of desire to leave welfare that caused them to remain on welfare. Rather, it was the type of employment that left these individuals impoverished. As Mink stated, "Minimum wage is likely to produce about an $11,000 or $12,000 income for that individual."[29] That wage "is not going to bring that family out of poverty."[30]

To make visible the structural conditions of poverty, Mink spoke of an "endemic problem of poverty in our country."[31] Her diagnosis contrasted with that of the critics of welfare. They frequently evoked the language of infection to describe the "epidemic of illegitimacy" or the "epidemic of fatherless babies" or the epidemic of dependency.[32] Such language evoked gender blaming by connecting reproduction outside of marriage and heteronormative kinship structures as the explanation for economic dependency. Mink offered instead a gendered analysis of economic discrimination. She pointed out that women received lower wages than men of similar educational backgrounds, and they tended to have higher childcare responsibilities (as evidenced by the numbers of single women with children on AFDC). In other words, they were structurally burdened due to gender, both in the labor market and in terms of kinship responsibilities. These impacts rendered mother-headed households more likely to be impoverished, more so when mothers were simultaneously subject to racism.

Statistics on children revealed this feminization and racialization of poverty. The US Department of Health and Human Services reported that in 1992, "among children in female-headed families, the [poverty] rate was 54 percent; among children in families with a male present, the rate was 11 percent."[33] In another report authored by Vee Burke, the 1992 census data showed that of the 14.6 million poor children in the country, 9 million were white (constituting one out of every sixteen white children), 4.9 million were Black (translating to almost one-half of all Black children), and 4.1 million were Hispanic (or one in three).[34]

Poor mothers who experienced economic discrimination and heightened family obligations found it difficult to escape poverty. Jason DeParle, a *New York Times* journalist who covered the welfare debates extensively, noted that "poor women leave the welfare rolls for jobs much more often than was previously thought, but the low-paying and sometimes unattractive work rarely provides a long-term solution. . . . Most of the women soon quit or lose the jobs and return to the welfare rolls."[35] Women who returned to welfare "complained that the low-paying jobs left them nearly as poor as they had been on welfare, and in some cases caused them to lose their children's health insurance."[36]

To address these issues, Mink advocated both big-picture changes and targeted support programs. She had long critiqued the economic inequality that women faced, the cultural attitudes that constrained women, and the lack of female political representation. In terms of welfare specifically, Mink proposed providing increased educational opportunities, job training, and childcare support for mothers who had some work experience or a high school degree. Mink also argued for continuing these services, even after women left welfare, so that those who were just above the AFDC threshold might continue to receive the necessary support to gain greater financial stability.

Some elements of Mink's plan were initially part of Clinton's proposal, but she maintained the importance of these measures in the face of political pressure. In contrast, Clinton and his supporters decided to pull back on supporting childcare, especially given the costs involved for young mothers with young children.[37] When the radical Republicans took charge of Congress after the 1994 elections, welfare benefits were stripped even further. The Personal Responsibility Act that Gingrich spearheaded reduced access to health insurance, Supplemental Security Income for children with disabilities, food stamps, and school lunches for poor families.[38] The Republican strategy was to reallocate these services to the states. However, the federal government also allowed state governments the leeway to deny benefits. In fact, the legislation encouraged them to cut off benefits by incentivizing the reduction of welfare caseloads. As Mink pointed out in her comments to Congress, "This bill . . . eliminate[s] all Federal standards."[39] In a letter to a constituent in Hawaiʻi, Mink characterized the bill as "the most violent assault on low-income women and children in recent memory."[40]

In response, Mink offered two alternative welfare bills. The first she introduced in the first round of welfare debates and the second after the Republicans took charge. In the 1994 "Job Start for America" bill that focused on older mothers with older children, Mink maintained her firm commitment to government-subsidized childcare—a position she had advocated since the 1960s. As she explained to a supporter of the moderate Republican plan, which did not budget for childcare, "We would like to spend less money on welfare, but child care must be provided for the two-thirds of welfare recipients who are children. If child care is not expanded, who will take care of the preschoolers while mom works? Who will take care of the 6–14 year olds after school if mom works? . . . Who will care for all the children during the summer months?"[41]

Very importantly, Mink did not mandate a two-year deadline for welfare benefits, and she did not support forcing recipients into government-funded jobs afterwards to retain welfare benefits. Her goal was not to get people off welfare within a certain time and into low-paying jobs. Instead, she envisioned the government offering support for those seeking better livelihoods for themselves and their families. As Mink stated, "When we are talking about welfare reform, we ought to be talking about poverty."[42] Further, in order for poverty to be addressed, larger issues related to "gender equity and economic equity and employment equity" needed to be tackled. Otherwise, "the very people that we are dealing with in . . . welfare reform are the very women that we are going to victimize again with low pay." In essence, Mink believed that effective welfare reform needed to address economic and social systems that enforced poverty.

Mink did not ignore younger mothers in her plan but instead offered a different approach to address their needs. In a letter to George Stephanopoulos, then the senior advisor to the president, Mink explained, "To begin with the youngest recipients who have no job experience and require the most costly child care for young children will only set us up for failure."[43] For these individuals, she also believed in education and job training. At the same time, she valued the labor of mothering. In response to Republican proposals to remove poor children from poor mothers, Mink countered, "We pay a foster parent $650.00 a month to care for a foster child. Why can't we pay a foster child. Why can't we pay a single parent at least as much to nurture her own child? The loving care of a single parent is not sinful. Yet in most places the welfare family receives only $375.00 a month. And now there are proposals to take the child away."[44]

The importance that Mink placed on motherhood and childhood challenged three fundamental assumptions of welfare reform. First, she believed that welfare mothers could be good mothers. As she stated, "The current debate on welfare reform is being fueled by the misconception that all welfare families are out to take advantage of the system.

Welfare mothers care about their children and making a better life for them, just as we do."[45] Second, she believed that mothering children is valuable and essential labor that should in itself be compensated. Third, Mink believed that children deserved financial support, independent of their family structure. When she asked, "Why can't we pay a foster child?" she was arguing for a system of government support for all children. Considering that more than one in five children in the United States was poor, Mink's proposal suggested that their welfare should not depend on the vagaries of their family context. Children needed a minimum level of sustenance, which the government could guarantee.

In essence, Mink affirmed the value of reproductive care by mothers and the state. This has been a key insight of feminist thinkers. Maternalist feminists believe that women as nurturers should play a protective role in the broader society. Radical feminists, as part of their challenge to normative ideas of gender and kinship arrangements, illuminate how women often provide reproductive care and that this form of labor tends to be devalued in a capitalist society. These critiques point out that raising children and caring for the home, essential aspects of all societies, are both idealized and simultaneously relegated to unpaid or underpaid labor. Just as Mink did not seek to push welfare mothers into low-paying jobs that reinscribed their marginalized status, she argued that motherhood held value that should be recognized and financially supported. If individual families/mothers could not make ends meet, then the government needed to provide income support in recognition of mothers' caregiving work in families, as well as to counter the impoverishing effect of low wages in the labor market.

Mink also believed that younger mothers deserved the right to define their family, to choose where and with whom they reside. In response to the efforts to mandate the establishment of paternity in order to either secure child support or pressure women into marriage, Mink queried, "Suppose the child's father was physically abusive . . . or worse, suppose the woman conceived the child through an unfortunate act of incest. Would it be right to cease providing her benefits because she can't marry the father of her child or doesn't wish to go through further trauma of identifying the father?"[46] Mink questioned the presumption that the heteronormative unit necessarily secured the safety and well-being of impoverished families.

Advocates seeking to bring visibility to domestic violence supported the argument that the middle-class nuclear family cannot serve as the panacea to poverty. The National Task Force on Violence against Women pointed out that there is "clear and compelling evidence of the profound correlation and interrelationship between family violence and poverty."[47] On the one hand, "poverty . . . intensifies family violence"; also, women seeking to escape "violence often . . . [experience] an impoverishing effect."[48] If these women, who survive battery, rape, or incest, have limited options for a safety net outside of their families, then the "restrictive and punitive welfare policies will only force these poor women to choose between living with abuse or escaping abuse and being denied the food and shelter benefits for themselves and their children."[49]

In advocating for government resources, Mink offered single mothers and their children the means to exit abusive situations. They could rely on government support rather than the privatized family. After all, members of biological and heteronormative kinship units did not all experience economic and/or emotional security. In fact, for those experiencing abuse, the home served as the site of trauma and violence. So, requiring poor mothers and children to depend on private kinship arrangements to survive could exacerbate their suffering.

A Welfare Movement

Mink's ideas emerged and developed in conversation with welfare and poverty advocates. Some of her political allies were members of Congress, and others were based in social service agencies, religious organizations, academia, research institutions, and among the poor. In working with these individuals and groups, Mink elevated their authority as political commentators and policy makers. She amplified their voices, at a time when her opponents fueled a representational war against the impoverished and against women.

Patsy and Wendy Mink, then a faculty member in political science at the University of California–Santa Cruz, collaborated to inject feminist research and perspectives into the welfare policy debates. In October 1993, they organized a day-long conference entitled "Women and Welfare Reform: Women's Poverty, Women's Opportunities, and Women's Welfare." The event featured the who's who among feminist welfare scholars, such as historian Linda Gordon, independent scholar Ricki Solinger, social work researcher Mimi Abramovitz, philosopher Nancy Fraser, and sociologist Diana Pearce, who coined the phrase "feminization of poverty." Co-organized by the Institute for Women's Policy Research, the conference also featured the institute's founder, economist Heidi Hartmann. One memo from Hartmann and her collaborators explained the scope of their research sources and methodology, which emerged from years of detailed study: "For the past several years we have been engaged in extensive research on the AFDC population using 1984–1990 data from the Survey of Income and Program Participation, a Census Bureau data set. By combing panels of data we have generated a data set of 1,200 single AFDC mothers who represent 2.8 million single mothers receiving AFDC nationwide."[50] Like Patsy, these feminist thinkers conducted extensive research in order to "break myths and create solutions," the stated goals of the conference.[51]

The conference also featured speakers from grassroots organizations. Marian Kramer, a civil rights and antipoverty activist, represented the National Welfare Rights Union (NWRU). Described as "an organization, of, by, and for the poor in the United States and beyond," the NWRU served as a reincarnation of the National Welfare Rights Organization, a group that played a pivotal role in the welfare-rights movements of the 1960s and 1970s.[52] The executive director of Mi Casa, Dorothy Trujillo, also spoke during the conference. Latinas in Denver founded the organization to support their educational, employment, and entrepreneurial goals.[53] Maxine Waters, a Black congresswoman from Los Angeles and leading advocate of welfare protection, and Lynn Woolsey, a white congresswoman from the Bay Area and a former welfare recipient, co-sponsored the conference. However, it was Patsy Mink, her daughter, and staff who primarily organized this opportunity to feature women of color activists and feminist scholars. Wendy eventually edited a volume based on the conference, and Patsy circulated the publication among her congressional colleagues to influence welfare debates.[54]

The collaboration with community advocates also led to an important letter that Mink and her political allies sent to President Clinton. In November 1993, a coalition of antipoverty advocates requested meetings with the lead aides of Bernie Sanders, Patsy Mink, and other supportive legislators. These community leaders sought to encourage collaboration across the "Progressive/Black/Hispanic/Women's caucus coalition." They wanted to foster this collective voice in order to "let the Administration know now that there are a solid group of liberal Dems that are interested in making sure welfare is not totally punitive and really does something to move people toward self-sufficiency."[55]

Just five days later, a group of progressive congressional leaders circulated a letter to be sent to President Clinton on welfare reform. Mink, Sanders, Waters, and Woolsey were among the key authors and supporters of the letter. They noted that their "principles [for welfare reform] mirror those adopted by the Coalition on Human Needs, an alliance of over 100 national organizations dedicated to promoting public policies which address the needs of low-income Americans."[56] Eighty-eight legislators eventually signed the letter, dated November 23, 1993. Mink requested members of the CCWI to cosign, but they would not do so as a group.

The collective letter outlined three major principles that needed to be recognized in the welfare debates. First, the focus should be placed on reducing the need for welfare by creating a meaningful antipoverty strategy. This included investing in education and training opportunities as well as facing the realities of the labor market. In the 1990s, the US economy was "increasingly dominated by low-wage, part-time and temporary jobs that cannot support a family."[57] Second, it asserted the importance of encouraging welfare recipients to "work for wages not for welfare." The letter critiqued moderate legislative proposals that offered the option of having welfare recipients work in publicly funded positions, since "requiring work in exchange for welfare benefits would create a permanent underclass of impoverished parents who would not enjoy the basic rights to which all other American workers are entitled." Instead, allowing working parents to receive benefits without penalty enabled them to "retain more of their earnings and to save for future needs." Finally, the letter identified the need for an "adequate safety net for children and their families." Cutting off access to welfare without additional support "will only increase poverty and hurt needy families." The letter ended by emphasizing that "the welfare system must treat people with dignity."

Women on welfare broadcast a similar message. One group of recipients met twice a week at the Chicago Commons Employment Training

Center to study the Clinton proposal and develop detailed critiques of it. An article published in the *Washington Post* described the political leadership and vision that emerged from this community: "With a minimum of prompting by their teacher, they [the welfare recipients] engage in spirited arguments over narrow aspects of the plan until they reach a consensus on what they feel would be best for those who will be affected most by welfare reform."[58] Importantly, the recipients and the director of the center emphasized the need for "flexibility in meeting individual needs and not imposing one-size-fits-all solutions."[59] As the statistics on women on welfare indicated, and as women in the center experienced, some may need more support than others in order to address the "appalling range and depth of problems" that impoverished women experience.[60] Welfare mothers were often the objects of political debate and media representation. Rarely were they perceived as experts who could help formulate a better welfare system. As one participant expressed, "When you aren't invited to the table, sometimes you have to set your own."[61]

These voices were precisely those that feminist scholars and political advocates sought to include and foreground. To spotlight social-justice approaches to welfare policy, they formed the Women's Committee of 100 in the spring of 1995. Wendy helped co-organize the group in collaboration with scholar activists and the NOW-Legal Defense and Education Fund. Patsy recruited some of her feminist colleagues in Congress to join. The organization brought together "over 700 women . . . to raise their voices against punitive welfare legislation."[62] The Women's Committee contested the Republicans' Contract with America, arguing that the Republican effort "undoes progressive social legislation in force since the New Deal," while noting that the "centerpiece of the Contract is the *Personal Responsibility Act*."[63] To fight retrenchment of social provision for low-income mothers, the Women's Committee sought to create a feminist alliance across class and racial divides. As their correspondence to potential supporters expressed, "Right now we face a glass ceiling for high achieving women and a bottomless abyss for women denied all opportunity. Let's raise the floor at the same time as we lift the ceiling."[64] The slogan of the organization encapsulated the desire for a broad women's movement by arguing that "a war against poor women is a war against all women."[65]

Figure 9.2. Patsy Mink speaks at a Capitol Hill rally convened by the National Organization for Women on March 22, 1995. Protesting welfare legislation that harmed low-income mothers, Mink was joined by scholar activists and social-justice advocates. Source: AP Photo/Joe Marquette photographer.

The intention of building a broad movement met with limited success, however. In a letter to a disappointed voter, Mink pointed out the cracks in the women's coalition: "I agree with you that being Pro-Choice is not enough. In the House, the women had the opportunity to vote for my welfare substitute. . . . You will note that while all Black, Hispanic, and Asian Democratic women voted for my substitute. . . . [only six] White Democratic women voted for it."[66] The issues of poverty and race revealed the divides that existed even among more liberal sectors of the Democratic Party and among women. Nevertheless, Mink emphasized the need to continue building a women's coalition. She pointed out that "I agree with you that women must work to create hope for all women rather than the grim choices of poverty, homelessness, hunger and destitution."[67]

Patsy Mink and her antipoverty allies analyzed the classed and racialized assumptions of good and bad motherhood as well as the structural forms of economic exclusion that resulted in the feminization and racialization of poverty. Working with feminist partners, Mink raised a legislative voice against the demonization of welfare recipients and in support of the just use of government resources. When Mink stood before Congress and reminded her colleagues that welfare is a women's issue, she was speaking in partnership with those who were not invited to the table but insisted on setting a place for themselves anyway.

The Costs of Welfare Reform

The critics of welfare sought to alleviate financial burdens on the government budget and by extension US taxpayers. This was a common refrain evoked by political leaders and "average" Americans. Their letters and postcards expressed anger for having their hard-earned wages reallocated to support so-called welfare queens. Those who wanted welfare reform recognized that there were costs, both political and financial, for reducing welfare. The more moderate and progressive proposals acknowledged that the government could not abandon those in poverty. Funding was needed to support job training, public work opportunities, and subsidized childcare. In other words, getting people off welfare rolls entailed government resources. An article in the *Brookings Review* described this conundrum as "the money trap."[68]

Author Kent Weaver explained, "The AFDC money trap is simple: any reform likely to improve the prospects for poor children means spending more money than the public thinks is necessary or Congress wants to spend. Most people already think that too many people receive AFDC and that it is too costly. They think welfare reform should save money immediately. But few reform proposals would do that."[69] The solution that welfare critics coalesced upon was to reduce expenditures for groups already impoverished or deemed even less worthy of government support—immigrants.

Aside from the progressive welfare solutions that Mink and allies championed, the other proposals all argued for the need to curtail immigrant benefits. As the *Washington Post* reported on March 24, 1994, "A group of 90 moderate and conservative House Democrats has joined with Republicans in urging that welfare benefits for most noncitizens should be eliminated to pay for welfare reform."[70] The proposed cuts included cutting Supplemental Security Income and Medicaid for immigrants. As scholar Lynn Fujiwara points out, "The 1996 reform law explicitly made citizenship status a criterion of eligibility for public benefits."[71] This ban targeted documented immigrants, while refugees were exempt from these exclusions for the first few years after their arrival in the United States.

Historically, new arrivals had to prove that they could be self-sufficient. Those designated as "likely to be a public charge," or "LPC," were refused entry. Sponsors had to prove that they could support the newcomers, if needed. In other words, immigrants were legally constructed as the ultimate neoliberal subjects. They offered their labor, contributing economically, but they could not receive financial support from their adopted country. The new proposals in the mid-1990s extended the refusal of government support for a longer period of time and to a larger group of immigrants.[72] As Dave McCurdy (D-Oklahoma), leader of the moderate Democrats, stated, "We believe American citizens are the priority."[73]

Mink and other political leaders who challenged Republicans and moderate Democrats on welfare reform also criticized the call to reduce support for immigrants. As Charles Wheeler, directing attorney of the Los Angeles–based national Immigration Law Center pointed out, this coalition between moderates and conservatives emerged because they "want to save money and . . . see immigrants as a vulnerable group that doesn't vote and is out of favor right now."[74] Aware of the impending proposals to cut off immigrant access to welfare, Mink, Woolsey, Nydia Velazquez (D–New York), Ron Dellums (an African American congressman, D-California), Bernie Sanders, and sixty other members of Congress cosigned a February 28, 1994, letter. Their criticism was encapsulated by the title "Let's Not Finance Welfare Reform on the Backs of the Poor!"[75] The legislators pointed out that doing so "defeats the very purpose of reforming the welfare system. It is like robbing Peter to pay Paul, or in this case robbing Patty to pay Pauline."[76] The letter goes on to advise, "Cutting or taxing other programs such as food stamps, housing assistance, and assistance to elderly and indigent legal immigrants only threatens to make many individuals, especially the working poor, worse off."[77] Through this letter, Mink and her allies insisted on protecting and advocating for those consistently marginalized in the political process: women, children, people of color, and immigrants.

Searching for Reproductive Justice

The defense of these marginalized groups ultimately did not gain enough political traction. Despite the efforts of Mink and others to present alternative perspectives about poverty and government responsibility, they did not have enough allies in Congress, especially after the Republican Revolution. Their political opponents drew from long-standing racialized and gendered assumptions about the "undeserving poor." Women, children, people of color, and immigrants have historically occupied the margins of the US polity. Social norms across the country regarded these individuals and groups as undeserving of rights and resources. In the context of the 1990s, with an increasing emphasis on neoliberal approaches to governance, calls for societal responsibility and structural solutions were easily dismissed as wasteful and ineffective. The War on Poverty that Mink helped to enact in the 1960s became transformed into a war on the impoverished.

The 1996 Personal Responsibility Work Opportunity Reconciliation Act succeeded in removing the poor from government support but not in alleviating poverty. Nearly ten years after the welfare reforms, one study of programs in Florida and Connecticut noted that the governments saved "approximately $28,000 per recipient over her life-time."[78] The same study also noted a "statistically significant difference in the measured death rates," which was higher for welfare recipients under TANF (Temporary Assistance for Needy Families) compared to AFDC.[79] Also, as a result of TANF, "nearly one million immigrants" lost "their food stamp benefits, resulting in a documented rise in hunger in immigrant families."[80] Half a million "elderly, disabled, and blind im-migrants" lost access to Supplemental Security Income.[81] Nearly three-quarters of those immigrants (72 percent) were women.

The battle over welfare as an "entitlement" exposed fundamental be-liefs about who constituted rights-bearing subjects in the United States. When Mink sent a newsletter about the congressional debates to restrict "entitlements," her constituents expressed strong opinions regarding the word. Mink responded by explaining that an entitlement is a legal com-mitment, a social contract between the state and the individual or group. An entitlement signaled a guaranteed right, recognized by the govern-ment. Her constituents tended to regard an "entitlement" as a special privilege, an arrangement that gave preference to particular people, such as welfare mothers and children. These critics challenged welfare for poor women and children, but not for themselves through programs like Social Security. They also tended to accept government subsidies for those perceived as deserving of support, such as farmers, suburban homeowners, casino operators, and corporations. This outrage about the "entitlement" of a particular form of welfare reflected a broader effort to draw the boundaries of US society to exclude the poor, the racialized, and the immigrant, particularly when these identities dovetailed with recipients being women and children.

Patsy Mink helped to coalesce and mobilize a coalition that crossed racial and class boundaries. Since the mid-1960s, around the time when Mink entered federal political office, Asian Americans were often ra-cialized as model minorities. Perceived as individuals and communities who did not protest social inequalities, their presumed success proved that the American promise of equal opportunity was a reality. Mink's ef-forts to speak for and with the impoverished demonstrated her efforts to identify structural forms of inequality and to politically ally with other women of color and racialized immigrants. She challenged the model minority image by demanding political change, and she declared her solidarity with those who were reviled and targeted. The legislation that passed, that Mink and others opposed, had brutal real-life consequences for millions of poor women and children. However, their efforts to demand economic and reproductive justice introduced important political ideas into national public discourse and helped mobilize collective resistance.

"NO, WHERE ARE YOU *REALLY* FROM?"

Growing up in Hawai'i in the 1950s and 1960s, I was acutely aware of racial divides, ethnic stratification, cultural pride, and resistance to white dominion. Experiences and observations in childhood trained my impulses toward racial justice and interracial solidarity, as did parental example. But they did not prepare me for the anti-Asian racism that my mother and I would live with daily once we moved to Washington, DC, in December 1964. Eventually named "microaggressions," the daily put-downs, othering, devaluing, and erasure directed at us because we were of Asian descent taught me that many in the white majority did not consider us fellow Americans. At its most benign, anti-Asian racism treated us as if we didn't belong to the US political community—invisible. At its most virulent, it inflamed violence against us as trespassers in US economic and political life—"yellow peril."

Anti-Asian sentiment directed against individual Asian Americans demeaned and disempowered us, first by belittling us and then by marking us as foreign and even dangerous. Everyday anti-Asian tropes and stereotypes endured by individuals could be summoned to serve larger, geopolitical ends, as in US trade wars, first with Japan and later with China.[1] The idea that Asians are "inscrutable" and "sneaky" invigorated attacks on Japan's economic prowess summed up in "buy American" campaigns of the 1970s, '80s, and '90s.[2] Hostility toward Asian-origin goods bled into hate toward Asian-heritage people, sometimes leading to white violence against Asian Americans, such as the 1982 murder of Vincent Chin.

Sometimes latent, at other times overt, hair-trigger racism against Asians in the United States has dogged our history since the 1850s. By the 1990s, Asian Americans had been assigned at least two unflattering profiles, neither immune from anti-Asian hate. According to a late-twentieth-century profile, Asian Americans were the model minority—hard-working but docile, successful but "not management material." A second profile, resilient for more than a century, cast Asians and Asian Americans as untrustworthy, devious, and unreadable.

Two episodes in the late 1990s spotlighted the second racial profile. The first arose from a campaign finance scandal involving the Democratic National Committee and the Clinton-Gore reelection campaign in 1996. Gross irregularities and outright legal violations in fundraising by the DNC involved Asian American and Asian donors and fundraisers as central players. While my mother did not excuse the donors or fundraisers their mistakes or transgressions, she did rise to the defense of Asian Americans in general and immigrants of all backgrounds when they were punished for a scandal they had no part in. Chair of the Asian Pacific American Congressional Caucus at the time, my mother told *Asian Week*, "There is a lot of race baiting and the concentration of the articles on the Asian aspects of the fundraising, it just goes on and on. I don't think this whole thing started in Congress, but they are just lapping up the juicy elements of it. It's the media."[3]

At one extreme, the *National Review* whipped up anti-Asian racism with a magazine cover caricaturing President Clinton and Hillary Clinton as slit-eyed and buck-toothed, Hillary dressed like Mao and Bill wearing a "coolie" hat.[4] More mainstream outlets used more subtle imagery, but still communicated the xenophobic and racist message that Asians are sinister.[5] Press coverage focused on individual donors with Asian-sounding surnames rather than the big picture of soft money loopholes and campaign finance abuses. When Asian American advocates protested the abundance of racist tropes in media coverage of the scandal, many in the media played dumb. On the *Today Show*, for example, Daphne Kwok of the Organization of Chinese Americans asserted, "This brings back the whole yellow peril of more than 100 years ago when the Chinese became the target of anti-Chinese sentiment, leading to the lynching and mobbing of the Chinese on the West Coast." Mystified, Matt Lauer responded, "Explain to me why it's racist, Miss Kwok."[6]

The DNC itself followed a similar pattern, interrogating individual donors with Asian-sounding names about their credit history, jobs, and citizenship. This treatment of individual Asian Americans as illegitimate participants in politics was not only insulting but chilling. Worse was the DNC's cure for the scandal: banning campaign contributions from legal immigrants who were not citizens. Asian American advocates were enraged, as was my mother.[7]

Eventually, the House of Representatives mirrored the DNC's example with legislation to amend the Federal Election Campaign Act by prohibiting contributions to campaigns by noncitizens, including green-card-holding legal residents.[8] My mother was the first to speak in opposition during the floor debate: "I rise in opposition to H.R. 34, cynically misnamed the Illegal Foreign Contributions Act. The title of this bill is there to lure Members into thinking that it deals with illegal foreign contributions. That is simply not the case. What this bill does is to prohibit legal residents who are living here in the United States legally, working, paying their taxes, fighting in the military, giving up their lives, denying the right to participate in the political process in this country. That is absolutely unconstitutional."[9]

One hundred law professors and all major Asian American advocacy organizations—including the Asian Pacific American Labor Alliance, the Organization of Chinese Americans, and the National Asian Pacific American Legal Consortium—opposed the effort to choke off political participation by Asian American immigrants.[10] But on the House floor, my mother felt pretty lonely in her opposition. Over a quick dinner in the Member's Dining Room the night of the debate, my mother and I discussed the impending vote. She lamented that few self-identified liberals or progressives were willing to stand up for the political rights of legal immigrants and against a sham call to outlaw "foreign influence" in campaigns—not even Bernie Sanders, who was in the House at the time. On the roll call vote, only forty-three members voted with my mother against the bill, thirty-seven of them Democrats.[11]

Dubbed "Chinagate," the campaign finance controversy left the impression that the Chinese government attempted to purchase influence in American politics using the services of Chinese Americans. Investigations ensued, dragging out inconclusively through 1997 and 1998 and preheating the political climate for more anti-Asian discrimination and hate. When a second major anti-Asian scandal broke in March 1999, both government actors and the public were primed to believe that a naturalized American of Chinese descent was a sleeper agent for the People's Republic of China. Eager to distance itself from the seedy campaign finance episode, the Clinton administration was happy to catch a "Chinese spy."

On March 6, 1999, the *New York Times* published an explosive story under an all-caps headline alleging espionage for China by a Chinese American. Vaunted journalists James Risen and Jeff Gerth reported that a spy at Los Alamos National Laboratory had given nuclear secrets to China, and described the spy as a "Chinese-American" who "stuck out like a sore thumb."[12]

Four days later, the *New York Times* exposed Wen Ho Lee as the alleged spy after energy secretary Bill Richardson fired him from his Los Alamos job.[13] No charges had been filed against him when Dr. Lee was unmasked as the prime suspect; nor were any charges brought for another nine months. When Lee was arrested in December 1999, he was not charged with nuclear espionage; the FBI could not find evidence of espionage. But to "imply spying," the government lodged fifty-nine felony counts of mishandling restricted data.[14] Once under arrest, Lee was denied bail, held in pretrial solitary confinement, his wrists and ankles shackled during his one hour of exercise each day, and forbidden to speak Mandarin to his family.[15] My mother and other Asian American advocates appealed to the attorney general either to allow Lee to be released on bail or to relax the conditions of confinement.[16] Even before his arrest, they protested the frenzy of suspicion surrounding Lee as racial profiling.[17]

Lee won a bail hearing in August 2000 after eight months in pretrial solitary confinement. In a stringent rebuke of the FBI and the prosecution, the judge called out the FBI for presenting misleading and unreliable evidence, questioned the "unfair manner" in which Lee had been held in custody, and released Lee on home detention.[18] In September 2000, the government dropped fifty-eight of the fifty-nine charges leveled against Wen Ho Lee, while Lee pled guilty to one count of downloading restricted data.

Wen Ho Lee didn't get his life back, but he did win back his freedom. Shortly after Lee's release on September 20, 2000, my mother took to the floor of the House of Representatives to challenge the Justice Department to answer for its anti-Chinese racial profiling. She asked, "Was his apprehension in the first place triggered because he was an Asian?" Suggesting that Lee was a victim of selective, race-based prosecution, she continued: "Others at the Los Alamos laboratory committed even more serious violations with respect to secret, classified documents . . . yet these people were not investigated, were not put through the same extent of inquiry as Dr. Lee was." Calling on Congress to prevent the unjust treatment suffered by Wen Ho Lee from ever happening again, she spoke as an Asian American too familiar with being regarded as not American enough: "It is a terrible thing. The Asian community feels burdened with this suspicion, and the wreckage of this whole incident has sort of fallen on all Asians, not just Chinese Americans, but all Asians."[19]

Although certain Clinton administration actions either aroused or inflamed anti-Asian hostility during the late 1990s, other actions promoted Asian Americans and shone a light on Asian American issues. In June 1997,

President Clinton nominated Bill Lann Lee assistant attorney general for civil rights, the top civil rights position in the Justice Department, which had been held previously by Deval Patrick. Son of immigrants, Lee would become the first Asian American appointed to the position, and as such the first civil rights chief from outside the white-Black binary. Clinton's selection of Bill Lann Lee was a momentous development for Asian Americans, signaling recognition of the Asian American community as a whole. As Karen Narasaki of the National Asian Pacific American Legal Consortium observed, "We believe it's sending a message to the Asian-American community that's been feeling pretty battered over the whole campaign finance scandal that, in fact, the Administration still is committed to the community."[20] The Republican-controlled Senate blocked Lee's confirmation, however, chiefly because Lee had been an outspoken defender of affirmative action in California. What followed was a years-long tug of war over Lee's confirmation. Lee served as acting assistant attorney general, his nomination continually rebuffed by the Republican Senate, until President Clinton finally installed him as the bona fide occupant of the job through a recess appointment just four months before all Clinton appointees would leave office.[21]

The struggle to secure, preserve, and legitimize Bill Lann Lee's leadership of the civil rights division engaged the Asian American advocacy community throughout Clinton's second term. Strategizing was ongoing among advocates, congressional allies like my mother, and the White House. Asian American advocates aimed for visibility for their issues, something that the elevation of Bill Lann Lee advanced. Clinton Democrats were interested in welcoming larger numbers of Asian Americans into the Democratic Party, something they thought recognition might accomplish.

In mid-1999, with eighteen months left in his presidency, Clinton promulgated an executive order establishing the White House Initiative on Asian Americans and Pacific Islanders (AAPI). A new office dedicated to AAPI issues was charged with increasing Asian American participation in federal programs and outreach to the underserved. The executive order creating the AAPI initiative was the first executive order pertaining to Asian Americans since Executive Order 9066 incarcerated Americans of Japanese ancestry during World War II.[22]

My mother's trusted legislative director, Laura Efurd, moved over to the White House to assist with raising the profile of Asian American communities and issues. The executive order asked each federal agency to develop objectives to better serve the AAPI community. In May 2000, President Clinton created the first-ever President's Advisory Commission on Asian Americans and Pacific Islanders, which took testimony from AAPI grassroots activists and community members to prepare a report on recommendations and priorities. The report, issued just as the Clinton presidency ended, highlighted four key themes: (1) AAPI invisibility at the table, in data, as participants in history, and in popular culture; (2) marginalization of Native Hawaiians and Pacific Islanders; (3) the damaging "model minority" stereotype; and (4) our status as "forever aliens" in the public imaginary.[23]

Clinton's move to signify Asian Pacific Americans as actual Americans headed in the right direction but was no antidote to toxic suspicion of Asian Americans as untrustworthy Americans. The government that gave us our own "Initiative" and invited us to enumerate priorities was also the government that ginned up inferences that Wen Ho Lee was a spy and that sponsored his inhumane incarceration. The media that got called out for sensationalizing rather than reporting the Los Alamos story also was the media that got away with an apology for journalistic mistakes in lieu of an apology for inflaming anti-Chinese racism. After Wen Ho Lee's release in September 2000, the New York Times published a non-apology apology noting that "passages of some articles also posed a problem of tone" but declined to take responsibility for the ensuing racism and its injuries.[24] Then, in February 2001, the Times published a snide reexamination of the Wen Ho Lee case that strongly implied that he might have been a national security risk after all.[25]

10

The Cost of Belonging

In 1996, the same year that the Personal Responsibility welfare reform law passed, Congress and President Clinton also authorized the Illegal Immigration Reform and Immigrant Responsibility Act (IIRIRA). The two bills overlapped in political approach, as the repetition of the term "responsibility" suggests. Welfare reform curtailed the claims of impoverished individuals on the US state, setting limits on who can access benefits and for how long. The law specifically prevented documented immigrants from utilizing certain social services. The 1996 immigration law sought to secure US borders from undocumented individuals. Doing so, though, made both documented and undocumented migrants more susceptible to detention, deportation, and racial harassment. Furthermore, the debates that resulted in IIRIRA initially proposed limiting all immigration, regardless of status. Racial anxieties clearly underlay the resentment towards newcomers. Individuals arriving after the 1965 Hart-Celler Act came predominantly from Asian and Latin American countries rather than Europe. The 1996 welfare and immigration laws worked in conjunction to strengthen internal and external borders of the United States.

During Patsy Mink's last twelve years of congressional service, she participated in vociferous debates regarding the nation's borders. These political disputes reflected anxieties regarding the identity of the American people and the appropriate limits of political and economic rights. Along with other pro-immigrant advocates, Mink argued against the political positions that regarded welfare recipients and noncitizens as undeserving of rights. She challenged the rhetoric that portrayed newcomers as threats to the US nation, and she fought for a more humane asylum process to include those fleeing political persecution and gender-based violence. Yet, in response to efforts to tarnish and banish newcomers, regardless of status, she and other political allies maintained a distinction between the documented and the undocumented.

The costs of belonging to the nation-state are revealed by analyzing how Mink navigated these debates about the legitimacy and enforcement of US borders. As a legislator, she was committed to the law. Mink understood her mission as expanding the possibilities of inclusion and equity within the US polity. At the same time, she acknowledged distinctions between those who had legal standing versus those who did not. This balance between reimagining and upholding the law was in evidence as Mink navigated the turmoil of immigration politics of the mid-1990s.

Immigrant Children and Unwanted Families

In the mid-1990s, nativist political leaders and pundits were simultaneously beholden to and preying upon constituent anxieties regarding immigration. The calls for restriction frequently focused on the children and family members of newcomers. These individuals might be immigrants themselves (documented as well as undocumented), or they might be American-born citizens. To deter the growth of unwanted communities, xenophobic campaigns communicated the message that the kin of immigrants were not welcome in the United States. In response, Mink and other allies countered these attacks by advocating for educational and welfare services to support the young and the impoverished.

Both immigration and welfare reforms targeted children by focusing on the social and fiscal costs of reproducing racialized families in the United States. Critics of the rise in Latin American and Asian populations pursued a variety of measures: banning bilingual education, restricting free lunches for students from low-income families, denying public education and medical services to the undocumented, deputizing school staff and healthcare providers to identify immigrants without status, and challenging the validity of birthright citizenship. The cumulative impact of these attacks, akin to the detonation of cluster bombs, targeted the children connected to immigrant families. Fundamentally, the racial and cultural identity of the children made them and their parents vulnerable.

Republican representative Dana Rohrabacher from southern California was a leading proponent of these initiatives. In 1994, California voters had approved Proposition 187, a ballot initiative that banned undocumented immigrants from using nonemergency health care and denied access to public schools. Twelve years earlier, the Supreme Court had ruled in *Plyler v. Doe* (1982) that states cannot deny public education to students based on their immigration status. The court found that undocumented immigrants had limited legal standing, due to their illegality. Additionally, *Plyler v. Doe* pronounced that education is not a fundamental right, which would trigger the requirement for heightened scrutiny for rights violations. Despite these important caveats, a majority of the Supreme Court (5–4) decided that preventing undocumented youth from attending public school imposed "a lifetime hardship on a discrete class of children not accountable for their disabling status."[1] The narrow majority in *Plyler* suggested that the decision was susceptible to reversal. So California nativists, Governor Pete Wilson and Dana Rohrabacher among them, rallied anti-immigrant support for Proposition 187.[2] Ultimately declared unconstitutional in 1997, the law nevertheless set the political tone for the state and, increasingly, the country.

Rohrabacher led the charge to transpose these initiatives to the national political stage. Emphasizing the theme of "responsibility," he decried that "these people are illegal by their willful and conscious illegal act. They are not entitled to any social welfare benefits and Congress' continued silence concerning their eligibility is a standing invitation for more and more illegal aliens to enter our country."[3] Rohrabacher accused parents of willfully breaking the law. In making this argument, he also implied that services to citizen-children of undocumented parents had a similar impact. Any provision of educational, health, or welfare benefits to unauthorized newcomers and their kids encouraged undocumented migration. This accusation fueled the "anchor baby" charge, that pregnant mothers entered the country in order to gain opportunities for their US-born children. In short, the political targeting of children tended to subsume citizen children into the undocumented status of their parents. What mattered was their membership within mixed-status families, especially families of color.

In these debates, Mink advocated for immigrant families. She consistently defended access to education and health care and food for impoverished school children, as well as cultural and linguistic diversity. In March 1994, Mink cosigned a statement to "Support Bilingual

Education!" The other key endorsers included California congressional representatives Norman Mineta and Robert T. Matsui, as well as Hawai'i representative Neil Abercrombie. Together, they emphasized the importance of bilingual education for the "3.6 million school-aged children with limited English Proficiency (LEP)."[4] Federal funding, the group argued, is "essential in helping school districts provide equitable educational opportunity."[5] Recognizing the demographic trend in the country, the letter emphasized that "the number of students who need bilingual assistance will continue to grow during the coming decade."[6]

Just two months later, the signers formed the core membership of the Congressional Asian Pacific American Caucus (CAPAC). Given the low numbers of Asian American and Pacific Islander representatives and senators, the caucus included congressmembers who served significant AAPI constituencies. For example, Nancy Pelosi (D-California), who eventually became the first female speaker of the House, represented San Francisco and was a founding member of the CAPAC. Mineta served as the caucus's first chair, and Mink succeeded him.

Members of the Congressional Hispanic Caucus (CHC) and organizations representing Latinx communities also played an active role in denouncing the campaign known as "English First." Joined by supportive political leaders and educational associations, they pointed out that "the utilization of both English and a student's native language as the child is transitioned into purely English instruction promotes learning English, as well as student achievement in other subjects like math and science, raising prospects for overall success in school."[7] Bilingual education communicated a message of welcome and a willingness to help students new to US schools. In contrast, English only, as Jose E. Serrano (D–New York), who served as the CHC chair, pointed out, "would subject citizen and permanent resident children from racial and ethnic backgrounds to discrimination and humiliation."[8]

The targeting of children reinforced the restrictive intent of immigration exclusion. The laws that guarded US borders sought to socially engineer the composition of US residents. Mandating English-only in schools forced children from multilingual and non-English-speaking households to assimilate. Doing so without providing bilingual support led to curtailed educational achievements. Targeting children discouraged racialized immigrants from pursuing biological and social reproduction in the United States; attacking children cut off immigrant futurity.

Admissible Kin

The exclusion of unwanted families became a central goal of immigration reform. Nativist advocates proposed narrowing the scope of admissible kin to stem the phenomenon of chain migration. Without these restrictions, one citizen or immigrant could sponsor numerous family members for entry. These attempts aroused opposition from pro-immigration advocates, who in response framed their arguments by supporting citizen rights to family reunification.

In 1994, Representative Lamar Smith (R-Texas) and Senator Alan Simpson (R-Wyoming) introduced companion bills designed to restrict documented as well as undocumented immigration. Arrivals based on kinship connections (461,725) constituted almost 60 percent of the total (804,416) admitted that year.[9] Seeking to reduce immigration overall and to prioritize the formation of nuclear families, the House legislation proposed an overall cap of 535,000, approximately one-third less than the 1994 total. This decrease followed the recommendations of the Commission on Immigration Reform that Congress established in 1990. Within this lowered quota, 330,000 slots were reserved for family. To achieve the reduction, the legislation proposed eliminating family-reunification eligibility for certain kinship categories. Only spouses and minor children of US citizens and immigrants, as well as parents of adult US citizens, were deemed admissible; adult children and siblings were not.

US immigration law did not always promote family reunification. The 1875 Page Law and the 1882 Chinese Exclusion Law sought to curtail unwanted entry and growth of these communities. Excluding women among predominantly male populations served as a prophylactic.[10] Under the 1924 national-origins-quota system, which continued bans from Asia while favoring immigrants from northern and western Europe, immediate relatives (spouses, minor children) had been able to enter without being counted towards the overall quota. In the aftermath of World War II and during the Cold War, with the increasing presence of the US military abroad, new legislation allowed US soldiers to bring home their "foreign" or "war" brides. The 1965 Johnson-Reed Act codified the principle of family reunification by reserving 75 percent of admissions for family members. Under this law, parents, adult children, and siblings could be admitted, along with spouses and minor children. Proponents of family reunification initially believed that this avenue would benefit individuals of European descent. Due to the skew of the national-origins quota, immigrants from Ireland, the United Kingdom, and Germany were entitled to 70 percent of the visas on the eve of the 1965 immigration reform. However, the 1965 reforms, particularly the family reunification pathways, paved the way for the shift towards Latin American and Asian entries.

Given the trajectory towards expanded kinship migration, the 1990s efforts to eliminate admissible family categories drew protest from a variety of circles, including some Republicans. Howard Berman (D-California), Chris Smith (R–New Jersey), Dick Chrysler (R-Michigan), Sam Brownback (R-Kansas), and others authored a series of "Dear Colleague" letters that explained "The Facts on Immigration." Letter number eight, entitled "Is Your Child Part of Your Nuclear Family?," questioned the proposed legislation for asserting a false divide between "extended family members" and "nuclear families." Their critique pointed out that "according to this legislation, if your only son or daughter turns 21 then he or she ceases to be part of your 'nuclear' family and must meet prohibitive requirements to immigrate—and would never be able to immigrate once he or she turns 26."[11] The memo points out that under the proposed law, "if you have a brother or sister, they're not part of your nuclear family either."[12] Also, speaking to the concerns about the welfare costs of the elderly, the authors indicate that "if your mother or father cannot afford the exorbitant bond or the type of health and nursing home care required in the bill—which the Justice Department has said virtually no one can obtain—then your mom and dad aren't part of your nuclear family either."[13] The legislators asked, "Who considers their daughter, sister or mother part of their 'extended family,' as opposed to their nuclear family? The answer is virtually no one, which is why this part of H.R. 2202 is so anti-family."[14] The signers of the memos, all white and male, articulated a more expansive understanding of family than the proponents of the Lamar Smith bill did. They argued instead that "our country has not grown too small for the mothers and fathers, sons and daughters, brothers and sisters of U.S. citizens."[15] As their argument reveals, the group focused on the rights of citizens to reunite with family. Working in conjunction with each other and other legislative partners, they coauthored amendments to remove the antifamily provisions and to divide H.R. 2202 in order to treat undocumented immigration issues separately from policies regarding documented immigrants.[16]

Communities of color also articulated similar concerns about family separation and the conflation of citizens, documented immigrants, and undocumented immigrants. In March 1996, Mink, as chair of the CAPAC, authored a "Dear Colleague" letter expressing that "Asian Pacific Americans Oppose Restrictions on Legal Immigration."[17] As the title suggests, Mink and the CAPAC protested limiting "*legal* immigration" (emphasis in the original) while acknowledging that "the Asian Pacific American community does not dispute the need for reasonable efforts to restrict illegal immigration."[18] Equally important, Mink spoke on behalf of the caucus to highlight how the proposed legislation "undercuts family reunification," especially since "it is estimated that one in five Asian Pacific American families will be adversely impacted."[19]

Other organizations and advocates within the Asian American community echoed similar sentiments. The National Asian Pacific American Bar Association, the Chinese American Committee of 100, the Gujarati Society, the Organization of Chinese Americans, and the Asian Pacific American Labor Alliance all issued statements that communicated their desire to protect family reunification and the need to distinguish between "legal" and "illegal" forms of immigration. In fact, thirty Asian American, Pacific American, and ethnic-specific organizations worked together to sponsor a lobbying week that attracted "hundreds of Asian Pacific Americans from around the country" to Washington, DC.[20] The title of their press release signaled their wish "to defend family immigration" and thus protect the rights of "Asian Pacific American citizens."[21] Reminding audiences that many Asian Americans and Pacific Islanders are citizens put their demands for family reunification on firmer political grounds. After all, the United States had a long-standing practice of regarding these groups as either forever foreigners or faraway natives.

These statements responded to escalating xenophobia during the 1990s. Organizations like the Federation of American Immigration Reform (FAIR) justified their nativist politics by distorting the history of

immigration restriction. For example, FAIR distinguished prior generations of overwhelmingly white immigrants from the new Latin American
and Asian immigrants. In a publication asking, "Doesn't Congress
Realize How Times Have Changed?" FAIR contrasted the contexts of
past and present. During the "Great Immigration Wave" of the late nineteenth and early twentieth centuries, FAIR maintained, there was "plenty
of cheap land and resources."[22] The organization did not acknowledge
that the US government and military dispossessed land from Indigenous
and Mexican peoples to make it available for Anglo settlers. Also, FAIR
claimed that earlier generations of immigrants were welcomed into the
"melting pot," which fostered "assimilation and 'Americanization.'"[23]
However, during the late nineteenth and early twentieth centuries, antagonism against southern and eastern Europeans, along with Asians, led to
laws designed to reduce their numbers or ban them from entry. Glossing
over this history, FAIR asserted that the 1990s immigrants rejected assimilation, represented lower-skilled workers at a time when "land and
resources" were "much more limited and expensive," and took advantage
of taxpayer-funded welfare programs. On the basis of this comparison,
the memo called for legal changes to limit undesirable groups from entering the United States.

Mink recalled the toxic political environment that curtailed possibilities and forced rear-guard defensive maneuvers. In response to a request
to extend the H-1A visa program for foreign nurses, Mink indicated her
disappointment that "my amendment was not adopted." She also explained the difficult political context, since "the current anti-immigration
atmosphere in the GOP-controlled Congress makes it difficult to do anything to help immigrants nowadays."[24] This was not just a Republican-led
charge, however. Some Republicans supported immigration, and some
Democrats also participated in the escalation of xenophobic attacks
against Asians and Latinx immigrants.

In the suffocatingly hostile political environment, the defenses of
children, citizenship rights, and authorized immigrants were easier, but
still not easy, cases to make. The letters calling for family reunification
argued that "law-abiding" Asian Pacific American citizens deserved
"fairness," meaning an opportunity to reunite their families through
immigration. But the language of civil rights and appeals to fairness
advanced constrained arguments that principally applied to those with

legal status. This focus postponed protecting the most vulnerable immigrants, those who for one reason or another lacked documented status.

Advocating for People in the Shadows

Being undocumented was conflated primarily with Latinx peoples but also extended to Asians. In 1996, approximately five million unauthorized immigrants resided in the United States.[25] A government report indicated that the majority came from Mexico (54 percent) and other countries in the Western hemisphere (80 percent), including Canada. Yet, at least four Asian countries—the Philippines (ninety-five thousand migrants), Pakistan (forty-one thousand), India (thirty-three thousand), and Korea (thirty thousand)—were in the top twenty nations where undocumented migrants originated.[26] To respond to the racialization of illegality, AAPI and Latinx organizations called for "fairness" not just for citizens or documented immigrants but for those seeking asylum as well as those presumed to be criminals.

The 1993 *Golden Venture* scandal, an attempt to smuggle in 286 Chinese by boat, sparked inflammatory accusations that equated Chinese people with illegality. Even Chinese American journalist Melinda Liu fanned the flames of these allegations. In an article entitled "How to Play the Asylum Game, Immigration: The Chinese Have It Figured Out," she pointed out that "smuggling by Chinese gangs has become a hot topic since the grounding of the freighter Golden Venture off New York City last month. . . . The influx is not new. Chinese illegal aliens have been crossing U.S. borders for years."[27] In response to these charges, the Organization of Chinese Americans (OCA) stated that "in times of economic hardships, the need to find a scapegoat has turned public sentiment, once again, against the Chinese/Chinese Americans."[28] To challenge the presumption of illegality, OCA called for "the nondiscriminatory investigation and vigorous prosecution to the full extent of the law, of all persons, regardless of national origin, involved in smuggling and indenturing people for profit."[29] At the same time, the organization issued the reminder that "all undocumented immigrants be granted full due process under national and international law, and that these individuals be accorded fair and humane treatment."[30]

Mink and other AAPI leaders also called for due process and compassion, thereby separating their positions from those of hard-core immigration critics like Dana Rohrabacher. Mink cosponsored and supported various amnesty bills for specific groups of undocumented immigrants, all to no avail. But in pronouncements on the public record, Mink usually used the negative formulation "does not dispute" to characterize how people in the "Asian Pacific American community" understood "the need for reasonable efforts to restrict illegal immigration."[31] In correspondence with a constituent, Mink indicated that she did "not support undocumented immigration" but believed that the focus on unauthorized entries was exaggerated. Similarly, the National Asian Pacific American Bar Association (NAPABA) emphasized that the organization "recognizes the need to address issues of undocumented persons in the United States—but with reason, intelligence, common sense and compassion."[32] The NAPABA again used the negative formulation "we would not oppose legislation that addresses undocumented persons in a humane and fair manner and with due process."[33]

These proclamations underscored that Asian and Pacific *Americans* were on the "right" side of the law. As citizens and authorized immigrants, they would not oppose the enforcement of federal policy against people who violated its admissions process. Simultaneously, Mink and others reminded political leaders and the American public that the due process clause of the Fourteenth Amendment applied to all "persons," not citizens only. They called for fairness and compassion—in essence a recognition of humanity—for those deemed outside the pale of the US polity.

Defending Women

Mink voted against the escalation of border enforcement, but she did help pass H.R. 3355, the Violent Crime Control and Law Enforcement Act of 1994 (Crime Bill). As the title indicates, the legislation expanded the state's carceral capacity, which included reinforcing the Border Patrol and the police. Mink pointed out that the bill "appropriated $181 million to control our borders. It also includes, for example: (1) a criminal alien tracking center; (2) enhancement of penalties for those failing to depart or re-entering after final order of deportation; (3) guidelines relating to the expeditious deportation for denied asylum applicants; (4) stricter penalties for passport and visa offence; and (5) a provision to ensure that aliens who are incarcerated are immediately deportable."[34] In addition to this impact on policing the national border, as Michelle Alexander argues, the legislation escalated mass incarceration, particularly of African American men. Just as Clinton wanted to out-Republican the Republicans by calling for welfare reform, he conveyed the message that he, too, was "tough on crime." Quoting a study by the Justice Policy Institute, Alexander underscored how the law, endorsed by the president, contributed to the "largest increases in federal and state inmate populations of any president in American history."[35]

Given Mink's critical stance on the US security state and her compassion for immigrants, why did she vote for the bill? The primary reason appears to be the Violence against Women Act (VAWA), which was attached to the Crime Bill. One of the original cosponsors of VAWA, Mink was invested in revising the legal apparatus to support women and children experiencing domestic and sexual violence. When the Crime Bill was first taken up by the full House of Representatives in the fall of 1993, it passed on a voice vote—no amendments, no roll call. Mink was not a member of the Judiciary Committee, which had jurisdiction, so she had no opportunity to influence the bill's specifications other than VAWA, which originally had been free-standing legislation. Like a majority of Democrats, she ended up supporting the final conference bill, in spite of its worst parts and because of its better ones. John Lewis, the civil rights activist, did not vote for the final Crime Bill. Neither did Maxine Waters, one of Mink's frequent allies. Other members of the Black Caucus voted for the bill, as did white progressives like Bernie Sanders.

Through the roll call votes on H.R. 3355, it is possible to discern Mink's opposition to particular aspects of the bill. Spearheaded by Senator Joe Biden and developed with substantial White House input, the crime bill's thirty-three titles touched nearly every aspect of the federal criminal justice system. When the House considered the conference measure, it took a series of roll call votes to instruct the conferees how to respond to differences between the two chambers.[36] Mink voted multiple times against a $10.5 billion authorization for prison construction and the requirement of mandatory sentencing. She voted consistently to strengthen the ability to prosecute sex crime offenses and expand protections for elderly and disabled victims of violence. Notably, Mink voted with a minority of the Democrats to block Dana Rohrabacher's motion to prevent "people not lawfully present within the U.S." from receiving payment from federal programs. The motion nevertheless passed with the majority of Democrats and Republicans voting in favor. In essence, Mink did not support funding for prison construction or mandatory sentencing and disagreed with the funding ban for undocumented immigrants. She voted in favor of VAWA provisions.

Feminist activists and scholars have critiqued VAWA for fostering carceral feminism, defined as "a reliance on policing, prosecution, and imprisonment to resolve gendered or sexual violence."[37] In bringing attention to partner and familial violence against women, the advocates of VAWA demanded legal recognition of these harms and access to resources to better respond to these forms of violence. Initially introduced in 1991, with Mink as a cosponsor, VAWA was eventually embedded as part of the 1994 Crime Bill. This process, as Nancy Whittier argues, illuminates the tensions between the intersectional feminist advocates of the bill and the lawmakers who eventually authorized the law predominantly through a "gendered crime" framework.[38]

Mink was among the advocates who sought to address violence against women through an intersectional approach. Whittier noted that the coalition that advocated for VAWA focused on "sexual and intimate partner violence against immigrants, same-sex partners, transgender people, and Native Americans."[39] In centering these communities, the supporters foregrounded an "intersectional feminist approach [that] emphasizes how social, economic, and political forces interact to shape different experiences and necessary solutions to violence."[40] That means recognizing that "law enforcement responses to violence against women can perpetuate violence against groups that are heavily policed based on race, class, or immigration status, while social services that treat violence primarily in terms of gender do not work well for women of color, non-English speakers, immigrants, and low income women."[41] In other words, the activists who demanded legal recognition of these harms sought a variety of methods to address partner violence. These solutions went beyond incarceration. VAWA supported training for lawyers, judges, and police officers as well as treatment for offenders. Funding was allocated for shelters to expand their work and improve their ability to meet the needs of diverse women. The policy also created a legal definition of sexual violence to allow civil rights remedies. This last component, eventually invalidated by the Rehnquist Supreme Court in 2000, provided an alternative to the criminal justice system.[42]

In contrast to these intersectional feminist advocates, many legislators who supported VAWA often prioritized a "gendered crime" perspective. This framework viewed crime as a harm that women experienced and that men tended to perpetrate. The proposed solutions to address these harms emphasized incarceration. The "gendered crime" framework explains why VAWA eventually passed as part of the Crime Bill. Whittier, who studied the hearings to pass VAWA in 1994 and then to reauthorize it in 2000, 2006, and 2013, noted that the gendered crime arguments dominated the hearings, with Republicans the "most frequent users of crime frames."[43] Women's advocates also discussed gendered crimes, but they were the only ones to use feminist frames. Also, the intersectional arguments disappeared after 2000, making the crime framework even more dominant over time. The displacement of intersectionality with a focus on criminality constitutes a form of what Wendy Mink described earlier as "topic extinction."

Nevertheless, Patsy Mink, a veteran of campaigns to pass and reauthorize VAWA, described the legislation as "a great victory for women."[44] She recognized the pervasiveness of violence against women throughout the country. The Department of Justice published national statistics indicating that "in 1994 there were 1 rape for every 270 women, 1 robbery for every 240 women, and 1 assault for every 29 women."[45] Furthermore, "in 1994 women were about two-thirds as likely as men to be victims of violence," and "women are more likely to be victimized by someone they know than by a stranger."[46] In fact, "in 1992–1993 a majority of women victims (78%) indicated that the offender who victimized them was a person known to them (sometimes intimately)."[47] This contrasts with men who are almost equally likely to be attacked by "a stranger (49%) as by someone they know (51%)."[48] Feminist advocates also note that these statistics very likely undercounted incidents of violence against women, given the prevalence of underreporting both by the survivors who experience these harms and by law enforcement agencies, which tend to dismiss these incidents.[49]

Mink was aware that Hawai'i was not immune to these national trends. She wrote to a local supporter that "VAWA is needed now more than ever, in light of alarming reports such as Monday's announcement by Hawaii Attorney General Margery Bronster upon the release of a new study that found an alarming number of domestic violence–related homicides resulting in the deaths of wives and girlfriends. . . . According to the study, 29% of homicides between 1985 and 1994 were domestic violence cases, and of these homicides, 63% involved female victims. We must do all we can to prevent and reduce these horrible crimes against women."[50] Mink was particularly invested in securing the resources from VAWA for Hawai'i. After the bill's passage, she helped to advocate for an increase in minimum funding from two hundred to four hundred thousand dollars for "small" states.[51] This entailed building support among political representatives of seventeen states and Washington, DC; some states, like Alaska and Montana, were large in terms of geographical size but deemed "small" on the basis of population.[52] As Mink pointed out, "Small states have the same pressing needs as large states to provide adequate services for women who have been the victims of domestic violence."[53] Her efforts reflected her long-standing interest in ensuring that her home state, particularly women's advocates, received access to resources that she fought for at the federal level.

The emphasis on crime and prosecution, however, shaped the overall funding allocation for VAWA. After its passage, a new Violence Against Women Office was created within the Department of Justice's National Institute of Justice. Also, an Advisory Council on Violence against Women was established with cochairs from the offices of the attorney general and the secretary of health and human services.[54] These two offices, one located in the Department of Justice (DOJ) and the other in the Department of Health and Human Services (HHS), symbolized the main components of the bill: law enforcement and social services. In 1995, the DOJ received $26 million and allocated approximately $426,000 to each state. A quarter of this amount went to law enforcement, a second quarter to prosecution, a third to nonprofit "victim services," and a fourth was to be allocated at the state's discretion.[55] In contrast, only $1 million was authorized to the HHS in 1995 to support the development of a national domestic violence hotline. These funding disparities persisted in subsequent years. In fiscal year 1996, the

DOJ received $175 million, while the HHS received $54 million.[56] Mink noted these differences in resource allocation and promised to "continue to support full funding for VAWA programs."[57] Given the disparity in resources, it is clear that Mink recognized that HHS projects were in greater need.

Mink's support for VAWA revealed the difficult political compromises that she made. She advocated for VAWA "and other efforts to prevent abuse of and violence against women in our society."[58] She noted that "there is no doubt that our current system does not always treat women and children fairly or appropriately."[59] In response, Mink partnered with others to "eliminate the stigmatism associated with sexual assault, child abuse and incest."[60] VAWA, Mink believed, would play an important role. The expansion of law and the allocation of resources, Mink underscored, provided survivors of violence with more options. In other words, incarceration was not the primary goal but part of an array of alternatives to empower women. Despite Mink's intersectional feminist understanding of VAWA and her critiques of the carceral aspects of the Crime Bill in which VAWA was housed, the omnibus legislation ultimately resulted in the escalation of the police state that disproportionately impacted people of color.[61]

Gendering Borders

The passage of VAWA did provide leverage for Mink and other advocates to critique proposed immigration changes that impacted women and children experiencing abuse. As a memo published by the National Immigration Forum pointed out, "At one time, men were far more likely than women to migrate to the U.S. However today, and each year for the last decade, *almost half of the immigrants coming to the U.S. have been women*" (emphasis in the original).[62] Given this demographic shift, the organization advocated for adjustment in immigration policy, in legislation addressing violence against women, and in the process of recognizing gender-based crimes as a basis for asylum application. In other words, there needed to be a gender reframing of law based on the recognition of women's experiences. As the Lamar Smith bill moved forward in Congress, feminist groups presented detailed analyses of the proposed changes. These writings exposed how anti-immigrant proposals made battered women more vulnerable. In turn, these advocates also pointed out how VAWA could be revised to better serve migrant women.

The organization Ayuda and the Family Violence Prevention Fund (FVPF), for example, issued a statement pointing out three anti-immigrant provisions that would "have an especially destructive impact on the safety and well-being of battered and abused immigrant women."[63] First, the "deeming" provision mandated that immigrants seeking government support, such as AFDC, Medicaid, Supplemental Security Income (SSI), or food stamps, would face higher barriers in order to qualify for assistance. Under the proposed law, government agencies would consider not only the immigrant's own income and resources but also the assets of the immigrant's partner for seven years after permanent residency. In other words, "battered women who do not meet the tests and cannot survive economically on their own will have to stay with or return to their abusers."[64]

Second, the Lamar Smith bill's proposed requirement to settle claims prior to naturalization mandated that immigrants who receive support from any government programs had to repay the state before applying for naturalization. This measure, like the previous one, sought to zero out any potential costs that immigrants might incur at the federal, state, or local levels. As the memo pointed out, "The settlement of claims provision is particularly harmful to battered immigrant women who may need the support of publicly-funded programs to escape their abusers and whose abusers may deliberately attempt to block their spouses' naturalization by refusing to pay claims for funds extended in support of the abused partner's escape from the violent situation."[65]

Finally, the advocacy groups critiqued the deportation of those who need "too much" assistance. This section of Smith's proposed bill made legal immigrants eligible for deportation if, "within seven years of entering the United States, they need more than a total of twelve months of assistance from any the following programs: AFDC, Medicaid, Food Stamps."[66] The authors pointed out that the list "could include some shelter programs," making the provision "especially harmful to battered and abused women who may not be able to access shelter and may be forced to choose between remaining with their abusers and being deported from the United States."[67] They pointed out that women who leave their abusers tend to be especially vulnerable for a two-year period, so a one-year limit would cut off access to shelter programs that could "provide them with the safety and support that they need."[68]

As Ayuda and FVPF critiqued the proposed reforms, they also highlighted how VAWA offered some protections for immigrant women. In collaboration with the National Immigration Project based in Boston, the three organizations formed the National Network on Behalf of Battered Immigrant Women (National Network). As the US Senate considered immigration reform, the three organizations conveyed the importance of maintaining the VAWA-authorized rights for "'self-petitioning' for permanent residency or applying for suspension of deportation."[69] Both provisions allowed immigrant women experiencing abuse to independently seek an adjustment to their status. In other words, these women would not have to rely on their partners, who might have greater legal standing as permanent residents or citizens but also might be enacting abuse.

The National Network pointed out that targeting undocumented individuals weakened VAWA protections. For example, prohibiting newcomers without status from receiving lawful permanent residency takes away the right to self-petition for undocumented women. Similarly, unauthorized entry would void the possibility of suspension of deportation. In addition, requiring those without visas to return to their originating countries to obtain the necessary paperwork and increasing the penalty for staying in the United States while trying to adjust status made it prohibitively difficult for battered women to gain legal standing.

The National Network also took the opportunity to point out the ways in which VAWA fell short in supporting immigrant women. These included

1) the excessively burdensome evidentiary requirements on good moral character required for eligibility for VAWA;

2) the difficulty in accessing work authorization needed so that women will have the economic self-sufficiency to successfully leave her abuser;

3) the strict documentary requirements demanded for women whose abusers often control needed papers and information and who often flee violent relationships under exigent circumstances;

4) the ability of the abuser to recapture control over the victim's immigration status by changing his own immigration status; and

5) the definition of battering, which . . . does not provide enough guidance to Service examiners in the actual regulation and a total lack of
guidance on the type of evidence that could be presented to prove
extreme cruelty.[70]

While VAWA, in the eyes of these advocates, was an imperfect tool, the
legislation nevertheless served as a benchmark to critique pending anti-
immigrant legislation.

Winning VAWA entailed political trade-offs. VAWA sought government recognition, access to resources, and legal protections for women,
including undocumented immigrant women, who experienced violence. At the same time, the passage of the law containing VAWA, the
1994 Crime Bill, heightened border enforcement and advanced mass
incarceration. The Crime Bill did not invent either problem—mass incarceration was well underway by the 1980s—but it certainly fueled their
persistence. Mink's overall political track record revealed her ability to
navigate the structures of political liberalism in order to offer radical
possibilities. Yet in the instances of immigration policy and VAWA, the
efforts to support women who experience violence were subsumed by a
project to expand state capacity to enact violence and incarcerate. Mink's
advocacy for VAWA did not include advocacy for the punitive, carceral
consequences of the broader crime bill. Yet, as a legislator faced with binary choices—yes or no on legislation containing both good and bad—
she worked in a universe of constraint.

Model Immigrants

The upswell of xenophobic sentiment in the mid-1990s set political limits on how to argue for legal recognition and inclusion. Some immigrant
advocates responded by focusing on the "good" immigrants, those who
follow the rules, contribute to the US economy, and do not serve as a
"drain." Their reputed capacity to give and not take justified their ability,
however limited, to enter the nation. Mink used elements of these arguments, but she also emphasized the rights of immigrants to access the
welfare state.

Given the high rates of poverty among noncitizens, statistics from the
early 1990s show that they did utilize social services at both the federal

and state level. They did so, though, at a rate below their actual needs. A Congressional Research Service report pointed out that "the vast majority of non-citizens receive no assistance from Federal or State welfare programs."[71] They comprised 6 percent of the overall population but 11 percent of those living below poverty. And, they accessed social services below their poverty rate for SSI recipients (10 percent), AFDC families (7 percent), Medicaid recipients (8 percent), and food stamp recipients (8 percent). In two program categories, noncitizens comprised a greater percentage of participants compared to their poverty rates. They represented 16 percent of SSI recipients for those sixty-five years or older and 12 percent of families receiving state assistance. The greater utilization of SSI reveals how immigrants used this program to support the elderly. The higher usage of state welfare programs reveals that noncitizens accessed these programs at a rate more commensurate to their poverty rates, in contrast to their underutilization of federal programs.

Although noncitizens tended to use welfare programs below their actual economic needs and naturalized citizens exhibited poverty rates lower than US-born citizens, any reported reliance on these programs stoked criticism. The US Business and Industrial Council, for example, argued that immigration led to escalating crime and irresponsible dependence on social welfare. Kevin Kearns, the president of the organization, argued, "Dramatic increases in both legal and illegal immigration have contributed to exploding entitlement costs. . . . In California's public hospitals, 40% of the births are to illegal aliens, with taxpayers picking up most of the tab. In fact, 20 percent of all immigrants are now on welfare. A study done by Professor George Borjas of Harvard University shows that legal immigrants alone cost taxpayers a net $25 billion per year in cash and non-cash welfare benefits."[72] At least some, if not all, of these allegations and supporting statistics were inaccurate. Nevertheless, conservative pundits and lobbyists repeated the information to justify policy changes.

The charge that immigrants were criminals led to the criminalization of immigrants. The 1996 IIRIRA made crossing the border a criminal, not civil, violation. Undocumented immigrants who committed misdemeanors prior to the passage of the law became subject to deportation. Similarly to the 1994 Crime Bill, the 1996 immigration reforms expanded the reach of the state and the state's ability to punish. As a result, the law ironically helped create and expand the legal category of illegality.[73]

These anti-immigrant sentiments fueled welfare reform as well as counterresponses to retain access. In September 1995, the National Asian Pacific American Legal Consortium (NAPALC) issued a news release announcing its collaboration with the Council of Jewish Federations, the National Council of La Raza, and the US Catholic Conference. Together, the organizations blasted "Congress and President Clinton for legislation that would deny legal permanent residents and other immigrants access to government funded programs." In the words of NAPALC executive director Karen Narasaki, "How can the Senate pass, with no objection from President Clinton, a bill that contains a provision that creates an official second-class citizenship by denying assistance to new immigrants even after they become naturalized citizens? . . . It is an insult to those who have worked hard, paid taxes and contributed to our society to discriminate against them on the basis of their route to citizenship."[74] Mink also believed that immigrants should be able to access social welfare programs as a matter of equity. She worked to secure undocumented immigrants' access to the Women, Infants, and Children program (WIC) and was part of the "Fix 96" coalition effort to restore documented immigrants' eligibility for SNAP (Supplemental Nutrition Assistance Program, which replaced the Food Stamps Program) and other public benefits. Additionally, in the TANF Reauthorization bill she introduced in 2001, which did not pass, Mink specifically eliminated the five-year ban on documented immigrant participation in the federal program.

Mink, Narasaki, and other leaders in the immigrant-advocacy community extolled the contributions of immigrants, people who work hard and play by the rules. In a letter to a critic seeking the curtailment of immigration, both documented and undocumented, Mink responded, "Our economy would suffer under an immigration moratorium. Legal immigrants start new businesses and create jobs at a higher rate than U.S.-born Americans and pay $27.4 billion more in taxes than they consume in government services. Growth industries essential to U.S. job creation would find that their overseas competitors had snapped up the most talented scientists and academics, thereby weakening America in the world marketplace."[75] Mink's argument, echoed by other advocates, reveals how the price of belonging depends upon immigrant ability to fulfill expectations of neoliberal, upwardly mobile subjects. Newcomers to the nation are scripted to contribute to the US economy and enable its global competitiveness. At the same time, these immigrant advocates did not stop at this model portrayal. Instead, they demanded measures to relax stringent deportation triggers for more vulnerable immigrants and support for those experiencing economic precarity. In contrast, antiwelfare forces generally argued that immigrants were less deserving of state resources and more deserving of discipline; at the extreme, reactionaries like Dana Rohrabacher and Lamar Smith treated absolute deprivation of social assistance as a stepping stone toward absolute exclusion.

The immigration politics of the 1990s transpired within narrow constraints and involved whack-a-mole action to fight policies that promised both incremental and wholesale oppression and exclusion of immigrants. In response to a cost-benefit critique of newcomers to the United States, pro-immigrant advocates often pointed to self-reliant, economic-success stories, even as they also defended access to social programs for economically vulnerable immigrants. Mink and other immigrant allies demanded full rights of personhood and membership, which entailed access to a robust welfare state.

The Price of Belonging

The violent-crime, welfare, and immigration laws of the mid-1990s worked in conjunction to strengthen external and internal borders in the United States. The lawmakers who promoted these policies sought to restrict who resided in the United States and determine who constituted rights-bearing subjects. The titles of the welfare and immigration laws reveal their didactic function—to instill personal responsibility and immigrant responsibility. By focusing on the presumed irresponsible behaviors of welfare recipients and newcomers, the US government denied its obligation to address poverty, acknowledge international standards of human rights, or enforce the equal protection clause of the Fourteenth Amendment for any person (regardless of citizenship) in the country. Through the laws passed during the mid-1990s, the US state acquired resources and authorizations, many still in effect, to detain and deport those perceived as unable to fulfill their responsibilities.

Mink believed in the social welfare and activist state. She challenged the broader implications of the racial and gendered politics of the border and immigration. She and other defenders of immigrants centered upon three archetypes: children, women, and economic contributors. In each instance, Mink responded to conservative rhetoric that rendered these groups as threats to the US nation. She and other pro-immigration allies attempted to expand the legal protections of the state to all persons and not just citizens. Yet as a legislator, she also recognized that there were people who remained outside of the law, and she at times utilized model-immigrant narratives to argue for the rights of racialized newcomers.

As her long political career reveals, Mink believed in the democratic process of law making and the need to expand the collective understanding of who constituted people deserving of rights and resources in the United States. She also recognized the protracted timeline of passing laws, authorizing funding, and refining and reevaluating imperfect laws. Mink chose to be in the midst of these political battles, because she believed that they mattered. But even good outcomes were never complete victories, and the compromises meant that struggles for justice never ended.

"STAY SAFE, PATSY"

I began writing this vignette while confined to my mother's Capitol Hill pied-á-terre, now my home, on the fifteenth day of Washington, DC's coronavirus pandemic lockdown. I spent a lockdown in this space once before, when two planes flew into the World Trade Center in New York, a third plane hit the Pentagon, and a fourth plane aimed at the seat of government was crashed by heroic passengers. Like the coronavirus pandemic, the 9/11 trauma altered everyday life and routine politics in ways big and small, skewing national priorities toward surveillance and security while imperiling civil liberties. In a way, 9/11 brought my mother's political life full circle, with old bigotries unleashed against new targets and new inroads against liberty forged by old mantras of patriotism. The 9/11 trauma also marked the beginning of what turned out to be my mother's final year: on September 28, 2002, she lost her life to a vicious virus that literally took her breath away.

A beat before 9:00 a.m. on Tuesday, September 11, 2001, I strolled into my mother's office in the Rayburn House Office Building. I lived in Penn Quarter, only a short metro ride from the House side of the Hill, but caught a cab that morning for no particular reason. My choice of transportation was fortuitous, though, as I might well have been stuck underground for a few hours had I traveled by metro. I popped into my mother's office hoping to check in with her before heading over to a welfare-rights briefing that was scheduled for 10:00 a.m. in the Gold Room of the Rayburn Building.[1] Upon entering the reception area of my mother's office, I greeted the intern who sat at the front desk, staring entranced at his computer screen. He didn't look up. Nosy, I twisted around to see what transfixed him. His screen showed images of skyscrapers billowing smoke above a "breaking news" chyron that I couldn't quite make out. I was about to needle the young man for watching movies while on the job when he looked at me, ashen, and said, "This just happened." The staff were gathered in various corners of the office, where televisions were tuned to CNN. My father sat at his table in my mother's private office, clipping Hawai'i newspapers as he often did in the morning, still unaware of events. But when a second plane deliberately crashed into the south tower of the World Trade Center, the rumble of shock and panic in the staff rooms grabbed his attention and he joined us to await reassurance from the morning news anchors.

For many minutes, we did not know that what had happened in New York City was part of a concerted attack. But as the words "hijacking" and "terror" hit the airwaves shortly before 9:15 a.m., I began to wonder whether precautions were needed to protect the staff and my parents. My mother was out of the office. In her absence, we all sort of awaited instructions from Capitol security, but none came. Buzzers go off in the congressional office buildings all the time when the Congress is in session, but no buzzers went off that morning either to convene the Congress or to alert personnel to danger. No one phoned to say shelter in place; no one emailed instructions to duck and cover; and no one ran up and down hallways urging evacuation. Stone-cold silence from authorities left everyone guessing whether to proceed with business as usual or to flee. In my mother's absence, someone had to make the call to send the staff home. Though uncertain, at 9:30 a.m. my mother's chief of staff and I declared an end to the business day. My father joined the exodus at my urging, heading on foot to my parents' apartment ten blocks away. As he did every other morning when he was in DC, he walked across the Capitol grounds heading north, unaware that forty heroic passengers would soon give their lives to take down a plane headed toward his path.

My mother was at the House beauty salon, two blocks away on the first floor of the Cannon House Office Building. The beauty shop was old-fashioned—quiet, staid, and sealed off from the whirligig of current events. It was the kind of place you could still get a bouffant hairdo in the twenty-first century and where clients routinely spent time in curlers under the plastic dome of a hooded hairdryer. This was the last day of the pre-Blackberry era in Congress, and there were no TVs in the salon, so there was no way my mother would find out about the twin towers on her own.[2]

I couldn't reach her cell so I called her on the salon phone to alert her about events. With circumstances still opaque, my attempt to describe the emergency to my mother over the phone did not go well, because what I was saying made no sense. When I explained that two passenger aircraft had intentionally flown into the World Trade Center, she thought my report was metaphor or hyperbole and asked me to translate. When I told her I thought we should evacuate she protested that she couldn't go anywhere because she had to attend a meeting of Democratic conferees for the No Child Left Behind bill, George Bush's signature education initiative. When I told her the meeting would be canceled, she said she also needed to stop by the Rayburn Gold Room to show support for the grassroots welfare groups whose press briefing was scheduled for 10:00 a.m. Frustrated by my failure to communicate, I told her that I would run over to the beauty shop to explain everything on the walk back to the office. As we walked the subterranean corridors between Cannon and Rayburn, I reported on events of the morning. In the Rayburn elevator we were joined by a senior army officer. Dispensing with pleasantries, my mother asked, "General, is it true?" He nodded, and as we exited the elevator said solemnly, "Stay safe, Patsy." Hearing those words from that person in that moment, she finally assimilated the information I had given her.

We arrived back at the office to learn that the Pentagon had been hit, probably by a plane. Rumors of a fire at the State Department and smoke on the Mall added to fear and foreboding. When we got word a few minutes later that the Capitol had been evacuated, we packed up the work my mother anticipated needing over the next while, offered rides to a couple of staff who had stayed behind, and headed to the Rayburn garage. As we exited the garage onto C Street and turned toward Independence Avenue, we realized belatedly that evacuating by car was a fool's errand. Traffic was stalled in all directions, sirens and horns inflamed desperation in drivers, and nobody in our car could get a cell signal. It took more than an hour to travel to my parents' neighborhood on the north side of Capitol Hill, where my father was frenzied with worry because he couldn't fathom how it could take more than five minutes to drive ten blocks. We spent the rest of the day watching televised horror unfold on the Manhattan skyline and at the Pentagon, trying to understand what had happened and what the Congress would seek to do about it.

The Congress and the city shut down for just a few days, though everyone remained on high alert for much longer. By week's end Congress had declared war on the terrorists responsible for the attacks, delegating broad authority to the president to use military force against parties who waged or abetted the devastation (the Authorization of the Use of Military Force, or AUMF). A month later, Congress designed legislation to pump up federal surveillance and investigative capacities, both domestic and international (PATRIOT Act).

My mother struggled with the AUMF, a fateful decision about militarization and intervention that was rushed to the House floor just three days after the attacks. On the one hand, she knew the United States had to respond militarily to the 9/11 perpetrators, Al Qaeda and the Taliban. On the other hand, she also was wary that granting the president plenary authority to wage a "war on terror" would put us on an open-ended war footing, consign peace to a last resort, and further erode Congress's constitutional war-making power. Other Democrats shared these concerns, pushing back against the wide discretion sought by President Bush to "deter and pre-empt *any* future acts of terrorism or aggression against the United States" (italics added for emphasis). A compromise between the president and Congress, hawks and doves, Republicans and Democrats, the 2001 AUMF resolution enacted by Congress applied to the 9/11 attack only, though in the end it authorized a twenty-year war in Afghanistan. It gave the president power to pursue "nations, organizations, or persons" that "planned, authorized, committed, or aided the terrorist attacks that occurred on September 11, 2001."[3] My mother was not happy to delegate war authority to the president, but was persuaded that the AUMF was not intended to be a blank check to pursue military action whenever an action adverse to the United States could be labeled "terrorism."[4] With 419 other House members, she voted to pass the AUMF; only Barbara Lee (D-California) voted against it.[5]

Legislatively speaking, the 2001 AUMF resolution was just the opening salvo in a year-long series of policy initiatives responding to the 9/11 attacks. In short order, Congress took up legislation to proliferate counterterrorism tools available to law enforcement, intelligence services, the military, and the judicial system. In between enactment of the AUMF on September 18 and passage of the PATRIOT Act on October 26, the nation was set on edge by an apparent bioterror attack that infected twenty-two people, killing five. Letters containing anthrax spores arrived at several national news headquarters in New York City in late September, infecting a few individuals and spreading fright. In mid-October, letters containing more potent doses of anthrax arrived at the United States Senate, designated for Senate majority leader Tom Daschle (D–South Dakota) and Senate judiciary chair Patrick Leahy (D-Vermont). Congressional mail shut down as a result and congressional office buildings were evacuated. A sweep of the office buildings for contamination showed traces of anthrax in the Longworth and Ford buildings on the House side of the Capitol complex, prolonging the evacuation period.

For several weeks, House members and skeletal staffs were relocated to a General Services Administration (GSA) building in DC's Chinatown area. Even after they returned to the congressional office buildings, the mail system remained compromised for quite some time. Also, even after the buildings were declared safe, some constituents were nervous to receive mail from congressmembers' DC offices. So, members found alternative locations from which to originate their mail. My mother had all mail sent from her Honolulu office, for example, each outgoing piece stamped with a red label indicating Honolulu as the point of origin.[6] As for incoming mail to DC congressional offices: thenceforth, it was detoured offsite to be baked and irradiated.[7]

In this jittery climate, Congress turned its attention to the PATRIOT Act.[8] To advance the war on terror, the PATRIOT Act expanded and intensified the federal government's search, surveillance, seizure, detention, and deportation powers, while also defining a range of new crimes and increasing penalties for existing ones. Critics condemned the act's multiple deprivations of privacy and other civil liberties, including due process for immigrants.[9]

My mother agreed with the critics. She objected to the expansion of government's investigative powers without due process safeguards. She was horrified by the act's guilt-by-association premises that permitted surveillance of innocent persons. She deplored the violations of habeas corpus triggered by provisions for the indefinite detention of immigrants. She abjured plans to allow grand jury and other sensitive information to be shared among law enforcement and intelligence agencies without a court order. For these reasons, she joined sixty-five House members in voting against passage of the PATRIOT Act.[10]

Related issues arose nine months later when the Congress took up legislation to create the Department of Homeland Security. The bill moved a wide range of federal agencies from existing bureaucratic locations into a new behemoth to promote "national security." Agencies seemingly unrelated to terrorism and national security, such as FEMA and the Animal and Plant Health Inspection Service, were destined for the new DHS, along with the Coast Guard and Immigration and Naturalization Service. My mother had many reservations, from administrative overload to Freedom of Information Act exemptions to the displacement of immigrant services by immigration control.[11]

In what would be her next-to-last vote in Congress, on July 26, 2002, Mom voted against the Homeland Security bill along with 131 other House members.[12] Two weeks before, she had voted no on the Arming Pilots Against Terrorism bill.[13] As it was the height of congressional midterm election season, it was no surprise that her political detractors tried to make hay of her dissenting legislative votes. Following her PATRIOT Act vote the previous fall, a right-wing Republican who aspired to her seat denounced her as "soft on terrorism." When she voted against a concurrent resolution[14] urging the president to extend the war on terror to Palestinians, he invoked George Bush's warning: "Either you're with us, or you're with the terrorists."[15] "Soft on terrorism" became a refrain deployed against her, as had "soft on communism" nearly fifty years before. When she returned to Hawai'i for the August congressional recess, she had to defend her record as often against the smear as on the merits.

During the August recess Mom engaged with keiki (children), an activity that always brought her joy. During the school year, she periodically visited second or third grade classes to read to students and buoy their developing love of books. During children's summer holiday, she interacted with them in other public spaces where they gathered—clinics, parks, summer school. Perhaps from a child whom she encouraged to read, or perhaps from an adult whom she urged to vote, somehow Mom acquired a contagious virus, chicken pox. Like the coronavirus, chicken pox can be dire for older folk, especially if it develops into viral pneumonia. A child of the sparsely populated Maui countryside, neither she nor her brother had had chicken pox growing up. At age seventy-four, she proved susceptible to its pulmonary ravages.

Epilogue

Ripples

Over the 2002 Labor Day weekend, in the midst of her reelection campaign, Patsy Mink was hospitalized with varicella pneumonia as a result of exposure to chicken pox. She died on September 28, 2002.

Her life partner, John Mink, visited her grave regularly at the National Memorial Cemetery of the Pacific at Punchbowl in Honolulu. They had maintained a true collaboration, ever since meeting at the University of Chicago in 1950. Laura Efurd, Patsy's legislative director from 1990 to 1999, recalled that John would come almost every day to the congressional office, when he was in Washington, DC:

> You know . . . every day, well, when John was there . . . , he'd come into the office at about four o'clock, and, you know, that was always nice. . . . John . . . had his relationship with the staff too, you know? . . . He would just kind of, you know, . . . talk about books, or movies. . . . We'd work pretty late to like maybe ten o'clock. And then we'd all go out to dinner together, right? So, it had kind of this family atmosphere.[1]

John supported Patsy, serving as her political confidant. Laura recalled, "I think Wendy and John were the only people in the world who could say no to Patsy. . . . Like if anybody else said no to her, she wouldn't accept that."[2]

Just as her constituents did not release Patsy from service when they elected her posthumously in 2002, John also retained his daily communion with her, until his death three years later. Amy Isaacs, who worked with Patsy at Americans for Democratic Action, became a friend and ally over the long haul. She recalled that her daughter stayed with John while doing research in Hawai'i. Rachel Isaacs told her mother, "'Do you know what happened, mom?' And, I said, 'No.' She said, 'He died of a

Figure E.1. Patsy and John, forever partners in all things, at the Hawai'i State Democratic Party annual convention, June 2, 2002. Source: Honolulu Star Advertiser Photo.

broken heart.' . . . Every morning before he did anything else, he went to the cemetery and talked to Patsy. So that's a marriage."[3]

The House of Representatives and the US Senate held a joint memorial session in Patsy's honor. Seventy-two members of the House and two members of the Senate, including all the elected officials from the State of Hawai'i, spoke to recognize her life. Maxine Waters, a sister woman of color from California, celebrated Patsy's role as a feminist leader: "Patsy was on the cutting edge of the women's movement. Patsy was there when all of the great strategies were formed, when all the great organizations got started. Patsy was there with Bella Abzug and Gloria Steinem and women who dedicated their lives so that women could have justice and equality in America."[4]

Waters elaborated by highlighting two important achievements of Mink. First, Waters celebrated the impact of Title IX, which was renamed the Patsy T. Mink Equal Opportunity in Education Act shortly after her death. "It was just a few months ago that I sat at the WNBA All Star Game where Patsy was honored for 30 years' recognition of Patsy's work. As I looked at all of those strong, tall women out there playing and my dear child, Lisa Leslie, who won the All-Star honor that evening, I thought it was a short, little woman who caused this tall, big woman to be able to realize her dreams, to be able to hone her talents."[5]

Second, Waters emphasized Mink's advocacy for welfare and impoverished women and families: "Patsy was an expert on any number of subjects and certainly on education, but the mark of this woman was the fact that this brilliant woman devoted her time to poor women. . . . She fought for poor women to have a safety net as we debated welfare reform. . . . She simply talked about the need for poor women and their children to have a place to live and food to eat."[6]

Established a year after Mink's death, the Patsy Takemoto Mink Foundation carries on her commitment to low-income women with children. Administered by Wendy Mink, the foundation joins allies from welfare-justice struggles with trusted family and friends. Patsy's niece and Eugene's daughter, Jo Ann Kagawa, is one of the guardians of this legacy. Each year, the foundation offers scholarships to assist low-income women with children who seek college educations.[7]

Nydia Velazquez, a congressional ally from New York, also eulogized Mink, foregrounding her transgressive advocacy in terms of race, gender, and antimilitarism. Speaking of Mink, Velazquez shared, "She fought for civil rights in an era of segregation. . . . She opposed a war before it made headlines. . . . She was the first in so many things, the first female student body president, the first Japanese-American woman to practice law in Hawaii, the first woman of color to serve in the U.S. Congress, all things we take for granted today. We should always remember it was Patsy who fought to get us here, especially women."[8]

Fast forward to the summer of 2020, when another Latinx legislator from New York took to the House floor to denounce the culture of sexism in Congress. Historian and family friend Dana Frank remembered how "fifty years ago, Patsy Mink paved the way for Alexandria Ocasio-Cortez." After all, "Congresswomen of color have always fought back against sexism."[9] Their intersectional identities as women of color amplified experiences of exclusion and sharpened their desire to fight for and demand respect, not just for themselves but for others similarly marginalized.

Eni Faleomavaega, the nonvoting congressional delegate from American Samoa, contextualized Mink's commitment to justice by speaking of the US government's willingness to disregard the political rights of racialized American citizens: "I can remember, remember and well imagine the hardships Patsy had to endure, especially after the sudden attack of Pearl Harbor by Japanese war planes [when] Americans of Japanese ancestry [were] immediately, herded like cattle and placed in what was then described as relocation camps but I consider them as concentration camps, I have no doubt that Patsy and her family were severely affected socially and psychologically. How [can] a Nation . . . unilaterally terminate the constitutional rights of its citizens solely on the basis of their race[?]"[10] While Faleomavaega highlighted the denial of constitutional rights of Japanese Americans in paying tribute to Mink, he undoubtedly drew connections to the marginalized status of his own community. American Samoans live in a permanent state of political exclusion. They are legally defined as nationals, not citizens, and have to navigate a burdensome process to naturalize. Unlike American Samoans, citizens of other territorial jurisdictions are also citizens of the United States. But, like American Samoans, residents of territories like Guam or Puerto Rico cannot vote in US presidential elections.

Daniel Akaka, the first Native Hawaiian senator, elaborated on Mink's significance for the Pacific. He pointed to her activism against nuclear testing in Amchitka and her subsequent court case to strengthen the Freedom of Information Act. As he stated, "The case gained tremendous historical significance when the U.S. Supreme Court cited it as a precedent for the release of the Watergate tapes."[11] Her activism against nuclear testing persisted into the 1990s. Akaka recounted, "I recall her leadership in 1996 on a successful boycott of a joint session speech by French President Jacques Chirac, in protest of French nuclear testing in the Pacific, much in line with our shared commitment to championing the disenfranchised peoples of the Pacific."[12]

Daniel Inouye, who had a history of disagreements with Mink, nevertheless spoke of her as "an honorable colleague."[13] He recounted her original desire to be a doctor and her rejection from medical schools. Instead of accepting "defeat, the strong-willed Patsy set out to eliminate the societal barriers of the day, and ran for office in the U.S. House of Representatives."[14] Inouye highlighted that Mink retained her passion for politics and justice throughout her long career. Just the summer before her death, Inouye and Mink spoke at a fundraiser event in Hawaiʻi. "She mingled and talked with constituents with her trademark vim and vigor. Her deep love for her constituents and her Nation was evident. She was focused on the future and continuing her service to the people of Hawaii."[15]

Mink's ally and friend Nancy Pelosi also spoke of her departed colleague's passionate interest in the future, most notably expressed through Patsy's commitment towards children and education: "She was enthusiastic about America's children. She worked her heart out for them. She literally gave her life ministering to their needs, visiting a clinic for poor children where she contracted chicken pox. . . . She lives in the spirit of young girls playing sports all over America. She lives in the school rooms of America for all she did for America's children."[16] Mink would not live to see her friend rise to the speakership of the House. But, Patsy avidly supported Pelosi's first steps towards that powerful role by supporting her campaign to become minority whip in 2001. Pelosi evoked their mutual commitment to children when she was sworn in twice as speaker of the House. She invited her grandchildren and all other children of Congress to join her at the podium in 2007 and again in 2019. In 2007, Pelosi announced, "We are going to make children the centerpiece of this Congress."[17] In 2019, she proclaimed, "I now call the House to order on behalf of all of America's children."[18]

Like Pelosi, Mink had to navigate contradictory expectations of women in politics. Mink was labeled too tough for not being deferential. She was denigrated as too hormonal to assume traditionally masculine forms of leadership. In response, Mink showed through actions and words that she had to be taken seriously. She did not forsake her gender identity and gender politics. She brought gender and race strategically from the political margins to the legislative table and fought for what she believed, not taking no for an answer.

Spanning nearly three-quarters of a century, Mink's life both tracked and contributed to profound shifts in US society and politics. She was born in 1927, just seven years after the Nineteenth Amendment prohibited the denial of women's right to vote. However, twenty-five years would pass before her own grandmother could access the ballot, as Japanese immigrants could not become US citizens until 1952. Mink was a young mother and pathbreaking attorney when she first entered public life, advocating, among other things, for Hawai'i's transition to statehood in 1959. Still in her thirties, she was a seasoned legislator and political activist when she first won election to Congress in 1964. She ran for the presidency in 1972, joining Shirley Chisholm as one of the first two women to seek the presidential nomination in a major political party. Once Mink returned to Congress in 1990, she demanded respect for female leadership and forced attention on women's issues.

Growing up in a plantation society, Mink developed a keen awareness of racial and class divides as well as the central role of women in work and family. Inspired by the ideals of Franklin Delano Roosevelt and the New Deal vision of government, she embraced the Great Society's efforts to eradicate poverty and advance civil rights for racial minorities and women. She was an islander who sought to protect the waters, lands, and people of the Pacific, often forgotten or taken advantage of by political leaders in Washington, DC. She lived the last twelve years of her life back in Congress fighting for this expansive vision of the US polity and against the chokeholds of neoliberalism and conservatism.

Mink was a radical in liberal guise. Various scholars have critiqued the inherent limitations of political liberalism. Some of Mink's votes and causes reinforce this interpretation. Yet she also saw political possibilities. She advocated for legal protections and economic security measures, believing that rights and resources could make a difference in people's lives.

Calvin Tamura, Patsy's cousin, gave the final words of her memorial service in Hawai'i. A storyteller, he shared, "And so a story has been told in the Great Pacific Ocean. A stone has fallen into the deep blue water. And even as it comes to rest, the ripples from the journey will shape our future forever."[19]

ACKNOWLEDGMENTS

During the many years we worked on this book, family, friends, and colleagues indulged our frequent requests for information, recollection, and feedback. We have told the story of Patsy's origins and background with confidence thanks to generous and responsive discussions with Patsy's brother, Eugene Takemoto, and with her cousins, Ruth Mukai, Jean Igarashi, Maureen Farineau, Phyllis Takara, Julie Tamura, and Calvin Tamura.

The comprehensive biographic narrative of Patsy's public service and political life that we provide here was enabled by specialists and archivists at the Library of Congress, where the complete papers of Patsy Takemoto Mink reside. The brilliant, intersectional historical sensibility of Barbara Bair, the mad skills of then-archivist Margaret McAleer, and the gracious and informative guidance provided by Janice Ruth together made the Mink Papers accessible and indispensable.

Both Wendy and Judy are deeply appreciative of Ilene Kalish, Sonia Tsuruoka, and Alexia Traganas at New York University Press for supporting and shepherding this project. We also benefited from the meticulous attention that Emily Wright provided as our copyeditor and from David Luljak's care in indexing the book.

Wendy owes a huge debt to friends willing to read her work. They helped in so many ways, from correcting granular inaccuracies to synthesizing grand themes to whipping up her confidence to write in the first person. Dana Frank, always generous with her time, read every vignette with care and offered unerring insight about all things historical as well as about voice and rhythm. No less essential to the project were long-time friends, some of them writers and all of them politically engaged. All either knew Patsy or knew Wendy across many of the decades covered here. Wendy will always be grateful to them for reading and commenting on her work: Aline Kuntz, Cynthia Harrison, Jane George, Patti Blumer, Tahi Mottl, Joan Manke, Barbara Bair, William Tetreault,

Burton Reist. No less essential than friends willing to read, Wendy's extended family eased her path, always ready to share a memory or provide a quick fact check. Jo Ann Kagawa, Patsy's only niece, and her partner, Brian Wong, sustained her with their kindnesses and patience during the many years of research and writing. Conversations with David Lee and Juliet Kono, Watters Martin, Russell Kudo, and Richard Port refreshed and enriched Wendy's understanding of Hawai'i politics, and also nourished her with ono kau kau.

Judy is grateful to the communities of scholars and friends who helped to give birth to this manuscript. Writing can be such an isolating experience, but she was guided by the intellectual insights, companionship, and, whenever possible, the joys of eating together with friends. Foremost, she wants to acknowledge members of her Asian American women historians writing group (Connie Chen, Monisha Das Gupta, Kelly Fong, Dorothy Fujita-Rony, Jane Hong, Valerie Matsumoto, Isa Quitana, and Susie Woo). She also thanks the members of the "Waterways and Worldviews: Rethinking Regions Defined by Oceans and Seas" research residency group sponsored by the University of California–Irvine's Humanities Research Commons and led by Jeff Wasserstrom; the "Radical Transnationalism: Reimagining Solidarities, Violence, Empire" feminist research seminar sponsored by the Institute for the Research of Women and Gender at the University of Michigan and co-led by Karen Leong and Laura Briggs and in community with Maile Arvin, Maylei Blackwell, Stanlie M. James, Ikue Kina, Rosamond King, and Nadine Naber; the "Gender, the State, and the 1977 International Women's Year Conference" National Endowment for the Humanities Summer Seminar hosted by Leandra Zarnow and Nancy Young; the "Rethinking Transnational Feminisms" residential research cluster sponsored by the University of California Humanities Research Institute and co-led by Maylei Blackwell and in intellectual communion with Monisha Das Gupta, Rachel Fabian, Grace Hong, Rana Jaleel, Zeynep Korkman, Karen Leong, and Jessica Millward; the Asian American and Pacific Islander History Symposium Workshop organized by Connie Chen, Lon Kurashige, and David Yoo; the University of California Consortium on Women's, Gender, and Sexuality Histories of the Americas (WGSHA) co-led by Ellen Hartigan-O'Connor, Lisa

Materson, and Rebecca Jo Plant; and the "Gender and the Trans-Pacific World" workshop and retreat led by Catherine Ceniza Choy.

During the last push to complete the manuscript in the midst of the COVID-19 pandemic, Judy is especially grateful for the virtual writing communities that sustained her. Rena Goldstein and Darby Vickers have been leading a nurturing writing and mentoring group, inspired by the approach of Barbara Sarnecka's *Writing Workshop*. Judy is grateful to write regularly with Qianru Li and Nima Yolmo as well as Nancy McLaughlin, Laura Mitchell, Inez Tan, and Roberta Wue. In addition, the Association for Asian American Studies Feminisms section seamlessly transitioned from a planned in-person writing retreat to a virtual intellectual community co-led by Kimberly McKee and Patty Chu and in companionship with Juliann Anesi, Kavita Daiya, Tammy Ho, Lynn Itagaki, SueJeanne Koh, Yaejoon Kwon, Christine Peralto, Courtney Sato, Ashanti Shih, Catherine To, Adrienne Winans, and others. More recently, Judy has benefited from the discussions about writing brought together by feminist scholars of nuclearism, a group formed with Lorraine Bayard de Volo, Anne Harrington, Tiara Na'puti, and Lauren Wilcox. And, Lynn Itagaki and Katherine Marino help Judy start her Monday mornings right by focusing on scholarship.

In addition to these writing partners, Judy thanks all those who provided helpful feedback (including the two anonymous reviewers of the manuscript), moral support, and opportunities to present her work. These individuals include Amanda Alexander, Jason Arthur, Melissa Blair, Deborah Blackwell, Brooke Blower, Eileen Boris, Cathleen Cahill, Keith Camacho, Gordon Chang, Kyle Ciani, Genevieve Clutario, Ian Coller, Anastasia Curwood, Claire Delahaye, Ed Dimendberg, Yuri Doolan, Theodora Dragostinova, Nathalie Duval, Christopher Elias, David Farber, Lilia Fernandez, Jaimey Fisher, Alfred Flores, Estelle Freedman, Kara French, Diane Fujino, Julie Gallagher, Susan Goodier, Kaaryn Gustafson, Annelise Heintz, Nicholas Grant, Anna Guevarra, Nicole Guidotti-Hernandez, Nina Ha, Michelle Haberland, Sherine Hamdy, Susan Hartmann, Nancy Hewitt, Erin Hiebert, Madelyn Hsu, Adria Imada, Noriko Ishii, Wesley Jackson, Marth Jones, Rabie Kadri, Miliann Kang, Aaron Katzeman, Christine Keiner, Scott Kurashige, Meredith Lee, Steven Lee, Mitch Lerner, Julia Lim, Mimi Long,

Laura Lovett, Mary Lui, Shadee Malaklou, Doreen Mattingly, Sinead McEneaney, Julia Mickenberg, David Milne, Kaeten Mistry, Robin Morris, Lucy Murphy, Kristina Myers, Cindy Ng, Jamie Nisbet, Jocelyn Olcott, Lorena Oropeza, Juno Parrenas, Monica Perales, Claire Potter, Sarah Potter, Helene Quanquin, Einav Rabinovitch-Fox, Renee Raphael, Sarah Rawley, Gayatri Reddy, Amira Rose Davis, Vicki Ruiz, Virginia Scharff, Sara Schwebel, Jay Sexton, Haley Seif, Nayan Shah, Naoko Shibusawa, Jeannie Shinozuka, CeCe Sloan, Bradley Smith, Seema Sohi, Bryant Simon, Karen Su, Julie Suk, Lisa Tetrault, Jessie Tromberg, Myla Vicenti Carpio, Jamie Wagman, Naoko Wake, Leigh Ann Wang, Kim Warren, Emily Westkaemper, Tiffany Willoughby-Herard, Barbara Winslow, Rumi Yasutake, and Natasha Zaretsky.

Judy benefited enormously from giving talks and receiving helpful feedback. These include the international exchange program sponsored by the Organization of American Historians and the Japanese Association for American Studies and visits to Konan and Sophia Universities. Other invaluable visits include Agnes Scott College, Berea College, Boston University, Brandeis University, California State University, Long Beach, Harvey Mudd College, Laguna Woods Village's International Women's Day, Loyola University, Ohio State University, Osher Lifelong Learning Institute, ProQuest/Alexander Street Press, Saint Olaf College, Scripps College, Soka University, Stanford University, Université de Lille and Université Paris-Est Marne-la-Vallée, University of California–Davis, University of California–Irvine, University of California–Los Angeles, University of California–San Diego, University of California–Santa Barbara, the University of East Anglia, the University of Illinois, Chicago's Global Asian Studies Program, and the Virginia Polytechnic Institute and State University.

Judy is also grateful to have had the opportunity to publish portions of this biography and reflections on this project in "Reflections on 'The U.S. 1968: Third-Worldism, Feminisms, and Liberalism,'" published in *American Historical Review*; *Asian American Feminisms and Women of Color Politics* (2018), edited by Lynn Fujiwara and Shireen Roshanravan; *The Conversation* with editor Catesby Holmes; *Journal of American History* as part of a "Sex, Suffrage, and the Nineteenth Amendment" interchange; *Meridians: Feminism, Race, Transnationalism*'s special issue on "Radical Transnationalism:

Reimagining Solidarities, Violence, Empires," guest edited by Laura Briggs and Robyn Spencer; *Our Voices, Our Lives: New Dimensions of Asian American and Pacific Islander Women's History* (NYU Press, 2020), edited by Shirley Hune and Gail Nomura; *Politico* magazine for a column on "Who Should Be on the Next Mount Rushmore?"; *Suffrage at 100: Women in American Politics since 1920* (2020), edited by Stacie Taranto and Leandra Zarnow; *Time* magazine with Olivia Coleman; and *Verge Journal*, edited by Tina Chen. Judy also shared her insights on Patsy Mink for the documentary series *Asian Americans* for episode 3, directed by Leo Chiang; a C-Span interview at the Organization of American Historians conference; and a podcast conversation with Laura Boersma for *She's History*. She also benefited from the opportunity to create a digital map about Mink's life as part of a digital humanities working group at the University of California–Irvine led by Danielle Kane with Audrey Fong, Marcie Hague, Dwayne Pack, Deanna Shemek, and Amanda Swain.

Judy wants to especially acknowledge the graciousness of those who supported her research by sharing resources and providing shelter. Kimberlee Bassford generously made available her interviews based on the groundbreaking documentary *Ahead of the Majority*, and Robin Lung, who conducted research for the film, also offered insights and encouragement. Julie Martinez, Katja and Mischa David-Fox, and Tobie Meyer-Fong in Washington, DC, welcomed Judy for multiple visits and meals over the years. Mari Yoshihara shared her condo and was a motivating exercise partner in Honolulu. Judy's Uncle John and Aunt Helen Huang in Minneapolis also provided her with a home away from home. Gulsah and Berke Torunoglu were ideal hosts in Turkey, when Judy participated in the International Congress on Women and Politics in the Global World. Rina Carvalho, Jennifer Choy, Peter Cibula III, Robert Escalante, Ryan Gurney, and Jasmine Robledo have provided essential administrative support. Jenny Fan and Tonie Zhu are inspirations for their dedication to social justice and mentorship. Thuy Vo Dang has been a wonderful conversation partner and friend who has sustained Judy through meaningful collaborations and weekly walks. And, Stephanie Narrow has been an invaluable research assistant—reading, formatting, and offering insights about this manuscript—all with such good cheer and enthusiasm.

This project has received research funding from Ohio State University's Division of Arts and Humanities, Coca-Cola Critical Difference for Women Faculty Grant for Research sponsored by the Women's, Gender, and Sexuality Studies Department, the University of California Humanities Research Institute, the University of California–Irvine's Chancellor's Fellowship funds, Humanities Commons, and School of Humanities.

Judy is especially grateful to Patsy Mink's friends and colleagues who granted interviews: Amy Agbayani, Doris Ching, Laura Efurd, Amy Isaacs, Juliet Kono, David Lee, Herb Lee, Jim and Joan Manke, Watters Martin, Mari Matsuda, Marilyn Moniz-Kahoohanohano, and Richard Port. Lynn Demyan offered invaluable transcription services. This project could not have proceeded without Wendy Mink's willingness to collaborate and educate. Judy deeply thanks her and her cousins Jo Ann, Brian, Julie, and Calvin for their aloha and many fabulous meals. It was a joy for Judy to participate in the 2018 dedication of the Patsy Mink statue in Honolulu with her family and many supporters.

Judy started this project in 2012, when her kids (Konrad and Langston) were still shorter than she. She is profoundly grateful for her husband, Mark Walter, for his love and care of their family, especially as she had to travel extensively for archival research and as the Walter-Wus relocated from Ohio to California with a year-long stop-over in Germany. She also thanks the extended Walter family and Huang family for their hospitality and care. Judy would like to honor her parents. Her father—John Yu-Pu Wu—passed away in April 2020 and was always proud and eager to read her work. Her mother—Betty Chao-Hua Wu—is a fierce caregiver who is finding her way after over fifty-six years of marriage.

NOTES

INTRODUCTION

1 Patsy T. Mink, "Statement by Congresswomen Patsy T. Mink in the House of Representatives Celebrating the 30th Anniversary of Title IX of the Education Act Amendments of 1972," Patsy T. Mink Papers, Box 2041/Folder 2, Library of Congress, Manuscript Division, Washington, DC (hereafter MP box/folder).

2 Mink, "Statement," p. 1.

3 Mink, "Statement," p. 4.

4 Mink, "Statement," p. 5.

5 Mink, "Statement," p. 5.

6 Mink, "Statement," p. 1.

7 Amira Rose Davis, *All-American Welfare Queens: Race, Politics, and Sports in the Time of Title IX* (forthcoming).

8 "First Arrivals, First Reactions," History, Art & Archives, The United States House of Representatives, https://history.house.gov/

9 Barbara Winslow, *Shirley Chisholm: Catalyst for Change* (New York: Routledge, 2013); Leandra Ruth Zarnow, *Battling Bella: The Protest Politics of Bella Abzug* (Cambridge, MA: Harvard University Press, 2019).

10 Rachel Laura Pierce, "Capitol Feminism: Work, Politics, and Gender in Congress, 1960–1980," PhD diss., University of Virginia, 2014, 4.

11 Anastasia Curwood, "Black Feminism on Capitol Hill: Shirley Chisholm and Movement Politics, 1968–1984," *Meridians* 13:1 (2015): 204–32. Also see Belinda Robnett, "African American Women in the Civil Rights Movement, 1954–1965: Gender, Leadership, and Micromobilization," *American Journal of Sociology* 101:6: 1661–93.

12 Becky Thompson, "Multiracial Feminism: Recasting the Chronology of Second Wave Feminism," *Feminist Studies* 28:2 (Summer 2002): 336–60.

13 Stephanie Gilmore and Sara Evans, *Feminist Coalitions: Historical Perspectives on Second-Wave Feminism in the United States* (Urbana: University of Illinois Press, 2008).

14 Chela Sandoval, "U.S. Third World Feminism: The Theory and Method of Oppositional Consciousness in the Postmodern World," *Genders*, no. 10 (Spring 1991): 1–24.

15 Kimberlé Crenshaw, "Demarginalizing the Intersection of Race and Sex: A Black Feminist Critique of Antidiscrimination Doctrine, Feminist Theory, and Antira-

cist Politics," *University of Chicago Legal Forum* 1989:1 (1989): 139. Also see "Mapping the Margins: Intersectionality, Identity Politics, and Violence against Women of Color," *Stanford Law Review* 43:6 (July 1991): 1241–99.

16 Candace Fujikane and Jonathan Y. Okamura, eds., *Asian Settler Colonialism: From Local Governance to the Habits of Everyday Life in Hawai'i* (Honolulu: University of Hawai'i Press, 2008); Dean Saranillio, "Colliding Histories: Hawai'i Statehood at the Intersection of Asians 'Ineligible to Citizenship' and Hawaiians 'Unfit for Self-Government,'" *Journal of Asian American Studies* 13:3 (October 2010): 283–309; Haunani-Kay Trask, *From a Native Daughter: Colonialism and Sovereignty in Hawaii*, rev. ed. (Honolulu: University of Hawai'i Press, 1999).

17 Audre Lorde, *Sister Outsider: Essays and Speeches* (Berkeley: Crossing Press, 1984).

18 Mink, "Statement," p. 6.

PART I. THE PARTY OF THE PEOPLE

1 Epigraphs are from P. Mink, "Which Party Shall I Choose? From a National Viewpoint . . . ," Speech, Girls' State, Punahou School, Wilcox Hall, American Legion Auxiliary, June 28, 1963, MP 13/9; and "Convention Cheers Patsy Mink's Plea for Strong Civil Rights Plank," *Honolulu Star-Bulletin*, n.d., MP 5/4.

2 Patsy Takemoto Mink, "Speech," Democratic National Convention, as reported in "Convention Cheers Patsy Mink's Plea for Strong Civil Rights Plank," *Honolulu Star-Bulletin*, n.d., MP 5/4.

3 Bob Considine, "On the Line: Golden Gate," *Seattle Times*, July 19, 1960, MP 5/4.

CHAPTER 1. PLANTATION SOCIETY

1 The Big Five consisted of the companies Castle & Cooke, Alexander & Baldwin, C. Brewer & Co., American Factors, and Theo H. Davies & Co.

2 Eiichiro Azuma, "The Lure of Military Imperialism: Race, Martial Citizenship, and Minority American Transnationalism during the Cold War," *Journal of American Ethnic History* 36:2 (Winter 2017): 72–82.

3 Misc. Notes about Family Genealogy, MP 2638/folio: "Tateyama Family Genealogical Material Miscellany ca. 1971–ca. 1988, n.d."

4 "Passenger Manifest" for Yamada, Tsuru, January 30, 1898, "Ships Passenger Manifest," Immigration and Naturalization Service (INS), U.S. National Pacific Region (San Francisco), San Bruno, California (hereafter "Ships Passenger Manifest").

5 "Passenger Manifest" for Tateyama, G., September 11, 1999, "Ships Passenger Manifest."

6 "Passenger Manifest" for Yamada, Tsuru; Misc. Notes about Family Genealogy, MP 2638/folio: "Tateyama Family Genealogical Material Miscellany ca. 1971–ca. 1988, n.d."

7 Ronald Takaki, *Strangers from a Different Shore: A History of Asian Americans*, updated and revised edition (Boston: Little, Brown, 1998).

8   Native Hawaiians constituted 97 percent of the island's population in 1853 but only 16 percent by 1923. "Hawaii: Life in a Plantation Society," https://www.loc.gov/classroom-materials/immigration/japanese/hawaii-life-in-a-plantation-society/.

9   Misc. Notes about Family Genealogy, MP 2638.

10 "Passenger Manifest" for Yamada, Tsuru, and Yamada, Sootsuchi, January 30, 1898.

11 Yuji Ichioka, *The Issei: The World of the First-Generation Japanese Immigrants, 1885–1924* (New York: Free Press, 1988).

12 One sibling died from drowning in his early twenties and another from a bad cold at three years old. Misc. Notes about Family Genealogy, MP 2638.

13 Brenda J. Child, *Boarding School Seasons: American Indian Families, 1900–1940* (Lincoln: University of Nebraska Press, 2000); Alfred P. Flores, "U.S. Colonial Education in Guam, 1899–1950," *Oxford Research Encyclopedia of American History* (Oxford University Press, 2019); Denise K. Lajimodiere, *Stringing Rosaries: The History, the Unforgivable, and the Healing of Northern Plains American Indian Boarding School Survivors* (Fargo: North Dakota State University Press, 2019).

14 Chinese immigrants, arriving in the mid-nineteenth century before Japanese immigrants, tended to move off the plantations earlier as well. They created an economic niche by operating family-run businesses, and their children took advantage of educational opportunities in Hawai'i.

15 Sue Davidson, *A Heart in Politics: Jeannette Rankin and Patsy T. Mink* (Seattle: Seal Press, 1994), p. 103.

16 "Tateyama Family . . . Then and Now," p. 27.

17 "Ruth Mukai," interviewed by Kimberlee Bassford, *Ahead of the Majority*, timecoded transcript, Kula, Maui, February 8, 2007, Take 00, p. 1.

18 "Ruth Mukai," p. 1.

19 "Eugene Takemoto," interviewed by Kimberlee Bassford, *Ahead of the Majority*, timecoded transcript, Honolulu, Hawai'i, February 6, 2007, Take 00, p. 3.

20 "Eugene Takemoto," pp. 3, 5.

21 "Eugene Takemoto," p. 6.

22 "Calvin Tamura," interviewed by Kimberlee Bassford, *Ahead of the Majority*, timecoded transcript, Honolulu, Hawai'i, February 5, 2007, Take 37, p. 5.

23 "Eugene Takemoto," p. 2.

24 "Eugene Takemoto," p. 2.

25 "Eugene Takemoto," p. 2.

26 "Calvin Tamura," pp. 3–4.

27 Esther K. Arinaga and Rene E. Ojiri, "Patsy Takemoto Mink," in *Called from Within: Early Women Lawyers of Hawai'i*, ed. Mari J. Matsuda (Honolulu: University of Hawaii Press, 1992), 255.

28 "Harriet Holt," interviewed by Kimberlee Bassford, *Ahead of the Majority*, timecoded transcript, Kula, Maui, February 8, 2007, Take 22, p. 1.

29 "Harriet Holt," p. 7.

30 "Ruth Mukai," p. 4.

31 Arinaga and Ojiri, "Patsy Takemoto Mink," p. 255.

32 Arinaga and Ojiri, "Patsy Takemoto Mink," p. 255.

33 James R. Barrett and David Roediger, "Inbetween Peoples: Race, Nationality, and the 'New Immigrant' Working Class," *Journal of American Ethnic History* 16:3 (Spring 1997): 3–44.

34 "Elmer Cravalho," interviewed by Kimberlee Bassford, *Ahead of the Majority*, timecoded transcript, Kahului, Maui, February 9, 2007, Take 00, p. 1.

35 "Harriet Holt," Take 23, pp. 3–4.

36 "Burns, John A., Oral History Project: Interview—Elmer Cravalho," August 10, 1977, "Burns Oral History Project," John A. Burns and Dan Boylan Collection, 1/folio: "Elmer Cravalho," Hawaii Congressional Papers Collection, University of Hawaii, Manoa, Archives and Manuscripts (hereafter cited as BBC).

37 Lynn Langway, "When Patsy Mink Was an Outsider," *Honolulu Bulletin*, March 26, 1970, Hiram Fong Papers, Hawaii Congressional Papers Collection, University of Hawai'i, Manoa, Archives and Manuscripts, 14/folder: "Mink 1968."

38 W. H. Anderson, "The Question of Japanese-Americans," *Los Angeles Times*, February 1942.

39 "Tateyama Family . . . Then and Now, 1989," p. 28.

40 "Ruth Mukai," p. 6.

41 "Tateyama Family . . . Then and Now, 1989," p. 28.

42 Langway, "When Patsy Mink Was an Outsider."

43 "Tateyama Family . . . Then and Now, 1989," p. 28.

44 Arinaga and Ojiri, "Patsy Takemoto Mink," p. 254.

45 "Ruth Mukai," p. 7.

46 "Students Speak at A.A.U.W. Meet: Aspects of Internationalism Occupy Talks of Trio at Wilson College Meeting," [no title identified], n.d., MP O. 12/Red Scrapbook.

47 "Avis Condict, Patsy Takemoto, Jacqueline Rasqui Speak at Open Meeting of I.R.C.," [no title], October 11, 1946, MP O. 12/Red Scrapbook.

48 Patsy Takemoto, "To the Editor," "Letterip," [no title], n.d., MP O. 12/Red Scrapbook

49 Takemoto, "To the Editor."

50 "Island Girl Home from Midwest: Tells of Fight on Discrimination," *Honolulu Star-Bulletin*, n.d., MP, O. 12/Red Scrapbook.

51 Takemoto, "To the Editor."

52 "Island Girl Home from Midwest."

53 "Island Girl Home from Midwest."

54 Patsy Takemoto, "An enemy threatens . . . ," [no title], n.d., MP, O. 12/Red Scrapbook.

55 Takemoto, "An enemy threatens."

56 Takemoto, "An enemy threatens."

57 "Three Women Students Capture Top ASUH Oratory Prizes in Contest," [no title], n.d., MP, O. 12/Red Scrapbook.

58 Patsy Takemoto, "Dr. William Welch, beloved dean . . . ," n.d., MP, O. 12/Red Scrapbook.

59 "Statehood Forum Begins Tomorrow," [no title], n.d., MP, O. 12/Red Scrapbook.

60 "Radio Script," n.d., "Statehood Forum Begins Tomorrow," [no title], n.d., p. 7, MP, O. 12/Red Scrapbook.

61 Davidson, *A Heart in Politics*, pp.116–17.

62 Regina Morantz-Sanchez, *Sympathy and Science: Women Physicians in American Medicine* (Chapel Hill: University of North Carolina Press, 2005).

63 "'One World' under One Roof: A Design for Living; International House," *Chicago Sun-Times*, March 8, 1950, p. 26, MP 11/13.

64 Renee Christine Romano, *Race Mixing: Black-White Marriage in Postwar America* (Cambridge, MA: Harvard University Press, 2003), p. 45.

65 Peggy Pascoe, *What Comes Naturally: Miscegenation Law and the Making of Race in America* (New York: Oxford University Press, 2009); Deenesh Sohoni, "Unsuitable Suitors: Anti-Miscegenation Laws, Naturalization Laws, and the Construction of Asian Identities," *Law & Society Review* 41:3 (September 2007): 587–618.

66 Patsy Takemoto, "Justice & Equality: Discussion of Trade Unionism in Hawaii, U.S.A.," Paper, University of Chicago Law School, May 23, 1951, MP 15/2.

67 Takemoto, "Justice & Equality."

68 Takemoto, "Justice & Equality."

69 Takemoto, "Education: Foundation for Peace," MP 15/2.

"PINK MINK"

1 "Nuclear Rocket Test Near Oahu," *Honolulu Advertiser*, August 1, 1958, p. 1; "Thousands of Islanders Witness Bright Blast," *Honolulu Star-Bulletin*, August 1, 1958, p. 1.

2 "Lack of Test Blast Warning Is Protested," *Honolulu Star-Bulletin*, August 1, 1958, p. 1.

3 UPI wire report by Charles Bernard, MP 10/ 2.

4 Defense Nuclear Agency, US Department of Defense, *Operation Hardtack I, 1958*, p. 271 (Washington, DC, December 1982).

5 *Operation Hardtack*, quoting the *Honolulu Star-Bulletin*, August 12, 1958.

6 Albert Bigelow, *The Voyage of the Golden Rule* (New York: Doubleday, 1959).

7 U.S. v. Albert Smith Bigelow et al., Cr. No. 11,243, warrant for arrest of defendant, United States District Court for the District of Hawaii, May 1, 1958, MP 9/12.

8 Letters from Ben Norris, Religious Society of Friends of Honolulu, Hawaii, March 17, 20, 1958, MP 9/11.

9 "Mrs. Mink Urges Isles Give Pacifists Rousing Welcome," *Honolulu Star-Bulletin*, April 9, 1958, p. 1.

10 The Editor, "Still No Protest to Moscow," *Honolulu Star-Bulletin*, May 6, 1958, MP 10/2.

11 Letters to the Editor, *Honolulu Star-Bulletin* and *Honolulu Advertiser*, April 23, 24, 26, 1958, MP 10/2.

12 H.R. No. 15 passed the Territorial House of Representatives on February 21, 1957. "Halt Bomb Test, T.H. Asks," *Honolulu Star-Bulletin*, February 21, 1957, MP 10/2; "Nisei Woman's H-Bomb Crusade," *Yomiuri Shimbun*, April 27, 1957, MP 9/11.

13 The Editors, "Dangers of Radioactive Fallout," *Honolulu Star-Bulletin*, May 11, 1957, p. 4.

14 Patsy T. Mink, Letter to Delegate John Burns, MP 9/11.

15 Patsy T. Mink notes and clippings on the effects of radioactive fallout, MP 10/1, 2.

16 "Fallout Alarms Woman Legislator," *Honolulu Advertiser*, April 25, 1957, MP 10/2.

17 Letters to the Editor, *Honolulu Advertiser* and *Honolulu Star-Bulletin*, April–May 1957, MP 10/1.

18 Patsy T. Mink, Letter to Judith Ontai, May 14, 1957, MP 9/11.

19 Patsy T. Mink, "Peace Rally Speech," May 13, 1962, GMP.

CHAPTER 2. A DEMOCRATIC REVOLUTION

1 "Patsy Takemoto Breaks Trail into Law Field for Nisei Women," *Honolulu Star-Bulletin*, August 19, 1953, p. 10.

2 Patsy T. Mink, "Letter to Edward N. Sylva," [1954?], MP 3/15.

3 Even though she was third generation, or sansei, the newspapers tended to mistakenly report her as a Nisei.

4 Mark Waters, "Do Portias Face Life? Most of Isle Lady Lawyers Prefer Government Service," *Honolulu Star-Bulletin*, February 24, 1956.

5 Waters, "Do Portias Face Life?"

6 Waters, "Do Portias Face Life?"

7 "Mrs. John A. Burns," interviewed by Dan Boylan and Paul Hooper, February 11, 1976, p. 11, BBC, 1/folio: "Beatrice Burns."

8 "Honolulu Police Department: Espionage Bureau," MP 1/8.

9 "Purposes," MP 1/8.

10 Jonathan Rinehart, "Citizen Inouye," reproduced from *USA *1 Monthly News and History* (August 1962), Democratic Party of Hawaii Collection, Special Collections, University of Hawaii 14/folio: "Inouye, Daniel," p. 3.

11 Rinehart, "Citizen Inouye," p. 5.

12 Rinehart, "Citizen Inouye."

13 Rinehart, "Citizen Inouye."

14 Patsy Takemoto Mink, "Letter," December 7, 1953, MP 17/1.

15 Mink, "Letter," December 7, 1953.

16 Committee of Three, "Letter," December 22, 1953, MP 17/1.

17 Committee of Three, "Letter."

18 "Meeting Notes," held January 28, 1954, MP 17/1.

19 Territorial Central Committee Meeting, "Minutes," September 11, 1954, p. 3, BBC, 2/folio: "Post-War Political Organizing 1954–1956."

20 Norman Meller and Anne Feder Lee, "Hawaiian Sovereignty," *Publius* 27:2 (Spring 1997): 170.

21 Meller and Lee, "Hawaiian Sovereignty," 170.

22 Patsy T. Mink, "Letter," May 5, 1955, MP 3/16.

23 Stuart Gerry Brown and Daniel Boyland, Interview with Thomas P. Gill, November 7, 1976, p. 20, BBC.

24 Brown and Boyland, interview with Gill, pp. 19–20.

25 Unknown, "The Fifth District," [1962], MP 3/10.

26 Patsy Takemoto Mink, "My Political Beliefs," Campaign Brochure, MP 1/11.

27 Mink, "My Political Beliefs."

28 Mink, "My Political Beliefs."

29 Mink, "My Political Beliefs."

30 Patsy Takemoto Mink, "My Background," Campaign Brochure, MP 1/11.

31 Mink, "My Background."

32 Patsy Takemoto Mink, "Speech Blurbs," MP 2/3. For discussions of Cold War gender roles and maternalist politics, see Elaine Tyler May, *Homeward Bound: American Families during the Cold War* (New York: Basic Books, 1988); Joanne J. Meyerowitz, *Not June Cleaver: Women and Gender in Postwar America, 1945–1960* (Philadelphia: Temple University Press, 1994); Amy Swerdlow, *Women Strike for Peace: Traditional Motherhood and Radical Politics in the 1960s* (Chicago: University of Chicago Press, 1993).

33 Kuihelani Mahikoa Brandt, "Letter," April 18, 1955, MP 3/16.

34 Patsy T. Mink, "Letter," May 13, 1955, MP 3/16.

35 Patsy Takemoto Mink, "AJA Woman Tells How She Won Nomination," *Honolulu Advertiser*, October 31, 1956, p. 35.

36 John Mink, "Diaries," September 19, 1956, MP R 2637.

37 Patsy T. Mink, "Letter," June 12, 1957, MP 9/9.

38 This phrase is borrowed from Mary L. Dudziak, *Cold War Civil Rights: Race and the Image of American Democracy* (Princeton, NJ: Princeton University Press, 2000).

39 Setsu Shigematsu and Keith L. Camacho, *Militarized Currents: Toward a Decolonized Future in Asia and the Pacific* (Minneapolis: University of Minnesota Press, 2010), p. xxix.

40 Patsy T. Mink, "Letter," February 25, 1957, MP 9/11.

41 Mink, "Letter," February 25, 1957.

42 Mink, "Letter," February 25, 1957.

43 Patsy Takemoto Mink, "Letter," May 2, 1957, MP 9/11.

44 Patsy T. Mink, "Letter," May 14, 1957, MP 9/11.

45 Dan K. Inouye, "Letter," March 3, 1957, p. 6, 5/folio: "Daniel Inouye Correspondence, 1957–1960," BBC.

46 Lorrin P. Thurston, "Communism Does Not, and Never Will, Control Hawaii," MP 4/12.

47 Patsy Takemoto Mink, "Statehood Message to Democratic National Conference," February 15–16, 1957, MP 4/12.

48 Mink, "Statehood Message."

49 Patsy Takemoto Mink, "Letter," October 29, 1957, MP 17/10.

50 Patsy T. Mink, "Letter," November 15, 1957, MP 17/10.

51 "Mrs. Mink Takes High Court Oath," *Honolulu Advertiser*, January 21, 1958, MP 11/14.

52 "See It Now—Edward Morrow: 'Statehood for Alaska and Hawaii?'" *TV Guide*, listing for March 2, 1958, p. A-17, MP 11/14.

53 Democratic National Committee, "Press Release," December 16, 1957, MP 17/11.

54 Helene Hale, "Letter," January 26, 1958, MP 19/3.

55 Patsy Takemoto Mink, "Young Political Leaders Conference," August 8, 1958, MP 13/8.

56 Mink, "Young Political Leaders Conference."

57 Mink, "Young Political Leaders Conference."

58 Mink, "Young Political Leaders Conference."

59 John Mink, "Diaries," October 1, 1958.

60 John Mink, "Diaries," October 29, 1958.

61 John Mink, "Diaries," October 29, 1958.

62 "'Equal Pay' Bill Is Put Off Again," [unidentified newspaper], April 27, 1959, MP 11/1.

63 "Lee Vote Blocks 'Equal Pay' Bill," [unidentified newspaper], April 25, 1959, MP 11/1.

64 Patsy T. Mink, "Letter," March 16, 1959, MP 19/4.

65 Patsy T. Mink, "Speech," January 1959, MP 13/8.

66 George Cooper and Gavan Daws, *Land and Power in Hawaii: The Democratic Years* (Honolulu: University of Hawai'i Press, 1990); Saranillio, "Colliding Histories," 296.

67 Saranillio, "Colliding Histories," 299; John S. Whitehead, "The Anti-Statehood Movement and the Legacy of Alice Kamokila Campbell," *Hawaiian Journal of History* 27 (1993): 43–63.

68 Saranillio, "Colliding Histories," 302.

69 Patsy T. Mink, "Letter," August 6, 1959, MP 2/16.

70 Brian Casey, "Inouye Switches Aims to Seat in U.S. House," *Honolulu Advertiser*, May 26, 1959, MP 2/20.

71 Casey, "Inouye Switches Aims."

72 Casey, "Inouye Switches Aims."

73 Mink, "Letter," August 6, 1959.

74 Hank Sato, "Democrats in 'Battle of Sexes': Inouye Supporter and Mrs. Mink 'Spar' at Puunene Rally," *Maui News*, June 20, 1959.

75 Sato, "Democrats in 'Battle of Sexes.'"

76 Sato, "Democrats in 'Battle of Sexes.'"

77 John Mink, "Diaries," July 13, 1959.

78 Gwendolyn Mink, interviews with author, Washington, DC, 2013.

79 Kiyoshi Takasaki, "Letter," June 18, 1959, MP 2/16.

80 John Mink, "Diaries," June 28, 1959.

81 Patsy T. Mink, "Letter," August 10, 1959, MP 2/16.

82 Patsy T. Mink, "Letter," August 8, 1960, MP 2/12.

83 Bob Considine, "On the Line: Golden Gate," *Seattle Times*, July 19, 1960, MP 5/4.

84 "Senator in Miami: 'Mrs. Hawaii' Aiming High," *Miami News*, April 17, 1959, MP 18/11.

85 "Senator in Miami."

86 "Senator in Miami."

87 "When a Speaker Is Speechless," *Los Angeles Examiner*, August 24, 1963; Harry Johanesen, "Plush Hawaii Tour: How Lawmakers Live It Up," *San Francisco Examiner*, August 25, 1963, MP 7/9.

88 "When a Speaker Is Speechless."

89 Patsy T. Mink, "Letter," September 11, 1963, MP 7/9.

90 Patsy T. Mink, "Letter," September 19, 1963, MP 6/4.

91 Patsy T. Mink, "Speech," MP 3/13.

92 "Press Release," n.d., MP 16/7.

93 Patsy T. Mink, "Speech," November 19, 1964, MP 13/10.

94 Mink, "Speech," November 19, 1964.

95 John Mink, "Diaries," October 5, 1964.

96 John Mink, "Diaries," October 13, 1964.

PART II. A GREAT SOCIETY AT WAR

1 Epigraphs are from Frances Spatz Leighton, "A Rare Mink: Congresswoman from Hawaii, Patsy Mink, Is New Glamour Girl in Capital," *New York Sunday News*, March 7, 1965, p. 19, MP 754/ 2; and "Mrs. Mink's Strategy," *Honolulu Star-Bulletin*, October 28, 1975, Spark M. Matsunaga Papers 14/folio: "Mink July–December 1975," CPC.

2 Frances Spatz Leighton, "Congress' New Glamor Girl," *Pittsburgh Press*, "Sunday ROTO," March 7, 1965, p. 6.

3 "The Honorable Patsy T. Mink: A Bright New Face in Congress," *IPS Photo Bulletin*, no. 13 (February 1965), p. 183, MP 753/6.

4 "Patsy Tells Grads: Don't Be Machines," *Honolulu Advertiser*, June 11, 1965, MP 755/9.

5 "Patsy Mink: Education Key to Great Society," *Honolulu Star-Bulletin*, September 9, 1965, MP 755/12.

6 "Patsy Mink: Education Key."

7 "Patsy Calls on AJAs to Lead Rights Fight," *Honolulu Advertiser*, February 1, 1965, MP 755/6.

8 "Patsy Calls on AJAs."

9 William Petersen, "Success Story, Japanese-American Style," *New York Times Magazine*, January 9, 1966; Ellen Wu, *The Color of Success: Asian Americans and the Origins of the Model Minority* (Princeton, NJ: Princeton University Press, 2014).

"I SEE YOU HAVE APPOINTMENT WITH VIETCONG"

1 "G.O.P. Nominee's Views, in His Own Words, on Major Issues of Campaign," *New York Times*, July 18, 1964, p. 6.

2 "Goldwater Calls for Drive to Finish War in Vietnam, Implies Johnson Did Not Go Far Enough in Air Attacks on Reds," *New York Times*, August 11, 1964, p. 1.

3 Mitchell Lerner, "Vietnam and the 1964 Election: A Defense of Lyndon Johnson," *Presidential Studies Quarterly* 25:4 (Fall 1995): 752.

4 "Vietnam Puzzle," *New York Times*, February 28, 1965, p. E1; "Wider War," *New York Times*, March 7, 1965, p. E1.

5 Letter to the President signed by Sixteen Democrats, March 26, 1965, MP 497/13.

6 Patsy T. Mink, Remarks, May 10, 1967, MP 508/1.

7 Patsy T. Mink, Remarks relating to Vietnam, August 25, 1965, MP 508/1.

8 Letter to Constituent, September 29, 1965, MP 500/7.

9 The whole Johnson family called my mother "Miss Patsy." At one of the White House Easter egg rolls I attended, I was greeted by Johnson's daughters, who exclaimed, "This is Miss Patsy's daughter!" and then dragged me over to meet their mother, who cooed, "Miss Patsy's daughter! We all love her here. So nice to meet you."

10 "Text of President's Message on Funds for Vietnam," *New York Times*, May 5, 1965, p. 18.

11 "$1.7 Billion More Asked for Viet War," *Los Angeles Times*, August 5, 1965, p. 1.

12 US House of Representatives, H. Res. 560, September 20, 1965, endorsed the unilateral use of force in the Western hemisphere to thwart "the intervention of international Communism." *Congressional Record*, September 20, 1965, pp. 24347–64, https://www.congress.gov.

13 "10,000 to Protest War in Viet-Nam with Rally, Parade," *Washington Post*, April 17, 1965, p. A4.

14 The chair of the House Armed Services Committee, for example, was Mendel Rivers, Democrat of South Carolina. He began serving in Congress in 1941. Unabashedly pro-war and antiprotest, Rivers sped a bill through Congress in the late summer of 1965 to assign a ten thousand dollar fine or five years in prison to anyone caught burning his draft card. "Johnson Signs Bill on Draft Card Burning," *Los Angeles Times*, September 1, 1965, p. 2.

15 "Michigan Faculty Created Teach-In," *New York Times*, May 9, 1965, p. 43; "Johnson Signs Bill on Draft Card Burning," *Los Angeles Times*, September 1, 1965, p. 2; "10,000 March on 5th Avenue in Viet Protests," *Washington Post*, October 17, 1965, p. A1.

16 Patsy T. Mink, "Opening Address by Representative Patsy T. Mink to First National Conference on Asian American Studies," April 16, 1971, University of Southern California, MP 242/2.

17 "Agnew Vetoed Daughter's Plan to March," *Washington Post*, October 24, 1969, p. A4.

18 "'Our Children Have Never Lived a Single Day of Peace': A Report from the Paris Meeting between Congresswomen Bella Abzug, Patsy Mink, and Ministers Nguyen Thi Binh and Xuan Thuy," *Women Strike for Peace: Memo* 2:3 (Spring 1972), MP 510/4.

19 "Interview with Madame Nguyen Thi Binh," transcript, MP 510/5.

20 Abzug and Mink draft press release, April 23, 1972, MP 510/5.

21 "Reds 'Earnest,' Rep. Mink Says," *Honolulu Advertiser*, April 23, 1972, p. 2; "Mrs. Mink Urges Mass Peace Rallies," *Honolulu Star-Bulletin*, April 24, 1972, p. 1; "GOP Head Scores Rep. Mink's Stand," *Honolulu Advertiser*, April 26, 1972, p. 14.

22 Correspondence dated April 25, 1972, MP 499/3.

CHAPTER 3. A DOVE AMONG HAWKS

1 The resolution responded to two alleged attacks against the USS *Maddox*, a destroyer conducting clandestine operations in the Gulf of Tonkin. The first attack occurred because the destroyer was in another country's waters. The president privately questioned whether the second attack actually took place, and US internal military reports confirmed that it had not. However, US government officials testified and lobbied Congress to respond to both attacks.

2 "Mrs. Mink Voted for All Key Bills," *Honolulu Star-Bulletin*, August 20, 1965, MP 755/11.

3 This group supported "the President on 89 percent of 12 selected 'Great Society' key votes and 83 percent of the 66 roll call votes." "Mrs. Mink Voted for All Key Bills."

4 J. B. Neilands, "Vietnam: Progress of the Chemical War," *Asian Survey* 10:3 (March 1970): 209; George E. Brown et al., "Letter to the President," March 26, 1965, MP 49/11.

5 "Letter to the President," March 25, 1965, in "Reviewing the Record on Vietnam," *Congressional Record: Proceedings and Debates of the 89th Congress, Second Session*, MP 508/2.

6 The signers included Jonathan Bingham (D–New York), Benjamin Rosenthal (D–New York), Donald M. Fraser (D-Minnesota), Paul Todd (D-Michigan), George E. Brown Jr. (D-Michigan), Patsy T. Mink (D-Hawaiʻi), Leonard Farbstein (D–New York), Richard W. McCarthy (D–New York), Phillip Burton (D-California), John G. Dow (D–New York), Don Edwards (D-California), Robert Kastenmeier (D-Wisconsin), James Scheuer (D–New York), Edith Green (D-Oregon), William Folder Ryan (D–New York), Henry Reuss (D-Wisconsin), and John Conyers (D-Michigan).

7 Jonathan Bingham et al., "Letter to Honorable Lyndon B. Johnson," December 11, 1965, MP 496/11.

8 Patsy T. Mink, "Statement relating to South Vietnamese Execution," March 15, 1966, MP 508/2.

9 Mink, "Statement relating to South Vietnamese Execution."

10 Patsy T. Mink, "Statement relating to South Vietnam Elections," May 11, 1966, MP 508/4.

11 Mink, "Statement relating to South Vietnam Elections."

12 Mink, "Statement relating to South Vietnam Elections."

13 "Peace in Our Time," October 17, 1966, MP 508/2.

14 Patsy T. Mink, "Remarks," May 10, 1965, p. 1, MP 508/1.

15 Mink, "Remarks," May 10, 1965, MP R 2637.

16 Mink, "Remarks," May 10, 1965, p. 2.

17 Mink, "Remarks," May 10, 1965.

18 John Mink, "Diaries," August 13, 1965, MP R 2637.

19 John Mink, "Diaries," August 24, 1965.

20 John Mink, "Diaries," August 24, 1965.

21 Patsy T. Mink, "Remarks relating to Vietnam," August 25, 1965, MP 508/1.

22 Mink, "Remarks relating to Vietnam."

23 Mink, "Remarks relating to Vietnam."

24 Mink, "Remarks relating to Vietnam."

25 Mink, "Remarks relating to Vietnam."

26 "The Vietnam War: Military Statistics," Gilder Lehrman Institute of American History, https://www.gilderlehrman.org.

27 General William C. Westmoreland, the commander of US forces in Viet Nam, and Henry Cabot Lodge, the US ambassador to the RVN, also attended.

28 John Mink, "Diaries," February 6, 1965.

29 John Mink, "Diaries," February 27, 1965.

30 John Mink, "Diaries," February 27, 1965.

31 "Democratic Study Group Celebrates," *Roll Call*, August 12, 1965, MP 755/11.

32 "News Release," March 1, 1967, MP 508/3.

33 Office of William F. Ryan, "Press Release," February 28, 1967, MP 508/3.

34 Office of William F. Ryan, "Press Release."

35 Office of William F. Ryan, "Press Release."

36 Pope John XXIII, "Pacem in Terris," April 11, 1963.

37 William D. Laffler, "U.S. Businessmen to Peace Meeting," [no title], May 21, 1967, MP 517/2; Marquis Childs, "Apostles of Peace Start a Dialogue," *Washington Post*, May 22, 1967, MP 517/2.

38 Patsy T. Mink, "I believe that I am invited . . . ." Handwritten Statement, MP 517/3.

39 Theodore H. Draper, "A Special Supplement: Vietnam; How Not to Negotiate," *New York Review of Books*, May 4, 1967.

40 John Mink, "Diaries," March 21, 1968.

41 John Mink, "Diaries," March 18, 1968.

42 John Mink, "Diaries," March 21, 1968.

43 "Patsy Mink Gives Address by Phone," *Honolulu Star-Bulletin*, June 8, 1968, p. A-12, MP 758/2.

44 John Mink, "Diaries," January 19, 1969.

45 John Mink, "Diaries," January 19, 1969.

46 Office, Chief of Legislative Liaison, Department of the Army, "Memorandum for Members of Congress," November 23, 1969, MP 511/10.

47 Patsy T. Mink, "Letter to William E. Miller," December 17, 1969, MP 511/10.

48 Patsy T. Mink, "Statement concerning the Lt. Calley Verdict," April 1971, MP 508/10.

49 Patsy T. Mink, "Speech," in *Congressional Record*, April 22, 1971, E3357, MP 508/10.

50 Mink, "Speech," in *Congressional Record*.

51 Mink, "Speech," in *Congressional Record*.

52 Mink, "Speech," in *Congressional Record*.

53 Mink, "Speech," in *Congressional Record*, E3358.

54 Patsy T. Mink, "After Ten Years . . . ," [n.d.], p. 3, MP 509/1.

55 Michael Liu, Kim Geron, and Tracy Lai, *The Snake Dance of Asian American Activism: Community, Vision, and Power* (Lanham, MD: Lexington Books, 2008); Daryl Joji Maeda, *Rethinking the Asian American Movement* (New York: Routledge, 2011).

56 Yen Le Espiritu, *Asian American Panethnicity: Bridging Institutions and Identities* (Philadelphia: Temple University Press, 1992).

57 R. W. Apple, "Lessons from the Pentagon Papers," *New York Times*, June 23, 1996.

58 Zarnow, *Battling Bella*.

59 Patsy T. Mink, "Remarks concerning Resolution of Censure for President Nixon," MP 497/9.

60 Jessica M. Frazier, *Women's Antiwar Diplomacy during the Vietnam War Era* (Chapel Hill: University of North Carolina Press, 2017); Mary Hershberger, *Traveling to Vietnam: American Peace Activists and the War* (Syracuse, NY: Syracuse University Press, 1988); Swerdlow, *Women Strike for Peace*; Judy Tzu-Chun Wu, *Radicals on the Road: Internationalism, Orientalism, and Feminism during the Vietnam Era* (Ithaca, NY: Cornell University Press, 2013).

61 John Mink, "Diaries," April 23, 1972.

62 John Mink, "Diaries, April 27, 1972.

63 Donald R. Dana, "Letter to Mink," April 25, 1972, MP 510/4.

64 Dana, "Letter to Mink."

65 Patsy T. Mink, "Letter to Donald R. Dana," May 2, 1972, MP 510/4.

66 Shola Lynch, dir., *Unbought and Unbossed* (2004); Winslow, *Shirley Chisholm*.

67 John Mink, "Diaries," April 10, 1972.

68 John Mink, "Diaries," June 24, 1972.

69 Mink, "Diaries," June 24, 1972.

"YOU MUST BE A WOMEN'S LIBBER"

1 "Welcome Is Urged for Mississippi's Vote Protest Group," *Washington Post*, January 3, 1965, p. D22.

2 "Letter to Martin Luther King, Jr.," January 7, 1965, MP 74/9.

3 "Letter to Martin Luther King, Jr."

4 "Letter to Martin Luther King, Jr."; Phyllis Segal, "Memo to Delegation of Women to Chairman Larry O'Brien," MP 684/15.

5 Patsy T. Mink, "Equal Rights for Women—A National Priority," Testimony before the Committee on National Priorities of the Democratic Policy Council, April 30, 1970, MP 682/4; Christopher Lydon, "Role of Women Sparks Debate by Congresswoman and Doctor," *New York Times*, July 26, 1970; Nancy L. Ross, "The Leadership Potential of Women," *Washington Post*, July 29, 1970, p. B1.

6 Letters to my father, July 30 and 31, 1970, MP R2636.

7 Patsy T. Mink, Letter to Allen Trubitt, October 18, 1971, MP 685/1; Malcolm Barr, "Isle Democrats Get 'Worst' Reform Rating," *Honolulu Star-Bulletin*, October 14, 1971, MP 685/4.

8 Gerry Keir, "Isle Boycott of Demo National Meet Weighed," *Honolulu Advertiser*, October 7, 1971, MP 685/4.

9 "Nomination and Election of the President and Vice President of the United States, including the Manner of Selecting Delegates to National Political Conventions," Report prepared for the Office of the Secretary of the Senate (Washington, DC: US Government Printing Office, 1972), pp. 87–88.

10 Gerry Keir, "Demo 'Reform' Rules Basis of Isle Challenge," *Honolulu Advertiser*, May 24, 1972, MP 685/1; Patsy T. Mink, Memo to the Credentials Committee, 1972 Democratic National Convention, MP 685/1.

11 "Clean Sweep for Burns Forces," *Honolulu Advertiser*, May 13, 1968, p. 1.

12 James S. Burns, Memo to Patricia Roberts Harris, Acting Chair, Credentials Committee, MP 685/2.

13 Hawaii Women's Political Caucus, Memo to the Credentials Committee concerning the Proper Delegation to Represent the State of Hawai'i at the 1972 Democratic National Convention, May 27, 1972, MP 685/1.

14 Frank C. Newman, "Findings of Fact," MP 685/2.

15 "A 'Surprise' for Hawaii," *Honolulu Advertiser*, June 23, 1972; Gerry Keir, "Hawaii Demos Back Down, Name Woman to Committee," *Honolulu Advertiser*, June 24, 1972. Both in MP 685/5.

16 Warren Weaver, "3 Slate Challenges Lost by Reformers," *New York Times*, June 28, 1972.

17 Eileen Shanahan, "Caucus to Seek Equal Number of Women Convention Delegates," *New York Times*, November 10, 1971.

18 Henry Willis, "Patsy Mink's Name May Go on Ballot," *Eugene Register-Guard*, August 16, 1971.

19 Becky Little, "'Unbought and Unbossed': Why Shirley Chisholm Ran for President," December 4, 2018, History.com website.

CHAPTER 4. A FEMINIST LEGISLATOR

1 Lesbian feminists called for women-identified women, meaning women who sought love, companionship, and political support from other women. Some also promoted the creation of lesbian-separatist communities. Adrienne Rich, "Com-

pulsory Heterosexuality and Lesbian Existence," in *Blood, Bread, and Poetry* (New York: Norton, 1994). Also see Emily K. Hobson, *Lavender and Red: Liberation and Solidarity in the Gay and Lesbian Left* (Oakland: University of California Press, 2016).

2 Socialist feminists examined how the free-market system relied upon gendered wage disparity as well as the unpaid and oftentimes invisible labor that women performed for their families. This analysis posited that achieving gender equality necessitated transforming the economic organization of capitalist society.

3 Maylei Blackwell, *¡Chicana Power! Contested Histories of Feminism in the Chicano Movement* (Austin: University of Texas Press, 2011); Benita Roth, *Separate Roads to Feminism: Black, Chicana, and White Feminist Movements in America's Second Wave* (Cambridge: Cambridge University Press, 2003); Kimberly Springer, *Living for the Revolution: Black Feminist Organizations, 1968–1980* (Durham, NC: Duke University Press, 2005).

4 Describing Mink as a woman of color, an Asian American, or a feminist to characterize her politics utilizes categories that emerged after she already entered the US Congress. Activists conceptualized, named, and promoted these collective identifications, particularly from the mid- to late 1960s onward. Mink's sense of identity, given her upbringing in Hawai'i, and her politics, preceded these categories. However, Mink also worked synergistically with these new political movements, given her beliefs in racial and gender equality.

5 Roth, *Separate Roads to Feminism*; Springer, *Living for the Revolution*; Thompson, "Multiracial Feminism."

6 Stephanie Gilmore and Sara Evans, *Feminist Coalitions: Historical Perspectives on Second-Wave Feminism in the United States* (Urbana: University of Illinois Press, 2008); Stephanie Gilmore, ed., *Feminist*; Sandoval, "U.S. Third World Feminism"; Anne M. Valk, *Radical Sisters: Second-Wave Feminism and Black Liberation in Washington, D.C.* (Champaign: University of Illinois Press, 2010).

7 Pierce, "Capitol Feminism," p. 4.

8 Curwood, "Black Feminism on Capitol Hill."

9 "Patsy, 2 Colleagues Call for Equal Gym Rights," *Honolulu Advertiser*, February 7, 1967, MP 694/5.

10 Albert Thomas, "Letter to Dear Colleagues," March 25, 1965, MP 694/5.

11 Jack Anderson, "These Congresswomen Say the Men of the House Are Unfair," April 23, 1967, MP 694/5.

12 "Fight Belle Bars: Gals Muscle In on House Gym," *Detroit News*, February 7, 1967, 5; and Tom Stewart, "Patsy Seeking to Exercise Woman's Right to Exercise," *Hawaii Tribune Herald*, February 7, 1967.

13 Anderson, "These Congresswomen."

14 Anderson, "These Congresswomen."

15 Anderson, "These Congresswomen."

16 Edith Green, "Letter," April 4, 1973, p. 5, MP 244/3.

17 Green, "Letter," p. 1.

18 National Women's Political Caucus, "History: Early History," https://www
.nwpc.org.

19 "Gym-Dandy Congress Gals," *Daily News*, February 7, 1967, p. 3; and "3 Find Gym
in House Only for Him, Not Her," *New York Times*, February 7, 1967, MP 694/5.

20 Patsy T. Mink, "Equal Rights for Women: A National Priority," *Congressional
Record*, June 1, 1970, MP 678/8.

21 Mink, "Equal Rights for Women."

22 Mink, "Equal Rights for Women."

23 Mink, "Equal Rights for Women."

24 Transcript of Patsy T. Mink Testimony, Committee on National Priorities, Democratic National Council, April 30, 1970, p. 50, MP 678/8.

25 Transcript of Patsy T. Mink Testimony.

26 Transcript of Patsy T. Mink Testimony, p. 51.

27 Transcript of Patsy T. Mink Testimony.

28 Clare Crawford, "Fear of Female Hormones Wrapped in Power: Democrats Feud
over Women's Place," *Washington Daily News*, July 29, 1970, MP 678/7.

29 Christopher Lydon, "Doctor Asserts Women Are Unfit for Top Jobs," *New York
Times*, July 26, 1970, MP 678/7.

30 Edgar Berman, Letter to Patsy T. Mink, July 14, 1970, MP 677/6.

31 Nancy L. Ross, "Democrat Hits Views of Berman," *Washington Post*, July 30, 1970,
MP 678/7.

32 Ross, "Democrat Hits Views of Berman."

33 "Patsy Mink Wins Battle with Doctor over Hormones," *Honolulu Star-Bulletin*,
August 1, 1970, MP 678/7.

34 "Her Side of It!" *Honolulu Star-Bulletin*, July 28, 1970, MP 678/7.

35 John P. MacKenzie, "Carswell Repudiates '48 Speech Supporting 'White Supremacy,'" *New York Post*, January 22, 1970, MP 389/2.

36 MacKenzie, "Carswell Repudiates."

37 "Hits Carswell on Women's Rights Case," *New York Post*, January 1970, MP 389/2.

38 Katherine Turk, *Equality on Trial: Gender and Rights in the Modern American
Workplace* (Philadelphia: University Pennsylvania Press, 2016).

39 Patsy T. Mink, "Statement in Opposition in the Confirmation of G. Harrold
Carswell to the Supreme Court of U.S. before the Senate Committee on Judiciary,"
January 27, 1970, MP 389/1.

40 Mink, "Statement in Opposition," p. 1.

41 Ellen Lee, "Patsy Takemoto Mink's Trailblazing Testimony against a Supreme
Court Nominee," *Atlantic Monthly*, September 16, 2018.

42 Mink, "Statement in Opposition," p. 5.

43 Mink, "Statement in Opposition," pp. 5–6.

44 Mink, "Statement in Opposition," p. 6.

45 Mink, "Statement in Opposition."

46 Mink, "Statement in Opposition," pp. 9–10.

47 "New Hearings for Woman in Carswell Case," *Honolulu Star-Bulletin*, March 2, 1970, MP 389/2.

48 Patsy T. Mink, "Notecards," MP 560/4.

49 Mink, "Notecards."

50 Mink, "Notecards."

51 Patsy T. Mink, "Federal Legislation to End Discrimination against Women," *Valparaiso University Law Review* (1971): 397–98.

52 Julie C. Suk, *We the Women: The Unstoppable Mothers of the Equal Rights Amendment* (New York: Skyhorse, 2020).

53 Mink, "Federal Legislation," p. 400.

54 Patsy T. Mink, "Remarks relating to Supplementary Educational Programs in Day Care Centers," January 21, 1969, MP 71/1.

55 Patsy T. Mink, "Statement to the Joint Hearing of the House Subcommittee on Select Education, Senate Subcommittee on Children and Youth, Senate Subcommittee on Employment, Poverty, and Migratory Labor concerning the Child and Family Services Act," March 3, 1975, MP 72/2.

56 Ronald Takaki, *Pau Hana: Plantation Life and Labor in Hawaii* (Honolulu: University of Hawaiʻi Press, 1983).

57 Mink, "Statement."

58 John Mink, "Notecard," MP 560/4.

59 Mary Dublin Keyserling, Letter to Patsy T. Mink, May 26, 1967, MP 68/7.

60 Organizers formed "the National Committee for the Day Care of Children," and "the Day Care and Child Development Council of America" as well as a variety of locally based organizations. Parents and educators created experimental childcare facilities and developed early childhood education curriculum. Advocates also publicized childcare practices in other countries and sometimes traveled internationally to observe and bring back lessons from these initiatives.

61 "A Woman's Right," *Voice for Children Newsletter* 3:2 (February 1970): 7, MP 66/5.

62 "A Woman's Right."

63 Richard Nixon, "President Nixon's Veto Message (S. 2007)," December 9, 1971, p. 2, MP 66/8.

64 Patsy T. Mink, Telex to Frank Fasi, December 3, 1971, MP 69/9.

65 Roberta M. Hall and Bernice R. Sandler, *The Classroom Climate: A Chilly One for Women?* (1982) and Bernice R. Sandler and Roberta M. Hall, *The Campus Climate Revisited: Chilly for Women Faculty, Administrators, and Graduate Students* (1986), both published by Association of American Colleges (now AAC&U), Washington, DC.

66 Kristina Chan, "The Mother of Title IX: Patsy Mink," *The She Network* (sponsored by the Women's Sports Foundation), April 24, 2012. https://www.womenssports-foundation.org.

67 Susan Kakesako, "Memo," July 10, 1975, MP 185/2.

68 42 Cong. Rec. 23123 (1975).

69 Bella Abzug et al., "Dear Colleague," MP 184/7.

70 Julianne Densen-Gerber, "Letter," August 8, 1975, MP 184/7.

71 Eric Wentworth, "Ban on Sex Integration Is Rejected," *Washington Post*, July 19, 1975, MP 184/7.

72 *Congressional Record—House*, June 8, 1972, H 20282.

73 US House of Representatives, 92nd Congress, 2nd Session, Roll Call #451, June 8, 1972.

74 Patsy T. Mink, Letter to Marjean Davis, January 27, 1972, MP 168/8.

75 *Congressional Record—House*, December 4, 1974, H 11282.

76 Patsy T. Mink, "Letter," December 30, 1974, MP 183/10.

77 Susan Ware, *Title IX: A Brief History with Documents* (Boston: Bedford/ St. Martin's, 2007).

78 Maegan Olmstead, "Title IX and the Rise of Female Athletes in America," *The She Network* (sponsored by the Women's Sports Foundation), September 2, 2016. https://www.womenssportsfoundation.org.

79 Ware, *Title IX*, pp. 1–2.

80 "Celebrating the 30th Anniversary of Title IX," *Congressional Record*, June 19, 2002, MP 1693/6.

81 Nancy K. Schlossberg, "Testimony before the Committee on Labor and Public Welfare, Subcommittee on Education, U.S. Senate," October 17, 1973, p. 1, MP 194/5.

82 Bernice Sandler, "Testimony before the Subcommittee on Equal Opportunities," July 25, 1973, p. 3, MP 194/5.

83 Sandler, "Testimony."

84 Sandler, "Testimony," pp. 2–3.

85 Schlossberg, "Testimony," p. 2.

86 Susan Kakesako, "Memo to Patsy T. Mink," October 11, 1973, MP 205/2.

87 Arlene Horowitz, "Memo to Patsy T. Mink," November 9, 1973, MP 205/2.

88 Patsy T. Mink, "Letter to Ruth Whitney," April 30, 1974, MP 205/5.

89 Patsy T. Mink, "Remarks in the U.S. House of Representatives concerning ESEA Extension Bill's Provision on Women's Educational Equity," MP 205/5.

90 Andrew Fishel, "Chapter III: Sex Discrimination and the Legislative Process; The Enactment of the Women's Educational Equity Act," Draft Manuscript, MP 207/3. It was eventually published in Andrew Fishel and Janice Pottker, *National Politics and Sex Discrimination in Education* (Lanham, MD: Lexington Books, 1977).

91 Fishel, "Chapter III," 1.

92 Fishel, "Chapter III."

93 Fishel, "Chapter III," 7.

94 Fishel, "Chapter III," cover page.

95 Judy Tzu-Chun Wu, "Envisioning the National Women's Conference: Patsy Takemoto Mink and Pacific Feminism," in *Suffrage at 100: Women in American Politics since 1920*, ed. Stacie Taranto and Leandra Zarnow (Baltimore, MD: John Hopkins University Press, 2020, 257–73).

96 The "territories" represented at the conference were American Samoa, the District of Columbia, Guam, Puerto Rico, Virgin Islands, and the Trust Territories. American Women on the Move: National Women's Conference, November 18–21, 1977, Houston, Texas, conference program.

97 Robert Self, *All in the Family: The Realignment of American Democracy since the 1960s* (New York: Hill & Wang, 2012).

98 Jeanne Quan, "Congresswoman Patsy Takemoto Mink," in *Asian Women* (Berkeley: University of California, 1971; Asian American Studies Center, University of California, Los Angeles, 3rd printing, October 1975), 106.

MAUCH CHUNK

1 "Jim Thorpe, Pa., No Tourist Lure, May Change Name," *New York Times*, July 22, 1964, p. 36; John Luciew, "Town of Jim Thorpe Is Ready to Fight for Identity It Adopted 56 Years Ago," *Patriot-News*, August 2, 2010.

2 "Rep. Patsy T. Mink to Address Dinner-Dance at Flagstaff," *Jim Thorpe Times-News*, MP 702/4.

3 Event ticket, MP 702/4.

4 Trump won 65 percent of the vote in Jim Thorpe's Carbon County in 2016 and 2020.

5 "Foes Single Out Mink in Protest," *Honolulu Star-Bulletin*, April 9, 1975, MP 326/7.

6 "2 Mine Groups Boycott Hawaii," *Honolulu Advertiser*, April 30, 1975, MP 326/7.

7 Federal Bureau of Investigation teletype, October 24, 1975, MP 327/1.

8 Memo from SAC, Albany, to Director, FBI, MP 327/1.

CHAPTER 5. A PACIFIC ENVIRONMENTALIST

1 Patsy T. Mink, "Letter to T. C. Yim," April 15, 1976, MP 244/9.

2 Friends for Patsy Mink for U.S. Senate Committee, "Patsy T. Mink, U.S. Congress: Hawaii's Concerned Voice for Our Environment," n.d., MP 232/3.

3 Leilani Nishime and Kim D. Hester Williams, *Racial Ecologies* (Seattle: University of Washington Press, 2018) and Laura Pulido, "Rethinking Environmental Racism: White Privilege and Urban Development in Southern California," *Annals of the Association of American Geographers* 90:1: 12–40.

4 Elizabeth M. DeLoughrey, "The Myth of Isolates: Ecosystem Ecologies in the Nuclear Pacific," *Cultural Geographies* 20:2: 167–84.

5 Philip D. Carter, "Aleutian Wildlife Preserve New Nuclear Test Site," *Honolulu Star-Bulletin* April 13, 1969, D-8, MP 51/3.

6 US Department of Energy, National Nuclear Security Administration, "Surface Completion Report for Amchitka Underground Nuclear Test Sites: Long Shot, Milrow, and Cannikan," Revision No. 1 (September 2006), p. 13.

7 Cynthia Enloe, *Bananas, Beaches, and Bases: Making Feminist Sense of International Politics* (Berkeley: University of California Press, 2000); Vernadette Vicuna Gonzalez, *Securing Paradise: Tourism and Militarism in Hawai'i and the Philippines* (Durham, NC: Duke University Press, 2013); Setsu Shigematsu and Keith

L. Camacho, *Militarized Currents: Toward a Decolonized Future in Asia and the Pacific* (Minneapolis: University of Minnesota Press, 2010).

8 Mansel G. Blackford, "Environmental Justice, Native Rights, Tourism, and Opposition to Military Control: The Case of Kahoʻolawe," *Journal of American History* 91 (2004): 544–71, and *Pathways to the Present: U.S. Development and Its Consequences in the Pacific* (Honolulu: University of Hawaiʻi Press, 2007); Catherine Ceniza Choy and Judy Tzu-Chun Wu, eds., *Gendering the Trans-Pacific World* (Leiden, The Netherlands: Brill, 2017); David Igler, "Commentary: Re-Orienting Asian American History through Transnational and International Scales," *Pacific Historical Review* 76, no. 4 (2007): 611–14; and *The Great Ocean: Pacific Worlds from Captain Cook to the Gold Rush* (New York: Oxford University Press, 2013); Paul Lyons and Ty P. Kāwika Tengan, "Introduction: Pacific Currents," *American Quarterly* 67:3 (2015): 545–74; Matt K. Matsuda, *Pacific Worlds: A History of Seas, Peoples, and Cultures* (Cambridge: Cambridge University Press, 2018); Viet Thanh Nguyen and Janet Hoskins, *Transpacific Studies: Framing an Emerging Field* (Honolulu: University of Hawaiʻi Press, 2014); Gary Okihiro, *Island World: A History of Hawaiʻi and the United States* (Berkeley: University of California Press, 2008), and *Pineapple Culture: A History of the Tropical and Temperate Zones* (Berkeley: University of California Press, 2009); Yasuko Takezawa and Gary Y. Okihiro, *Trans-Pacific Japanese American Studies: Conversations on Race and Racializations* (Honolulu: University of Hawaiʻi Press, 2016).

9 US Atomic Energy Commission, "The Use of Amchitka Island for Underground Testing," [1969], p. 1, MP 47/folio: "Amchitka Background Information, 1969–1972, n.d. (1 of 2)."

10 US Atomic Energy Commission, "The Use of Amchitka Island for Underground Testing," pp. 3–4.

11 W. H. Kupau, Letter to Atomic Energy Commission, September 24, 1969, reprinted in *Congressional Record—House*, H 8704 (September 30, 1969), MP 47/folio: "Amchitka Background Information, 1969–1972, n.d. (1 of 2)."

12 "Earthquakes and Nuclear Tests: Playing the Odds on Amchitka," *Science*, August 22, 1969, p. 773.

13 Dale Trenhail, Telegram to Mink, November 3, 1971, MP 49/folio: "Amchitka Correspondence, Hawaii, 1971, Nov. (1 of 2)."

14 Patsy T. Mink, Letter to Richard M. Nixon, September 24, 1969, MP 50/1.

15 Patsy T. Mink, Letter to Rogers B. Morton, October 13, 1971, MP 50/2.

16 Patsy T. Mink, Letter to Richard M. Nixon, June 23, 1971, MP 50/2.

17 Association on American Indian Affairs, Statement, July 26, 1971, MP 49/folio: "Amchitka Correspondence, General, 1971, Sept.–Nov."

18 Association on American Indian Affairs, Statement.

19 "Prehistoric Settlement: Sure Victim If Amchitka Shot Goes," *Tundra Times*, August 4, 1974; and John P. Cook, Letter to Patsy T. Mink, September 29, 1971, MP 50/2.

20 "Prehistoric Settlement."

21 Kaare R. Gundersen and Paul K. Bienfang, "Kahoolawe: The Unique Potential of the Hawaiian Island, Kahoolawe, as a Site for a Central Thermonuclear Power Plant and Aqua-and Agricultural Development," Proposal [1970] in MP, 128/3; "Defense Navy Kahoolawe Island Background Information, 1969–1976"; and Patsy T. Mink, Letter to E. Hebert, June 17, 1974, MP 128/6.

22 Patsy T. Mink, Letter to John H. Chafee, September 30, 1969, MP 128/5.

23 Mink, Letter to John H. Chafee.

24 Mink, Letter to John H. Chafee.

25 Writing on behalf of the secretary of the navy, Paul Nitze explained to Mink that new preventative measures had been instituted as a result of the mistake. These included requiring all pilots "to familiarize themselves during daylight hours with the target before they are permitted to make a night bombing attack" (Paul Nitze, Letter, October 9, 1965, MP 129/9). The fact that such an obvious protocol was not instituted prior to the mistake reveals how few safety precautions the navy required, even as it conducted war games in the proximity of the people in Hawai'i.

26 Nitze, October 9, 1965.

27 Jean King, Letter to Patsy Mink, July 19, 1976, MP 129/1.

28 Patsy T. Mink, Press Release, September 16, 1969, MP 116/5.

29 Mink, Press Release.

30 Yen Le Espiritu, *Body Counts: The Vietnam War and Militarized Refugees* (Oakland: University of California Press, 2014).

31 Simeon Man, *Soldiering through Empire: Race and the Making of the Decolonizing Pacific* (Oakland: University of California Press, 2018).

32 Mink, Letter to Edward Hebert.

33 Director FBI, Teletype to Legat Tokyo, October 25, 1975, MP 327/1.

34 Jimmy Carter, "Letter to Patsy Mink," August 15, 1977, MP 327/2.

35 Yu-Fang Cho, "Nuclear Diffusion: Notes toward Reimagining Reproductive Justice in a Militarized Asia Pacific," *Amerasia Journal* 41:3 (2015): 2–24, and "Remembering Lucky Dragon, Re-membering Bikini: Worlding the Anthropocene through Transpacific Nuclear Modernity," *Cultural Studies* 33:1 (2019): 122–46.

36 Gerald R. Ford, "Press Release," May 20, 1975, MP 329/6.

37 Patsy T. Mink, "Remarks in Support of the Environmental Education Act in the U.S. House of Representatives," August 3, 1970, MP 231/4.

38 Jim Rathlesberger, "Special Alert: Conference Report on Surface Mining," May 7, 1975, MP 329/6.

39 Duncan Spencer, "Strip Mining . . . It All Depends on the Eye of the Beholder," *Washington Star*, April 21, 1975, MP 327/3.

40 Spencer, "Strip Mining."

41 Spencer, "Strip Mining."

42 Lynda G. Hubbard, "Letter to Patsy Mink," March 27, 1975, MP 328/4.

43 Spencer, "Strip Mining."

44 Ben A. Franklin, "Strip Mine Workers Protest in Capital," *New York Times*, April 8, 1975, MP 327/3.

45 "That's the Question: To Strip or Not . . . ," *Kentucky Coal Journal,* June 1975, 4, MP 327/4.

46 Gerardo Jovinelli, "Mink's Stand on Strip-Mining Praised," *Honolulu Star-Advertiser,* May 9, 1975, MP 327/4.

47 Patsy T. Mink, "Statement," May 8, 1973, MP 330/5.

48 Mink, "Statement," May 8, 1973.

49 Trask, *From a Native Daughter*; Candace Fujikane and Jonathan Y. Okamura, eds., *Asian Settler Colonialism: From Local Governance to the Habits of Everyday Life in Hawai'i* (Honolulu: University of Hawai'i Press, 2008).

50 Jodi Byrd, *The Transit of Empire: Indigenous Critiques of Colonialism* (Minneapolis: University of Minnesota Press, 2011), p. xix.

51 Dean Itsuji Saranillio, *Unsustainable Empire: Alternative Histories of Hawai'i Statehood* (Durham, NC: Duke University Press, 2018), p. 21.

52 "Let's Not Holler before We Are Hurt," *Garden Island,* March 24, 1965, section I, p. 4, MP 129.

53 "The Matter of Kaula Rock," *Garden Island,* March 31, 1965, Section I, p. 4, MP 129.

54 Patsy T. Mink, Letter to Gerald K. Machida, May 31, 1975, MP 128/9; also see Patsy T. Mink, Letter to Robert J. Shallenberger, June 22, 1974; Patsy T. Mink, Letter to Peter J. Connally, July 16, 1974, MP 128/9.

55 Maile Arvin, Eve Tuck, and Angie Morrill, "Decolonizing Feminism: Challenging Connections between Settler Colonialism and Heteropatriarchy," *Feminist Formations* 25:1 (Spring 2013): 8–34.

56 Noelani Goodyear-Ka'ōpua, "Introduction," in *A Nation Rising: Hawaiian Movements for Life, Land, and Sovereignty,* ed. Noelani Goodyear-Ka'ōpua, Ikaika Hussey, and Erin Kahunawaika'ala Wright (Durham, NC: Duke University Press, 2014).

57 Osorio, "Hawaiian Souls," in *A Nation Rising,* p. 146.

58 Mansel G. Blackford, *Pathways to the Present: U.S. Development and Its Consequences in the Pacific* (Honolulu: University of Hawai'i Press, 2007), p. 30.

59 This occupation represented the first of a series of five protests conducted in 1976 and 1977.

60 Patsy T Mink, Letter to Noel Gayler, December 17, 1974, MP 129/3.

61 Mink, Letter to Noel Gayler.

62 Mink, Letter to Noel Gayler.

63 Anne Harpham, "Kahoolawe Holdouts Arrested: 2 Claim Isle 'Desecrated,'" *Honolulu Advertiser,* January 7, 1976, MP 129/1.

64 Harpham, "Kahoolawe Holdouts Arrested."

65 Harpham, "Kahoolawe Holdouts Arrested."

66 Harpham, "Kahoolawe Holdouts Arrested."

67 Osorio, "Hawaiian Souls," p. 144.

68 Osorio, "Hawaiian Souls," p. 150.

69 Harpham, "Kahoolawe Holdouts Arrested."

70 Harpham, "Kahoolawe Holdouts Arrested," p. 137.

71 Clara Ku, Mary Lee, Rose Wainui, Lani Kapuni, and William Wainui Sr., Letter to Patsy Mink, March 15, 1976, MP 129/3.

72 Ku et al., Letter to Patsy Mink.

73 Ku et al., Letter to Patsy Mink.

74 Ku et al., Letter to Patsy Mink.

75 Ku et al., Letter to Patsy Mink.

76 Patsy T. Mink, Letter to Ralph S. Wentworth Jr., April 15, 1976, MP 129/3.

77 Osorio, "Hawaiian Souls," p. 148.

78 Osorio, "Hawaiian Souls," pp. 148–49.

79 Osorio, "Hawaiian Souls," p. 148.

80 Charles K. Maxwell, Letter to Patsy T. Mink, July 27, 1973, MP 128/7.

81 Patsy T. Mink, Letter to Inez Ashdown, February 19, 1976, MP 129/1. A number of Native Hawaiian organizations participated in the movement and differed in their political strategies and goals as well.

82 Patsy T. Mink, "Telex to Secretary Sidney K E Leong," July 9, 1973, MP 345/5.

83 Patsy T. Mink, Letter to Pearl Kaauwai, June 24, 1974, MP 345/8.

84 Mink, Letter to Pearl Kaauwai.

85 Patsy T. Mink, Letter to Rene La Plante, July 9, 1974, MP 345/8.

86 Mink, Letter to Rene La Plante.

87 Lisa Kahaleole Hall, "Strategies of Erasure: U.S. Colonialism and Native Hawaiian Feminism," *American Quarterly* 60:2 (June 2008): 273–80.

88 Hall, "Strategies of Erasure."

89 Hall, "Strategies of Erasure."

90 Hall, "Strategies of Erasure."

91 Patsy T. Mink, Letter to the Council of Hawaiian Organizations, January 27, 1976, MP 129/1.

92 Mink lost the campaign for the US Senate in 1976. She continued her interest in Kahoʻolawe, however, into the 1990s. Native Hawaiian activist accounts of the late 1970s point to Daniel Inouye as the leading political figure who sometimes aided and at other times worked at cross-purposes with the Kanaka Maoli.

93 For an example of the ongoing trans-Pacific antimilitarism feminist activism, please see the International Women's Network against Militarism (IWNAM).

PART III. OCEANS AND ISLANDS

  1 Epigraphs are from "DRAFT—WCF Statement for Senate press conference," MP 817/7; and Brian Sullam, "Patsy Mink: A Farewell to House Work," *Hawaii Observer*, August 3, 1976, pp. 6–7, MP 815/6.

  2 M. J. Rymsza-Pawlowska, *History Comes Alive: Public History and Popular Culture in the 1970s* (Chapel Hill: University of North Carolina Press, 2017) and Natasha Zaretsky, *No Direction Home: The American Family and the Fear of National Decline, 1968–1980* (Chapel Hill: University of North Carolina Press, 2007).

  3 "Women's Campaign Fund" brochure, MP 817/7.

  4 "DRAFT—WCF Statement for Senate press conference."

5 Jerry Burris, "Two Less Active Than Colleagues in Senate Races," *Honolulu Star-Bulletin Advertiser*, December 14, 1975, MP 815/6.

6 "Inouye Sees 'Blood' in Senate Primary," *Honolulu Star-Bulletin*, August 11, 1975, MP 815/6.

7 "Matsunaga, Mink Both Plan to Run," *Honolulu Star-Bulletin*, August 16, 1975, MP 815/6.

8 Marcia Reyonlds, "No Blood-Bath: Mink Won't Spar Directly with Matsunaga," *Hawaii Tribune-Herald*, August 22, 1976, MP 815/6.

9 "Matsunaga Apologizes for Error in Political Flier," *Garden Island*, October 1, 1976, MP 815/6.

10 "Press Release," MP 816/2.

11 "Press Release."

12 "Matsunaga, Mink Judged on Voting," *Hawaii Tribune-Herald*, February 15, 1976, MP 815/6.

13 "Matsunaga, Mink Judged on Voting."

14 "Matsunaga, Mink Judged on Voting."

15 John E. Simonds, "How Matsunaga and Mrs. Mink Voted," *Honolulu Star-Bulletin*, October 31, 1975, MP 815/6.

16 "Patsy T. Mink, Democrat, Candidate for U.S. Senator, Announcement Statement," MP 816/2.

17 Sullam, "Patsy Mink: A Farewell to House Work."

18 Simonds, "How Matsunaga and Mrs. Mink Voted."

19 John Lau, "Matsunaga Meets Mink," *Maui Hi-Notes*, June 4, 1976, p. 3, MP 815/6.

20 Lau, "Matsunaga Meets Mink."

21 Lau, "Matsunaga Meets Mink."

22 "Patsy T. Mink, Democrat, Candidate for U.S. Senator, Announcement Statement."

23 Sullam, "Patsy Mink: A Farewell to House Work."

24 Sullam, "Patsy Mink: A Farewell to House Work."

25 Sullam, "Patsy Mink: A Farewell to House Work."

26 "Primaries Roundup: Rep. Patsy Mink Loses in Hawaii," [newspaper title unknown], October 4, 1976, MP 815/6.

27 "Primaries Roundup."

VIOLATED

1 Letter from Marluce Bibbo, M.D., DES Program Director, Chicago Lying-In Hospital, dated January 29, 1976, MP R2631.

2 Mink (Gwendolyn) v. University of Chicago, 727 F. 2d 1112, No. 83–179 (August 1983), "Statement of the Case (appellate filing)," MP R2633/9.

3 Mink (Patsy Takemoto) et al. v. University of Chicago and Eli Lilly & Company, No. 77 C 1431, Amended Complaint (April 3, 1978), MP R2631.

4 John V. Long, "Memorandum of Conference with Dr. Marluce Bibbo, DES Program Director at the Chicago Lying-In Hospital" (April 5, 1976), MP R2632/4.

5 Marlene Cimons, "DES Suit Highlights Victims' Plight," *Los Angeles Times*, May 5, 1977, p. 35.

6 Patsy T. Mink letter to Sidney Wolfe, MD (September 24, 1976), MP R2632/4.

7 Lynda Collins and Heather McLeod-Kilmurray, "Toxic Battery: A Tort for Our Time?" *Tort Law Review* 16 (2008): 135–48.

8 Patsy Takemoto Mink et al. v. University of Chicago et al., 460 F. Supp. 713, No. 77C 1431, Memorandum Opinion (March 17, 1978).

9 Letter from Marian M. Hubby, DES Project Coordinator, Chicago Lying-In Hospital (July 23, 1982), MP R2635/3.

10 Collins and McLeod-Kilmurray, "Toxic Battery"; Christopher McAuliffe, "Resurrecting an Old Cause of Action for a New Wrong: Battery as a Toxic Tort," *Boston College Environmental Affairs Law Review* 20:2 (1993): esp. 285–89.

11 Around the time of our DES litigation, legal controversies burned regarding employers' restrictions on pregnant or potentially pregnant women's employment to protect fetuses from toxic exposure. One such controversy began as a class action in 1984 and made its way to the Supreme Court in 1991, United Autoworkers v. Johnson Controls, 499 U.S. 187 (1991). For a discussion of the issues in the moment, see Mary E. Becker, "From Muller v. Oregon to Fetal Vulnerability Policies," *University of Chicago Law Review* 53 (1986): 1219–73.

CHAPTER 6. A PROGRESSIVE POLITICAL VISION

1 "Carter and Human Rights, 1977–1981," *Milestones: 1977–1980*, Office of the Historian, Department of State, US Government.

2 Claiborne Pell, "The Nomination of Frederick Irvine, of Rhode Island, a Foreign Service Officer of Class 1, to Be Assistant Secretary of State for Oceans and International Environmental and Scientific Affairs," *Hearing before the Committee on Foreign Relations, United States Senate*, March 23, 1976 (Washington, DC: US Government Printing Office, 1976), p. 5, MP 921/10.

3 "Bureau of Oceans and International Environmental and Scientific Affairs" flow chart, January 11, 1977, MP 919/8; Douglas Woo, "Senate Unit Oks Mink," *Honolulu Advertiser*, March 23, 1977, MP 924/2; Akio Konoshima, "For Mink, It's a Happy Interlude," *Honolulu Star-Bulletin*, April 17, 1977, MP 924/2.

4 Woo, "Senate Unit Oks Mink."

5 Dorothy Austin, "The Working Woman: Career Road Rough for Mink," *Milwaukee Sentinel*, December 2, 1977, MP 924/2.

6 Austin, "The Working Woman."

7 Austin, "The Working Woman."

8 William V. Shannon, "Guessing Game," *New York Times*, December 7, 1976, MP 924/2.

9 Shannon, "Guessing Game."

10 Shannon, "Guessing Game."

11 Shannon, "Guessing Game."

12 Shannon, "Guessing Game."

13 Nancy Hicks, "Feminists Critical of Carter on Jobs," *New York Times*, February 8, 1977, MP 921/10.

14 Shannon, "Guessing Game."

15 "Mink's Good Job," *Honolulu Advertiser*, January 8, 1977, MP 924/2.

16 "Mink's Good Job."

17 Saleem H. Ali and Helena Voinov Vladich, "Environmental Diplomacy," *The Sage Handbook of Diplomacy*, 601, edited by Costas M. Constantinou, Pauline Kerr, and Paul Sharp (Los Angeles: Sage, 2016).

18 Mink, "Confirmation Testimony," Question 2, p. 4, March 22, 1977, MP 921/6.

19 "Mink: Everybody 'Counts' in Politics," *Pacific Citizen*, February 17, 1978, p. 1, MP 924/3.

20 "Patsy Takemoto-Mink Urges JAs to Shun Socializing for Activism," *Rafu Shimpo*, February 9, 1978, MP 924/3.

21 Patsy T. Mink, Note to Tom, October 6, 1977, MP 920/4.

22 Mink, Note to Tom.

23 Patsy T. Mink, "Speech at Federal Day Awards Luncheon," June 24, 1977, p. 9, MP 924/10.

24 Patsy T. Mink, "Speech," United Nations Environment Program, Nairobi, Kenya, May 11, 1977, MP 924/10.

25 Mink, "Speech," United Nations Environment Program.

26 Cyrus Vance, Outgoing Telegram, "Presidential Message on Whales," June 1977, MP 926/4.

27 "The Bowhead Controversy: Leadership or Hypocrisy," *Washington Post*, September 28, 1977, A9, MP 924/2.

28 Iwao Fujita and Hideo Omura, "The Whaling Industry of Japan and International Whaling," September 12, 1977, MP 926/4.

29 S. Lynn Sutcliffe, "Letter to Cyrus Vance," October 10, 1977, MP 926/4.

30 Sutcliffe, "Letter to Cyrus Vance."

31 Patsy T. Mink, Memo regarding Telephone Conversation with Doug Bennett, October 12, 1977, MP 926/4.

32 Donald M. Fraser, "Letter to Cyrus Vance," October 14, 1977, MP 926/4. Fraser also wrote a letter to the editor of the *Washington Post*.

33 Patsy T. Mink, Memo regarding Telephone Conversation with Dave Keaney, October 12, 1977, MP 926/4.

34 David O. Hill, "Letter to Anne Wickham," October 13, 1977, MP 926/4.

35 Hill, "Letter to Anne Wickham."

36 David R. Brower, "Letter to Patsy Mink," September 28, 1977, MP 926/4.

37 Patsy T. Mink, "Letter to Donald M. Fraser," October 31, 1977, MP 926/4.

38 Mink, "Letter to Donald M. Fraser."

39 Carl Zimmerman, "Mink Defends Whale Quota," *Honolulu Star-Bulletin*, December 30, 1977, MP 924/2.

40 Zimmerman, "Mink Defends Whale Quota."

41 Pell, "The Nomination of Frederick Irvine," p. 5.

42 Pell, "The Nomination of Frederick Irvine," p. 13.

43 Hubert Humphrey, "The Nomination of Frederick Irvine, of Rhode Island, a Foreign Service Officer of Class 1, to Be Assistant Secretary of State for Oceans and International Environmental and Scientific Affairs," *Hearing before the Committee on Foreign Relations, United States Senate*, March 23, 1976 (Washington, DC: US Government Printing Office, 1976), p. 12, MP 921/10.

44 T. Keith Glennan, "Technology and Foreign Affairs: A Report by Dr. T. Keith Glennan to Deputy Secretary of State Charles W. Robinson," December 1976, MP 924/5.

45 Glennan, "Technology and Foreign Affairs," pp. vii and 39.

46 Glennan, "Technology and Foreign Affairs," p. 35.

47 Glennan, "Technology and Foreign Affairs."

48 Glennan, "Technology and Foreign Affairs."

49 Patsy T. Mink, Note to Tom, August 19, 1977, MP 919/10.

50 Patsy T. Mink, Letter to Thomas M. Franck, February 8, 1977, MP 922/9.

51 Patsy T. Mink, Letter to Anita Steckel, August 27, 1977, MP 922/9.

52 Patsy T. Mink, Note to Tom, October 28, 1977, MP 920/1.

53 Patsy T Mink, Note to Bob, undated, MP 920/5.

54 Patsy T. Mink, Note to Bob, December 13, 1977, MP 920/1.

55 Mink, Note to Bob, December 13, 1977.

56 Mink, Note to Bob, December 13, 1977.

57 Christine Keiner, *Deep Cut: Science, Power, and the Unbuilt Interoceanic Canal* (Athens: University of Georgia Press, 2020).

58 Patsy T. Mink, Statement beginning with "The Congress was absolutely correct in 1973," MP 924/8.

59 Mink, Statement beginning with "The Congress was absolutely correct in 1973."

60 Bill Drummond, "Asian-Americans Seeking Policy Clout," *Honolulu Advertiser*, May 5, 1978, A-13, MP 924/3.

61 Patsy T. Mink, "We Can Meet the Challenge of the Right Wing—and Win!" *ADA World* 33:4 (November 1978): 2, MP 858/1.

62 George McGovern, "A Vision of Positive Government," June 17, 1978, p. 1, MP 857/6.

63 . McGovern, "A Vision of Positive Government," p. 2.

64 McGovern, "A Vision of Positive Government," p. 6.

65 McGovern, "A Vision of Positive Government," p. 1.

66 McGovern, "A Vision of Positive Government."

67 McGovern, "A Vision of Positive Government."

68 "Agenda," June 15, 1978, MP 854/4.

69 Mink, "We Can Meet," p. 1.

70 Mink, "We Can Meet," p. 2.

71 "A Litany of Regression," *ADA World* 33:4 (November 1978): 2.

72 Leon Shull, "Memorandum," December 28, 1978, MP 853/5.

73 Leon Shull, "Memorandum," January 13, 1979, MP 853/5.

74 Americans for Democratic Action, "The FY 1980 Budget," Adopted Resolution, January 14, 1979, MP 853/5.

75 "ADA President Attacks Carter Budget, Press Conference Scheduled," January 22, 1979, MP 853/5.

76 Patsy T. Mink, "Memorandum," April 13, 1979, MP 852/6.

77 Mink, "Memorandum," April 13, 1979.

78 Patsy T. Mink, "Letter," April 13, 1979, MP 852/6.

79 Patsy T. Mink, Letter to Cardiss Collins, June 25, 1980, MP 852/9.

80 Mink, Letter to Cardiss Collins.

81 Mink, Letter to Cardiss Collins.

82 Patsy T. Mink, "Speech" beginning with "In Biblical times," MP 852/3.

83 Mink, "Speech" beginning with "In Biblical times."

84 "ADA Opposes Anti-Abortion Riders," July 31, 1980, MP 857/6.

85 "ADA Opposes Anti-Abortion Riders."

86 Maya, Letter to Leon Shull, June 15, 1978, MP 852/5.

87 Maya, Letter to Leon Shull.

88 Jesse Jackson, "How We Respect Life Is the Over-Riding Moral Issue," *Right to Life News* (January 1977).

89 George Simson, Letter to Patsy T. Mink, December 10, 1983, MP 853/3.

90 Patsy T. Mink, Letter to George Simson, December 28, 1983, MP 853/3.

91 Mink, Letter to George Simson.

92 Patsy T. Mink, "Banquet Speech" to the Independent Voters of Illinois, June 9, 1979, MP 853/4.

93 Mink, "Banquet Speech."

94 Mink, "Banquet Speech."

95 Mink, "Banquet Speech."

96 Stina Santiestevan, "Patsy Mink—ADA Ambassador, Lobbyist, Organizer, Fund Raiser & President Extraordinary," *ADA World* 36:2 (Summer 1981): 23, MP 858/2.

97 John Kenneth Galbraith, Letter to Mink, July 9, 1981, MP 853/2.

98 Walter Chilman, Letter to Patsy T. Mink, June 24, 1980, MP 852/9.

99 Vega H. Rohne, Letter to Patsy T. Mink, April 11, 1981, MP 853/1.

100 Patsy T. Mink, "Notes," MP 852/3.

101 Barbara A. Koppe, "Liberals Lament Reagan's Election," *Milwaukee Journal*, November 17, 1980, MP 852/10.

CHAPTER 7. PRACTICING "WE" POLITICS

1 Karleen Chinen, "The Political Animal in Patsy Mink: Waipahu Is Home for the Veteran Democrat," *Hawaii Herald: Hawaii's Japanese American Journal*, "Waipahu Issue," February 3, 1989, p. 9, MP 908/4.

2 Victor Lipman, "Patsy Mink," *Honolulu Magazine*, May 1985, p. 42, MP 908/1.

3 Chinen, "The Political Animal in Patsy Mink," p. 9.

4 Chinen, "The Political Animal in Patsy Mink."

5 Chinen, "The Political Animal in Patsy Mink."

6 Chinen, "The Political Animal in Patsy Mink."

7 Election Coverage, "Honolulu," *Honolulu Star-Bulletin*, November 3, 1982, MP 907/6.

8 Election Coverage, "Honolulu."

9 Election Coverage, "Honolulu."

10 Election Coverage, "Honolulu."

11 Patsy T. Mink, "Toward Open City Government for Honolulu," *Honolulu Advertiser*, January 4, 1983, MP 907/7.

12 Mink, "Toward Open City Government."

13 Mink, "Toward Open City Government."

14 "Mink's Views on Council Issues," *Honolulu Star-Bulletin*, January 27, 1983, MP 907/7.

15 "Mink's Views."

16 "Trust Patsy Mink," Political Ad, *Honolulu Advertiser*, September 15, 1988, MP 908/4.

17 "Patsy Mink's Candidacy," *Honolulu Star-Bulletin*, April 7, 1982, MP 907/6.

18 Mink, "Toward Open City Government."

19 Michael Schmicker, "Putting on the Gloves: The Mink Council Has Come Out Fighting on the Thorny Issue of Affordable Housing," [Publication not identified], n.d., MP 908/4.

20 Mink, "Toward Open City Government."

21 "Patsy Takemoto Mink: Woman Pioneer in Politics," *Ka Huliau*, April–May 1984, p. 11, MP 907/8.

22 "Putting on the Gloves."

23 Jerry Burris, "Scrimmage Is On for Title of Hizzoner of Honolulu," *Honolulu Advertiser*, May 8, 1988, MP 908/4.

24 Peter Wagner, "Councilman Iwase Opens His Drive to Topple Mayor Fasi," *Honolulu Star-Bulletin*, March 11, 1988, MP 908/4.

25 Dan Boylan, "Going after Frank—Part II," *Honolulu Magazine*, June 1988, p. 31, MP 908/4.

26 "Fasi's Victory Surprises City Council: Members Find Prospects 'Interesting,'" *Honolulu Star-Bulletin*, November 7, 1984, MP 907/8.

27 Patsy T. Mink, "City Council Lauds Tight, No-Nonsense Budget," *MidWeek*, February 27, 1985, MP 908/1.

28 Mark Matsunaga, "5 Give Up on Bid to Oust Mink," *Honolulu Advertiser*, April 5, 1985, MP 908/1.

29 Matsunaga, "5 Give Up on Bid to Oust Mink."

30 Mark Matsunaga and Jerry Buris, "3 Dems Convert to GOP," *Honolulu Advertiser*, June 7, 1985, MP 908/1.

31 Matsunaga and Buris, "3 Dems Convert to GOP."

32 Matsunaga and Buris, "3 Dems Convert to GOP."

33 Matsunaga and Buris, "3 Dems Convert to GOP."

34 Mark Matsunaga, "Mink Wants 3 Defectors Recalled," *Honolulu Advertiser*, June 8, 1985, MP 908/1.

35 "City Council: 3 'Outsiders' May Be Given Leadership Posts," *Honolulu Advertiser*, April 8 1983, MP 907/7.

36 T. W. Keithley, "Arrogance of Power," *Honolulu Advertiser*, October 2, 1985 [misdated 1982], MP 907/6.

37 Donna Reyes, "Narvaes Calls Recall Drive 'Sour Grapes': Mink Canvassing against Defectors," *Honolulu Advertiser*, June 9, 1985, MP 908/1.

38 Reyes, "Narvaes Calls Recall Drive 'Sour Grapes.'"

39 Matsunaga, "Mink Wants 3 Defectors Recalled."

40 Gregg K. Kakesako, "Ariyoshi: Vote Is Vindication," *Honolulu Star-Bulletin*, October 7, 1985, MP 908/1.

41 Kakesako, "Ariyoshi: Vote Is Vindication."

42 Boylan, "Going after Frank—Part II."

43 Boylan, "Going after Frank—Part II."

44 Boylan, "Going after Frank—Part II."

45 Donna Reyes, "Big Debate Turns into Mini-Talks," *Honolulu Advertiser*, September 11, 1986, MP 908/3.

46 Reyes, "Big Debate Turns into Mini-Talks."

47 A. A. Smyser, "Don't Count Mink Out," *Honolulu Star-Bulletin*, June 30, 1986, MP 908/2.

48 Smyser, "Don't Count Mink Out."

49 Boylan, "Going after Frank—Part II," p. 30.

50 Smyser, "Don't Count Mink Out."

51 Gerry Keir, "Bornhorst Ahead, but Dem Race for Mayor Wide Open," *Honolulu Advertiser*, September 11, 1988, MP 908/4.

52 Keir, "Bornhorst Ahead."

53 Jerry Burris, "Bornhorst Gets Backing of Isle Women's Group," *Honolulu Advertiser*, May 27, 1988, MP 908/4.

54 Keir, "Bornhorst Ahead."

55 Gerry Keir, "Mink Barely Cuts into Bornhorst Lead," *Honolulu Advertiser*, September 14, 1988, MP 908/4.

56 Keir, "Mink Barely Cuts into Bornhorst Lead."

57 Chinen, "The Political Animal in Patsy Mink," p. 9.

58 Chinen, "The Political Animal in Patsy Mink," p. 9.

59 Chinen, "The Political Animal in Patsy Mink," p. 9.

60 Chinen, "The Political Animal in Patsy Mink," p. 9.

61 Chinen, "The Political Animal in Patsy Mink," p. 9.

PART IV. A NATIONAL RECKONING

1 Epigraphs are from Patsy Takemoto Mink, "In Celebration of the 30th Anniversary of Title IX of the Education Amendments of 1972," *Congressional Record*, July 17, 2002, 148: 97, H 4860, 4862, 4863, MP 1692/9; and Patsy Takemoto Mink, Speech appearing in *Patsy Mink: Ahead of the Majority*, DVD, directed by Kimberlee Bassford (Women Make Movies, 2008).

2 Lisa Levenstein, *They Didn't See Us Coming: The Hidden History of Feminism in the Nineties* (New York: Basic Books, 2020).

3 Levenstein, *They Didn't See Us Coming*.

"NOBODY AROUND HERE IS INTERESTED"

1 "Patsy Mink Swearing-In," Clip of House Session, September 27, 1990, C-SPAN.

2 Julia Ernst, "The Congressional Caucus for Women's Issues: An Inside Perspective on Lawmaking by and for Women," *Michigan Journal of Gender and Law* 12:2 (2006): 190–274.

3 From 1985 to 1991, Cardiss Collins (D-Illinois) was the lone Black woman in the House of Representatives.

4 Price Waterhouse v. Hopkins, 490 U.S. 228 (1989); Wards Cove Packing Co. v. Atonio, 490 U.S. 642 (1989); Martin v. Wilks, 490 U.S. 755 (1989); Lorance v. AT&T Technologies, 490 U.S. 900 (1989); Patterson v. McLean Credit Union, 491 U.S. 164 (1989).

5 Griggs v. Duke Power Co., 401 U.S. 424 (1971).

6 David Lauter, "Civil Rights Bill Vetoed by Bush: Job Bias," *Los Angeles Times*, October 23, 1990.

7 Civil Rights Act of 1866, 42 USC 1981.

8 Steven A. Holmes, "Senate to Vote Today on Override of Bush's Veto of Civil Rights Bill," *New York Times*, October 24, 1990; Lynn Ridgeway Zehrt, "Twenty Years of Compromise: How the Caps on Damages in the Civil Rights Act of 1991 Codified Sex Discrimination," *Yale Journal of Law and Feminism* 25:2 (2013): 249–318.

9 NOW Legal Defense and Education Fund, "Dear Members," February 26, 1991, MP 2069/3.

10 Hearings on H.R.1, the Civil Rights Act of 1991: Hearings before the H. Comm. on Education and Labor, 102d Congress (1991) (hearings were held on February 27 and March 5, 1991), p. 26.

11 Joan Biskupic, "Bill Passes House, Not Muster: Next Chance Is in the Senate," *Congressional Quarterly*, June 8, 1991, pp. 1498–1503.

12 "Testimony by Rep. Patsy T. Mink before the Senate Judiciary Committee on the Nomination of Judge Clarence Thomas," MP 1072/8.

13 Nina Totenberg, "A Timeline of Clarence Thomas–Anita Hill Controversy as Kavanaugh to Face Accuser," National Public Radio, September 23, 2018.

14 Annys Shin and Libby Casey, "Anita Hill and Her 1991 Congressional Defenders to Joe Biden: You Were Part of the Problem," *Washington Post*, November 22, 2017; Naureen Khan, "These Congresswomen Protested Clarence Thomas: Here's What They're Doing about Kavanaugh," *Vice News*, October 1, 2018.

15 Laura Kurtzman, "Case a Lightning Rod for Women's Complaints of Mistreatment on the Job," *San Jose Mercury News*, October 11, 1991, p. 1A.

16 Patricia Schroeder quoted in Shin and Casey, "Anita Hill and Her 1991 Congressional Defenders to Joe Biden."

17 "Thomas Outcome Haunts Females in Congress," *Sunday Star Bulletin & Advertiser*, October 27, 1991, MP 1072/7.

18 Civil Rights Act of 1991, Pub. L. No. 102–166, § 102(b)(3).

19 Quoted in Zehrt, "Twenty Years of Compromise," fn. 329, p. 299.

20 Civil Rights Act of 1991, Roll Call #386, November 7, 1991.

21 *Congressional Record*, 102nd Congress, 1st Sess., November 7, 1991, p. H9510.

CHAPTER 8. THE THIRD WAVE

1 Rebecca Walker, "Becoming the Third Wave," *Ms. Magazine* 41 (1992).

2 Patsy T. Mink, "Statement in Opposition in the Confirmation of G. Harrold Carswell to the Supreme Court of U.S. before the Senate Committee on Judiciary," January 27, 1970, MP 389/1.

3 Patsy T. Mink, "Testimony before the Senate Judiciary Committee on the Nomination of Judge Clarence Thomas," September 20, 1991, p. 1, MP 2074/1.

4 Mink, "Testimony."

5 Mink, "Testimony," p. 2.

6 Mink, "Testimony."

7 Mink, "Testimony," p. 3.

8 Mink, "Testimony."

9 Mink, "Testimony," p. 4l

10 Mink, "Testimony."

11 Mink, "Testimony."

12 Marjorie J. Spruill, *Divided We Stand: The Battle over Women's Rights and Family Values That Polarized American Politics* (New York: Bloomsbury, 2017) and Karissa Haugeberg, *Women against Abortion: Inside the Largest Moral Reform Movement of the Twentieth Century* (Urbana: University of Illinois Press, 2017).

13 Mink, "Testimony," p. 1.

14 Mink, "Testimony," pp. 4, 2.

15 Patsy T. Mink, "Letter to Aileen Wood," October 31, 1991, MP 1072.1.

16 Mink, "Letter to Aileen Wood."

17 Mink, "Letter to Aileen Wood."

18 Mink, "Letter to Aileen Wood."

19 Mink, "Letter to Aileen Wood."

20 Maureen Dowd, "The Senate and Sexism," *New York Times*, October 8, 1991, p. A21.

21 Catherine Stimpson, "Letter to New York Times," October 20, 1991, requoted in "Congressional Inquisition," *Women's International Network News*, MP 2073/9.

22 "Thomas' Confirmation Galvanizes the Public," *Honolulu Advertiser*, October 16, 1991, MP 1072/8.

23 Patsy T. Mink, "Letter to Maxine Slade," October 21, 1991, MP 1072/7.

24 Patsy T. Mink, "Letter to Sharon Anolik," June 11, 1992, MP 1072/7.

25 Linda Hosek, "Mink Backs Attack on Ovarian Cancer," *Hawaii Star Bulletin*, March 4, 1991, MP 1049/1.

26 Congressional Caucus for Women's Issues, "The Women's Health Equity Act of 1991," MP 1049/1.

27 Janet LaFleur and Nan Foster Burns McClellan, "National Experts in Biomedical and Behavioral Sciences Calls for Multidisciplinary 'Centers of Excellence' for Research on Women's Health," December 6, 1990, p. 1, MP 1049/1.

28 LaFleur and McClellan, "National Experts."

29 Laura Lorenzen, "Minutes from February 6 Executive Committee Meeting," February 7, 1991, MP 1049/1.

30 Lorenzen, "Minutes."

31 "The Women's Health Equity Act of 1991," p. 3.

32 Patsy T. Mink, "Letter to Paul and Vanessa Gamboda," September 24, 1992, MP 1063/5.

33 Lorenzen, "Minutes."

34 "Family and Medical Leave Act of 1993, Draft Copy of Report," 103rd Congress, 1st Session, MP 1222/1.

35 "Family and Medical Leave Act," p. 2.

36 "Family and Medical Leave Act," p. 2.

37 Mack McLarty, Letter to William D. Ford and Christopher J. Dodd, January 5, 1993, MP 1222/1.

38 "Congresswoman Mink Joins President Clinton at White House Bill Signing Ceremony," February 5, 1993, MP 1222/3.

39 Patsy T. Mink, "Introduction of the Gender Equity in Education Act," *Congressional Record*, April 21, 1993, 139:51, H1953, MP 1151/10.

40 Mink, "Introduction."

41 Laura Efurd, Memo to Patsy Mink, February 28, 1992, MP 1151/7.

42 Congressional Caucus for Women's Issues, "Dear Colleague" letter, June 22, 1993, MP 1151/5.

43 Congressional Caucus for Women's Issues, "Dear Colleague" letter.

44 Congressional Caucus for Women's Issues, "Dear Colleague" letter.

45 Laura Efurd, "Meeting Report," August 3, 1992, MP 1151/3.

46 American Association of University Women Program and Policy Department, "Fact Sheet: Women's Educational Equity Act & Office of Women's Equity H.R. 1743," June 1993, MP 1151/3.

47 Laura Efurd, "Memo," April 8, 1993, MP 1151/3.

48 Efurd, "Memo."

49 Efurd, "Memo."

50 "Kelso's Retirement," *Honolulu Star-Bulletin*, April 22, 1994, MP 1138/4.

51 "Kelso's Retirement."

52 "Kelso's Retirement."

53 Mink, "Introduction."

54 Gary Peller, "For Girls, High School Sometimes Feels like Tailhook," *Washington Post*, July 25, 1993, MP 1151/9.

55 Mink, "Introduction."

56 Mink, "Introduction."

57 Patsy T. Mink, Letter to Schroeder, October 26, 1994, MP 1289/9.

58 Mink, Letter to Schroeder.

59 Beverly LaHaye, "Legislative Action Memorandum," September 1993, MP 1151/5.

60 LaHaye, "Legislative Action Memorandum."

61 Heritage Foundation, "Mandate for Leadership," January 1981, MP 1152/3.

62 "Feminist Network Fed by Federal Grants," *Conservative Digest*, April 1982, p. 26, MP 1152/3.

63 "Feminist Network."

64 "Feminist Network."

65 "Feminist Network."

66 Judy Mann, "Two-Faced," September 14, 1983, MP 1153/3.

67 Christina Hoff Sommers, "The Myth of Schoolgirls' Low Self-Esteem," *Wall Street Journal*, October 3, 1994, MP 1151/9.

68 Patsy T. Mink, Letter to A. S. Warinner, October 31, 1994, MP 1151/10.

69 Patsy T. Mink, *Congressional Record* 140, MP 1151/10.

70 Mink, *Congressional Record* 140.

71 Mink, *Congressional Record* 140.

WELFARE IS A WOMEN'S ISSUE

1 Aida Hurtado names the problem in *The Color of Privilege: Three Blasphemies on Race and Feminism* (Ann Arbor: University of Michigan Press, 1996), 135, 166; Mary Hawkesworth demonstrates the problem in the congressional context in "Congressional Enactments of Race-Gender: Toward a Theory of Raced-Gendered Institutions," *American Political Science Review* 97:4 (November 2003): 529–50.

2 Center for American Women in Politics, "History of Women in the U.S. Congress." https://cawp.rutgers.edu.

3 Hawkesworth, "Congressional Enactments of Race-Gender."

4 Late-twentieth-century welfare reform is explained and my mother's role described in Felicia Kornbluh and Gwendolyn Mink, *Ensuring Poverty: Welfare Reform in Feminist Perspective* (Philadelphia: University of Pennsylvania Press, 2018).

5 See, especially, David Ellwood, *Poor Support: Poverty in the American Family* (New York: Basic Books, 1988).

6 Materials related to the conference can be found in MP 1373.

7 "Statement on President Clinton's Welfare Reform Proposal," June 14, 1994, signed by forty-one Democrats, MP 1382/8.

8 Memo to Laura Efurd, February 14, 1994, MP 1257/2.

9 William J. Eaton, "Shalala Revives 'Murphy Brown' Pregnancy Issue," *Los Angeles Times*, July 15, 1994.

10 Jason DeParle, "From Pledge to Plan: The Campaign to End Welfare," *New York Times*, July 15, 1994, p. 1.

11 Women's Committee of One Hundred, "Women's Pledge on Welfare Reform: Eliminating Poverty for Women and Their Children," MP 1879/7.

12 Special Orders is speaking time reserved for congressmembers after legislative business has been completed but before the House adjourns for the day.

13 Gwendolyn Mink, "Feminist Policy Scholars Intervene in Welfare Debate," *Social Justice* 30:4 (2003): 108.

14 "Cosponsors of Mink Welfare Substitute (as of March 17, 1995)," MP 1878/6.

15 Bruce Horovitz, "Hooters' Most Embarrassing Moments over 30 Years," *USA Today*, October 4, 2013. https://www.usatoday.com

16 See, e.g., Nancy Johnson's (R-Connecticut) "Fathers Count Bill," HR 3073, U.S. House of Representatives, 106th Congress, 1st Session, 1999. The bill was cosponsored by senior Ways and Means Committee Democrats Bob Matsui (D-California) and Pete Stark (D-California), among others.

17 National Organization for Women, "Fathers Count Act of 1999, HR 3073: Talking Points," November 9, 1999, MP 1654/4.

18 Women's Committee of One Hundred, "An Immodest Proposal: Rewarding Women's Work to End Poverty," March 23, 2000, GMP.

19 Felicia Kornbluh and I discuss this feminist legislative initiative at length in *Ensuring Poverty*, chapter 6.

20 Katherine Seligman, "Sex, Justice on Trial at Santa Cruz," *San Francisco Examiner*, July 25, 1993, p. 1.

21 Office for Civil Rights, Department of Education, Letter to Maria Blanco, Esq., Equal Rights Advocates, June 15, 1994, GMP.

22 Gwendolyn Mink, "Misreading Sexual Harassment Law," *New York Times*, op-ed, March 30, 1998, p. A17; Gwendolyn Mink, "Should the Truth Faze Feminists?" *New York Times*, op-ed, August 18, 1998, p. A19.

CHAPTER 9. BATTLING POVERTY

1 "Welfare Reform: The Gender Issue," *Congressional Record* 140:27 (March 11, 1994), MP 1255/5.

2 The phrase was introduced on October 23, 1991, at a speech at Georgetown University. Jason DeParle, "The Clinton Welfare Bill Begins Trek in Congress," *New York Times*, July 15, 1994, MP 1256/6.

3 "Welfare Reform: The Gender Issue."

4 "Welfare Reform: The Gender Issue," H1311.

5 Nancy Gibbs, "When Young, Single Women Have Children, It Almost Guarantees They Will Be Poor; Can Welfare Reform Break the Pattern?" *Time Magazine*, June 20, 1994, p. 27.

6 Kornbluh and Mink, *Ensuring Poverty*, p. 58.

7 Patsy T. Mink, "Statement by U.S. Representative Patsy T. Mink (2nd-HI) Subcommittee on Human Resources House Committee on Ways and Means, H.R. 4498, The Job Start for America Act," July 27, 1994, MP 1256/2.

8 Dorothy Roberts credits a Black feminist caucus at a 1994 pro-choice conference for coining the term. Reproductive justice went beyond a focus on accessing birth control; the term encompassed "not only a woman's right not to have a child, but also the right to have children and to raise them with dignity in safe, healthy, and supportive environments. This framework repositioned reproductive rights in a political context of intersecting race, gender, and class oppressions." Dorothy Roberts, "Reproductive Justice, Not Just Rights," *Dissent*, Fall 2015.

9 "Entitlement Law and Legal Definition," U.S. Legal, https://definitions.uslegal.com.

10 Lynn Fujiwara, *Mothers without Citizenship: Asian Immigrant Families and the Consequences of Welfare Reform* (Minneapolis: University of Minnesota Press, 2008).

11 Vee Burke, "Time-Limited Welfare Proposals," Congressional Research Service Issue Brief, December 3, 1993, p. 10, MP 1256/3.

12 Fujiwara, *Mothers without Citizenship*, and Ira Katznelson, *When Affirmative Action Was White: An Untold History of Racial Inequality in Twentieth-Century America* (New York: Norton, 2006).

13 Burke, "Time-Limited Welfare Proposals," p. 2, and Fujiwara, *Mothers without Citizenship*.

14 Burke, "Time-Limited Welfare Proposals," p. 10.

15 "Women in the Labor Market," *Focus* 20:1 (Winter 1998–1999): 1.

16 Fujiwara, *Mothers without Citizenship*, p. 31.

17 "Welfare as We Know It," *New York Times*, June 19, 1994, MP 1256/7.

18 "United States: Population by Race," *CensusScope*.

19 Fujiwara, *Mothers without Citizenship*.

20 Eric Pianin, "Formerly United House Republicans Split over Welfare Reform Package," *Washington Post*, April 29, 1994, MP 1256/7.

21 "Also in Washington: Welfare Reform," *USA Today*, March 25, 1994, MP 1256/7.

22 *Official Report of the Nineteenth Annual Conference of Charities and Correction* (1892), 46–59. Reprinted in Richard H. Pratt, "The Advantages of Mingling Indians with Whites," *Americanizing the American Indians: Writings by the "Friends of the Indian," 1880–1900*, 260–71 (Cambridge, MA: Harvard University Press, 1973).

23 "National Association of Black Social Workers Position Statement on Trans-Racial Adoptions," September 1972, https://cdn.ymaws.com.

24 "The Harm in Family Welfare Caps," *New York Times*, June 9, 1994, MP 1255/6.

25 Vee Burke, "Information for Dear Colleague Letter on Welfare Reform," February 25, 1994, MP 1255/7.

26 "Welfare Reform: The Gender Issue," H1313.

27 "Mink Introduces Job Start for America Act: A Bill to Reform the Welfare System," News Release, May 25, 1994, MP 1256/7.

28 "Mink Introduces Job Start for America Act."

29 "Welfare Reform: The Gender Issue."

30 "Welfare Reform: The Gender Issue."

31 "Welfare Reform: The Gender Issue."

32 James M. Talent, Y. Tim Hutchinson, and Charles T. Canady, "Dear Colleague Letter," March 22, 1994, MP 1255/7; Mary McGrory, "Orphanage Idea Has Many Parents," December 13, 1994, MP 1256/6; Richard A. Cloward and Frances Fox Piven, "Punishing the Poor, Again: The Fraud of Workfare," *Nation*, May 24, 1993, MP 1256/6.

33 "Facts Related to Welfare Reform: Aid to Families with Dependent Children (AFDC)," US Department of Health and Human Services, June 1994, MP 1255/5.

34 Vee Burke, "Poverty and Welfare among Urban Children: A Fact Sheet," Congressional Research Service Report for Congress, February 17, 1994, MP 1256/3.

35 Jason DeParle, "Welfare Mothers Find Jobs Easy to Get but Hard to Hold," *New York Times*, October 24, 1994, MP 1256/6.

36 DeParle, "Welfare Mothers."

37 "The Threat to Welfare Reform," *New York Times*, May 2, 1994, MP 1255/6.

38 Patsy T. Mink's Statements for "Conference Report on H.R. 4, Personal Responsibility Act of 1995," December 21, 1995, *Congressional Record* 141:206, MP 1373/4.

39 Patsy T. Mink's Statements.

40 Patsy T. Mink, "Letter to Karen Young," December 27, 1995, MP 1373/4.

41 Patsy T. Mink, "Letter to Georgette Steven-Begley," April 14, 1994, MP 1255/8.

42 "Welfare Reform: The Gender Issue."

43 Patsy T. Mink, "Letter to George Stephanopoulos," April 9, 1994, MP 1255/5.

44 Patsy T. Mink, "Letter to David M. Douglas," February 5, 1994, MP 1255/8.

45 "Mink Introduces Job Start for America Act."

46 Patsy T. Mink, "Letter to Marie Kodelsky," November 28, 1994, MP 1255/3.

47 National Task Force on Violence against Women, "Dear Policymaker," February 1995, MP 1373/4.

48 National Task Force on Violence against Women, "Dear Policymaker."

49 National Task Force on Violence against Women, "Dear Policymaker."

50 Roberta Spalter-Roth, Heidi Hartmann, and Beverly Burr, Memorandum to Bonnie Dean, MP 1373/6.

51 "Women and Welfare Reform," Conference Schedule, MP 1373/6.

52 National Welfare Rights Union website.

53 "Our Story," Mi Casa Resource Center website.

54 Gwendolyn Mink, editor, *Women and Welfare Reform: Women's Poverty, Women's Opportunities, and Women's Welfare Conference Proceedings* (Washington DC: Institute for Women's Policy Research, 1994).

55 Laura Efurd, "Meeting Report," November 5, 1993, MP 1255/6.

56 Patsy T. Mink et al., "Dear Colleague," November 10, 1993, MP 1255/6.

57 Patsy T. Mink et al., "Dear William J. Clinton," November 23, 1993, MP 1255/6. All subsequent quotations in this paragraph are from this document.

58 William Claiborne, "On the Receiving End of Welfare Reform: Chicago Mothers Say Clinton Doesn't Understand the Problems They Face," *Washington Post National Weekly Edition*, April 18–24, 1994, MP 1256/7.

59 Claiborne, "On the Receiving End."

60 Claiborne, "On the Receiving End."

61 Claiborne, "On the Receiving End."

62 "About the Co-Sponsors of the December 15, 1995, Press Conference," MP 1379/7.

63 Committee of One Hundred, "Dear Friend," May 2, 1995, MP 1379/7.

64 Committee of One Hundred, "Dear Friend."

65 Committee of One Hundred, "Dear Friend."

66 Patsy T. Mink, "Letter to Lynn Phillips," October 17, 1995, MP 1373/4.

67 Mink, "Letter to Lynn Phillips."

68 Kent Weaver, "Old Traps, New Twists," *Brookings Review*, Summer 1994, p. 19, MP 1256/7.

69 Mink, "Letter to Lynn Phillips."

70 William Claiborne, "Immigrants' Benefits at Risk: House Alliance Wants Funds for Welfare Reform," *Washington Post*, March 24, 1994, MP 1257/1.

71 Fujiwara, *Mothers without Citizenship*, p. 22.

72 One Republican proposal would allow those seventy-five years or older to receive benefits, thereby increasing the age requirement before an immigrant could qualify for welfare. President Clinton's plan proposed extending the period, from three to five or ten years, during which sponsors would be financially responsible for immigrants.

73 Nancy Gibbs, "Cycle," *Time*, June 20, 1994, MP 1256/7.

74 Gibbs, "Cycle."

75 Patsy T. Mink et al., "Let's Not Finance Welfare Reform on the Backs of the Poor," February 28, 1994, MP 1255/6.

76 Mink et al., "Let's Not Finance Welfare Reform on the Backs of the Poor."

77 Mink et al., "Let's Not Finance Welfare Reform on the Backs of the Poor."

78 Kornbluh and Mink, *Ensuring Poverty*, p. xi.

79 Kornbluh and Mink, *Ensuring Poverty*.

80 Fujiwara, *Mothers without Citizenship*, p. xv.

81 Fujiwara, *Mothers without Citizenship*, p. xv.

"NO, WHERE ARE YOU *REALLY* FROM?"

1 Jay Matthews, "Economic Invasion by Japan Revives Worry of Racism," *Washington Post*, May 14, 1982.

2 Dana Frank, "Our History Shows There's a Dark Side to 'Buy American,'" *Washington Post*, January 30, 2017.

3 Frank Wu, "D.C. Officials React to Asian Bashing," *Asian Week*, March 28, 1997, p. 8.

4 *National Review* (cover), March 24, 1997.

5 E.g., "The Asian Connection," *Newsweek*, October 28, 1996, p. 24.

6 *Today Show*, March 21, 1997, transcript.

7 Brian Blomquist, "Asian-Americans Say Funds Scandal Spawns Stereotypes," *Washington Times*, March 13, 1997.

8 H.R. 34, "Illegal Foreign Contributions Act of 1998," US House of Representatives, *Congressional Record* (March 30, 1998), p. H1739 ff.

9 H.R. 34, "Illegal Foreign Contributions Act of 1998."

10 Law Professors' Letter on Campaign Finance Reform and the Rights of Legal Permanent Residents," March 20, 1998, reprinted in *Congressional Record* (March 30, 1998), p. H1741-2.

11 U.S. House of Representatives, 105th Congress, 2nd Session, Roll Call #82, March 30, 1998.

12 James Risen and Jeff Gerth, "Breach at Los Alamos: A Special Report," *New York Times*, March 6, 1999, p. A1.

13 James Brooke, "This Man Is the Talk of Los Alamos," *New York Times*, March 10, 1999, p. A6.

14 Walter Pincus, "Surrounding the Lee Case, Questions about Fairness," *Washington Post*, September 14, 2000, p. A4.

15 Karen Narasaki, Director, National Asian Pacific American Legal Consortium, Memorandum to Attorney General Janet Reno, January 30, 2000, MP 1618/5.

16 Patsy T. Mink, letter to Attorney General Janet Reno, January 7, 2000, MP 1618/5.

17 National Asian Pacific American Bar Association, Letters to Attorney General Janet Reno and President Bill Clinton, August 18, 1999; Patsy T. Mink, Letter to NAPABA, August 20, 1999, MP 1616/8.

18 Pincus, "Surrounding the Lee Case, Questions about Fairness."

19 Patsy T. Mink, "Investigation and Treatment of Wen Ho Lee," US House of Representatives, *Congressional Record*, October 12, 2000, 146:127, pp. H9880-H9883.

20 Steven A. Holmes. "Asian-American Is Named to Top Civil Rights Position," *New York Times*, June 12, 1997, p. B16.

21 Christopher Marquis, "Clinton Sidesteps Senate to Fill Civil Rights Enforcement Job," *New York Times*, August 4, 2000, p. A14.

22 Executive Order 13125, June 7, 1999, reprinted in *Federal Register*, 64:111, June 10, 1999.

23 President's Advisory Commission on Asian Americans and Pacific Islanders, *Asian Americans and Pacific Islanders: A People Looking Forward; Action for Access and Partnerships in the Twenty-First Century—Interim Report to the President and the Nation*, January 2001.

24 "The Times and Wen Ho Lee," *New York Times*, September 26, 2000.

25 Matthew Purdy, "The Making of a Suspect: The Case of Wen Ho Lee," *New York Times*, February 4, 2001, p. 1.

CHAPTER 10. THE COST OF BELONGING

1 Larry M. Eig, "The Right of Undocumented Alien Children to Basic Education: An Overview of *Plyler v. Doe*," *CRS Report for Congress*, October 21, 1994, MP 1345/4.

2 Phillip J. Cooper, "*Plyler* at the Core: Understanding the Proposition 187 Challenge," *Chicana/o Latina/o Law Review* 17:1 (1995): 64-87.

3 Dana Rohrabacher, "The Greatest Unfunded Mandate of All," March 21, 1994, MP 1145/8.

4 Norman Y. Mineta, Patsy T. Mink, Neil Abercrombie, and Robert T. Matsui, "Support Bilingual Education!" MP 1145/5.

5 Mineta et al., "Support Bilingual Education!"

6 Mineta et al., "Support Bilingual Education!"

7 "Vote No on the Roth Amendments: Support Local Control of Education!" March 8, 1994, MP 1145/5.

8 Jose E. Serrano, "Oppose the Rohrabacher Amendments to HR 6," March 2, 1994, MP 1145/5.

9 Joyce Vialet et al., "Immigration Legislation in the 104th Congress," *CRS Report for Congress*, August 16, 1995, MP 1145/4.

10 But the Contract Labor Law of 1885 and the nativist national-origins-quota laws of the 1920s exempted spouses and minor children from restrictions.

11 Howard L. Berman et al., "The Facts on Immigration #8: Is Your Child Part of Your Nuclear Family?" MP 1342/3.

12 Berman et al., "The Facts on Immigration #8."

13 Berman et al., "The Facts on Immigration #8."

14 Berman et al., "The Facts on Immigration #8."

15 Berman et al., "The Facts on Immigration #8."

16 Surprisingly, though, some of the Republican authors of this series of memos did end up voting to support the Smith Bill.

17 Patsy T. Mink, "Asian Pacific Americans Oppose Restrictions on Legal Immigration," March 15, 1996, MP 1344/2.

18 Mink, "Asian Pacific Americans Oppose Restrictions."

19 Mink, "Asian Pacific Americans Oppose Restrictions."

20 Organization of Chinese Americans, "Asian Pacific Americans Gather in D.C. to Defend Family Immigration: Congressional Representatives to Speak at Press Conference," February 29, 1996, MP 1344/2.

21 Organization of Chinese Americans, "Asian Pacific Americans Gather in D.C."

22 Federation of American Immigration Reform, "Doesn't Congress Realize How Times Have Changed?" MP 1342/3.

23 Federation of American Immigration Reform, "Doesn't Congress Realize?"

24 Patsy T. Mink, "Letter to Sylvia Boecker," February 26, 1996, MP 1341/5.

25 "Illegal Alien Resident Population," Department of Homeland Security, https://www.dhs.gov.

26 "Illegal Alien Resident Population." The undocumented population has more than doubled since the mid-1990s, and Asian immigrants constitute the fastest-growing group among both the documented and the undocumented. In 2020, the undocumented population is estimated at between 10.5 and 12 million. Elaine Kamarck and Christine Stenglein, "How Many Undocumented Immigrants Are in the United States and Who Are They?" November 12, 2019, *Policy 2020*, Brookings Institute. A 2017 study estimate that at least 1.7 million undocumented Asian

Americans live in the United States, constituting the fastest-growing undocumented population. "One out of Every 7 Asian Immigrants Is Undocumented," September 8, 2017, *Data Bits: A Blog for AAPI Data.*

27 Melinda Liu, "How to Play the Asylum Game, Immigration: The Chinese Have It Figured Out," *Newsweek*, August 2, 1993, p. 23.

28 Ginny Gong, National President of Organization of Chinese Americans, quoted in "OCA Opposes Clinton Administration Asylum Restrictions," July 27, 1993, MP 1245/5.

29 "The Organization of Chinese Americans Resolution on Immigration Policy Regarding Undocumented Aliens," passed by OCA General Membership, July 17, 1993, MP 1245/5.

30 "The Organization of Chinese Americans Resolution."

31 Mink, "Asian Pacific Americans Oppose Restrictions on Legal Immigration."

32 Paul W. Lee, "Letter to Orrin G. Hatch," February 27, 1996, MP 1344/2.

33 Lee, "Letter to Orrin G. Hatch."

34 Patsy T. Mink, "Letter to Chester E. Whitcomb," September 14, 1994, MP 1343/6.

35 Michelle Alexander, *The New Jim Crow: Mass Incarceration in the Age of Colorblindness* (New York: New Press, 2010), p. 71.

36 "H.R. 3355—Violent Crime Control and Law Enforcement Act of 1994," 103rd Congress (1993–1994).

37 Alex Press, "#MeToo Must Avoid 'Carceral Feminism,'" *Vox*, February 1, 2018; Emily Thuma, *All Our Trials: Prisons, Policing, and the Feminist Fight to End Violence* (Champaign: University of Illinois Press, 2019).

38 Nancy Whittier, "Carceral and Intersectional Feminism in Congress: The Violence against Women Act, Discourse, and Policy," *Gender and Society* 30:5 (October 2016): 791–818.

39 Whittier, "Carceral and Intersectional Feminism," 793.

40 Whittier, "Carceral and Intersectional Feminism."

41 Whittier, "Carceral and Intersectional Feminism."

42 United States v. Morrison, 529 U.S. 598 (2000).

43 Whittier, "Carceral and Intersectional Feminism," 800.

44 Patsy T. Mink, "Letter to Carol C. Lee," October 1, 1994, MP 1220/3.

45 Diane Craven, "Female Victims of Violent Crime," *Bureau of Justice Statistics: Selected Findings*, December 1996, MP 1350/11.

46 Craven, "Female Victims of Violent Crime," pp. 1, 2.

47 Craven, "Female Victims of Violent Crime," p. 2. "About 9% of female victims reported that the offender was a relative; 29% an intimate (which includes spouse or ex-spouse, boyfriend or girlfriend, and ex-boyfriend or ex-girlfriend); and 40%, an acquaintance."

48 Craven, "Female Victims of Violent Crime."

49 The DOJ utilized statistics from the National Crime Victimization Survey (NCVS), conducted by the Bureau of Justice Statistics in conjunction with the Census Bureau, as well as the FBI's Uniform Crime Reporting (UCR) system.

50 Patsy T. Mink, "Letter to Victoria D. Peters," June 4, 1996, MP 1350/14.

51 Patsy T. Mink, "Letter to Carol C. Lee," September 4, 1996, MP 1350/10.

52 The states included Alaska, Delaware, Hawaiʻi, Idaho, Maine, Montana, Nebraska, Nevada, New Hampshire, New Mexico, North Dakota, Rhode Island, South Dakota, Utah, Vermont, West Virginia, and Wyoming. Neil Abercrombie, Patsy Mink, Michael Castle et al., "Letter to William Goodling," September 11, 1996, MP 1350/10.

53 Neil Abercrombie, Patsy Mink, and Michael Castle, "Dear Colleague," MP 1350/10.

54 Suzanne Cavanagh and David Teasley, "Violence against Women: Recent Development," *CRS Report for Congress*, June 11, 1996, MP 1350/14; "Clinton Administration Acts to Prevent Violence against Women," *HHS Fact Sheet*, February 21, 1996, US Department of Health and Human Services, MP 1350/14.

55 Cavanagh and Teasley, "Violence against Women," p. 3.

56 Cavanagh and Teasley, "Violence against Women," p. 4.

57 Patsy T. Mink, "Letter to Moana Asam," June 21, 1996, MP 1350/14.

58 Patsy T. Mink, "Letter to Darleen Plavan," July 30, 1994, MP 1220/3.

59 Patsy T. Mink, "Letter to Lily T. Lai," December 9, 1993, MP 1220/3.

60 Mink, "Letter to Lily T. Lai."

61 Chandan Reddy characterizes these tensions not as contradictions but as interwoven aspects of political liberalism. *Freedom with Violence: Race, Sexuality, and the U.S. State* (Durham, NC: Duke University Press, 2011).

62 National Immigration Forum, "Issue Brief: Immigrant Women," MP 1345/2.

63 Ayuda is a community organization that advocates for and serves low-income immigrants in the Washington, DC, Maryland, and Virginia area. The Family Violence Prevention Fund helped to develop VAWA and also wrote the Platform for Action at the United Nations Conference on Women in Beijing. "Family Violence Prevention Fund," *Changing the Present*, https://changingthepresent.org; "Action Alert," MP1345/2.

64 "Action Alert."

65 "Action Alert," p. 2.

66 "Action Alert."

67 "Action Alert."

68 "Action Alert."

69 National Network on Behalf of Battered Immigrant Women, "Re: VAWA Oversight Hearing before the Senate Judiciary Committee," May 22, 1996, MP1345/2.

70 National Network on Behalf of Battered Immigrant Women, "Re: VAWA Oversight Hearing," p. 2.

71 National Network on Behalf of Battered Immigrant Women, "Re: VAWA Oversight Hearing," Summary.

72 Kevin L. Kearns, "Letter to Dear Representative," March 14, 1996, MP 1345/3.

73 Mae M. Ngai, *Impossible Subjects: Illegal Aliens and the Making of Modern America* (Princeton, NJ: Princeton University Press, 2004).

74 "NAPALC Blasts Congress and Administration on Welfare Reform," September 27, 1995, MP1345/4.

75 Patsy T. Mink, "Letter to Horace V. Beazlie," March 28, 1996, MP 1345/3.

"STAY SAFE, PATSY"

1 Grassroots Organizing for Welfare Leadership, "National Grassroots Policy Briefing," September 11, 2001, 10:00 a.m.–noon, 2168 Rayburn House Office Building, Washington DC, Gwendolyn Mink files.

2 "For Congress, an Abrupt Introduction to the Mobile Office," *New York Times*, November 8, 2001, p. G8.

3 Authorization for the Use of Military Force, PL 107–40, Sec. 2.

4 Statement of Senator Harry Byrd, *Congressional Record*, October 1, 2001, p. S9949: "[T]he use of force authority granted to the President extends only to the perpetrators of the September 11 attack. It was not the intent of Congress to give the President unbridled authority . . . to wage war against terrorism writ large without the advice and consent of Congress. That intent was made clear when Senators modified the text of the resolution proposed by the White House to limit the grant of authority to the September 11 attack."

5 US House of Representatives, 107th Cong., 1st Sess., Roll Call #342, September 14, 2001.

6 "Mink's Mail Not from DC," *Honolulu Advertiser*, November 5, 2001, p. B6.

7 Steve Twomey, "A Recipe for Safe Mail," *Washington Post*, January 30, 2002.

8 USA PATRIOT Act of 2001, PL 107–56.

9 E.g., "Testimony of Professor David Cole on Civil Liberties and Proposed Anti-Terrorism Legislation before the Subcommittee on the Constitution, Federalism, and Property Rights of the Senate Judiciary Committee," October 3, 2001, reprint in MP 1750/1.

10 Patsy T. Mink, Floor Statement on the PATRIOT Act, *Congressional Record*, October 12, 2001, MP 1750/1; Letter to Constituent, November 30, 2001, MP 1750/1; US House of Representatives, 107th Cong., 1st Sess., Roll Call #398, October 24, 2001.

11 Patsy T. Mink, "Statement before the Government Reform Committee on the President's Department of Homeland Security Proposal," June 20, 2002, MP 1674/6; Letter to Constituent, July 3, 2002, MP 1674/6.

12 US House of Representatives, Roll Call #367, July 26, 2002.

13 US House of Representatives, Roll Call #292, July 10, 2002.

14 H. Con. Res. 280, "Expressing Solidarity with Israel in the Fight against Terrorism," US House of Representatives, 107th Cong., 1st Sess., December 5, 2001.

15 "Political Rival Labels Mink Soft on Terrorism," *Honolulu Star-Bulletin*, December 12, 2001; "McDermott Insulted Mink's Patriotism" and "Charge against Mink Was a GOP Smear," letters to the editor, *Honolulu Star-Bulletin*, December 16, 2001, p. D4.

EPILOGUE

1 Laura Efurd, interview with author, April 13, 2013, San Francisco, California.
2 Efurd interview.
3 Amy Isaacs, interview with author, April 7, 2015, Washington, DC.
4 Maxine Waters, in "Memorial Addresses and Other Tributes for Patsy T. Mink," September 30, 2002, 107th Congress.
5 Waters, in "Memorial Addresses."
6 Waters, in "Memorial Addresses."
7 Patsy Takemoto Mink Education Foundation for Low-Income Women and Children (https://www.patsyminkfoundation.org/).
8 Nydia M. Velazquez, in "Memorial Addresses and Other Tributes for Patsy T. Mink," September 30, 2002, 107th Congress.
9 Dana Frank, "Congresswomen of Color Have Always Fought Back against Sexism," *Washington Post*, July 31, 2020.
10 Eni Faleomavaega, in "Memorial Addresses and Other Tributes for Patsy T. Mink," September 30, 2002, 107th Congress.
11 Daniel K. Akaka, "Proceedings in the Senate," in "Memorial Addresses and Other Tributes for Patsy T. Mink," September 30, 2002, 107th Congress.
12 Akaka, "Proceedings in the Senate."
13 Daniel Inouye, "Tribute to Congresswoman Patsy T. Mink," in "Memorial Addresses and Other Tributes for Patsy T. Mink," October 1, 2002, 107th Congress.
14 Inouye, "Tribute."
15 Inouye, "Tribute."
16 Nancy Pelosi, in "Memorial Addresses and Other Tributes for Patsy T. Mink," September 30, 2002, 107th Congress.
17 William Branigin, "Pelosi Sworn In as First Woman Speaker of the House," *Washington Post*, January 4, 2007.
18 Kelly McLaughlin, "Nancy Pelosi Invited 'All Children' Up to the Podium as She Was Sworn In as House Speaker," *Business Insider*, January 3, 2019.
19 Calvin Tamura, "Patsy Takemoto Mink, 1927–2002, in Memoriam," October 4, 2002.

SELECTED BIBLIOGRAPHY

CITED ARCHIVES

Bassford, Kimberlee. *Ahead of the Majority*. Oral history interviews. Private Papers.

Democratic Party of Hawaiʻi Collection. University of Hawaiʻi, Manoa. Special Collections.

Hawaiʻi Congressional Papers Collection (cited as CPC).

Hiram Fong Papers. Hawaiʻi Congressional Papers Collection. University of Hawaiʻi, Manoa. Archives and Manuscripts.

Immigration and Naturalization Service (INS). US National Pacific Region (San Francisco).

John A. Burns and Dan Boylan Collection (cited as BBC). Hawaiʻi Congressional Papers Collection. University of Hawaii, Manoa. Archives and Manuscripts.

Mink, Gwendolyn, Private Papers. Washington, DC (cited as GMP).

Mink, Patsy T. Papers. Library of Congress, Manuscript Division. Washington, DC (cited as MP box/folder).

BOOKS AND ARTICLES

Alexander, Michelle. *The New Jim Crow: Mass Incarceration in the Age of Colorblindness*. New York: New Press, 2010.

Ali, Saleem H., and Helena Voinov Vladich. "Environmental Diplomacy." In *The Sage Handbook of Diplomacy*, 601–16. Edited by Costas M. Constantinou, Pauline Kerr, and Paul Sharp. Los Angeles: Sage, 2016.

Arinaga, Esther K., and Rene E. Ojiri. "Patsy Takemoto Mink." In *Called from Within: Early Women Lawyers of Hawaiʻi*, 251–80. Edited by Mari J. Matsuda. Honolulu: University of Hawaii Press, 1992.

Arvin, Maile, Eve Tuck, and Angie Morrill. "Decolonizing Feminism: Challenging Connections between Settler Colonialism and Heteropatriarchy." *Feminist Formations* 25:1 (Spring 2013): 8–34.

Azuma, Eiichiro. "The Lure of Military Imperialism: Race, Martial Citizenship, and Minority American Transnationalism during the Cold War." *Journal of American Ethnic History* 36:2 (Winter 2017): 72–82.

Barrett, James R., and David Roediger. "Inbetween Peoples: Race, Nationality, and the 'New Immigrant' Working Class." *Journal of American Ethnic History* 16:3 (Spring 1997): 3–44.

Bigelow, Albert. *The Voyage of the Golden Rule*. New York: Doubleday, 1959.

Blackford, Mansel G. "Environmental Justice, Native Rights, Tourism, and Opposition to Military Control: The Case of Kahoʻolawe." *Journal of American History* 91 (2004): 544–71.

———. *Pathways to the Present: U.S. Development and Its Consequences in the Pacific.* Honolulu: University of Hawaiʻi Press, 2007.

Blackwell, Maylei. *¡Chicana Power! Contested Histories of Feminism in the Chicano Movement.* Austin: University of Texas Press, 2011.

Byrd, Jodi. *The Transit of Empire: Indigenous Critiques of Colonialism.* Minneapolis: University of Minnesota Press, 2011.

Chan, Kristina. "The Mother of Title IX: Patsy Mink." *The She Network*, April 24, 2012. https://www.womenssportsfoundation.org.

Child, Brenda J. *Boarding School Seasons: American Indian Families, 1900–1940.* Lincoln: University of Nebraska Press, 2000.

Cho, Yu-Fang. "Nuclear Diffusion: Notes toward Reimagining Reproductive Justice in a Militarized Asia Pacific." *Amerasia Journal* 41:3 (2015): 2–24.

———. "Remembering Lucky Dragon, Re-membering Bikini: Worlding the Anthropocene through Transpacific Nuclear Modernity." *Cultural Studies* 33:1 (2019): 122–46.

Choy, Catherine Ceniza, and Judy Tzu-Chun Wu, eds. *Gendering the Trans-Pacific World.* Leiden, The Netherlands: Brill, 2017.

Collins, Lynda, and Heather McLeod-Kilmurray. "Toxic Battery: A Tort for Our Time?" *Tort Law Review* 16 (2008): 135–48.

Cooper, George, and Gavan Daws. *Land and Power in Hawaii: The Democratic Years.* Honolulu: University of Hawaii Press, 1990.

Cooper, Phillip J. "*Plyler* at the Core: Understanding the Proposition 187 Challenge." *Chicana/o Latina/o Law Review* 17:1 (1995): 64–87.

Crenshaw, Kimberlé. "Demarginalizing the Intersection of Race and Sex: A Black Feminist Critique of Antidiscrimination Doctrine, Feminist Theory, and Antiracist Politics." *University of Chicago Legal Forum* 1989:1 (1989): 139–67.

———. "Mapping the Margins: Intersectionality, Identity Politics, and Violence against Women of Color." *Stanford Law Review* 43:6 (July 1991): 1241–99.

Curwood, Anastasia. "Black Feminism on Capitol Hill: Shirley Chisholm and Movement Politics, 1968–1984." *Meridians* 13:1 (2015): 204–32.

Davidson, Sue. *A Heart in Politics: Jeannette Rankin and Patsy T. Mink.* Seattle: Seal Press, 1994.

Davis, Amira Rose. *All-American Welfare Queens: Race, Politics, and Sports in the Time of Title IX.* Forthcoming.

DeLoughrey, Elizabeth M. "The Myth of Isolates: Ecosystem Ecologies in the Nuclear Pacific." *Cultural Geographies* 20:2: 167–84.

Dudziak, Mary L. *Cold War Civil Rights: Race and the Image of American Democracy.* Princeton, NJ: Princeton University Press, 2000.

Ellwood, David. *Poor Support: Poverty in the American Family.* New York: Basic Books, 1988.

Enloe, Cynthia. *Bananas, Beaches, and Bases: Making Feminist Sense of International Politics*. Berkeley: University of California Press, 2000.

Ernst, Julia. "The Congressional Caucus for Women's Issues: An Inside Perspective on Lawmaking by and for Women." *Michigan Journal of Gender and Law* 12:2 (2006): 190–274.

Espiritu, Yen Le. *Asian American Panethnicity: Bridging Institutions and Identities*. Philadelphia: Temple University Press, 1992.

———. *Body Counts: The Vietnam War and Militarized Refugees*. Oakland: University of California Press, 2014.

Fishel, Andrew, and Janice Pottker. *National Politics and Sex Discrimination in Education*. Lanham, MD: Lexington Books, 1977.

Flores, Alfred P. "U.S. Colonial Education in Guam, 1899–1950." In *Oxford Research Encyclopedia of American History*. Oxford University Press, 2019.

Frazier, Jessica M. *Women's Antiwar Diplomacy during the Vietnam War Era*. Chapel Hill: University of North Carolina Press, 2017.

Fujikane, Candace, and Jonathan Y. Okamura, eds. *Asian Settler Colonialism: From Local Governance to the Habits of Everyday Life in Hawai'i*. Honolulu: University of Hawai'i Press, 2008.

Fujiwara, Lynn. *Mothers without Citizenship: Asian Immigrant Families and the Consequences of Welfare Reform*. Minneapolis: University of Minnesota Press, 2008.

Gilmore, Stephanie, and Sara Evans. *Feminist Coalitions: Historical Perspectives on Second-Wave Feminism in the United States*. Urbana: University of Illinois Press, 2008.

Gonzalez, Vernadette Vicuna. *Securing Paradise: Tourism and Militarism in Hawai'i and the Philippines*. Durham, NC: Duke University Press, 2013.

Goodyear-Ka'ōpua, Noelani, Ikaika Hussey, and Erin Kahunawaika'ala Wright, eds. *A Nation Rising: Hawaiian Movements for Life, Land, and Sovereignty*. Durham, NC: Duke University Press, 2014.

Hall, Lisa Kahaleole. "Strategies of Erasure: U.S. Colonialism and Native Hawaiian Feminism." *American Quarterly* 60:2 (June 2008): 273–80.

Hall, Roberta M., and Bernice R. Sandler. *The Classroom Climate: A Chilly One for Women?* Washington, DC: Association of American Colleges, 1982.

Haugeberg, Karissa. *Women against Abortion: Inside the Largest Moral Reform Movement of the Twentieth Century*. Urbana: University of Illinois Press, 2017.

Hawkesworth, Mary. "Congressional Enactments of Race-Gender: Toward a Theory of Raced-Gendered Institutions." *American Political Science Review* 97:4 (November 2003): 529–50.

Hershberger, Mary. *Traveling to Vietnam: American Peace Activists and the War*. Syracuse, NY: Syracuse University Press, 1988.

Hobson, Emily K. *Lavender and Red: Liberation and Solidarity in the Gay and Lesbian Left*. Oakland: University of California Press, 2016.

Hurtado, Aida. *The Color of Privilege: Three Blasphemies on Race and Feminism*. Ann Arbor: University of Michigan Press, 1996.

Ichioka, Yuji. *The Issei: The World of the First-Generation Japanese Immigrants, 1885–1924.* New York: Free Press, 1988.

Igler, David. "Commentary: Re-Orienting Asian American History through Transnational and International Scales." *Pacific Historical Review* 76:4 (2007): 611–14.

———. *The Great Ocean: Pacific Worlds from Captain Cook to the Gold Rush.* New York: Oxford University Press, 2013.

Katznelson, Ira. *When Affirmative Action Was White: An Untold History of Racial Inequality in Twentieth-Century America.* New York: Norton, 2006.

Keiner, Christine. *Deep Cut: Science, Power, and the Unbuilt Interoceanic Canal.* Athens: University of Georgia Press, 2020.

Kornbluh, Felicia, and Gwendolyn Mink. *Ensuring Poverty: Welfare Reform in Feminist Perspective.* Philadelphia: University of Pennsylvania Press, 2018.

Lajimodiere, Denise K. *Stringing Rosaries: The History, the Unforgivable, and the Healing of Northern Plains American Indian Boarding School Survivors.* Fargo: North Dakota State University Press, 2019.

Lee, Ellen. "Patsy Takemoto Mink's Trailblazing Testimony against a Supreme Court Nominee." *Atlantic Monthly,* September 16, 2018.

Lerner, Mitchell. "Vietnam and the 1964 Election: A Defense of Lyndon Johnson." *Presidential Studies Quarterly* 25:4 (Fall 1995): 751–66.

Levenstein, Lisa. *They Didn't See Us Coming: The Hidden History of Feminism in the Nineties.* New York: Basic Books, 2020.

Liu, Michael, Kim Geron, and Tracy Lai. *The Snake Dance of Asian American Activism: Community, Vision, and Power.* Lanham, MD: Lexington Books, 2008.

Lorde, Audre. *Sister Outsider: Essays and Speeches.* Berkeley, CA: Crossing Press, 1984.

Lyons, Paul, and Ty P. Kāwika Tengan. "Introduction: Pacific Currents." *American Quarterly* 67:3 (2015): 545–74.

Maeda, Daryl Joji. *Rethinking the Asian American Movement.* New York: Routledge, 2011.

Man, Simeon. *Soldiering through Empire: Race and the Making of the Decolonizing Pacific.* Oakland: University of California Press, 2018.

Matsuda, Matt K. *Pacific Worlds: A History of Seas, Peoples, and Cultures.* Cambridge: Cambridge University Press, 2018.

May, Elaine Tyler. *Homeward Bound: American Families during the Cold War.* New York: Basic Books, 1988.

McAuliffe, Christopher. "Resurrecting an Old Cause of Action for a New Wrong: Battery as a Toxic Tort." *Boston College Environmental Affairs Law Review* 20:2 (1993): 265–301.

Meller, Norman, and Anne Feder Lee. "Hawaiian Sovereignty." *Publius* 27:2 (Spring 1997): 167–85.

Meyerowitz, Joanne J. *Not June Cleaver: Women and Gender in Postwar America, 1945–1960.* Philadelphia: Temple University Press, 1994.

Mink, Gwendolyn. "Feminist Policy Scholars Intervene in Welfare Debate." *Social Justice* 30:4 (2003): 108–9.

———, ed. *Women and Welfare Reform: Women's Poverty, Women's Opportunities, and Women's Welfare Conference Proceedings.* Washington, DC: Institute for Women's Policy Research, 1994.

Mink, Patsy T. "Federal Legislation to End Discrimination against Women." *Valparaiso University Law Review* 5:2 (1971): 397–414.

Morantz-Sanchez, Regina. *Sympathy and Science: Women Physicians in American Medicine.* Chapel Hill: University of North Carolina Press, 2005.

Ngai, Mae M. *Impossible Subjects: Illegal Aliens and the Making of Modern America.* Princeton, NJ: Princeton University Press, 2004.

Nguyen, Viet Thanh, and Janet Hoskins. *Transpacific Studies: Framing an Emerging Field.* Honolulu: University of Hawai'i Press, 2014.

Nishime, Leilani, and Kim D. Hester Williams. *Racial Ecologies.* Seattle: University of Washington Press, 2018.

Okihiro, Gary. *Island World: A History of Hawai'i and the United States.* Berkeley: University of California Press, 2008.

———. *Pineapple Culture: A History of the Tropical and Temperate Zones.* Berkeley: University of California Press, 2009.

Olmstead, Maegan. "Title IX and the Rise of Female Athletes in America." *The She Network*, September 2, 2016. https://www.womenssportsfoundation.org.

Pascoe, Peggy. *What Comes Naturally: Miscegenation Law and the Making of Race in America.* New York: Oxford University Press, 2009.

Pierce, Rachel Laura. "Capitol Feminism: Work, Politics, and Gender in Congress, 1960–1980." PhD thesis. University of Virginia, 2014.

Pulido, Laura. "Rethinking Environmental Racism: White Privilege and Urban Development in Southern California." *Annals of the Association of American Geographers* 90:1 (2000): 12–40.

Quan, Jeanne. "Congresswoman Patsy Takemoto Mink." In *Asian Women.* Berkeley: University of California, 1971. Asian American Studies Center, University of California, Los Angeles, 3rd printing, October 1975.

Reddy, Chandan. *Freedom with Violence: Race, Sexuality, and the U.S. State.* Durham, NC: Duke University Press, 2011.

Rich, Adrienne. "Compulsory Heterosexuality and Lesbian Existence." *Blood, Bread, and Poetry.* New York: Norton, 1994.

Robnett, Belinda. "African American Women in the Civil Rights Movement, 1954–1965: Gender, Leadership, and Micromobilization." *American Journal of Sociology* 101:6: 1661–93.

Romano, Renee Christine. *Race Mixing: Black-White Marriage in Postwar America.* Cambridge, MA: Harvard University Press, 2003.

Roth, Benita. *Separate Roads to Feminism: Black, Chicana, and White Feminist Movements in America's Second Wave.* New York: Cambridge University Press, 2004.

Rymsza-Pawlowska, M. J. *History Comes Alive: Public History and Popular Culture in the 1970s.* Chapel Hill: University of North Carolina Press, 2017.

Sandler, Bernice R., and Roberta M. Hall. *The Campus Climate Revisited: Chilly for Women Faculty, Administrators, and Graduate Students.* Washington, DC: Association of American Colleges, 1986.

Sandoval, Chela. "U.S. Third World Feminism: The Theory and Method of Oppositional Consciousness in the Postmodern World." *Genders* no. 10 (Spring 1991): 1–24.

Saranillio, Dean Itsuji. "Colliding Histories: Hawai'i Statehood at the Intersection of Asians 'Ineligible to Citizenship' and Hawaiians 'Unfit for Self-Government.'" *Journal of Asian American Studies* 13:3 (October 2010): 283–309.

———. *Unsustainable Empire: Alternative Histories of Hawai'i Statehood.* Durham, NC: Duke University Press, 2018.

Self, Robert. *All in the Family: The Realignment of American Democracy since the 1960s.* New York: Hill & Wang, 2012.

Shigematsu, Setsu, and Keith L. Camacho. *Militarized Currents: Toward a Decolonized Future in Asia and the Pacific.* Minneapolis: University of Minnesota Press, 2010.

Sohoni, Deenesh. "Unsuitable Suitors: Anti-Miscegenation Laws, Naturalization Laws, and the Construction of Asian Identities." *Law & Society Review* 41:3 (September 2007): 587–618.

Springer, Kimberly. *Living for the Revolution: Black Feminist Organizations, 1968–1980.* Durham, NC: Duke University Press, 2005.

Spruill, Marjorie J. *Divided We Stand: The Battle over Women's Rights and Family Values That Polarized American Politics.* New York: Bloomsbury, 2017.

Suk, Julie C. *We the Women: The Unstoppable Mothers of the Equal Rights Amendment.* New York: Skyhorse, 2000.

Swerdlow, Amy. *Women Strike for Peace: Traditional Motherhood and Radical Politics in the 1960s.* Chicago: University of Chicago Press, 1993.

Takaki, Ronald. *Pau Hana: Plantation Life and Labor in Hawaii.* Honolulu: University of Hawai'i Press, 1983.

———. *Strangers from a Different Shore: A History of Asian Americans.* Updated and revised edition. Boston: Little, Brown, 1998.

Takezawa, Yasuko, and Gary Y. Okihiro. *Trans-Pacific Japanese American Studies: Conversations on Race and Racializations.* Honolulu: University of Hawai'i Press, 2016.

Thompson, Becky. "Multiracial Feminism: Recasting the Chronology of Second Wave Feminism." *Feminist Studies* 28:2 (Summer 2002): 336–60.

Thuma, Emily. *All Our Trials: Prisons, Policing, and the Feminist Fight to End Violence.* Champaign: University of Illinois Press, 2019.

Trask, Haunani-Kay. *From a Native Daughter: Colonialism and Sovereignty in Hawaii.* Rev. ed. Honolulu: University of Hawaii Press, 1999.

Turk, Katherine. *Equality on Trial: Gender and Rights in the Modern American Workplace.* Philadelphia: University Pennsylvania Press, 2016.

Valk, Anne M. *Radical Sisters: Second-Wave Feminism and Black Liberation in Washington, D.C.* Champaign: University of Illinois Press, 2010.

Walker, Rebecca. "Becoming the Third Wave." *Ms. Magazine* 41 (1992).

Ware, Susan. *Title IX: A Brief History with Documents.* Boston: Bedford/St. Martin's Press, 2007.

Whitehead, John S. "The Anti-Statehood Movement and the Legacy of Alice Kamokila Campbell." *Hawaiian Journal of History* 27 (1993): 43–63.

Whittier, Nancy. "Carceral and Intersectional Feminism in Congress: The Violence against Women Act, Discourse, and Policy." *Gender and Society* 30:5 (October 2016): 791–818.

Winslow, Barbara. *Shirley Chisholm: Catalyst for Change.* New York: Routledge, 2013.

"Women in the Labor Market." *Focus* 20:1 (Winter 1998–1999).

Wu, Ellen. *The Color of Success: Asian Americans and the Origins of the Model Minority.* Princeton, NJ: Princeton University Press, 2014.

Wu, Judy Tzu-Chun. "Envisioning the National Women's Conference: Patsy Takemoto Mink and Pacific Feminism." In *Suffrage at 100: Women in American Politics since 1920,* 257–73. Edited by Stacie Taranto and Leandra Zarnow. Baltimore, MD: John Hopkins University Press, 2020.

———. *Radicals on the Road: Internationalism, Orientalism, and Feminism during the Vietnam Era.* Ithaca, NY: Cornell University Press, 2013.

Zaretsky, Natasha. *No Direction Home: The American Family and the Fear of National Decline, 1968–1980.* Chapel Hill: University of North Carolina Press, 2007.

Zarnow, Leandra Ruth. *Battling Bella: The Protest Politics of Bella Abzug.* Cambridge, MA: Harvard University Press, 2019.

Zehrt, Lynn Ridgeway. "Twenty Years of Compromise: How the Caps on Damages in the Civil Rights Act of 1991 Codified Sex Discrimination." *Yale Journal of Law and Feminism* 25:2 (2013): 249–318.

INDEX

Note: Page numbers in italic type indicate photographs.

ABOUT THE AUTHORS

Judy Tzu-Chun Wu is Professor of Asian American Studies at the University of California–Irvine and the Director of the Humanities Center. She received her PhD in US history from Stanford University. She is the author of *Dr. Mom Chung of the Fair-Haired Bastards: The Life of a Wartime Celebrity* (2005) and *Radicals on the Road: Internationalism, Orientalism, and Feminism during the Vietnam Era* (2013).

Gwendolyn Mink is the author or editor of nine books about social justice issues in US policy history and politics, including *The Wages of Motherhood: Inequality in the Welfare State* (1995), which won the 1996 Victoria Schuck Book Award of the American Political Science Association, and *Welfare's End* (1998, 2002). Most recently she published *Ensuring Poverty: Welfare Reform in Feminist Perspective* (2018) with coauthor Felicia Kornbluh.